The Quest for Love Divine

The Quest for Love Divine

—— Select Essays in Wesleyan Theology and Practice ——

Paul W. Chilcote

Foreword by
Randy L. Maddox

CASCADE Books • Eugene, Oregon

THE QUEST FOR LOVE DIVINE
Select Essays in Wesleyan Theology and Practice

Copyright © 2022 Paul W. Chilcote. All rights reserved. Except for brief quotations in critical publications or reviews, no part of this book may be reproduced in any manner without prior written permission from the publisher. Write: Permissions, Wipf and Stock Publishers, 199 W. 8th Ave., Suite 3, Eugene, OR 97401.

Cascade Books
An Imprint of Wipf and Stock Publishers
199 W. 8th Ave., Suite 3
Eugene, OR 97401

www.wipfandstock.com

PAPERBACK ISBN: 978-1-6667-3211-5
HARDCOVER ISBN: 978-1-6667-2543-8
EBOOK ISBN: 978-1-6667-2544-5

Cataloguing-in-Publication data:

Names: Chilcote, Paul Wesley, 1954–, author. | Maddox, Randy L., foreword.

Title: The quest for love divine : select essays in Wesleyan theology and practice / by Paul W. Chilcote ; foreword by Randy L. Maddox.

Description: Eugene, OR : Cascade Books, 2022 | Includes bibliographical references.

Identifiers: ISBN 978-1-6667-3211-5 (paperback) | ISBN 978-1-6667-2543-8 (hardcover) | ISBN 978-1-6667-2544-5 (ebook)

Subjects: LCSH: Wesley, Charles, 1707–1788. | Methodist Church—Doctrines. | Hymns, English—History and criticism. | Criticism, interpretation, etc. | Wesley, John, 1703–1791. | Methodist Church—England—Clergy. | Methodist women.

Classification: BX8332 .C46 2022 (print) | BX8332 .C46 (ebook)

07/22/22

For
my devoted partner in life

Janet

whose own quest for love
continues to inspire me
and calls me ever onward and upward

Contents

Foreword by Randy L. Maddox | ix

Preface | xiii

Acknowledgments | xvii

Introduction | xxi

Part 1: Charles Wesley's Lyrical Theology

1 Charles Wesley's Lyrical Credo | 3

2 Charles Wesley and the Language of Faith | 30

3 "All the Image of Thy Love": Charles Wesley's Vision of the One Thing Needful | 54

Part 2: John and Charles Wesley's Practical Divinity

4 Rethinking the Wesleyan Quadrilateral | 81

5 "Practical Christology" in John and Charles Wesley | 84

6 John and Charles Wesley on "God in Christ Reconciling" | 111

Part 3: Early Methodist Women

7 Biblical Equality and the Spirituality of Early Methodist Women | 129

8 An Early Methodist Community of Women | 143

9 Sanctification as Lived by Women in Early Methodism | 156

Part 4: Wesleyan Spiritual Practices

10 Spirituality in the Wesleyan Tradition | 171

11 Charles Wesley and Christian Practices | 189

12 A Faith That Sings: The Renewing Power of Lyrical Theology | 199

Part 5: Worship, Sacraments, and Leadership

13 John and Charles Wesley's Theology of the Sacraments | 217

14 The Integral Nature of Worship and Evangelism: Insights from the Wesleyan Tradition | 238

15 "Claim Me for Thy Service": Charles Wesley's Vision of Servant Vocation | 255

Part 6: Missional Ecclesiology and God's Rule

16 The Mission-Church Paradigm of the Wesleyan Revival | 277

17 Lessons from the "Society Planting" Paradigm of Early Methodist Women | 289

18 Charles Wesley and the "Peaceable Reign" of Christ | 305

Appendix A: A World Methodist Affirmation | 325

Appendix B: A Progressive Wesleyan Declaration | 328

Bibliography | 331

Foreword

IN 1786, NEAR THE end of his long and faithful ministry, John Wesley penned a short essay titled "Thoughts upon Methodism." In this essay, Wesley warned that the Methodist movement would become a dead sect—having the form of religion but lacking its power—unless they held fast to the crucial insights and practices that birthed the movement. Significantly, the first insight that he emphasizes which early Methodists drew from their broad study of Scripture was "That religion is an inward principle; that it is no other than the mind that was in Christ; or, in other words, the renewal of the soul after the image of God, in righteousness and true holiness," wrought in us "by the power of the Holy Ghost."[1]

Every quest or journey is oriented by its goal. The goal of early Methodists was to become faithful and mature disciples of Christ. This meant far more than just affirming Christ as their Lord or having an assurance of his pardoning love. They longed for what they saw promised in Scripture: the transformation of their sin-distorted attitudes and dispositions into ever greater conformity with Christ's abiding love for God, for neighbor, and for the whole creation. As Charles Wesley put it in hymnic prayers, they longed for the Spirit of Christ to "plant, and root, and fix in me / All the mind that was in thee";[2] or the Spirit of "Love divine, all loves excelling" to "set our hearts at liberty."

In other words, while the early Methodists celebrated the freedom *from* sin that comes in the new birth, they fervently desired that greater freedom *for* walking in God's life-giving ways and participating in God's saving mission. Implicit in this desire was their conviction that concern for transformation of the heart was not a distraction from or alternative to concern for the world around us. As John Wesley frequently reminded

1. J. Wesley, *Thoughts upon Methodism*, 258.
2. Wesley and Wesley, *Hymns and Sacred Poems* (1742), 222; "Hymn on Phil. 2:5," st. 10.

them, holiness of heart is reciprocally connected to holiness of life. As we experience the love of God transforming our lives, we are more inclined to engage the world around us in compassionate and transforming ways; and as we engage the world in these ways, empowered by the Spirit, our transformation in Christ-likeness is deepened!

Obviously, this is an ideal. It was my fortune to grow up in a congregation within the broad Wesleyan tradition that included some members whose lives embodied such growing transformation in love divine, and who extended that love to me. The congruence between the faith they articulated and their lives drew me into and grounded me in the Wesleyan tradition. Over the last four decades, as I turned to scholarly study of Wesleyanism, I continued to be drawn to those within it who emulate this congruence. I also increasingly appreciated students of the tradition who approached their subject with a desire not only to understand, but to encourage and help facilitate in the present church the quest for love divine.

Over the years, I have come to prize the author of this collection of essays in particular. Paul Wesley Chilcote is not just a careful and reliable historian of early Methodism, he embodies in his approach to the subject characteristic commitments of early Methodism. To begin with, as Chilcote notes in his helpful introductory study of the faith of John and Charles Wesley, *Recapturing the Wesleys' Vision* (2004), a prominent characteristic of the Wesleyan tradition has been to appreciate and seek to hold together themes and practices that are posed in opposition by some Christian writers or communities—such as: both faith *and* works in salvation; both individual piety *and* social transformation; or both the centrality of the Word *and* the prominence of the Eucharist. Far from a hazy (or lazy) eclecticism, Chilcote contends that this characteristic of Wesleyan theology reflects its concern to do justice to the full breadth of Scripture, the full range of Christian experience, and full salvific concern of the triune God.

But Chilcote does not just defend the "conjunctive" character of the Wesleyan tradition, he has extended it in ways that help correct imbalances in some scholarship on the tradition. One way he has done this is to give Charles Wesley (who is often nearly forgotten) more equal voice with his brother John, particularly probing areas where they differ. Note how this volume opens with a section on the younger brother before turning to essays that engage them both.

Going further, Chilcote has labored throughout his career to recover the stories and witness of the full early Methodist community, not just its leaders. His dissertation recovered the stories of early Methodist women preachers and, in edited collections like *Her Own Story* (2001) and *Early Methodist Spirituality* (2007), he introduces contemporary readers to the writings of several early Methodist women. Some of the fruits of this dimension of Chilcote's scholarship appear in the third section of the present volume.

In addition to the "conjunctive" character of the theology of John and Charles Wesley, recent scholarship has highlighted how they worked as "practical" theologians—valuing and focusing their efforts on formative expressions of theology like song, liturgy, sermons, etc. In the second section of this volume, Chilcote describes this characteristic of the brothers well. But I would encourage readers to check out how Chilcote *emulates* this same type of practical theology in the appendices to this volume and in books like *Praying in the Wesleyan Spirit* (2001).

One other way that Chilcote embodies the concern of early Methodism that is evident in this collection deserves mention. When the movement started, the Wesley brothers insisted that they were not trying to start yet another "church," but seeking to participate in God's work of breathing new life into the church as a whole. Similarly, in all of his writing on the Wesleyan tradition, Chilcote comes across not as seeking to defend or to recommend that tradition over others, but as trying to distill and offer the pastoral wisdom of Wesleyanism at its best to the larger church, in hopes of helping to heal some of the divides that continue to impede our communion with one another and undercut our witness to the world.

As one who shares this hope, and has been helped to understand the Wesleyan tradition in many ways by Chilcote's scholarship (as well as been enriched by his winsome spirit and deep spirituality), I gladly recommend this collection of his most salient essays.

Randy L. Maddox, PhD
William Kellon Quick Emeritus Professor of Wesley and Methodist Studies
Duke Divinity School

Preface

MY JOURNEY AS A serious student of John and Charles Wesley began around 1974. As a Methodist undergraduate student, majoring in theology and history at a Lutheran institution, I came to appreciate my middle name—Wesley—as never before. I loved my time at Valparaiso University. I enjoyed living inside a Christian tradition different from my own. But this juxtaposition pushed me to ask questions about my identity. What differences distinguished these two great Protestant traditions? What did they hold in common? I discovered, for example, that Lutherans retained a rich Eucharistic heritage, something lost in the ambiguities of the American frontier among Methodists and in need of recovery. Followers of Martin Luther helped me reclaim that lost treasure in terms of my own spirituality. So I began a rather intense study of the Wesleys in hopes of other discoveries that might emerge.

At around the same time, as a child of a Methodist parsonage, and having come through a period in which I claimed I would do anything other than go into the ministry, I was nudged by the Holy Spirit to rethink that judgment. Indeed, during the Advent season of 1974, and in the Chapel of the Resurrection at Valpo, I sensed a firm call to seminary to pursue a path into the United Methodist ministry. In my mind, I linked this call with a teaching vocation as well, so I began looking for a school that had a robust doctoral program, anticipating that I might want to pursue further studies beyond my ministerial training. In conversations about all this with my mentor, he advised me to leave the region of my birth—the Midwest—with hopes that such a change would raise my horizons and broaden my vision. Convinced that I wanted to do more in Wesley studies, I began my quest and quickly settled on Duke University, the divinity school of which provided the foundation for my ministerial pursuits, and the graduate school of which afforded the unique opportunity for me to study closely with both Frank Baker and Bob Cushman.

In my final year of my master of divinity degree program, I did not have as much clarity as this might suggest. In fact, I struggled with a divided mind. One part of me wanted to pursue doctoral studies in liturgical and ecumenical theology. I had a place in mind for that—Union Theological Seminary—and hopes of working with Geoffrey Wainwright, who was both a liturgical theologian and a Wesleyan scholar. But when I learned that Frank Baker, my beloved instructor in Wesley studies at Duke, was planning to retire a year beyond my graduation, that event made my decision for me. There was no way I could pass up the opportunity of studying with the foremost student of John and Charles Wesley in the late twentieth century. Having sat at his feet in his classroom and his home, I knew who this was. Dr. Baker represented two things, in particular, that I have always sought to emulate since those days: he was an exceptional scholar and an authentic follower of Jesus, academic excellence and genuine humility bound together in one person. Dr. Baker welcomed me with open arms as his last doctoral student.

When I launched into my studies, I never realized how many doors this would open. I always thought that obtaining a doctorate entailed drilling down and focusing in, not opening up and reaching out. I didn't know how much the personal connections I had made with other classmates, scholars, and leaders within the church, in particular, would lead me in totally unanticipated directions. So, after I completed my studies, the adventure began. In the course of it all, the most precious gift Frank Baker bestowed on me was, ironically, my own voice. He did all he could do to help me find that voice. He let me know when I was hiding it, perhaps in deference to scholars I considered high above me. He also affirmed it when he heard it. I can still hear him saying, "There it is. Can you hear it? That's your voice." He instilled my confidence in that voice by affirming me and made me feel more like a son than a student. After the committee deliberated over my dissertation defense, he was the one to invite me back into the room. He shook my hand, as is the custom, with the greeting, "Dr. Chilcote." He also said that I could now call him "Frank." But I found that so difficult. He was always Dr. Baker to me.

Dr. Baker produced a collection of his salient essays, and so did my theological mentor, Dr. Cushman. Those two volumes provided the impetus for me to consider the possibility of this present collection. I confess that it still feels somewhat self-serving, and I sit uncomfortably with that feeling. But many, particularly my students, convinced me that the breadth of this collection and the quality of the insights into the Wesleyan heritage it affords make this a worthwhile endeavor. I hope you find this to be true.

I hardly know where to begin to thank all those who have supported me along the way and who contributed to the development of this book over the years. But the words of St. Paul to the Philippians come immediately to mind.

> I thank my God every time I remember you, constantly praying with joy in every one of my prayers for all of you, because of your sharing in the gospel from the first day until now. I am confident of this, that the one who began a good work among you will bring it to completion by the day of Jesus Christ. It is right for me to think this way about all of you, because you hold me in your heart, for all of you share in God's grace. (Phil 1:3–7a)

I hope this book makes abundantly clear to you that Wesleyan theology and practice is all about grace and love. My research in Wesleyan studies put me inevitably into circles of beloved colleagues with sharp minds and open hearts. My students across several continents shaped my thinking, contributed their unique insights from their own contexts, and encouraged me in both my teaching and my scholarship. I come from a family with deep roots in the Wesleyan heritage, and my immediate family has encouraged and supported me more than any others, particularly my wife, Janet, to whom I dedicate this book. A special word of thanks to my dear friend and colleague, Randy Maddox, who graciously agreed to provide a foreword for this volume. He is one of the most dependable people I have ever known, and he has done a great honor to me in this. To all these dear colleagues, friends, and family members, I want you to know how much "I hold you in my heart" and will continue to do so as we engage in this quest for love divine together, in grace and with joy and peace in our hearts.

Paul W. Chilcote
July 11, 2021 (Day of St. Benedict)

Acknowledgments

ALL CHARLES WESLEY HYMN texts in this volume are cited from the Center for Studies in the Wesleyan Tradition website, Duke Divinity School, which has published a complete, definitive, and free-access edition of Wesley's published and manuscript poetry under the editorial direction of Randy L. Maddox, with the diligent assistance of Aileen F. Maddox: http://divinity.duke.edu/initiatives-centers/cswt/wesley-texts.

I-to Loh granted permission for the use of an excerpt from his hymn, "On the Shore of Galilee."

Simei Monteiro granted permission for the reprinting of excerpts from two of her hymns, "Tua Palavra na vida" (Your Word in Our Lives) and "Canção da caminhada" (If Walking Is Our Vocation).

Hope Publishing Company granted permission for the reprinting of excerpts from two hymn texts of Fred Pratt Green, "The Caring Church" and "Let the People Sing."

Essays in this volume that were previously published in journals and books are listed below. Some have undergone minor revision for the purpose of this volume, and permission has been granted for their reprinting in this book.

Abingdon Press

"A Faith that Sings: The Renewing Power of Lyrical Theology." In *The Wesleyan Tradition: A Paradigm for Renewal*, edited by Paul W. Chilcote, 148–62. Nashville: Abingdon, 2002.

"A World Methodist Affirmation." In *The Wesleyan Tradition: A Paradigm for Renewal*, edited by Paul W. Chilcote, 19–21. Nashville: Abingdon, 2002.

"A Progressive Wesleyan Declaration." In *Active Faith: Resisting 4 Dangerous Ideologies with the Wesleyan Way*, 75–76. Nashville: Abingdon, 2019.

Asbury Theological Journal

"The Integral Nature of Worship and Evangelism: Insights from the Wesleyan Tradition." *Asbury Theological Journal* 61.1 (Spring 2006) 7–23.

Epworth Press

"Charles Wesley and the Language of Faith." In *Charles Wesley: Life, Legacy, and Literature*, edited by Kenneth G.C. Newport and Ted A. Campbell, 299–319. London: Epworth, 2007.

General Board of Higher Education and Ministry—Wesley's Foundery Books

"'Practical Christology' in John and Charles Wesley." In *Methodist Christology: From the Wesleys to the Twenty-First Century*, edited by Jason Vickers, 1–35. Oak Park: Wesley's Foundery, 2020.

Good News Magazine

"Rethinking the Wesleyan Quadrilateral." *Good News Magazine* 38.4 (January/February 2005) 22–23.

Methodist History

"John and Charles Wesley on 'God in Christ Reconciling.'" *Methodist History* 47.3 (April 2009) 132–45.

"An Early Methodist Community of Women." *Methodist History* 38.4 (July 2000) 219–30.

"Sanctification as Lived by Women in Early Methodism." *Methodist History* 34.2 (January 1996) 90–103.

New York University Press

"John and Charles Wesley." In *Christian Theologies of the Sacraments: A Comparative Introduction*, edited by Justin S. Holcomb and David A. Johnson, 272–94. New York: New York University Press, 2017.

Priscilla Papers

"Biblical Equality and the Spirituality of Early Methodist Women." *Priscilla Papers* 22.2 (Spring 2008) 11–16.

Proceedings of the Charles Wesley Society

"'All the Image of Thy Love': Charles Wesley's Vision of the One Thing Needful." *Proceedings of the Charles Wesley Society* 18 (2014) 21–40.

"Charles Wesley and Christian Practices." *Proceedings of the Charles Wesley Society* 12 (2008) 35–47.

"Charles Wesley and the 'Peaceable Reign' of Christ." *Proceedings of the Charles Wesley Society* 21 (2017) ??–??

"Charles Wesley's Lyrical Credo." *Proceedings of the Charles Wesley Society* 15 (2011) 41–67.

"'Claim Me for Thy Service': Charles Wesley's Vision of Servant Vocation." *Proceedings of the Charles Wesley Society* 11 (2006–2007) 69–85.

Providence House Publishers

"The Mission-Church Paradigm of the Wesleyan Revival," in *World Mission in the Wesleyan Spirit*, edited by Darrell L. Whiteman and Gerald H. Anderson, 151–64. Franklin: Providence House Publishers, 2009.

Witness: Journal of the Academy for Evangelism in Theological Education

"Lessons from the 'Society Planting' Paradigm of Early Methodist Women." *Witness* 27 (2013) 5–30.

Introduction

I HAVE REFLECTED A lot recently on the statements I have made and repeated hundreds of times over the years about Wesleyan theology and practice. Here is a sampling of what I would consider to be some of the most salient themes:

- The movement of spiritual renewal under the direction of John and Charles Wesley was both an evangelical and a Eucharistic revival.
- The early Methodist people learned their theology by singing it.
- How the Wesleys did theology is as important as the theology that they did.
- The Wesleyan vision of the Christian life is "conjunctive"; it holds together aspects of the Christian faith often torn apart.
- Wesleyan theology can be described as a theology of grace upon grace.
- John and Charles's view of redemption is both forensic (about the forgiveness of sin) and therapeutic (about the restoration of God's image in our lives).
- If I had to summarize the essence of Wesleyan theology in a phrase, it would be "faith working by love leading to holiness of heart and life."
- If I had to summarize the essence of the Wesleyan tradition in two words, they would be "accountable discipleship."
- Early Methodism, for all intents and purposes, was a movement of women.
- The Wesleys established and nurtured *ecclesiolae in ecclesia* (little churches inside the church) that functioned as catalysts of renewal.
- The Wesley brothers embraced a holistic spirituality, combining practices of piety and practices of mercy.

- The golden thread that has stood the test of time in the Methodist heritage is the deep conviction that you must translate your faith into action.
- John and Charles Wesley rediscovered a missional vision of the church for their own time, centered in Jesus Christ, but spun out into the life of the world in mission and in service.
- Everything revolves around God's love for the Wesleys—love divine.

In this book, I am trying to bring these kinds of critical sound bites to life. I do not set out to examine Wesleyan themes and emphases in anything approaching an exhaustive fashion, although this volume covers a lot of territory. I intend primarily to showcase a number of salient themes that I believe bear directly on the life of faith today. In order to introduce this collection of essays in the most helpful way, I offer a brief overview of the Wesleyan movement of renewal, identify the salient themes of Wesleyan theology and practice, and reflect on the enduring legacy of this Wesleyan tradition. Having laid this foundation, I then discuss the organization of the material into six major sections, the contours of which reflect my personal passions about the Wesleyan heritage and its contemporary contribution.

The Wesleyan Movement

Throughout the course of John and Charles Wesley's adult lives, they remained inextricably bound to the Methodist connection they founded; their theology and practice shaped the movement, and Methodism shaped their theology and practice. They organized a network of Societies, divided into yet smaller groups of bands and classes. These structures for accountable discipleship liberated those awakened by the experience of God's grace, engendered faith, and provided nurture for growth in grace and love. Before too long Methodism established its identity as an "evangelistic order" within the Church of England. The Wesleys had stressed "holiness of heart and life" from the outset, but their evolving experience increasingly urged the importance of the fullest possible love of God and love of neighbor. Their attempt to live authentic lives in Christ, and the controversy that frequently swirled around them, sharpened their theology. John left a doctrinal standard for Methodism in his published *Sermons* and his *Explanatory Notes upon the New Testament*; Charles left an informal standard for theology and practice expressed in the 1780 *Collection of Hymns for the Use of the People Called Methodists*.

Charles's primary gift to the world was the production of some nine-thousand hymns and sacred poems through which the vast majority of people called Methodists learned their theology. His production of hymns for the movement began in earnest in 1739 with the advent of three successive collections of *Hymns and Sacred Poems*. But he produced many hymn collections on various theological themes such as the Trinity, Incarnation, Resurrection, and Pentecost, as well as practical lyrical reflections on many aspects of the Christian life. In 1749, he published his first solo hymnbook independent of his brother's editorial influence, a two-volume collection of *Hymns and Sacred Poems*. During a lengthy period of illness in 1762, he worked on a lyrical paraphrase of the Bible—*Short Hymns on Select Passages of the Holy Scriptures*—2,349 poems that function as a poetic biblical commentary. His 166 *Hymns on the Lord's Supper* demonstrate the centrality of the Eucharist in Wesleyan spirituality. While technically published by his brother, John, the 1780 *Collection of Hymns*, including over five hundred of Charles's own compositions, stands out as one of the most significant hymn books in the history of the church. For many years, this collection provided the standard poetic explication of virtually every dimension of Methodist theology and practice—it is the ultimate compilation of Charles's lyrical theology.

John published more than 450 separate items, ranging from brief pamphlets to full-blown theological treatises. The primary guidebook for his movement, *The Nature, Design, and General Rules of the United Societies*, saw no less than twenty-one editions during his lifetime. In the course of his sixty-six year ministry, he preached no fewer than forty-thousand sermons, publishing four volumes of *Sermons on Several Occasions* from 1746 to 1760. These sermonic essays continue to function as a distinctive "doctrinal standard" for most Methodists today. These "standard sermons" emphasize the centrality of grace, the view of faith as pardon and reconciliation, and the assurance of God's mercy confirmed by the Spirit of Jesus. They describe the way in which God works in the lives of faithful people to make them whole. While the sermons serve as the primary window into the theology and practice of the Wesleyan heritage, a number of the other apologetic theological writings provide balance and perspective. Three stand out: *The Character of a Methodist* (1742) and *A Plain Account of the People Called Methodists* (1749), both of which attempt to portray the Methodists as authentic Christians, and *A Plain Account of Christian Perfection* (1766), arguably John Wesley's magnum opus. Wesley's "quest for perfect love" was the single most consistent theme in his life and thought.

Salient Themes

The salient themes in Wesleyan theology and practice include the foundation of the grace and love of God, the way of salvation, accountable discipleship in a community of grace, and compassionate mission in God's world.

The Grace and Love of God

The Wesleys built their lives and their movement on the foundation of grace. The brothers draw an intimate connection between this grace and the loving God known to us as Father, Son, and Holy Spirit. For the Wesleys, grace is a relational term with which to talk about love, a word that embraces the full image of God, creation, and humankind. This expansive understanding of love and grace links theology and practice—our thoughts about God and our actions. John and Charles understood the Christian life, therefore, as a pilgrimage of "grace upon grace." The practice of Christianity begins in grace, grows in grace, and finds its ultimate completion in God's grace. Grace is God's unmerited love, restoring our relationship to God and renewing God's own image in our lives. Christian discipleship is, first and foremost, a grace-filled response to the free gift of God's all sufficient grace.

The Way of Salvation

The Wesleys constructed a theology oriented essentially around soteriology, or the doctrine of salvation. The so-called Wesleyan "way of salvation" consists of three dynamic movements: repentance, faith, and holiness.

- *Repentance.* John Wesley defines repentance as a true self-understanding akin to that experienced by the prodigal son who "came to himself" (Luke 15:17) in the realization that he was far from his true home. This acknowledgment is the first step toward restoration.
- *Faith.* Faith has to do with the capacity to entrust one's life fully to God. John and Charles both defined saving faith as a genuine trust and confidence in the mercy and love of God through Jesus Christ and a steadfast hope of all good things at God's hand.
- *Holiness.* Holiness is a shorthand term for the whole process by which God restores Christlike love in our lives through the power of the Holy Spirit. Holiness of heart and life, or sanctification, is the process that leads to the ultimate goal of perfect love.

Accountable Discipleship in a Community of Grace

The Wesleys developed the first Methodist Societies in Bristol initially as small groups that met weekly for worship, fellowship, prayer, and instruction. Mutual encouragement and genuine care marked these groups as places of support for those who sought to become loving disciples of Jesus. They were laboratories in which Wesleyan practices such as self-denial, transparency, simplicity, hospitality, and generosity were discussed and nurtured. In the intimacy of these small groups, the early Methodists learned what it meant to grow in Christ and, together, they plumbed the depths of God's love for them all. Above all, they cultivated a holistic spirituality that combined works of piety and works of mercy.

Fellowship in small groups was just one "means of grace" in a constellation of spiritual practices or disciplines, the purpose of which was richer communion with God through Christ. In addition to Christian fellowship, or conference, John Wesley also included prayer and fasting, Bible study, and participation in the Sacrament of Holy Communion among the "instituted means of grace." He called these "works of piety." The Wesleys found it impossible to separate their redemptive experience of God from their active role as agents of reconciliation and social transformation in the world. To the various works of piety, therefore, they added "works of mercy," included among the more expansive "prudential means of grace." The first two of the three "General Rules" enjoined the Methodists to "avoid evil" and to "do good," a rather simple and straightforward philosophy of life. Authentic Christianity, they believed, consists in a constant inward and outward movement. The combination of these practices nurtured and sustained the early Methodists and also provided the energy that fueled the Wesleyan movement as a powerful religious awakening.

The Wesleyan Revival was both "evangelical" (a rediscovery of God's word of grace) and "Eucharistic" (a rediscovery of the Sacrament of Holy Communion as a way to experience that grace). The Wesleys believed that sacramental grace and evangelical experience are necessary counterparts in both worship and the Christian life. The celebration of the Lord's Supper shaped their understanding of God's love for them and their reciprocal love for God, all powerfully symbolized for them in the sharing of a meal.

Compassionate Mission in God's World

The Wesleys rediscovered what is often described today as a missional church: a community of faith that reaches out to others intentionally to demonstrate the way of Jesus. The missional practices of the Wesleys mirrored their understanding of a God who was primarily missional in nature, always reaching out to others with love. Moreover, they firmly believed that God was active and at work in the world to save and restore all creation, to bring about the new creation promised in Scripture. These primary convictions led the Wesleys to reclaim mission as the church's reason for being and evangelism as the heart of that mission in the world. They developed a holistic vision of mission and evangelism that refused to separate faith and works, personal salvation and social justice, physical and spiritual needs. The Wesleys embraced a radical vision of God's activity in the world and lived in hope of the realization of God's reign in beloved community.

The Legacy

John and Charles Wesley influenced Christian thought and practice more than most people realize, leaving behind a robust legacy. Every age needs winsome spiritual mentors. The Wesleyan way affords a different vision of existence—a life of discipleship rooted in Jesus that points to an alternative way of being in the world for the sake of love. The dynamic nature of their Christian vision of redemption, discipleship, and mission, and their embrace of all who seek to serve Jesus by serving others in the world, stand in stark contrast to judgmental and exclusivist traditions that cast a shadow over genuine Christianity. The Wesleyan practices of hospitality, healing, and holiness attract all who seek to find abundant life in the service of love. At least six elements comprise the Wesleys' living legacy.

- *Commitment.* From their parents, John and Charles Wesley learned the importance of wholehearted dedication to God. God gave us God's all; we are called to offer back the whole of our selves—all we are and all we have—as a living sacrifice to God.

- *Orthodoxy.* The roots of this word actually mean "right praise." The Wesleys sought to praise God with every aspect of their being; head and heart and hands all worked together to praise the God of love. They viewed life as a song to be sung to the praise of God in gratitude for all that God has done.

- *Spirituality.* The Wesleys practiced a disciplined devotional life. The classic spiritual disciplines, from Bible study and Eucharist to helping the poor and waging peace, shaped their lives. They offer this holistic spirituality to all who would embrace it today.

- *Mission.* One of the most crucial insights that John and Charles carried with them throughout their lives was that the gospel—the good news of God's love revealed in Jesus—is a message for everyone. They understood themselves to be God's partners in a mission of love and in service to others.
- *Order.* It is in large measure due to John's organizational genius that the Wesleyan Revival developed into such a powerful religious awakening. Methodists lived as those who practiced the presence of God in an intentional and disciplined way.
- *Scripture.* The Wesleyan Revival was, for all intents and purposes, a rediscovery of the Bible. John and Charles Wesley helped others discover that this book was not simply "dead words" from long ago but God's "Living Word" to us today.

John and Charles Wesley viewed life as a way of devotion. All people, Christian or otherwise, are involved in a journey throughout the course of their lives. They seek to understand who they are and what their place is in this world. These brothers point to a spiritual path that all people can benefit from regardless of their religious heritage or perspective. John and Charles's contemplation of the God of grace and love led them both to be lost in wonder, love, and praise.

Overview of Contents

I prepared each chapter in this volume originally for separate presentation as a paper or publication in its own right. A couple essays here have never been published. I have revised much of the older material so as to reflect more recent and definitive research and sourcing. Some slight overlapping remains, mostly to retain the integrity of individual chapters, but I have tried to minimize redundancy. In order to avoid serious overlapping, I did find it necessary to omit two addresses I had hoped to include, delivered in November 2013 as the Inaugural Earl Robinson Memorial Lectures at William Booth College in Winnipeg: "Foundations of the Wesleyan Way" and "Gospel-bearing in the Wesleyan Way." The minimal redundancy that remains reveals, I am sure, some of the insights of other scholars that have shaped my thinking about the Wesleyan heritage definitively, as well as my own discoveries, of course, that appear and reappear due to their salient qualities.

Several of these essays I presented as keynote addresses at milestone events such as the tercentenary of Charles Wesley's birth. Others reflect invitations to provide plenary reflections at significant international events, such as a joint Methodist/Benedictine conference in Rome or an annual remembrance of the Wesleys in Seoul, South Korea. I delivered one of the papers as a presidential address before the Academy for Evangelism in Theological Education. It was my great honor to present another essay at the annual Wallace Chappell Lecture in Evangelism at Wesley Theological Seminary in Washington, DC. One-third of these chapters are linked in one way or another with The Charles Wesley Society, for which I served as president for eight years. Other papers I prepared for the sheer joy of working in this material and with hopes of offering discoveries that might just change lives. With regard to several papers I confess an eagerness to entertain or to exhort through them, given the circumstances of their delivery. But I hope these ulterior motives have never caused me to deviate from my determination to find and honestly present what I conceived to be the truth.

One of my life-long desires has been to extricate Charles Wesley out from under the long shadow of his older brother, John. So you will find equal treatment between these two great mentors in the Christian faith. Likewise, I have always felt that women in the life of the church deserve more attention than they have received. So women figure prominently here, as well. For me, the Christian faith is so much more than what we claim we believe. Our practices define who we are; the nature of our discipleship sets the trajectory of our lives. So my writings in the areas of discipleship, worship and liturgy, evangelism, and mission bring this volume to a fitting conclusion in action, with a couple appendices added that seek to translate my own points of learning into contemporary expression and action.

The six parts of this book reveal the various arenas within Wesleyan studies into which I have felt drawn. Parts 1 and 2 focus on the co-founders of the Methodist movement. Most studies related to the Wesleys begin invariably with John or exclude Charles entirely. This is understandable, but I open this collection of essays on Wesleyan theology and practice intentionally with Charles. I make an argument for this, not only because of the relative neglect of the younger brother, but because he functioned as the initiator of the revival in a number of ways. The younger brother launched the so-called "Holy Club" at Oxford University, the first "rise of Methodism," but deferred to John's leadership when he returned to his alma mater from Lincolnshire. Charles's "evangelical conversion" preceded his brother's famous Aldersgate Experience by three days. Methodists around the world know how John's heart was strangely warmed, but know nothing of the parallel experience of Charles. Once the revival under their direction commenced, Charles was the first to face mob violence in the "Black Country," Staffordshire. I could go on and on with this litany of firsts. But of greater significance is the fact that the Methodist people learned their theology, first, by singing it. While the proclamation of the gospel through the media of both song and sermon fueled the revival, a faith that sings permeates the life of the believer deeply. So I begin with Charles.

The three chapters of Part 1 introduce Charles as a lyrical theologian, demonstrate his dynamic conception of faith, and articulate his vision of a life of perfect love. Essentially, they lay a broad theological foundation and then highlight to the great foci of Wesleyan soteriology—faith and love (holiness of heart and life). Part 2 highlights several elements of the brothers' symbiotic theological perspective under the rubric of "practical divinity." In a very brief article, I provide an image to help understand the so-called Wesleyan quadrilateral as a normative model of authority. Chapter 5 outlines the contribution of both brothers to a practical understanding of the person and work of Christ. The third chapter in this section reveals the centrality of the concept of reconciliation to both brothers, particularly through the lens of the Incarnation and redemptive work of Christ.

I have devoted a lot of energy in my life to recovering the "lost history" of women in the Methodist movement. The three chapters of Part 3 may be aptly encapsulated in three words: equality, community, and sanctification. I argue that the Wesleys and the early Methodist women proclaimed a message of biblical equality that embraced the gifts of women who functioned as pioneers and preachers. Chapter 8 examines an early Methodist community of women under the direction of Mary Bosanquet that combined vital piety and social action. A prayer of Hester Ann Rogers provides the framework for an examination of the "lived holiness" of early Methodist women in the final chapter of this section.

Part 4 focuses on Wesleyan spiritual practices. The theology of the Wesleys shaped the practices in which Methodists engaged; the practices of the Methodist people shaped their theology. Chapter 10 provides a panoramic vision of the holistic spirituality developed within Methodism, combining works of piety and works of mercy. Charles Wesley inculcated a passion for spiritual practices through his hymns (ch. 11); Methodists sang what they practiced. Given the centrality of communal singing and the devotional use of lyrical texts in the Methodist tradition, chapter 12 explores a faith that sings and the renewing power of lyrical theology.

In virtually every movement of renewal in the history of the church, the innovators and pioneers enact important changes in worship and leadership. Part 5 examines this aspect of the Wesleyan project, illustrating the rediscovery and centrality of the sacramental in the Christian life (ch. 13), describing the integral connection between worship and evangelism (ch. 14), and highlighting a Wesleyan model of leadership based on the kenotic imagery of Jesus' life and ministry (ch. 15).

The volume concludes, then, with an exploration of the Wesleys' missional ecclesiology and emphasis on the reign of God (Pt. 6). The Wesleys discovered what they considered to be an authentic New Testament model of the church that faced the world rather than turning in on itself. This "mission-church paradigm," described in chapter 16, revolutionized the community of faith in their time. In a return to the contributions of women to the early Methodism, chapter 17 articulates the lessons learned from the "society planting" activities of these pioneers. Chapter 18 celebrates the central theme of the peaceable reign of Christ in the lyrical theology of Charles Wesley, painting a portrait of the ultimate goal of God's love in a universe of justice and peace.

John and Charles Wesley and the early Methodist people viewed life, essentially, as an adventurous quest for love divine. John preached that true religion is "living in eternity, and walking in eternity; and hereby walking in the love of God and [all people]."[3] Charles framed the Christian journey and its goal in his own inimitable way:

> Finish then thy new creation,
> > Pure and sinless let us be,
> Let us see thy great salvation,
> > Perfectly restor'd in thee;
> Chang'd from glory into glory,
> > Till in heaven we take our place,
> Till we cast our crowns before thee,
> > Lost in wonder, love, and praise![4]

My hope is that these collected essays on Wesleyan theology and practice cast light upon your path—a journey leading in this same direction.

---

3. J. Wesley, *Works*, 4:57–58.
4. C. Wesley, *Redemption Hymns*, 12 (no. 9.4).

Part 1
Charles Wesley's Lyrical Theology

Chapter 1

Charles Wesley's Lyrical Credo

Source note: A keynote address delivered before the 22nd Charles Wesley Society Meeting at Duke Divinity School in June 2011. "Charles Wesley's Lyrical Credo." *Proceedings of the Charles Wesley Society* 15 (2011) 41–67.

Introduction

DESPITE THE FACT THAT virtually everyone familiar with the Wesleyan tradition echoes the observation—early Methodists first learned their theology by singing it—scholars over the years have given much less attention to the lyrical theology of Charles Wesley than to the theology of his brother, John. Students of Charles have scrutinized particular aspects of his theology, to be sure, from its Trinitarian foundations to its millennialist speculations, from its vision of Christ's work of redemption to the presence of Christ in the worshiping community, from its articulation of faith as the means of salvation to its vision of *theosis* as the goal of the Christian life, from its presentation of sacramental grace and time in the Eucharistic hymns to its missiological ambiance in some of the most well-known texts.[1] But only a number of publications (many of them in the last quarter of the century) examine his

---

1. For essays and monographs on these respective topics as illustrative of such theological inquiry, see Vickers, "Making of a Trinitarian Theology"; Newport, "Premillennialism"; Tyson, "Charles Wesley's Theology of the Cross"; Gallaway, "Presence of Christ"; Chilcote, "Charles Wesley and the Language of Faith"; Kimbrough, "'Theosis' in the Writings of Charles Wesley"; Loyer, "Memorial, Means, and Pledge"; Meistad, "Missiology of Charles Wesley." Interest in Charles Wesley as a theologian is not completely novel. A volume entitled *The Theologians of Methodism*, edited by W.F. Tillet, included a brief essay: Herbert, "Charles Wesley: The Poet—Theologian of Methodism." For general studies of the theology of Wesley's hymns, see Dale, "Theological and Literary Qualities"; Lawson, *The Wesley Hymns*; and Yrigoyen, *Praising the God of Grace*.

theology as a coherent whole or have sought to answer the question, What kind of theologian was Charles Wesley? A quick survey of the books and articles that seek to address this issue reveals a variety of perspectives and characterizations of Charles Wesley as theologian.

J. Ernest Rattenbury, perhaps the most significant student of the Wesley corpus during the early twentieth century, described Charles as an "experimental theologian." In his monumental study of *The Evangelical Doctrines of Charles Wesley's Hymns*,[2] in particular, he developed a portrait of his subject in a spirit very similar to that of Albert Outler's depiction of Charles's brother, John, as a "folk theologian." Rather than a "formal theologian," in the conventional sense of that term, Charles functioned as a popular theologian who oriented his theological work around the needs of the common person of his day. Rattenbury demonstrated Charles's emphasis on the experience of God in his hymns; the theology of his hymns revolved around this experimental dimension of the Christian faith.

In his October 1989 address on "Charles Wesley as Theologian" at the Charles Wesley Publication Colloquium in Princeton, New Jersey, Tom Langford subordinated the younger brother's theological role in the Wesleyan Revival to that of his older brother, John. He viewed Charles as "a theologian in the same sense that anyone who thinks, sings, paints, or dances about God is a theologian."[3] While Charles served a "supportive, encouraging, and propagandizing role" within the life of the movement, he was not a "creative theologian."[4] Charles was at best, in Langford's view, a "practical theologian" like his brother, but of less immediate influence or abiding significance in matters of proper theology.

Langford was not unaware of Teresa Berger's groundbreaking dissertation in its original German form, *Theologie in Hymnen?*[5] published just a year prior to the conference, and that the two scholars differed in their conclusions. Berger argued that Wesley was a "doxological theologian," whose theological statements *to* God were of equal value to the theological affirmations of formal theologians *about* God. Unlike Langford, she viewed Wesley as a creative, first-order theologian whose hymns were theological documents of critical importance in the development of the Wesleyan theological heritage. Similarly, in his re-examination of Rattenbury's work on Charles, in an essay subtitled "The Theology of Charles Wesley's Hymns," Brian Beck confirms the theological weight of Charles's hymns in relation to the spiritual formation of

---

2. Rattenbury, *Evangelical Doctrines*.
3. Langford, "Charles Wesley as Theologian," 99.
4. Langford, "Charles Wesley as Theologian," 100.
5. Berger, *Theology in Hymns?*

the Methodist people. "We deceive ourselves," he maintains, "if we imagine that John Wesley's extensive theological writings were the decisive influence in the formation of the Methodist preachers or their hearers. . . . the words that lingered in the minds of the society members . . . were not snatches from [sermons or notes] . . . but [hymns]."[6]

Following this same basic line of argument, in an essay published in the tercentenary volume, *Charles Wesley: Life, Literature, and Legacy*, Ted Campbell imports a novel term to describe the character of Charles as a theologian. He resonates strongly with Berger and Beck, characterizing Wesley as *theologos*. He employs this Greek term in the same way Christians of the Eastern churches use it to honor those critical figures in the church who gave us words (*logoi*) about God (*theos*).[7] This description, Campbell argues, "allows us to claim more explicitly Charles Wesley's first-order work (*theologia prima*) of giving us words by which we can speak of God and indeed by which we can speak to God."[8] In a brief article on "The Theology of Charles Wesley's Hymns," John Tyson concurs with Berger and Campbell, asserting that Wesley's hymns make theological assertions *about* and *to* God.[9] His preferred descriptive title for Wesley is "praxis theologian," since Charles's fundamental concern, in his view, was how Christian theology is lived out in the world.

Despite detractors here and there who tend to argue the subordinate status of the hymn as a theological text, one can sense the development of a growing appreciation for Charles Wesley's theological significance today, a scenario parallel to the discovery of John Wesley as theologian a generation earlier. In addition to the descriptions of Charles as experimental, practical, doxological, praxis theologian and *theologos*, perhaps the most important recent characterization is that of Wesley as "lyrical theologian." The connection between the lyrical arts and theology is nothing new, of course. Scripture itself bears witness to the theological significance of sacred song in the community of faith from the Psalms to the hymn texts embedded in the narratives of the New Testament.[10] When Augustine made the claim that to sing is to pray twice, he was bearing witness to the fact that Christians define themselves and their theologies not simply on the basis of what they know or how they think, but by the forms and language they use to praise the One they love. In the current rediscovery of this conversation

6. Beck, "Rattenbury Revisited," 72.
7. Campbell, "Charles Wesley, 'Theologos.'"
8. Campbell, "Charles Wesley, 'Theologos,'" 265.
9. Tyson, "Theology of Charles Wesley's Hymns."
10. Greenman and Sumner, *Unwearied Praise*.

between theology and the arts, contemporary theologians such as William Dyrness[11] and Jeremy Begbie,[12] among many others, are expanding the vision of a *theologia poetica*, including the relationship between sacred song and theology. In the much-heralded book, *Resounding Truth: Christian Wisdom in the World of Music*, Begbie maintains that poetry expresses theology potently, but also announces and performs faith in a different voice. He argues the ancient conviction that art, in its multifarious forms, must be recognized as a genuine theological text.

In 1984, ST Kimbrough Jr. coined the term "lyrical theology" in reference to Charles Wesley. In three successive essays,[13] all reprinted in adapted form in his new book, *The Lyrical Theology of Charles Wesley: A Reader*, he refined the concept, defining it as "a theology couched in poetry, song, and liturgy, characterized by rhythm and expressive of emotion and sentiment."[14] He explores lyrical theology as both doxology and reflection—as both words to God and words about God. Charles expressed the doxological dimension of his theology primarily in hymns composed for the purpose of worship and devotion. In these texts, according to Kimbrough, "he was seeking a continual offering of the human heart and life to God. Hence, the lyrical theology of doxology is multifaceted, multidimensional, and filled with diverse themes."[15] But other hymns demonstrate "his way of working through theological issues, thought, and concepts, and of shaping theological ideas" through a poetic medium.[16] Charles used hymns to reflect on the discursive theology of his brother and other theologians of the church, as illustrated, for example, by his Eucharistic hymns, and on the meaning of significant historical events during his life, including the deaths of beloved friends. Through his poetic texts, Charles Wesley created "a vibrant, lyrical theological memory individually and corporately for Christians and the church as a whole."[17] Kimbrough's compilation of poetical selections from the Wesleyan corpus is an important step forward in an effort to uncover the rhythms, textures, and tones of his lyrical theology.

---

11. Dyrness, *Poetic Theology*.

12. Begbie, *Beholding the Glory*; and, with Guthrie, *Resonant Witness*.

13. Kimbrough, "Lyrical Theology"; "Lyrical Theology: Theology in Hymns"; and "Hymnody of Charles Wesley." Cf. Kimbrough, "Hymns Are Theology"; and "Charles Wesley's Dynamic, Lyrical Theology."

14. Kimbrough, *Lyrical Theology*, 3.

15. Kimbrough, *Lyrical Theology*, 53.

16. Kimbrough, *Lyrical Theology*, 54.

17. Kimbrough, *Lyrical Theology*, 72.

A "Lyrical Credo"

It should be immediately obvious that the exploration of Wesley's lyrical theology and any effort to discern its salient features, let alone to map it out in a coherent fashion, is a monumental task. Fortunately, the availability of the hymn corpus and Wesley's prose works in a much more definitive form now makes this kind of important work a real possibility. Perhaps what has happened in the world of John Wesley studies will capture the imagination of those who have interest in Charles, as well. If a full-blown lyrical theology of Charles Wesley stands somewhat beyond our reach at this point in time, however, some modest steps can be taken to discern the primary facets of his coherent theological vision. An important initial question to ask in this regard is, What does Charles Wesley explicitly claim to believe in his hymns? To state this question in a much more concrete form, Is there a "lyrical credo" that we can discern in those texts where Charles actually confesses "I believe" or "we believe"? These questions themselves raise several preliminary concerns that require brief examination.

A project on "Charles Wesley and the Language of Faith," the conclusions of which were published in the *Charles Wesley: Life, Literature, and Legacy* volume, involved a detailed analysis of Wesley's use of faith language as a lens through which to focus attention on the Methodist movement and to consider his understanding of faith.[18] This essay examined Charles's use of the term "faith" in the 1780 *Collection* and his published *Journal* and attempted to delineate the elements of a coherent "concept of faith" in those sources. A similar method is proposed here in an effort to discern Wesley's lyrical credo, recognizing the same limitations and dangers of this previous approach. This essay articulates Wesley's credo on the basis of his explicit confessions about it, rather than fitting his hymns into the structure of a traditional systematic theology, or of the Wesleyan *via salutis*, or of some other theological or doxological program. It focuses primarily on what Charles emphasizes by explicit reference to the language or confession of belief.

It is important to recognize that, in Wesleyan theology, a symbiotic relationship obtains between the faith by which one believes (*fides qua creditur*) and the faith in which one believes (*fides quae creditur*). While the previous study on "faith" alluded to above revealed Charles's implicit emphasis on subjective, living, or saving faith, this project examines more fully the objective aspect of faith in his hymns—the content of the faith in which Wesley believes. In order to construct his lyrical credo, therefore, every instance of the personal confession, "I believe," and the corporate

---

18. Chilcote, "Wesley and Faith."

confession, "we believe," has been identified in his published and manuscript hymns. Interestingly, these hymns make it abundantly clear that in Charles's theological vision, he seeks to move the singer from "propositional faith" to an "experience of faith." What the believer confesses, in other words, can have transforming power in life. Wesley's lyrical theology, to state the obvious, is much larger than any credo extracted from selected hymns. But Wesley's explicit language concerning belief can function as a window through which to view the salient themes of his personal credo more clearly. The working assumption is that when Charles employs language like "I believe," those within the worshiping community or in the context of intimate fellowship engaged those texts with greater attentiveness and a heightened sense of significance with regard to what they were singing or studying, much in the same way that a congregation stands as its members recite the historic Christian creeds.

It will be helpful to look at references to "I believe" separately from the first person plural forms, and then to examine the combined collections as a whole. In Charles Wesley's hymn corpus, there are forty-five instances of the confession, "I believe," in forty-one hymns.[19] The vast majority of these hymns are evenly distributed in three major collections, eleven hymns in each: *Hymns and Sacred Poems* 1742, *Hymns and Sacred Poems* 1749, and *Scripture Hymns* 1762. More than half of these hymns (27) are based upon explicitly identified biblical texts.[20] Given the fact that one in four of these sacred songs come from the *Scripture Hymns* 1762 collection, this should be no surprise. Wesley based seven hymns on texts from the Hebrew Scriptures; half of the New Testament documents (13 books) provided inspiration for the remaining twenty hymns. In a number of hymns, the words "I believe" simply fall naturally into the poetic line, but in more than half the texts, the line begins with the words "Jesu, I believe" (1), "Jesus, I believe" (2), or much more pervasively, "Lord, I believe" (20). In nine instances, the simple words "I believe" begin a poetic line. Of greater interest for us here, however, are those hymns in which these phrases begin a stanza (20 instances) or function as the opening words of what I will describe as a "credo hymn" (12 hymns). In these hymns, the confessional nature of the hymn as a whole tends to be much more pronounced.

---

19. The phrase also occurs three times in one hymn by Zinzendorf, translated by John Wesley. Zinzendorf, *Gesang-Buch der Herrnhuter*, 1136, no. 1258. This hymn has not been included in the analysis here.

20. Deut 6:5; Ps 7:1; 71; Isa 40:31; 56:1; Ezek 36:25ff; Dan 6; Matt 5:3–4, 6; 8:15; 14:36; Mark 9:24; Luke 18:1; John 3:18; 7:37–39; 8:12; Rom 4:16ff; 12:12; 1 Cor 10:11; 1 Tim 2:4; 2 Tim 4:5; Titus 2:14; Heb 4:9; 6:1; 1 John 1:9; 2:3; Jude 24; Rev 22:17.

Somewhat surprisingly—given the strong communal emphasis of the Wesleys—the collection of "we believe" hymns is somewhat smaller. Wesley uses this confession twenty-nine times in twenty-eight hymns—only one hymn has a double use of the phrase, concluding and beginning successive lines of two stanzas in a chiasmic structure. Examining these first person plural hymns in parallel fashion with the hymns couched in first person singular, we find a wide distribution across the Wesleyan corpus here, as well. The *Hymns and Sacred Poems* collections figure prominently, as do Wesley's *Scripture Hymns* 1762, from which one out of four of the hymns is drawn. Wesley based twelve hymns (8 of these in *Scripture Hymns* 1762) on biblical texts ranging from 2 Kings, Isaiah, Jeremiah, and Ezekiel in the Hebrew Scriptures to Matthew, John, 1 Thessalonians, Hebrews, 2 Peter, 2 John, and Revelation in the Greek Scriptures.[21] This particular collection of hymns tends to be much more diverse than the other group. Only two of these hymns actually begin with a declarative statement of belief, despite the fact that more than half the hymns (14) include "we believe" in the opening line of a stanza. Ten lines open with the words, "we believe," the majority of these (7) being the first line of a stanza. There are no credo hymns, as defined earlier, in which the hymn begins with the confession, "Lord, we believe," or a similar construction.[22] In these two collections of hymns taken together, therefore, Wesley employs the confessional language "I believe" or "we believe" seventy-four times in sixty-nine hymns.

General Observations

First, these poetic statements of faith are *rooted in Scripture*. A scriptural text accompanies or Wesley provides a scriptural title for nearly half the hymns (32) in this "credo" constellation. One in four of these sacred songs, as has been noted, comes from the *Scripture Hymns* 1762. As in all of Charles's hymns, the biblical message and/or narrative pervades these texts, shaping the content of belief.

Second, the vast majority of these hymns are set within the *context of prayer*. Nine lines of poetry in this corpus begin with the simple declaration, "I believe." There are no such parallels in the plural form. But

---

21. 2 Kings 19:10; Isa 40:8; Jer 6:16; Ezek 7:37; Matt 18:20; John 7:37; 1 Thess 4:13; Heb 6:12; 2 Pet 1:21; 3:12; 2 John 9; Rev 22:17.

22. In six instances, there are directly parallel lines of the singular and plural forms of the confession: "In Jesus I / we believe" (in two different hymns); "Lord, I / we believe the promise sure"; "Lord, I / we believe the promise true"; "Lord, I / we believe, and rest secure"; and, "The moment I / we believe."

Wesley explicitly couches nearly four times that number (33) in the form of prayer with the words, "Lord, or Jesus, I / we believe." Confession takes on a profoundly relational quality in these hymns. It arises out of the intimacy of a relationship and as an expression of devotion to a Person. It also reflects a "faith seeking understanding" posture of the believer or believing community.

Third, these hymns exhibit a profound *balance of individual and corporate confession*. The majority of texts clearly reflect what Robert Cushman described as the "enpersonalization of faith." On one level, all authentic believers express their faith in first person singular. But these hymns also demonstrate the importance of the corporate confession of faith and the centrality of a community in faithful praxis. While there are more hymns that express individual belief, Wesley balances these texts with substantial, plural, communal hymns.

Fourth, the hymns exhibit a *quality of existential trust* more than that of intellectual assent. It is interesting that none of these hymns falls into the genre of what are sometimes described as *lyra fidelium*: poetic translations of creedal statements.[23] Wesley neither indirectly nor intentionally paraphrases the historic creeds of the church or other primary doxological statements in poetic form in this particular constellation of hymns. This is not to say that he does not do this elsewhere. In *Redemption Hymns* 1747, for example, he provides a marvelous poetic paraphrase of the *Te Deum*.[24] In general, the first person hymns tend to be more existential and subjective—more urgent, whereas the plural hymns exhibit a more objective, even majestic quality—more timeless.

Fifth and similarly, rather than confessions of the *consensus fidelium*, these hymns tend to focus on *distinctive Wesleyan theological emphases*. The Wesleys shared a common theological heritage with Christians of every age and context—a biblical, apostolic faith evidenced in the life of the Christian community. Built upon and presupposing this foundation, the hymns in this credo constellation reflect a cluster of doctrinal emphases distinctive to John and Charles Wesley and their movement.

---

23. Martin Luther's "We All Believe in One True God" exemplifies this genre. First published in Johann Walther, *Geystliche gesangk Buchleyn* (Wittenberg, 1524), *Wir glauben all' an einen Gott* echoes explicit themes of the Nicene Creed.

24. C. Wesley, *Redemption Hymns*, 16–18 (no. 13).

Constituent Themes of the Lyrical Credo

Two hymns in this particular collection of texts related to Christian belief address the question of doctrine directly and describe its function in the life of the believer. In a hymn based on Second John 9, "He that abideth in the doctrine of Christ, he hath both the Father and the Son," Wesley explicates the meaning of doctrine. The opening stanza of the hymn reveals how propositional faith functions properly to elicit living faith. For belief to be real, it must be lived out in concrete actions in life, and this enacted belief unites the believer with God.

> We, only we believe indeed,
>> Our faith by our obedience shew,
>
> Who follow, by his Spirit led,
>> And walk as Jesus walk'd below,
>
> And in his ways continue still,
> And all his words with joy fulfil.[25]

Second, Wesley argues that intellectual assent to spiritual truth falls short of saving faith and can even impede a genuine, faith-filled relationship with God. In one of his texts from *Trinity Hymns* 1767, Charles distinguishes clearly between the faith of assent and a "true and lively faith" gifted to the believer by God.[26]

> But 'till our souls are born again,
> We to the truth assent in vain,
> By notions right ourselves deceive,
> And only fancy we believe.
>
> The Tri-une God we cannot know,
> Unless he doth the faith bestow,
> Faith which removes our mountain-load,
> And brings us to a pard'ning God:
>
> Sure evidence of things unseen,
> Which swallows up the gulph between,

---

25. C. Wesley, *Scripture Hymns*, 2:406; st. 1.

26. Wesley adheres to the teachings of the Church of England in this regard. See Newport, *Sermons of Charles Wesley*, 201; cf. Chilcote, "Wesley and Faith," 302–04.

> The light of life divine imparts,
> And forms Jehovah in our hearts.[27]

Charles Wesley dedicates theology, in other words, to the service of transformation.[28] Because of this fundamental orientation, mission claims a central place in Charles's life and work because the goal of Christian mission is a change from a condition of human existence contrary to God's purposes to one in which people are able to enjoy fullness of life in harmony with God. Texts such as these lay a groundwork for the construction of a lyrical credo, the purpose of which is to lead the believer into a dynamic relationship of love with the Creator through the Redeemer enabled by the Sustainer. The lyrical credo that emerges from this constellation of hymns consists of at least four constituent elements: trust in the God of promise; the work of grace experienced as forgiveness and pardon, liberation, and healing; the quest for holiness leading to Christian perfection; and ultimate rest or security in God. Those familiar with Wesleyan theology will immediately recognize the centrality of these salient themes.

Trust in the God of Promise

Charles Wesley's lyrical credo begins with the God of promise, goodness, and truth who can be trusted in all things. No fewer than seventeen hymns in this constellation celebrate this foundational truth. "Still we believe," Charles maintains, in a God "whose presence fills both earth and heaven."[29] His exposition of 2 Kings 19:10 celebrates the trustworthy nature of this God.

> Our God almighty to redeem
>   All-gracious we believe,
> And know, who humbly trust in him
>   He never can deceive.[30]

In several hymns, Charles simply expresses his belief in a God who is both good and true.[31]

---

27. C. Wesley, *Trinity Hymns*, 101, sts. 2–4.
28. See Langford, *Practical Divinity*, 24.
29. C. Wesley, *Trinity Hymns*, 43, st. 2.
30. C. Wesley, *Scripture Hymns*, 1:189.
31. Wesley and Wesley, *Hymns and Sacred Poems* (1742), 225, st. 1. Cf. C. Wesley, *Hymns and Sacred Poems* (1749), 1:187, st. 8.

Interestingly, he explicitly connects these aspects of the divine character with the primal issues of hunger and thirst, basic needs that are crucial in the development of trust in the lives of all human beings.

> Lord, we believe; and taste thee good,
>> Thee all-sufficient own,
> And hunger after heavenly food,
>> And thirst for God alone.[32]

In the only hymn included in the constellation of credo hymns presented here from *Hymns on the Lord's Supper* 1745, Charles extends this image of nourishment and applies it to "the holy mystery"—the Eucharistic feast:

> 'Tis God we believe,
>> Who cannot deceive,
> The witness of God
> Is present, and speaks in the mystical blood.
>
>> Receiving the bread
>>> On Jesus we feed,
>> It doth not appear
> His manner of working; but Jesus is here![33]

"If in Jesus we believe," he elsewhere urges, "let us on his mercies feast."[34]

Wesley emphasizes the centrality of God's promises in one of the "credo hymns" based on Isaiah 40:31.

> Lord, I believe thy every word,
>> Thy every promise true,
> And lo! I wait on thee, my Lord,
>> Till I my strength renew.[35]

---

32. Wesley and Wesley, *Hymns and Sacred Poems* (1740), 125, st. 6, from a hymn "To Be Sung at Meals." In the same collection, reflecting on Matt 5:3–4, 6, Charles sings: "Lord, I believe the promise sure, / and trust thou wilt not long delay; / Hungry, and sorrowful, and poor, / Upon thy word myself I stay" (Wesley and Wesley, *Hymns and Sacred Poems* (1740), 65, st. 6).

33. Wesley and Wesley, *Hymns on the Lord's Supper*, 79, sts. 5–6.

34. Wesley and Wesley, *Hymns and Sacred Poems* (1742), 156, st. 2.

35. Wesley and Wesley, *Hymns and Sacred Poems* (1742), 225, st. 1, the first of the so-called "Credo Hymns" to be cited, i.e., a hymn that opens with the words, "Lord, I / We Believe."

God's promises are manifold. God promises and gives the Spirit. In one of his many hymns for the Feast of Pentecost, Wesley confesses:

> Lord, we believe to us and ours
> > The apostolick promise given;
> We wait to taste the heavenly powers,
> > The Holy Ghost sent down from heaven.[36]

God promises to meet the followers of Jesus in prayer and to use that means of grace to encourage and empower them in the journey of faith. "Lord, we believe the promise true," he affirms, "The prayer of faith can all things do."[37] They can trust God, even when they "cannot see" and when their way is "dark, and dead, and comfortless." Even there the faithful one cries, "Jesus, I believe in thee."[38] God manifests these promises primarily in the "sure, irrevocable word" in which we believe.[39] God displays the restoring power of love through the promise of mercy.

> Lord, I believe thy mercy's power
> > Shall every obstacle remove,
> I trust thy promise to restore
> > In me the kingdom of thy love:
> Jesus, thy word cannot be vain;
> > Truth, power, and love divine thou art;
> And I shall love my God again,
> > With all my mind, soul, strength, and heart.[40]

Charles seems to be drawn inordinately to the promise of personal intimacy with God in Christ. A cluster of six hymns explore this theme of the nearness of God—God's immanence in human life. In his *Elegy on the Death of Robert Jones* he elevates the most fundamental aspect of his subject's life: "Lord I believe thou art—for thou art mine!"[41] A strong mystical quality tends to dominate all he writes on this subject. A participatory spirituality shapes his primary vision of the Christian life as the hymns bear witness to

---

36. Wesley and Wesley, *Hymns and Sacred Poems* (1742), 165, st. 5.
37. C. Wesley, *Hymns and Sacred Poems* (1749), 1:272, st. 2.
38. C. Wesley, *Scripture Hymns*, 2:252; a single-stanza hymn based on John 8:12.
39. Wesley, *Whitsunday Hymns*, 9, st. 5.
40. C. Wesley, *Scripture Hymns*, 1:91; a single-stanza hymn based on Deut 6:5. Cf. C. Wesley, *Hymns for Children*, 20, st. 3.
41. C. Wesley, *Elegy*, 7.

the possibility of intimacy with the Triune God. In a hymn based on Isaiah 56:1, Wesley reflects on the nearness of salvation and the immediate personal connection with Christ that it entails. "Jesus, I believe thee near," he writes, "I have my Lord within." He hastens "to embrace" Christ, who "dwells forever in [his] heart."[42] He celebrates the promise of Jesus' presence in the community of faith whenever the faithful call on his name.

> Can we believe this precious word,
> And not assemble in thy name,
> Sure, if we meet, to meet our Lord,
> And catch thy whisper, "Here I am!"
> Where two or three with faithful heart
> Unite to plead the promise given,
> As truly in the midst thou art,
> As in the countless hosts of heaven.[43]

True religion for Wesley includes a sense of overwhelming belonging, inner harmony, and connection. A stanza from his hymn, "For a Minister," expresses this intimacy with Jesus—this heart religion—using Jesus' own words of promise.

> Lord, I believe the promise true,
> "Behold, I always am with you";
> Always if thou with me remain,
> Hell, earth, and sin shall rage in vain.[44]

Charles yearns for greater intimacy with God in Christ.

> My Lord, thou wilt not long delay,
>   This inward calm proclaims thee near,
> Sorrow, and doubt are fled away,
>   My Lord shall in my heart appear.

---

42. C. Wesley, *Scripture Hymns*, 1:368–69. In one of his hymns, Charles reflects on the encounter between Jesus and Thomas, speaking intimately about his connections with the wounds of Christ. He concludes the hymn with the words of Thomas, "Thou art my Lord, my God!" (C. Wesley, *Hymns and Sacred Poems* (1749), 1:325).

43. C. Wesley, *Scripture Hymns*, 2:176; a single-stanza hymn based on Matt 18:20.

44. Wesley and Wesley, *Hymns and Sacred Poems* (1740), 112, st. 9.

> Jesu, my Saviour, brother, friend,
>   As I believe, so let it be;
> O make me patient to the end,
>   And then reveal thyself in me.[45]

In a hymn entitled "Waiting for the Promise," he simply proclaims, "I believe in Jesu's name," because he is the One in whom all God's promises come to ultimate fruition.[46] Charles Wesley, first and foremost, confesses belief in the God of promise.

The Work of Grace

> Stand we in the good old way,
>   Who Christ by faith receive,
> Heartily we must obey,
>   If truly we believe:
> Other way can none declare
> Than this from which we ne'er will move:
>   Sav'd by grace thro' faith we are,
>   Thro' faith that works by love.[47]

In this hymn based on Jeremiah 6:16, Charles articulates one of the most central themes in Wesleyan theology—faith working by love—a concept drawn from Galatians 5:6. True belief entails the experience of the work of grace in our lives. The hymns of the credo constellation reflect two dimensions of this saving grace. If those who seek God do not resist the gracious activity of the Spirit of Christ in their lives, then forgiveness and pardon define their lives as the disciples of Jesus. Secondly, God also seeks to liberate and heal through the work of grace; grace functions in a therapeutic manner to restore and make whole, as well. Three times as many hymns explore the former of these twin dimensions (15), but the therapeutic activity of God (articulated here in 5 hymns) spills over into the goal of perfect love, a third aspect of Wesley's lyrical credo to be explored more

---

45. Wesley and Wesley, *Hymns and Sacred Poems* (1742), 218, sts. 14–15. Wesley based this hymn on 2 Tim 4:5.

46. Wesley and Wesley, *Hymns and Sacred Poems* (1742), 238, st. 4. Cf. C. Wesley, *Elegy*, 7, in which he discusses the conversion of many to belief because of Jesus' own words.

47. C. Wesley, *Scripture Hymns*, 2:13, st. 1.

fully below. At its most rudimentary level, justification by grace through faith entails forgiveness and healing. The believer experiences God's grace as both pardon and liberation.

Forgiveness and Pardon

Charles articulates the essence of forgiveness in this lyrical paraphrase of Revelation 12:17—the Spirit's gift of the water of life.

> As soon as in him we believe,
> > By faith of his Spirit we take,
> And freely forgiven, receive
> > The mercy for Jesus's sake;
> We gain a pure drop of his love,
> > The life of eternity know,
> Angelical happiness prove,
> > And witness an heaven below.[48]

In a 1772 collection of hymns entitled *Preparation for Death*, Wesley expresses the ultimate prayer of the dying sinner.

> I long thy smiling face to see,
> > Who freely dost forgive
> Transgression, sin, iniquity,
> > The moment we believe.[49]

Through a gracious act of mercy, God does for sinners what they cannot do for themselves. Fallen and broken, the human being relies on God's free act of love in Christ to secure the forgiveness that true reconciliation with God, self, and others requires. First John 1:9 serves as the locus of Charles's vision of divine intervention: "If we confess our sins, he who is faithful and just will forgive us our sins and cleanse us from all unrighteousness." "Hast thou not revers'd my doom?" asks Charles, "Thou hast; and I believe: / Yet I still a sinner come, / That thou mayst still forgive." The concluding lines of this stanza, in which he describes the unredeemed child of God in search of forgiveness, leave no room for complacency.

---

48. C. Wesley, *Scripture Hymns*, 2:431, st. 2.
49. C. Wesley, *Preparation for Death*, 29 (no. 27.3).

> Wretched, miserable, blind,
>> Poor, and naked, and unclean,
> Still, that I may mercy find,
>> I bring thee nought but sin.[50]

God must subdue the rebel heart in order for the child of God to find her or his way home. "Self-desp'rate"—that is, despairing of one's own will, energy, and power—writes Charles, "I believe."[51]

In these hymns, Charles identifies both the source and the consequence of this work of grace. Forgiveness rests secure on the foundation of the *kerygma*—the proclamation of the death and resurrection of Christ and the affirmation of a God who brings life from death in all things. "In Jesus we believe," he confesses, "we believe, that Christ our head / for us resign'd his breath."[52] The costly sacrifice of Christ purchases this forgiveness; what God has done for us in Christ restores the possibility of a right relationship with God.

> O Saviour, whose blood
>> For sinners hath flow'd,
> I believe thou hast suffer'd, to bring me to God.
>
> My goodness thou art,
>> Impute and impart
> Thy virtue to quiet, and hallow my heart.
>
> The infinite store
>> Of thy merit runs o'er,
> For me thou hast purchas'd forgiveness, *and more.*
>
> I believe thou hast died
>> To redeem me from pride,
> From anger, desire, and all evil beside.
>
> And shall I not live
>> In full hope to receive
> All the graces and blessings the Lamb hath to give?[53]

50. Wesley and Wesley, *Hymns and Sacred Poems* (1742), 224, st. 2.

51. Wesley and Wesley, *Hymns and Sacred Poems* (1742), 252, st. 8; a hymn based upon Rom 4:16.

52. C. Wesley, *Hymns and Sacred Poems* (1749), 1:127, sts. 1–2.

53. C. Wesley, *Hymns and Sacred Poems* (1749), 1:225, sts. 1–5.

In a lengthy exposition of John 1:12, Wesley describes the threefold office of Jesus as prophet, priest, and king through which he instructs, atones, and reigns. "Lord, we believe thee still the same," he claims with regard to all these dimensions, "an utmost Saviour still."[54] In these hymns dealing with forgiveness and pardon, he focuses most of his attention on Jesus' priestly role—his atoning work. In a number of his texts from *Scripture Hymns* 1762, for example, he ponders the meaning of Christ's passion and the purchased forgiveness. "Lord, I believe thy sprinkled blood," he proclaims, "can quench the fever's fiercest fire."[55] Jesus' loving act relieves the burdens associated with sin. "Save me, gracious Lord, for why? / I believe thou canst, and wilt," pleads Wesley, "I on thee alone rely; / Purge, and wash out all my guilt."[56] Reflecting on Titus 2:14: "Who gave himself for us, that he might redeem us from ALL iniquity," he concludes the hymn:

> This is the dear redeeming grace,
> > For every sinner free:
> Surely it shall on me take place,
> > The chief of sinners me.
>
> From all iniquity, from all
> > He shall my soul redeem:
> In Jesus I believe, and shall
> > Believe myself to him.[57]

The believer experiences forgiveness as pardon. Wesley seems to have realized that most people struggle to accept the fact that they have been accepted by God in Christ. He makes this clear in a hymn that interfaces the reality of forgiveness provided and the experience of pardon accepted, reflecting on the pathos of the statement, "Lord, I believe; help thou my unbelief" (Mark 9:24).

> Lord, I believe, thou *wilt* forgive,
> > But help me to believe thou *dost*:

---

54. C. Wesley, *Hymns and Sacred Poems* (1749), 2:183, st. 8. See Maddox's discussion of the threefold office in reference to John Wesley's teaching in *Responsible Grace*, 109–14.

55. C. Wesley, *Scripture Hymns*, 2:152; a single-stanza hymn based on Matt 8:15. This is one of the "credo hymns," opening with the prayerful acclamation, "Lord, I believe."

56. C. Wesley, *Scripture Hymns*, 1:253; a single-stanza hymn based on Ps 7:1.

57. Wesley and Wesley, *Hymns and Sacred Poems* (1742), 247, sts. 11–12.

> The answer of thy promise give,
>> Wherein thou causest me to trust,
> The gospel-faith divine impart,
>> Which seals my pardon on my heart.[58]

He teaches that God desires all to experience this pardon in their lives. In a hymn on 1 Timothy 2:4, "God will have ALL men to be saved," he pleads for those with broken hearts to open them wide, for God offers "pardon to *all* that turn." The spiritual breakthrough comes in the second half of stanza nine of this sixteen-stanza hymn:

> Lord, I believe at last
> Thy promise and thy vow,
> Thy word and solemn oath are past,
> And thou *wilt* save me now.[59]

"Never, Lord, shall I believe it," Wesley confesses with the sinner, "till thou dost the power impart." That same sinner desires this experience with such desperation that he welcomes divine coercion in the hopes of peace. "Force my conscience to receive it," he pleads, "pardon stampt upon my heart."[60]

The signature hymn for this particular tenet of Wesley's lyrical credo comes from a hymn for "One Fallen from Grace" in *Hymns and Sacred Poems* 1749. It demonstrates how the struggle with sin in life continues even in the believer. God offers pardon to all who come to receive the gift of grace, however, whether for the first time or at any point in the journey.

> Jesu, I believe thee near:
>> Now my fallen soul restore,
> Now my guilty conscience clear,
>> Give me back my peace and power;
> Stone to flesh again convert,
> Write forgiveness on my heart.

---

58. C. Wesley, *Scripture Hymns*, 205; one of the "credo hymns" in the hymns explored here.

59. C. Wesley, *Hymns on God's Everlasting Love*, 48. The word "all" in the biblical verse is capitalized in this publication. In a similar hymn based on 1 John 2:3 in *Hymns on God's Everlasting Love* (1741), 31–32, Charles maintains that, if justice asks why any deserve the gift of pardon and peace they have received, they answer with confidence, "In Jesus I believe!" (123).

60. C. Wesley, *Hymns and Sacred Poems* (1749), 1:156, st. 3.

I believe thy pardning grace
    As at the beginning, free:
Open are thy arms t' embrace
    Me, the worst of rebels me;
All in me the hindrance lies,
Call'd I still refuse to rise.

Take this heart of stone away,
    Melt me into gracious tears,
Grant me power to watch and pray,
    'Till thy lovely face appears,
'Till thy favour I retrieve,
'Till by faith again I live.[61]

Liberation and Healing

The believer experiences God's work of grace not only as forgiveness and pardon, but also as liberation and healing. In the constellation of credo hymns presented here, Wesley exploits two familiar biblical images to describe the liberating experience of grace: the deliverance of the Israelites from bondage in Egypt and the deliverance of Daniel from the den of lions. The sinner cries to God for help, oppressed by sin and in bondage to evil. Like the ancient people of Israel, the prisoner desires freedom and seeks to escape "from the dire oppressor's land." "Drown all my sins in the Red Sea," prays Charles, "And bring me safe to land." His allegorization of the Exodus concludes with the simple testimony that pardon "and holy joy, and quiet peace" are his "The moment [he] believe[s]."[62] Danger surrounds the helpless sinner on every side. She lies "in the mire of sin." Like Daniel, "vain are all [her] hopes to flee / out of the lion's teeth." The Israelite puts all his trust in Yahweh; the supplicant quietly testifies, "In Jesus I believe."[63] God liberates

---

61. C. Wesley, *Hymns and Sacred Poems* (1749), 1:133–34, sts. 1–2, 6. In a hymn for "The Backslider," Wesley describes the torment of the soul separated from God. "Still thou seest my stormy breast, / My soul is as the troubled sea, / Never, never can I rest, / Till I believe in thee" (Wesley and Wesley, *Hymns and Sacred Poems* (1742), 62, st. 1).

62. C. Wesley, *Hymns and Sacred Poems* (1749), 1:43–44; quoting sts. 2, 4, and 6.

63. Wesley and Wesley, *Hymns and Sacred Poems* (1742), 211–12; quoting sts. 2 and 3.

souls bound in sin and nature's night. In a lyrical paraphrase of Psalm 88:8 in one of his manuscript collections, Wesley proclaims:

> The moment I believe;
> The chains of sin fall off my heart,
> And freed by love divine,
> My only Lord and God thou art,
> And I am wholly thine.[64]

The Great Physician also heals. "My spirit's desp'rate wound," Wesley acknowledges, "I cannot slightly heal."[65] And so, he expresses his deepest hope with regard to the work of grace:

> From sin, the guilt, the power, the pain,
> Thou wilt redeem my soul.
> Lord, I believe; and not in vain:
> My faith shall make me whole.[66]

Whereas this process of healing that leads to wholeness begins with the experience of forgiveness, pardon, and liberation, it is viewed most properly from the perspective of its goal. The fulfillment of the goal, however, requires this solid foundation of God's work of grace in Christ—this second tenet of Wesley's lyrical credo.

Sanctification and Christian Perfection

The path to Christian perfection and the *telos* of perfect love, then, represent a third important facet of his credo. Through the process of sanctification, the Spirit conforms the believer more and more to Christ. Charles, like his brother, emphasizes twin dimensions in this process: holiness of heart (internal holiness) or love of God (a vertical dimension) and holiness of life (external holiness) or love of neighbor (a horizontal dimension). He was not only concerned that people experience forgiveness for the brokenness in their lives (justification), he wanted them to move toward wholeness and

---

64. C. Wesley, *MS Scripture Hymns*, 62. Cf. C. Wesley, *MS Richmond*, 114–15, for a hymn in which Wesley discusses the faith of those imprisoned for righteousness sake, employing the same emancipatory language.

65. C. Wesley, *Hymns and Sacred Poems* (1749), 1:108, st. 11.

66. Wesley and Wesley, *Hymns and Sacred Poems* (1740), 74. Charles provides an extended reflection on 1 Cor 10:11 in this hymn.

healing as well (sanctification). According to Wesley, faith leads to love in the Christian life, and to be loving or holy is to be truly happy.

Reflecting on Isaiah 40:8, he describes what full conformity to Christ looks like.

> Lord, we believe, and wait the hour
> > Which all thy great salvation brings:
> The Sp'rit of love, and health, and power
> > Shall come, and make us priests and kings;
> Thou wilt perform thy faithful word,
> The servant shall be as his Lord.
>
> The promise stands for ever sure,
> > And we shall in thine image shine,
> Partakers of a nature pure,
> > Holy, and perfect, and divine,
> In Spirit join'd to thee the Son,
> As thou art with thy Father one.[67]

The Spirit sanctifies believers by indwelling their lives. The glorious liberty that accompanies the Spirit not only frees from sorrow, fear, and sin, but also liberates believers to love fully. In the process of sanctification there is, to use the language of the spiritual writers, an apophatic (emptying) and kataphatic (filling) rhythm. God empties the faithful of the old and fills them with the new. Wesley articulates this rhythm in the hymns.

> Lord, we believe; and wait the hour
> > That brings the promis'd grace,
> When born of God we sin no more,
> > But always see thy face.
>
> Since thou wouldst have us free from sin,
> > And pure as those above,
> Make haste to bring thy nature in,
> > And perfect us in love.[68]

---

67. Wesley and Wesley, *Hymns and Sacred Poems* (1742), 234, sts. 11–12.
68. C. Wesley, *Hymns and Sacred Poems* (1749), 2:189, sts. 5–6.

The Spirit consumes, blots out, erases, and drives out sins, emptying the disciple of all that separates him or her from God. With regard to this apophatic work, Charles proclaims, "I believe thou wilt remove, / thoroughly wash out all my stains."[69] A section of *Hymns and Sacred Poems* 1749 entitled "Hymns for Those that Wait for Full Redemption" supplies quite a number of hymns that illustrate this Christian goal. The closing stanzas of the second hymn in this section express the confidence of the believer in God's ability to perform this spiritual surgery.

> Bounds I will not set to thee,
>   Shorten thine almighty hand:
> Save from all iniquity,
>   Let not sin's foundations stand,
> Every stone o'erturn, o'erthrow;
> I believe it *may* be so.
>
> Wilt thou lop the boughs of sin,
>   Leaving still the stock behind?
> No, thy love shall work within,
>   Quite expel the carnal mind,
> Root and branch destroy my foe;
> I believe it *shall* be so.[70]

In Wesleyan theology, however, God empties for the purpose of filling. The Spirit fills the follower of Christ with the Lord's mind and righteousness, restores the image of Christ, and teaches the disciple how to love. "Into sin I cannot fall," observes Wesley, "while hanging on thy love."[71] "I even I believe in him," he confesses, in order that "thou wilt form thy Son in me, / and perfect me in him."[72] He underscores the kataphatic nature of perfection in one of his hymns on full redemption:

> Lord, we believe, and rest secure,
>   Thine utmost promises to prove,

---

69. Wesley and Wesley, *Hymns and Sacred Poems* (1742), 211, st. 6, the concluding stanza.

70. C. Wesley, *Hymns and Sacred Poems* (1749), 2:149, sts. 3–4.

71. C. Wesley, *Scripture Hymns*, 2:410; a single-stanza hymn on Jude 24.

72. Wesley and Wesley, *Hymns and Sacred Poems* (1742), 254, st. 19; reflections on Rom 4:16.

To rise restor'd, and throughly pure,
 In all the image of thy love,
Fill'd with the glorious life unknown,
Forever sanctified in one.[73]

Sanctification, in Charles's view, is a lengthy process. Few believers become fully loving all at once.[74] Reflecting on Hebrews 6:12, "Be followers of them, who through faith and patience, inherit the promises," he questions the instantaneity of this distinctive gift:

Nature would the crown receive
The first moment we believe,
But we vainly think to seize
Instantaneous holiness:
Faith alone cannot suffice,
Patience too must earn the prize,
Both insure the promise given,
Lead thro' perfect love to heaven.[75]

The Spirit enables believers to grow into authentic children of God. Charles holds to God's promise and expresses his confidence in God's power to accomplish this great work. In his hymn entitled "The Promise of Sanctification," based on Ezekiel 36:25, he defends this doctrine against its many detractors:

Hast thou not said, who canst not lie,
 That I thy law shall keep and do?
Lord, I believe, tho' men deny.
 They all are false, but thou art true.[76]

---

73. C. Wesley, *Hymns and Sacred Poems* (1749), 2:187, st. 8; the concluding stanza of no. 30. There may be multiple meanings associated with unity in this hymn, but Wesley makes it abundantly clear that the quest for perfection unites the community of faith, if it is genuine. In a reflection on Ezek 37:17, he writes: "Lord, thy promise we believe / Thou wilt perform the grace foretold, / All our jarring sects receive, / And blend us in one fold" (C. Wesley, *Scripture Hymns*, 2:54).

74. Charles engages in a lively debate throughout the course of his life with his brother over these issues, and they never fully resolve their differences. Over against John's more instantaneous view, Charles tended to emphasize the gift of perfect love in *articulo mortis*, "in the moment of death." On this issue, see Maddox, *Responsible Grace*, 186; and Tyson, *Charles Wesley on Sanctification*, 227–301.

75. C. Wesley, *Scripture Hymns*, 2:355–56.

76. C. Wesley, "Promise of Sanctification," 46, st. 13.

"Would my Saviour have me do / what he commands, in vain," questions Wesley in similar fashion. "Nay, but I believe thee, Lord, . . . as I hang upon thy word, thy word in me fulfill."[77] "Lord, we believe, and with calm zeal" continue on towards the goal for the prize of the heavenly call of God in Christ Jesus; this is the faith for which he contends.[78] In one of his hymns on the Trinity, he simply proclaims, "Lord, we believe the promise sure . . . To keep us pure in life and heart."[79] Charles embraces the scriptural promise for God to deliver the faithful fully from sin and to fill them completely with the love of Christ.

> In Jesus we believe,
> And wait the truth to prove,
> We shall, we shall receive
> The blessing from above,
> Fulness of love, and peace, and power,
> And live in Christ, and sin no more.[80]

The third feature of Charles Wesley's lyrical credo reflects his expectation for all believers to grow into the perfect love God has promised in Christ—the fullest possible love of God and neighbor.

A Rest of Lasting Peace

Whereas only a handful of hymns bear witness to a fourth and final theme in Wesley's lyrical credo, they deserve a status in their own right. These hymns reflect the confidence encapsulated in the familiar lyrical affirmation, "No condemnation now I dread, / Jesus, and all in him, is mine."[81] In a hymn entitled "Rejoicing in hope," he anticipates the rest promised to all who abide in Christ. Individual lines punctuate the vision.

---

77. C. Wesley, *Scripture Hymns*, 2:354; reflections on "Let us go on unto perfection" (Heb 6:1).

78. C. Wesley, *Hymns and Sacred Poems* (1749), 2:171, st. 15.

79. C. Wesley, *Trinity Hymns*, 38, st. 2.

80. C. Wesley, *Hymns and Sacred Poems* (1749), 2:328, st. 6. Wesley's profound optimism in the power of God's grace induces him to proclaim: "And if I believe in thee, / Nothing is too hard for me" (C. Wesley, *Scripture Hymns*, 2:230; a single-stanza hymn based on Luke 18:1).

81. These are the opening lines of st. 6 from "And can it be, that I should gain," one of the most famous hymns drawn from Wesley and Wesley, *Hymns and Sacred Poems* (1739), 118.

> With confidence I now look up (3:1)
>
> No longer am I now afraid (8:1)
>
> Confident now of faith's increase (11:1)
>
> Joyful in hope my spirit soars (16:1)
>
> I taste unutterable bliss, / and everlasting rest. (19:3–4) [82]

And the final stanza:

> Lord, I believe, and rest secure
> > In confidence divine,
>
> Thy promise stands for ever sure,
> > And all thou art is mine.[83]

One of his manuscript hymns exploits this image of rest and celebrates the One who offers all that he is to the believer.

> O Jesus, my Rest,
>
> How unspeakably blest
>
> Is the Sinner that comes to be hid in thy Breast!
>
> I come at thy Call,
>
> At thy Feet lo! I fall,
>
> I believe, I confess thee my GOD and my All.[84]

Hebrews 4:9, "There remaineth therefore a rest to the people of God," provides the impetus for Charles to explore the dimensions of this ultimate gift in the following credo hymn:

> Lord, I believe a rest remains
> > To all thy people known,
>
> A rest, where pure enjoyment reigns,
> > And thou art lov'd alone.
>
> A rest, where all our soul's desire
> > Is fixt on things above,

---

82. Wesley and Wesley, *Hymns and Sacred Poems* (1742), 180–82; lines from sts. 3, 8, 11, 16, and 19, respectively.

83. Wesley and Wesley, *Hymns and Sacred Poems* (1742), 182, st. 23.

84. C. Wesley, *MS Cheshunt*, 119, sts. 1–2.

>   Where doubt, and pain, and fear expire,
>   Cast out by perfect love.
>
> A rest of lasting joy and peace,
>   Where all is calm within:
> 'Tis then from our own works we cease,
>   From pride, and self, and sin.[85]

Conclusion

In the hymns discussed in this study, Charles Wesley affirms his trust in a God of promise, explicates God's work of grace, elevates the goal of perfect love, and celebrates a rest of lasting peace. If we were to articulate the lyrical credo based upon his hymns as a proposition, it might sound something like this: "We believe in the God of promise, goodness, and truth, who draws near to us in Jesus and through the power of the Holy Spirit offers forgiveness and pardon, liberation and healing, that we might love to the uttermost and rest in God's eternal peace." But there is power—transforming power—in the singing of these themes. The reality of these theological tenets penetrates to the core of our being in its lyrical form. One poetic masterpiece, the concluding hymn of the *Hymns and Sacred Poems* 1742, may be as close to a lyrical credo in one hymn as Charles Wesley ever came.

> 1. Lord, I believe, thy work of grace
>   Is perfect in the soul,
> His heart is pure, who sees thy face,
>   His spirit is made whole.
>
> 2. From every sickness by thy word,
>   From every sore disease
> Saved, and to perfect health restor'd,
>   To perfect holiness.
>
> 3. He walks in glorious liberty,
>   To sin entirely dead,

---

85. Wesley and Wesley, *Hymns and Sacred Poems* (1740), 204–05, sts. 1–3.

The truth, the Son hath made him free,
    And he is free indeed.

8. This is the rest, the life, the peace,
    Which all thy people prove,
Love is the bond of perfectness,
    And all their soul is love.

17. I feel, and know him now in part,
    His love my heart constrains,
Its near approach expands my heart,
    And fills with pleasing pains.

21. Come, O my God, thyself reveal,
    Fill all this mighty void,
Thou only canst my spirit fill:
    Come, O my God, my God!

22. Fulfil, fulfil my large desires,
    Large as infinity,
Give, give me all my soul requires,
    All, all that is in thee![86]

---

86. Wesley and Wesley, *Hymns and Sacred Poems* (1742), 301–04, sts. 1–3, 8, 17–18, 21–22.

Chapter 2

Charles Wesley and the Language of Faith

> Source note: An essay commissioned to mark the tercentenary of Charles Wesley's birth and published in *Charles Wesley: Life, Legacy, and Literature*, edited by Kenneth G.C. Newport and Ted A. Campbell, 299–319 (Peterborough: Epworth, 2007).

CHARLES WESLEY PREACHED, WROTE, and sang about faith. Christian faith defined his life and ministry. On August 31, 1748, an unnamed woman surrendered to God's grace under the influence of this Anglican priest/lyrical theologian who recorded her testimony in his journal.

> "I seem," said she, "to be laying hold on Christ continually. I am so light, so happy, as I never was before. I waked, two nights ago, in such rapture of joy, that I thought, 'Surely this is the peace they preach.' It has continued ever since. My eyes are opened. I see all things in a new light. I rejoice always." Is not this *the language of faith*, the cry of a new-born soul?[1]

While many themes pervade Wesley's literary corpus, perhaps none stands out quite so dramatically as faith. In the following hymn about the "Author of faith," Wesley describes the origins and nature of faith. He affirms the fact that faith is a gift, something related to the burning presence of the Spirit in the lives of the faith-ful. It is a source of knowledge concerning God and the way in which God offers salvation, hope, and healing to humanity. Faith illumines the child of God and enables spiritual vision. In short, for Charles, faith is a complex reality in the lives of people, rich in meaning and central to the Christian vision of life.

---

1. C. Wesley, *Manuscript Journal*, 2:541.

> Author of faith, eternal Word,
>> Whose Spirit breathes the active flame,
> Faith, like its finisher and Lord,
>> Today as yesterday the same;
>
> To thee our humble hearts aspire,
>> And ask the gift unspeakable:
> Increase in us the kindled fire,
>> In us the work of faith fulfil.
>
> By faith we know thee strong to save
>> (Save us, a present Saviour thou!)
> Whate'er we hope, by faith we have,
>> Future and past subsisting now.
>
> Faith lends its realizing light,
>> The clouds disperse, the shadows fly;
> Th'Invisible appears in sight,
>> And God is seen by mortal eye.[2]

For the student of Charles Wesley, of course, none of this is news. To assert that the concept of faith figures prominently in his poetic and prose works is tantamount to saying that Christianity exerted a profound influence on his life. It simply states the obvious. But the way in which Wesley employs the language of faith reveals, I believe, some of the most important insights with regard to the Wesleyan vision of Christianity. What I propose here, therefore, is a detailed analysis of "Charles Wesley and the language of faith" as a lens through which to focus attention on the essence of the Methodist movement and to contemplate anew the meaning of faith.[3]

---

2. J. Wesley, *Works*, 7:194–95, nos. 92.1–3, 6.

3. It is important for me to note at the outset that it is not my intention in this brief article to examine the differences between and debate about dogmatic speech and the language of faith, although there may be important implications the theologian wishes to draw from this study. For a helpful discussion of this debate, primarily in Protestant theology, see Berger, *Theology in Hymns*, 41–47. I use the phrase "language of faith" throughout in a much more literal sense as the way in which Charles Wesley employs the term "faith" and what we learn from his usage.

The parameters of this study need to be set out at this early point. The Wesleyan corpus, as may be deduced from other contributions to this volume, is immense. An exhaustive analysis of Wesley's "concept of faith" in a brief essay such as this is hardly thinkable. So I am imposing some rather serious limits on the study. First, I am examining Charles's use of the term "faith" in order to delineate his "concept of faith," rather than attempting to unearth the ideas that are reflected throughout his works. Second, I have restricted myself in this task to two primary sources: the 1780 *Collection of Hymns for the Use of the People Called Methodists* and the published journal. My methodology with regard to these sources has involved the identification of every instance of the term "faith" in this restricted corpus of material. Third, I have made important use of Wesley's *Sermons*[4] (a rich source hardly to be neglected in such a study), but have made no effort to survey this material in an exhaustive fashion with regard to language. Rather, I have focused my attention on those sermons in which Charles deals with the "subject of faith" and expounds his understanding in a definitive manner, for the benefit of the corroborative evidence and further interpretive insight this provides.[5] While I fully recognize the limitations and dangers of this design, I am convinced that its benefits are great. The portrait of faith that emerges, I trust, is both authentic and compelling.

I.

Despite the fact that we are not able here to discuss at any length the mass of detail that is, to be sure, relevant to this study, but are concerned rather with the big picture it provides, simply looking at the data does provide some interesting conclusions and confirmations. For example, an examination of the Jackson edition of the journal reveals that Charles uses the term "faith" 406 times between March 1736 and November 1756.[6] Despite the fact that the published journal material is uneven at best, and deficient at worst, over the course of these years, the extraordinary nature of the year 1738 stands out dramatically. Wesley's struggle with faith, his conversations

4. Newport, *Sermons of Charles Wesley*.

5. The principal sermons include Sermon 4 on 1 John 3:14 (particularly the second part of the sermon dealing with advices), Sermon 5 on "Faith and Good Works" (Titus 3:8), Sermon 6 on Rom 3:23–24, Sermon 7 on Rom 3:23–25, and Sermon 8 on Eph 5:14.

6. A detailed analysis of the journal reveals the following usage of the term faith: 1736 (8), 1737 (1), 1738 (153), 1739 (63), 1740 (37), 1741 (15), 1743 (28), 1744 (18), 1745 (14), 1746 (13), 1747 (14), 1748 (20), 1749 (2), 1750 (2), 1751 (5), 1753 (2), 1756 (11).

about faith, and his discovery and experience of living faith dominate his narrative account of this year. His record of 1738 reflects a veritable explosion of faith in his life. The language of faith permeates this narrative in particular (153 instances), representing more than one-third of the uses of the term in the published journal. In the context of that year itself, the fact that more than two-thirds of these references come from his account of the summer months, May through July, demonstrates the crucial significance of the "faith changes" Charles was undergoing in that period.

During the previous two years (1736-37), he only refers to faith nine times. The afterglow of Wesley's discoveries about faith in 1738 are reflected in the immediately subsequent years, 1739 with 63, and 1740 with 37 references. But his use of the term tapers off in the following decade (1741-51) with an average of only about thirteen references per year. Simply on the basis of his use of the term "faith," it is clear that 1738 represents a critical turning point with regard to Charles's engagement with the concept of and existential appropriation of faith.

The 1780 Collection, of course, represents a Wesleyan *summa pietatis* in that it is "A Little Body of Experimental and Practical Divinity." While it is impossible to examine Charles's use of the term "faith" in the hymns with reference to chronology, the dating and attribution of this poetic corpus being highly controverted issues, a detailed examination of the Collection reveals some interesting facts as well, leading to a broad but significant generalization. Wesley refers explicitly to faith in roughly one out of every four of the 525 hymns in the collection.[7] The vast majority of these uses of the

---

7. Despite the fact that the vast majority of these hymns are from Charles's pen, it must be acknowledged that not all of these texts can be attributed directly to him. See J. Wesley, *Works*, 7:31-8, "The Sources of the *Collection*," for a discussion of attribution. Regardless, Charles (and John as well) "owned" these hymns and their language. In the analysis of the hymns that follows, I draw no conclusions with regard to the meaning of "faith" from hymns other than those attributed incontrovertibly to Charles. Those hymns which directly reference faith are 1, 3, 4, 12, 14, 26, 37 (George Herbert), 50, 56, 58, 63, 71, 72, 73, 74, 77, 80, 81, 83, 86, 92, 107, 114, 116, 117, 118, 123, 124, 127, 129 (trans. of German hymn), 132, 134, 136, 137, 138, 142, 144, 146, 148, 158, 163, 166, 173, 176, 182 (trans. of German hymn), 184, 185, 186, 188 (trans. of German hymn), 192, 203, 208, 212, 219, 220, 226 (attrib. John Wesley), 231 (trans. of German hymn), 240, 249, 254, 259, 260, 264 (attrib. John Wesley?), 268, 269, 272, 274, 275, 277, 288, 289, 294, 297, 298, 303, 305, 314, 316, 318, 320, 324, 333, 337, 341 (attrib. John Wesley?), 343 (trans. of German hymn), 346, 347, 349, 350, 351, 354, 355, 357, 361, 364, 376, 378, 381, 382, 385, 386, 388, 391, 394, 402, 403, 408, 409, 419 (trans. of German hymn), 421, 433, 437, 442, 443, 444 (Henry More), 445 (Henry More), 446, 452, 453, 468, 471, 476, 477, 480, 484, 486, 489, 493, 497, 501, 505, 506, 507, 508, 509, 512, 515, 521, 523, and 525. I have provided parenthetical identifications for those twelve hymns that include references to "faith" but cannot be attributed indisputably to Charles Wesley. It can be assumed that all of the remaining hymns are of his composition.

term are singular, but a number of hymns function as commentaries on faith, as it were, with multiple references. Four hymns, in particular, might be designated as "hymns on faith" by virtue of Charles's pervasive use and interpretation of the term throughout.[8]

As might well be expected, more than half the hymns that reference faith (76 in all) are located in the major section of the collection "For Believers" (pt. 4). The largest concentration of these hymns (17) fall under the category "For Believers Groaning for Full Redemption." This provides tacit evidence at least for the fact that Charles places strong emphasis upon *sanctification* (as well as justification) *by faith*. The foundational Pauline/Reformation doctrine of justification by grace through faith is represented with nearly equal strength by hymns "For Believers Rejoicing" (16). Next in order of frequency, Wesley refers to faith in thirteen hymns related to "Praying for Mourners brought to Birth," in the separate Part 3 of the collection, also stressing the concept of salvation by faith. The next highest concentration of hymns featuring the language of faith comes from the final section of the collection (pt. 5), "For the Society, Praying" (11).

Despite the fact that the heaviest concentration of these hymns comes from the sections where one might well expect "faith" to be found, namely, in those crucial sections related to the Wesleyan *via salutis*, there is amazing balance throughout the entire collection in terms of proportional distribution.[9] The "hymns on faith," as I have described them, reflect this pervasive utilization of the language of faith, located, as it were, in four different major parts of the collection: "Describing Inward Religion" (pt. 1, no. 92), "Praying for Mourners brought to Birth" (pt. 3, no. 142), "For Believers Groaning for Full Redemption" (pt. 4, no. 350), and "For the Society, Praying" (pt. 5, no. 507). This detailed analysis of Charles's use of faith language simply confirms in rather dramatic fashion just how central the concept of faith was in the hymns and the experience of the early Methodist people. If the hymns of Charles Wesley communicated the essential doctrine of the movement, as many have argued persuasively,[10] then faith stood at the heart and core of the Wesleyan way.

8. See no. 92, "Author of faith"; no. 142, "Father of Jesus Christ the just"; no. 350, "Father of Jesus Christ my Lord"; and no. 507, "Let us plead for faith alone." In each of these "signature hymns," Wesley refers to faith five or more times.

9. In other words, regardless of the section in the collection, Wesley explicitly refers to faith in one out of four hymns, with the exception of the very brief second section (only eight hymns), as demonstrated by the data from each section: pt. 1 (20 out of 87 hymns or 23 percent), pt. 2 (1/8 or 12.5 percent), pt. 3 (23/86 or 27 percent), pt. 4 (76/283 or 27 percent), pt. 5 (21/61 or 34.5 percent).

10. The Methodist authority on the Wesleys, Prof. Richard P. Heitzenrater, observes: "It has long been a truism that the theology of the Wesleyan Revival was carried on the wings of the Wesleys' hymns perhaps more readily than on the words of their sermons"

These are some of the conclusions we can draw from the raw data, the minute detail, related to the presence of faith language in the journal and hymns, but of even greater significance are the major themes and powerful images that revolve around the language of faith in Charles Wesley's prose and poetic writings.

II.

Three particular themes—distinct but inseparable from one another—characterize Charles Wesley's understanding of faith and demonstrate the essential Anglican orientation of his lyrical theology and doctrinal language: the concept of true and lively faith, the doctrine of justification by faith, and the vision of faith working by love.

The Concept of True and Lively Faith

Charles Wesley distinguishes sharply between "dead faith" and "living faith." Both he and his brother, John, were well aware of the debates related to faith that led to the important definitions and distinctions of the Protestant scholastics. Philip Melanchthon, for example, differentiated between historical faith (which the devils also possess) and saving faith in Christ (defined as trust or assurance).[11] In his sermon on Romans 3:23-5, Wesley echoes the language of Augsburg.

> The faith which justifies is not purely an assent to things credible as known; it is not that speculative, notional, airy shadow which floats in the heads of some learned men; it is not a lifeless, cold, historical faith, common to devils and nominal Christians; it is not learnt of books or men; it is not a human thing, but a divine energy.[12]

(Kimbrough, *Heart to Praise*, 5); cf. J. Wesley, *Works*, 7:1-22 and Berger, *Theology in Hymns*, esp. pts. II and III.

11. See Article 20 of the Augsburg Confession, in particular, in which this distinction is articulated clearly: "the term 'faith' does not signify only historical knowledge—the kind of faith that the ungodly and the devil have—but that it signifies faith which believes . . . Augustine also reminds his readers in this way about the word 'faith' and teaches that in the Scriptures the word 'faith' is understood not as knowledge, such as the ungodly have, but as trust that consoles and encourages terrified minds" (Kolb and Wengert, *Book of Concord*, 57).

12. Newport, *Sermons of Charles Wesley*, 201. In his sermon on Rom 3:23-24, Wesley quotes Homily 3, "Of Salvation," extensively, including the statement: "Yet that faith which bringeth forth either evil works, or no good works, is not a right, pure and lively faith, but a dead, devilish counterfeit, and feigned faith. For even the devils know and

On several occasions in his journal, he refers to this shadow of a true faith, or faith improperly so-called, as the "faith of adherence." All of these references are pejorative. "I spoke closely to those who trusted to their faith of adherence," he wrote concerning a confrontation in May 1740, "and insisted on that *lowest mark* of Christianity, forgiveness of sins."[13] On other occasions he identifies this sub-species of faith with the view of certain Dissenters, half persuading one out of her aberrant view[14] and expressing triumph over another when his preaching "stripped her all at once of her self-righteousness, faith of adherence, and good works."[15] Wesley's attempt to disabuse some Baptists of their misconception of faith elicited a fairly concise definition of living faith and its consequences.

> I passed two hours with M. Powel, and another Baptist, whom I almost persuaded to give up their faith of adherence, so called, for the faith of the Gospel, which works by love, and is connected with peace, joy, power, and the testimony of the Spirit.[16]

In explicating this distinction, Wesley simply defended the conception of "true and lively faith" articulated by his church in the Anglican Articles of Religion and *Homilies*.[17] The English reformer and author of the Book of Common Prayer, Thomas Cranmer, embedded the same dynamic conception of faith in his *Homilies*, a rich theological reservoir in which Charles immersed himself and upon which he drew repeatedly as a source for his sermons and hymns.[18] In one of his most significant sermons on Christian faith, based upon Titus 3:8, Charles defines both dead and living faith by simply quoting at length from Homily 4.

> Faith is taken in scripture two ways. There is one faith which is called a dead faith, which bringeth not forth good works, but is dead, barren, and unfruitful. And this faith is a persuasion in man's heart whereby he knoweth there is a God, and agreeth to

believe all the Articles of our creed, and yet, for all this, they be but devils, remaining still in their damnable estate" (Newport, *Sermons*, 176).

13. C. Wesley, *Manuscript Journal*, 1:255 (May 10, 1740).
14. C. Wesley, *Manuscript Journal*, 1:264 (June 2, 1740).
15. C. Wesley, *Manuscript Journal*, 2:526 (March 14, 1748).
16. C. Wesley, *Manuscript Journal*, 2:511 (October 2, 1747).

17. The language "true and lively faith" comes from both sources, from Article XII, "Of Good Works," and from Homily 4, entitled "A Short Declaration of the True, Lively, and Christian Faith" ("Of Faith"). The 1662 Book of Common Prayer, which included the "39 Articles of Religion," shaped the Wesleys' lives and theology in innumerable ways.

18. See Leaver, "Charles Wesley and Anglicanism," 157–75; and Lawson, "Charles Wesley."

all truths maintained in holy scripture. And this is not properly called faith...

Another faith there is in scripture which is not idle, unfruitful, and dead, but worketh by love; and as the other vain faith is called dead, so may this be called a quick and lively faith. And this is not only the common belief of the Articles of our faith, but it is also a sure trust and confidence of the mercy of God through our Lord Jesus Christ, and a steadfast hope of all good things to be received at God's hand. This is a true, lively, and unfeigned Christian faith, and is not in the mouth and outward profession only, but it liveth and stirreth inwardly in the heart.[19]

That this faith must be stirred up and realized in fallen humanity by an external power Wesley make abundantly clear in the prayer of a spiritual pilgrim to the "hidden God":

> An unregenerate child of man,
> > To thee for faith I call;
> Pity thy fallen creature's pain,
> > And raise me from my fall.
>
> The darkness which through thee I feel
> > Thou only canst remove;
> Thy own eternal power reveal,
> > Thy Deity of love.
>
> Thou hast in unbelief shut up,
> > That grace may let me go;
> In hope believing against hope
> > I wait the truth to know.[20]

God must transform a dead faith into something that is living and vital. "The power of living faith impart," prays the lost child, "And breathe thy love into my heart."[21] "My want of living faith I feel," a tormented soul cries out, "Show me in Christ thy smiling face."[22] Reflecting on the meaning of John 5:24 and the transition from spiritual death to life, Wesley affirms

19. Newport, *Sermons of Charles Wesley*, 155.
20. J. Wesley, *Works*, 7:261 (no. 144.3–5).
21. J. Wesley, *Works*, 7:226 (no. 116.1).
22. J. Wesley, *Works*, 7:259 (no. 142.2).

that this change "belongs only to them that believe with a living, saving, justifying faith."²³ His overriding concern was for people to "know that we have passed from death to life" (1 John 3:14).

Before defining this living faith more fully and demonstrating its connection to justification, it is important to note a second, related distinction with regard to Wesley's concept of faith, associating it with belief. Nowhere in his writings does he distinguish explicitly between faith and belief, but the distinction is implied throughout his corpus. While failing to employ the classical terminology, Charles differentiates between the "faith in which one believes" (*fides quae creditur*) and the "faith by which one believes" (*fides qua creditur*). The contrast here is not so much between a dead and a living faith, as it is between an objective faith (what might be described as *the* faith, or a system of belief) and a subjective faith (what Wesley describes as a living or saving faith).²⁴

St. Augustine articulated the same distinction concisely in his monumental work *On the Trinity*: "For faith is not *that which is believed*, but *that by which it is believed*; and the former is *believed*, the latter is *seen*."²⁵ A true and lively faith enables spiritual perception, and it is not surprising, as we shall see later, that one of Charles's favorite images is "the eye of faith." Ancient Christian sources, upon which the Wesleys were highly dependent, frequently point to the heart as that locus of this spiritual vision.²⁶ And so, Wesley concludes the hymn quoted in part above:

> Speak, Jesu, speak into my heart
>
> What thou for me hast done!
>
> One grain of living faith impart,
>
> And God is all my own!²⁷

---

23. Newport, *Sermons of Charles Wesley*, 147.

24. I am indebted to Prof. Timothy J. Wengert, Ministerium of Pennsylvania Professor of Christian History at the Lutheran Theological Seminary at Philadelphia, for documenting the development of this distinction in the Lutheran tradition. One of the late seventeenth century scholastics, Johann Wilhelm Baier (1647–1695), distinguishes between "subjective" faith, "that by which one believes (faith, properly so-called, which dwells in a believer as a subject)" and "objective faith, or that which is believed (which is the doctrine of faith, and which is figuratively called faith, because it is the object of faith)." He used these terms in his major writings from which they were later taken over into common theological parlance. There is no evidence that either of the Wesleys had any knowledge of Baier's works.

25. *De Trinitate*, XIV.8.11. Italics mine.

26. As Robert Cushman observed: "What is *fides*? It is acknowledgment (*agnitio*) of the Word in the form of the Servant. Preeminently, it is love awakened by the lowly form of the historical. It is fundamentally 'a motion of the heart'" (Cushman, *Faith Seeking Understanding*, 20).

27. J. Wesley, *Works*, 7:261 (no. 144.10).

As important as it is to believe in certain things (the fundamental substance of faith), Wesley pointed to the act of faith, or that living faith by which one believes, as the foundation of the Christian life. While faith and belief are integral—never to be separated from one another—in the Wesleyan tradition, the "enpersonalization" of faith remains the key to authentic life in Christ; *the faith must become, at some point and in a dynamic way, my faith.*[28]

The Doctrine of Justification by Faith

Charles Wesley's essential discovery concerning life in Christ and the dominating theme of faith in his writings revolves around the classic Pauline text, Romans 3:23-24: "Since all have sinned and fall short of the glory of God; they are now justified by his grace as a gift, through the redemption that is in Christ Jesus." It should be no surprise to us that his discoveries with regard to justification by grace through faith were profoundly autobiographical. The doctrine and Wesley's own experience both bear close scrutiny.

With regard to the later sermons of Charles Wesley—i.e., the post-Pentecost 1738 collection, subsequent to his "evangelical conversion"— Newport maintains that "the one overriding concern is salvation and how it is achieved, and the one consistent answer given is that it is by faith in Christ, who has paid the price of human sin."[29] Of the several sermons in which Wesley explores the nature of faith, one of his two sermons from this period on the Romans 3:23-25 text, the longest of all his sermons to have survived, provides a vigorous account of his doctrine of justification by faith.[30] In his explication of justification, Wesley adheres closely to the language of the *Homilies* and *Articles*.[31] After having described the corrupt and fallen condition of the human creature, Wesley quotes nine

---

28. In his discussion of "the faithful life," Craig Dykstra observes: "To many people, faith means belief. Faith is, indeed, closely related to belief, but the relations between the two are complex . . . Faith involves more than believing *that* something is true, it also involves believing *in*, having confidence in, trusting. Trust and confidence in God and in God's promises have been classical Protestant emphases in describing faith" (Dykstra, *Growing in the Life of Faith*, 19–20). I explore these issues more fully in the next section on the doctrine of justification.

29. Newport, *Sermons of Charles Wesley*, 62.

30. Newport, *Sermons of Charles Wesley*, 183–210. Wesley's less protracted sermon on this text (Sermon 6 in *Sermons*, 167–82) obviously addresses the same subject, the preacher taking pains to demonstrate that all have sinned and fall short of the glory of God and that the cure of humanity's diseased condition is faith in the blood of Christ.

31. Indeed, 40 percent of the shorter version of this sermon (Sermon 6) consists in direct quotations from this source (Newport, *Sermons of Charles Wesley*, 68). It is not too much to say that he was rediscovering the established doctrine of his church and explaining it to his hearers through these sermons.

paragraphs from Homily 3, "Of Salvation," describing justification by faith as the remedy for this sickness, and tersely summarizes his position by quoting Article XI, "Of the Justification of Man."

> We are accounted righteous before God, only for the merit of our Lord Jesus Christ through faith, and not for our own works or deservings. Wherefore, that we are justified by faith only, is a most wholesome doctrine, and very full of comfort.[32]

Likewise, he imports the language of Homily 4, "On Faith," in order to define faith in this regard.

> The true, lively and converting faith, the sure and substantial faith which saveth sinners . . . is also a true trust and confidence of the mercy of God through our Lord Jesus Christ, and a steadfast hope of all good things to be received at God's hand. It is not in the mouth and outward profession only, but liveth and stirreth inwardly in the heart.[33]

That, in 1738, all of this was a discovery for Charles is a point that does not need belaboring. Attempts to interpret his awakening of faith on the Day of Pentecost and his poetical account of the experience in that year abound.[34] Suffice it to say that, on the threshold of that transformative experience, he was pondering the spiritual insight of his Anglican heritage, as is clear from his journal account:

> Who would believe our Church had been founded on this important article of justification by faith alone? I am astonished I should ever think this a new doctrine; especially while our Articles and Homilies stand unrepealed, and the key of knowledge is not yet taken away.
>
> From this time I endeavoured to ground as many of our friends as came in this fundamental truth, salvation by faith alone, not an idle, dead faith, but a faith which works by love, and is necessarily productive of all good works and all holiness.[35]

Having been convinced about the truth of this doctrine, God soon transformed his intellectual assent into a vital experience by virtue of which he could claim: "I saw that by faith I stood; by the continual support of faith,

---

32. Newport, *Sermons of Charles Wesley*, 199.
33. Newport, *Sermons of Charles Wesley*, 200.
34. See Rattenbury, *Conversion of the Wesleys*; Holland, "Conversions of John and Charles Wesley"; Tyson, *Charles Wesley*, 92–111; and Dixon, "Conversion Hymn," 43–47.
35. C. Wesley, *Manuscript Journal*, 1:104 (May 17, 1738).

which kept me from falling, though of myself I am ever sinking into sin."³⁶ One hears autobiographical echoes of this experience, particularly in his hymns for those groaning for full redemption.

> I hold thee with a trembling hand,
>
> But will not let thee go
>
> Till steadfastly by faith I stand,
>
> And all thy goodness know.³⁷

"By faith I every moment stand," sings Wesley, "Strangely upheld by thy right hand."³⁸

He explicitly refers to "justification by faith" nearly twenty times in his journal, primarily in his record of 1738 and 1739. More often than not, however, the term "faith" simply functions as a shorthand reference to the doctrine of justification by grace through faith. Whether described as the "doctrine of faith," the "experience of faith," "faith of the gospel," "life in the

---

36. C. Wesley, *Manuscript Journal*, 1:108 (May 21, 1738). In this brief essay, it is impossible to discuss one of the principle questions that consumed much of the Wesleys' time and apologetic energy in the months subsequent to these discoveries related to faith, namely, whether God can give faith instantaneously. On the basis of the scriptural evidence, the doctrine of their church, the witness of others, and their own experience, the brothers had become convinced of the validity of this claim. The fact that faith is God's gift, in fact, demanded the possibility. When Mrs. Delamotte accused John Wesley of "preaching an instantaneous faith," Charles sprang to his defense: "As to that," I replied, "we cannot but speak the things which we have seen and heard" (C. Wesley, *Manuscript Journal*, 1:125; June 26, 1738). A parallel concern that troubled many of the Wesleyan antagonists had to do with what they considered to be the "enthusiastic" claims of the Methodists with regard to assurance that accompanied the experience of justification by faith, an issue the Wesleys revisited on a number of occasions throughout their lifetimes and adapted accordingly. The close connection between justification and assurance in Charles Wesley's theology is explained, in part, by Rattenbury: "Saving faith is, as [John Wesley's] early sermon ('Salvation by Faith') shows, a trust in Christ as a Saviour; in this sense it is difficult to distinguish it either from Assurance or the Witness of the Spirit. Charles makes this clear in the hymn 'How can a sinner know.' In point of fact, if the two notions are kept in mind that faith is a gift of God and also an evidence of things unseen, it necessarily follows that the distinction between it and Assurance and the Witness of the Spirit is so tenuous as hardly to be worth making" (*Evangelical Doctrines*, 265).

37. J. Wesley, *Works*, 7:517 (no. 351.2). One also hears the echoes here of what might be claimed the greatest of all Charles Wesley's hymns, "Wrestling Jacob."

38. J. Wesley, *Works*, 7:524 (no. 355.6). If asked how this experience is mediated to the would-be believer, Wesley would most certainly have quoted Rom 10:17, "faith comes by hearing." He uses this phrase repeatedly in his journal. While "preaching faith" was essential to the appropriation of God's grace in the lives of the people to whom he ministered, Wesley also affirmed the mystery of faith and recognized the myriad ways in which his followers experienced God's love and grace through faith.

faith," "faith in the blood of Christ," or "spirit of faith," these expressions, and the term "faith" itself, connote the experience of having been accepted and pardoned by God through faith in Christ alone. The foundation of this concept, of course, is trust (*fiducia*). Faith is the gift of trust; the Spirit enabling the child of God to entrust his or her life into the care of the God of love. The center around which all else revolved for the Methodists was the shared experience of faith-as-trust and salvation by grace. Originally written to help distinguish the Wesleyan way from that of the Moravians, one of Wesley's "Hymns for One Convinced of Unbelief" celebrates this theme.

> Author of faith, to thee I cry,
> To thee, who wouldst not have me die,
>   But know the truth and live;
> Open mine eyes to see thy face,
> Work in my heart the saving grace,
>   The life eternal give.
>
> I know the work is only thine—
> The gift of faith is all divine;
>   But, if on thee we call
> Thou wilt the benefit bestow,
> And give us hearts to feel and know
>   That thou hast died for all.
>
> Be it according to thy word!
> Now let me find my pard'ning Lord,
>   Let what I ask be given;
> The bar of unbelief remove,
> Open the door of faith and love,
>   And take me into heaven![39]

The Vision of Faith Working by Love

In framing the Anglican Articles of Religion, and particularly the *Homilies*, Thomas Cranmer exemplified a twin concern. Not only did he seek to

---

39. J. Wesley, *Works*, 7:224–25 (no. 114.1, 3, 5).

establish the nature of salvation as God's free gift of grace received through faith, but he also demonstrated that salvation by faith alone need not lead to antinomianism and the abandonment of morality. Rather, he viewed good works, still, as an essential part of the Christian life. These entwined goals frame Homily 3, "Of Salvation," which, as we have already seen, figured prominently in Wesley's own sermons. The subsequent homilies, "Of Faith" and "Of Good Works," further elaborate the connection of faith and works in the Christian life.[40]

When Charles uses expressions like "practical faith" or the "full assurance of faith," or admonishes the believer to press on toward the "obedience," "triumph," or "righteousness of faith," he refers to the process by which faith is made effective in love. Standing squarely in his Anglican heritage, he affirms that faith—God's restoration of the capacity to entrust one's life to God—is the foundation of the abundant life, but also claims that faith is but a means to love's end. This dynamic conception of the interrelation of faith and love, or faith and works, is one of the primary contributions of the Wesleyan theological tradition. Charles explicates this vision of authentic Christianity repeatedly in all of his writings.

Joseph Williams offers a rare first-hand glimpse of Charles's synthesis of faith and works in his journal account of a sermon Wesley preached on 2 Corinthians 5:17–21 in 1739. After stressing the importance of justification by faith alone, according to Williams's report:

> Nor did he fail to inform them thoroughly, how ineffectual their faith would be to justify them in the sight of God, unless it wrought by love, purified their hearts, and reformed their lives: for though he cautioned them with the utmost care not to attribute any merit to their own performances, nor in the least degree rest on any works of their own, yet at the same time he thoroughly apprized them, that their faith is but a dead faith if it be not operative, and productive of good works, even all the good in their power.[41]

In all of his preaching Wesley defends his conviction that works come after faith and are the consequence and not the cause of divine acceptance. This, in

---

40. It is worth noting that Charles's brother, John, abridged these three homilies, the pamphlet extract of which he published in 1738. The value of this publication can hardly be overemphasized. For the definitive text of *The Doctrine of Salvation, Faith, and Good Works*, and discussion of this critical publication, consult J. Wesley, *Works*, 12:27–43; cf. Maddox, *Responsible Grace*, 174–76, for an excellent discussion of "faith working by love" in the theology of John Wesley.

41. Quoted in Newport, *Sermons of Charles Wesley*, 30–31.

fact, is the principal theme of his sermon on Titus 3:8.[42] In his exposition of this text, among the marks or effects of true faith, he includes inward peace of conscience; joy; liberty not only from the guilt, but from the power of sin; and love, for "faith works by love, and he that loveth not knoweth not God, for God is love."[43] He enforces this point in characteristic fashion at the conclusion of his sermon on 1 John 3:14 in a fifth word of advice.

> . . . show your faith in good works. Without these all pretensions to faith are false. These are the necessary effects or fruits or signs of a living faith. Necessary they are, not to justify us before God, but to justify us before man; or rather, not to make, but to show us acceptable; not as the cause but as the evidence of our new birth; not as conditions, but consequences and tokens of our salvation. The faith which worketh not by love, is an idle, barren, dead faith; that is, no faith at all.[44]

The biblical locus for this critical theme for both Wesley brothers is Galatians 5:6, "The only thing that counts is faith working through love." Charles frequently alludes to this text in his sacred verse:

> Happy the man that finds the grace
> The blessing of God's chosen race,
> The wisdom coming from above,
> The faith that sweetly works by love.[45]

Or again:

> O might we through thy grace attain
>   The faith thou never wilt reprove,
> The faith that purges every stain,
>   The faith that always works by love.[46]

While Wesleyan soteriology affirms the importance of justification by faith (the forensic dimension of salvation), it emphasizes the restorative process of salvation, the goal of which is the fullest possible love of God and neighbor (the therapeutic dimension of salvation). One of Wesley's "Hymns for Christian Friends" captures this dynamic movement of faith to love, elevates

---

42. See Newport, *Sermons of Charles Wesley*, 152–66.
43. Newport, *Sermons of Charles Wesley*, 160–61.
44. Newport, *Sermons of Charles Wesley*, 150–51.
45. J. Wesley, *Works*, 7:96 (no. 14.1).
46. J. Wesley, *Works*, 7:623 (no. 443.2).

the Eucharistic and eschatological dimensions of the journey, and celebrates the trilogy of faith, hope, and love:

> Come, let us ascend,
> My companion and friend,
> To a taste of the banquet above;
> If thy heart be as mine
> If for Jesus it pine
> Come up into the chariot of love.
>
> By faith we are come
> To our permanent home;
> By hope we the rapture improve;
> By love we still rise,
> And look down on the skies,
> For the heaven of heavens is love.[47]

This journey toward love, as Charles describes it in the hymn, requires a community of faithful companions. It takes a fellowship of believers, shaped by God's grace, to teach the children of God how to love. Wholeness means conformity to Christ in all things—holiness of heart and life. Faith is a means to the realization of this lofty goal. "Lord, I believe, and not in vain," claims Wesley, "My faith shall make me whole." And that faith makes it possible to prove, with all the saints, "What is the length, and breadth, and height, / And depth of perfect love."[48] He captures the essence of this quest in a one stanza reflection on Psalm 81:10.

> Give me the enlarged desire,
> And open, Lord, my soul,
> Thy own fullness to require,
> And comprehend the whole;
> Stretch my faith's capacity
> Wider and yet wider still;
> Then, with all that is in thee,
> My soul forever fill![49]

---

47. J. Wesley, *Works*, 7:673 (no. 486.1, 3).
48. J. Wesley, *Works*, 7:244–45 (no. 132.10–11).
49. J. Wesley, *Works*, 7:529 (no. 361).

Wesley's poetic reflections on Ephesians 2:8–10 provide the most memorable lyrical expression of this central theme. As ST Kimbrough has observed: "Unlike many of his other hymns, this text is not a prayer. It is an exhortation, an urging, an encouragement for all to plead for faith alone. But this faith 'forms the Savior in the soul.' The form of the Saviour, Jesus Christ, within us shapes our personalities, characters, attitudes, and demeanor. The essence of the Savior is love and his love becomes the very essence of our being."[50] The hymn describes faith as an ongoing, life-transforming experience, something for which the child of God yearns and stretches forward to receive as a gift.

> Plead we thus for faith alone,
> Faith which by our works is shown;
> God it is who justifies,
> Only faith the grace applies,
> Active faith that lives within,
> Conquers earth, and hell, and sin,
> Sanctifies, and makes us whole,
> Forms the Saviour in the soul.
>
> Let us for this faith contend,
> Sure salvation is its end;
> Heaven already is begun,
> Everlasting life is won.
> Only let us persevere
> Till we see our Lord appear;
> Never from the rock remove,
> Saved by faith which works by love.[51]

III.

A whole constellation of images, as can be easily seen, revolves around these three primary conceptions of faith. Wesley employs many other images, however, leaving us with a richly textured portrait of faith in his

---

50. Kimbrough, *Heart to Praise*, 128.
51. J. Wesley, *Works*, 7:698–99 (no. 507.3–4).

lyrical theology. Faith sustains, empowers, increases, assures; it is yearned for, called upon, and, though a gift, possessed; the arms of faith embrace, the unconquerable shield of faith guards and protects, the household of faith rejoices; faith leads the believer home. Of the many images Wesley uses to explore, illuminate, and communicate the mystery of faith, several call for particular attention because of their pervasiveness in his writings and their enduring significance. These include the image of faith as the door opening into a new world of spiritual vitality, faith as power (and its close relationship to prayer and healing), and faith as the source of spiritual vision (the eye of faith) and light.

The Door of Faith

The Wesleyan way of salvation consists essentially in three dynamic movements, summarized by John Wesley in an important piece of correspondence to Thomas Church: "Our main doctrines, which include all the rest, are three—that of repentance, of faith, and of holiness. The first of these we account as it were, the porch of religion; the next, the door; and third, religion itself."[52] Faith—or more precisely the experience of justification by grace through faith—is the door through which one enters the domain of true religion. The immediate biblical allusion upon which Charles draws is the apostles' report of their evangelistic labors upon return to Antioch and their celebration of the way in which God "opened a door of faith for the Gentiles" (Acts 14:27). The Spirit elicited faith among these Gentile converts when the followers of Jesus offered Christ to them through the preaching of the Word.

Indeed, one of the most pervasive expressions in Charles's journal is the simple entry: "I preached repentance."[53] "Fountain of unexhausted love, / Of infinite compassions, hear," he prays, "Repentance, faith and pardon give; / O let me turn again and live!"[54] He pleads for the Spirit to remove all barriers to genuine reconciliation:

> Still let the publicans draw near;
>
> Open the door of faith and heaven,
>
> And grant their hearts thy word to hear,
>
> And witness all their sins forgiven.[55]

52. Telford, *Letters of John Wesley*, 2:268.
53. Cf. C. Wesley, *Manuscript Journal*, 1:183 (August 7, 1739), 1:272 (June 30, 1740), 2:414 (August 2, 1744), and 2:449 (October 8, 1745).
54. J. Wesley, *Works*, 7:286 (no. 163.3).
55. J. Wesley, *Works*, 7:180 (no. 80.8).

The Power of Faith

Of greater mystery is the connection between faith and power, especially as this power is linked to prayer and to healing. One of Charles's favorite biblical images in this regard is the mustard-seed faith that possesses the ability to move mountains:

> That mighty faith on me bestow
> > Which cannot ask in vain,
> Which holds, and will not let thee go
> > Till I my suit obtain.
>
> On me that faith divine bestow
> > Which doth the mountain move;
> And all my spotless life shall show
> > Th'omnipotence of love.[56]

"Give me the faith which can remove," he prays, "And sink the mountain to a plain!"[57] The prayer of faith provides access to this capacity, this strength, as Charles makes clear in a lyrical reflection upon the whole armor of God.

> In fellowship, alone,
> > To God with faith draw near;
> Approach his courts, besiege his throne
> > With all the powers of prayer.[58]

The early Methodist people viewed their life as a journey with Christ in which, as in John Bunyan's classic account of the Christian pilgrim, progress is made only through struggle and even battle. And so, faith provides the resources for "believers fighting."

> That bloody banner see,
> > And in your Captain's sight
> Fight the good fight of faith with me,
> > My fellow-soldiers, fight.

---

56. J. Wesley, *Works*, 7:489–90 (no. 333.3, 6).
57. J. Wesley, *Works*, 7:596 (no. 412.1).
58. J. Wesley, *Works*, 7:402 (no. 260.1).

Tremendous impediments stand in the way of faith's journey toward love, but the "ancient conqueror" arms the faithful followers who shout in triumph in the end.

> This is the victory!
> Before our faith they fall;
> Jesus hath died for you and me!
> Believe, and conquer all![59]

Convinced of the necessity of total dependence upon Christ in the Church's quest for righteousness and truth, Charles, along with the gathered community of faith, intercedes on behalf of the church in the life of the world.

> Jesu, from thy heavenly place,
> Thy dwelling in the sky,
> Fill our Church with righteousness,
> Our want of faith supply;
> Faith our strong protection be,
> And godliness with all its power
> 'Stablish our posterity
> Till time shall be no more.[60]

Not only is the prayer of faith a personal discipline, it is a corporate action. Faith requires a community. "O let us stir each other up, / Our faith by works to approve," Wesley admonishes, for only through this corporate act of obedience in love can we hope to "Stretch out the arms of faith and prayer" and "reach" God "now!"[61] The prayer of faith is "incessant";[62] "effectual and fervent" prayer brings spiritual healing and liberation.[63] While "Faith to be healed thou know'st I have," claims Wesley before God, "For thou that faith hast given,"[64] the working of God's grace is a mystery, the depths of which can never to be fully plumbed. Not infrequently, therefore, prayer breaks forth into praise and faith takes on the wings of flight.

---

59. J. Wesley, *Works*, 7:412–3 (no. 268.3, 6).
60. J. Wesley, *Works*, 7:631–2 (no. 452.1).
61. J. Wesley, *Works*, 7:721 (no. 525.3).
62. J. Wesley, *Works*, 7:613 (no. 437.2).
63. J. Wesley, *Works*, 7:690 (no. 501.1).
64. J. Wesley, *Works*, 7:249 (no. 135.3).

> Angels and archangels all
> > Praise the mystic Three in One,
> Sing, and stop, and gaze, and fall
> > O'erwhelmed before thy throne.
>
> Vying with that happy choir
> > Who chant thy praise above,
> We on eagles' wings aspire,
> > The wings of faith and love.[65]

The Eye of Faith

Nearly twenty of Charles's hymns in the 1780 *Collection* refer explicitly to "the eye(s) of faith" or to the connection between faith and spiritual vision. It is not too much to claim that this is another of Charles's favorite expressions. His first use of this language in the journal comes in the rather moving entry of May 25 as he stands before the sacrament and continues to linger in the spiritual awakening of his Pentecost experience of 1738 and that of his brother from the previous day.

> I had no particular attention to the prayers: but in the prayer of consecration I saw, by the eye of faith, or rather, had a glimpse of, Christ's broken, mangled body, as taking [*sic*] down from the cross. Still I could not observe the prayer, but only repeat with tears, "O love, love!"[66]

The primary object of this vision is the crucified Lord, whose remembrance not only fixes the image of the crucifix in the mind's eye, but transforms the heart and soul:

> Vouchsafe us eyes of faith to see
> The Man transfixed on Calvary,
> > To know thee, who thou art—
> The one eternal God and true;
> And let the sight affect, subdue,
> > And break my stubborn heart.[67]

---

65. J. Wesley, *Works*, 7:346 (no. 212.2, 3).
66. C. Wesley, *Manuscript Journal*, 1:111 (May 25, 1738).
67. J. Wesley, *Works*, 7:228 (no. 118.2).

"Before my eyes of faith confessed," Charles sings, "Stand forth a slaughtered Lamb."[68]

The restoration of sight makes spiritual knowledge possible. Charles demonstrates great concern throughout his life for the intimacy involved in knowing God as God has known us. It should be no surprise, therefore, that the immediate consequence of the wrestler's discovery of God's "Pure Universal Love" in Wesley's famous hymn, "Come, O thou traveller unknown," is the unimpeded vision of God.

> My prayer hath power with God; the grace
>> Unspeakable I now receive;
> Through faith I see thee face to face;
>> I see thee face to face, and live!
> In vain I have not wept and strove—
> Thy nature, and thy name, is LOVE.[69]

His hymn on "Moses' Wish" articulates the same essential theme.

> Before my faith's enlightened eyes
>> Make all thy goodness pass!
> Thy goodness is the sight I prize—
>> O may I see thy smiling face!
> Thy nature in my soul proclaim!
> Reveal thy love, thy glorious name![70]

There is an interesting trajectory in the hymns of Charles Wesley that leads from faith to vision, from vision to knowledge, and from knowledge to the ultimate beatific vision of the God of love.[71] For Charles, as for John,

68. J. Wesley, *Works*, 7:235 (no. 124.6).
69. J. Wesley, *Works*, 7:252 (no. 136.8).
70. J. Wesley, *Works*, 7:422 (no. 274.2).
71. The parallels with the thought of Clement of Alexandria are rather startling: "There seems to me to be a first kind of saving change from heathenism to faith, a second from faith to knowledge, and this latter, as it passes on into love, begins at once to establish a mutual friendship between that which knows and that which is known" (Quoting *Stromateis*, VII.10.57.4, in Stevenson, *New Eusebius*, 199–200). The incisive analysis of Rex Matthews with regard to faith in the development of John Wesley's thought may be of particular interest here. He demonstrates three distinct conceptions of faith in Wesley's works, namely, faith as assent, faith as trust, and faith as an actual spiritual experience, his emphasis moving sequentially toward the latter understanding in the mature Wesley. While it is not possible to chart Charles Wesley's developing conception of faith with such precision, there may be parallels, and the concept of the "eye of faith" may point to this experiential dimension, grounded, as it is, in a spiritual

as we have seen, faith always moves towards love.[72] So despite the fact that "By faith we already behold / That lovely Jerusalem here,"[73] the community of the faithful yearn for that day "When faith in sight shall end," at the great marriage banquet of the Lamb and God brings "strength, life, and rest" to ultimate fruition in Jesus.[74] The vision of Moses, once again, springs immediately into Wesley's mind, and he plays with the image of his theophany in a hymn on the nature of prayer.

> The spirit of interceding grace
> > Give us in faith to claim,
> To wrestle till we see thy face,
> > And know thy hidden name.
>
> Then let me on the mountain top
> > Behold thy open face,
> Where faith in sight is swallowed up,
> > And prayer [is] endless praise.[75]

God illuminates the soul with the gift of faith. God restores sight to the blind and rescues those who dwell in darkness. Those who entrust their lives to God through Christ by faith pray for all the fullness of God in their lives. One of Charles Wesley's "redemption hymns" celebrates the language of faith and draws us ever upward to the amazing gift of faith working through love.

> Father of Jesus Christ, the just,
> > My Friend and Advocate with thee,
> Pity a soul that fain would trust
> > In him who lived and died for me.

---

sense. See the distillation of Matthews's analysis in "With the Eyes of Faith"; cf. Maddox, *Responsible Grace*, 127–28.

72. In light of this movement from faith to love, Gordon Wakefield once claimed that the Wesleyan spirituality is more "Catholic" than "Protestant," a claim borne out by a close study of Charles's hymns and prose writings. See Wakefield, *Methodist Spirituality*, where he maintains that Wesley's "spiritual theology was based more on 'love of God' than the 'faith in Christ' of continental and Puritan Protestantism. The Christian must aim for nothing less than perfect love" (24).

73. J. Wesley, *Works*, 7:170 (no. 71.3).

74. J. Wesley, *Works*, 7:340 (no. 208.5).

75. J. Wesley, *Works*, 7:440–41 (no. 288.3, 6).

But only thou canst make him known,
And in my heart reveal thy Son.

If drawn by thine alluring grace
    My want of living faith I feel,
Show me in Christ thy smiling face;
    What flesh and blood can ne'er reveal,
Thy coeternal Son display,
And call my darkness into day.

The gift unspeakable impart:
    Command the light of faith to shine,
To shine in my dark, drooping heart,
    And fill me with the life divine;
Now bid the new creation be!
O God, let there be faith in me!

Thee without faith I cannot please,
    Faith without thee I cannot have;
But thou hast sent the Prince of peace
    To seek my wandering soul, and save;
O Father, glorify thy Son,
And save me for his sake alone!

Save me through faith in Jesu's blood,
    That blood which he for all did shed;
For me, for me, thou know'st it flowed,
    For me, for me, thou hear'st it plead;
Assure me now my soul is thine,
And all thou art in Christ is mine![76]

---

76. C. Wesley published the first three verses of this hymn as cited in J. Wesley, *Works*, 7:259 (no. 142). The final two verses, restored here from *Redemption Hymns*, no. 14.4–5, are also retained in many of the subsequent hymnals.

Chapter 3

"All the Image of Thy Love"

Charles Wesley's Vision of the One Thing Needful

> Source note: Delivered as the keynote address for the joint Charles Wesley Society Meeting and the Wesley Week Lecture at Asbury University and Theological Seminary in Wilmore, Kentucky, September 23, 2014; subsequently published in *Proceedings of the Charles Wesley Society* 18 (2014) 21–40.

KNOWING OF MY KEEN interest in Christian piety, one of my professors in the Department of Theology at Valparaiso University took it upon himself to introduce this young Methodist to a proper study of holiness. I remember the day he thrust Adolf Köberle's *The Quest for Holiness* into my hands—his personal, well-worn copy—and said that this would be a good place to start. While I disagreed vehemently with some of this Lutheran theologian's conclusions (I was young), I was immediately drawn to his vision of holiness as something motivated entirely by the love of Christ and gratitude to God. Charles Wesley, like his older brother, John, most certainly considered the quest for holiness to be the keynote of his life and of the movement of spiritual renewal he co-founded.[1] He rooted holiness in God's grace; the fullest possible

---

1. Works that provide primary source material related to the themes of sanctification and holiness in the life and work of Charles Wesley, or explore these themes in part, include Kimbrough, *Orthodox and Wesleyan Spirituality*, 57–126; Kimbrough, *Lyrical Theology*, 177–212; Rattenbury, *Evangelical Doctrines*, 278–307; and Tyson, *Charles Wesley*, 360–97. Several articles are also of significance: Anderson, "Power of Godliness"; Kimbrough, "Charles Wesley and Sanctification"; Nicholson, "Holiness Emphasis"; Tyson, "One Things Needful"; and Watson, "Presentation of Holiness." The most important comprehensive examination of this theme is Tyson, *Charles Wesley on Sanctification*.

sanctification reflected the paradox of grace in Galatians 2:20.² Wesley always preferred the language of love, but by whatever language, he considered this grace-oriented pursuit the "one thing needful" (Luke 10:42).

Charles Wesley hardly stood alone in this conviction; rather, in emphasizing the lofty goal of holiness, he took his place in a lengthy succession of Christian disciples who became thoroughly captive to this biblical ideal. From the exclamation of Athanasius, "He was humanized that we might be deified,"³ to the song of the anonymous slave, "Lord, I want to be like Jesus, in my heart," disciples of Jesus have longed for a full, authentic Christlikeness that brings honor to God and true blessedness to life. Christian history pulsates with this profound desire, and the rediscovery of holiness, in one way or another, characterizes virtually every period of renewal.

Before we move to an examination of Charles Wesley's vision of the one thing needful, therefore, permit me to illustrate the rediscovery of holiness in two other significant Christian disciples, one ancient and one contemporary. I want to set the stage in this way because Wesley owed so much to the former, Thomas à Kempis, and contributed so much to the latter, Dallas Willard. I do not want this address simply to be an analysis of Wesley's thinking and singing about holiness and sanctification; I want you to be able to visualize this great poet-theologian as an important link in an ageless human chain of those who have sought holiness in this life. I also want to inspire and encourage you to become a participant in this quest, because I believe we live in an age pregnant with these same concerns. Our world yearns today for disciples of Jesus who are authentic witnesses to the love and grace of God—for men and women who are truly holy, who are transcripts of the divine, to use Charles Wesley's own phrase.⁴

During the late fourteenth century, the "modern devotion" movement in the Netherlands sought to establish a renewed spirituality for the common person based on an interior transformation, reforming the soul and rejuvenating the spirit.⁵ Quite simply, these "new devout," as they were sometimes

---

2. Donald M. Baillie coined this term in his classic study of Incarnation and atonement. "Its essence lies in the conviction which a Christian man possesses, that every good thing in him, every good thing he does, is somehow not wrought by himself but by God" (Baillie, *God Was in Christ*, 114).

3. Athanasius, *On the Incarnation*, ¶54, 107.

4. Charles Wesley described the Christian disciple as a "transcript of the Trinity." In his view, God writes God's self into the very being of disciples in such a way that others "read" their lives and perceive the presence of God in them. See multiple examples of this language in Wesley's poetry: Wesley and Wesley, *Hymns and Sacred Poems* (1739), 178; *Hymns and Sacred Poems* (1740), 188; *Hymns and Sacred Poems* (1749), 2:264; *Funeral Hymns*, 47; and *Hymns on the Trinity*, 63.

5. See the introduction to Chilcote, *Imitation of Christ*, xv–xxviii.

called, combined a religion of the heart with acts of loving service to others in "imitation of Christ." In his great devotional classic of that title, Thomas à Kempis emphasized holiness as the goal of the Christian journey. While forgiveness provides the foundation for human well-being and reconciliation with God, the authentic Christian pursues perfection in love, or holiness of heart and life. Those who are holy reflect the character of Jesus in their actual lives, giving evidence of their faith through active love. In our own time, Dallas Willard breathed this same spirit. In works such as *The Divine Conspiracy*, *The Great Omission*, and *Renovation of the Heart*, he claims that God's primary intention is for all his children to become Christ-like persons. He describes the Western church's neglect of sanctification as the great omission of our age. Willard describes sanctification—or spiritual transformation into Christlikeness—as "the process of forming the inner world of the human self in such a way that it takes on the character of the inner being of Jesus himself."[6] "*Single-minded and joyous devotion to God and his will, to what God wants for us—and to service to him and to others because of him—*" he also writes, "*is what the will transformed into Christlikeness looks like*."[7] With Charles Wesley, these kindred spirits conceived God's gift of salvation not only in terms of forgiveness, but also as sanctification or imparted holiness. From the perspective of all three, the primary goal of the Christian life is the "transformation of [believers'] dispositions and desires, enabling them to take on the 'mind of Christ' and the 'fruit of the Spirit.'"[8]

In his monumental study of *The Idea of Perfection in Christian Theology*, R. Newton Flew described his approach to a topic so large, and I feel compelled to emulate his method in this brief address, and especially given my assigned task.[9] I concern myself here with the content of Charles Wesley's vision—the ideal of holiness of heart and life—and do not "attempt any account of the different methods employed for the realization of the ideal."[10] Secondly, I attempt to state "the one thing needful" positively rather than negatively. Thirdly, like Flew, my personal interest in this topic is essentially evangelistic and missional. As he observed, "the truest evangelism is to preach the full ideal for which power is offered in the present life . . . A vast

---

6. Willard, *Renovation of the Heart*, 159.

7. Willard, *Renovation of the Heart*, 143.

8. Editorial introduction to Charles Wesley, "Promise of Sanctification" (1741), Charles Wesley's Published Verse, Duke Center for Studies in the Wesleyan Tradition, by Dr. Randy L. Maddox. All hymn texts in this article are taken from this source.

9. Flew, *Idea of Christian Perfection*.

10. Flew, *Idea of Christian Perfection*, xii. I have discussed the larger platform for the spiritual processes that characterized Wesleyan spirituality in Chilcote, *Recapturing the Wesleys' Vision* and "Charles Wesley and Christian Practices."

evangelistic advance can only be sustained if the Christian ideal for this life is steadily set forth in all its beauty and its fullness as being by the grace of God something not impossible of attainment . . . It is essential to the vitality and advance of the Christian message in this world."[11]

I. The Process of Sanctification

According to Charles Wesley, the term sanctification refers to that process by which the Spirit makes the child of God more and more like Jesus. The word simply means "to be made holy." Sanctification is the process; holiness is the goal. Like his older brother, Charles always defined holiness with reference to the two great commandments of Jesus, what we could call the twin dimensions of sanctification: holiness of heart, or love of God, and holiness of life, or love of neighbor (Matt 22:37–39). He was not only concerned that people experience forgiveness for the sin and brokenness in their lives (justification), he also wanted them to move toward the fullest possible wholeness and healing as well (sanctification), and he believed that God desired this for all in this life. Faith, he believed deeply, leads to love in the Christian life, and to be loving or holy is to be truly happy.

God accomplishes this great work in the life of the believer through the indwelling of the Holy Spirit. The glorious liberty that accompanies the Spirit not only frees from sorrow, fear, and sin, but also liberates those who follow Christ to love fully. Charles acknowledged a profound spiritual dynamic at work in those who pursue holiness earnestly, an apophatic (emptying) and kataphatic (filling) rhythm, to use the language of the spiritual writers. God expels or purges the "old" from those who seek holiness and fills them with the "new." The Spirit consumes, blots out, erases, and drives out sins, removing all barriers that separate us from God; the Spirit not only imputes, but imparts the mind and righteousness of Jesus, restores the image of Christ, and teaches us to love. In Charles's view, normally sanctification is a lengthy process. Few believers become fully loving all at once.[12] He questioned the instantaneity of this distinctive gift:

> Nature would the crown receive
>
> The first moment we believe,
>
> But we vainly think to seize
>
> Instantaneous holiness:

11. Flew, *Idea of Christian Perfection*, xiii–xiv.
12. See Maddox, *Responsible Grace*, 186; and Tyson, *Charles Wesley on Sanctification*, 227–301.

> Faith alone cannot suffice,
> Patience too must earn the prize,
> Both insure the promise given,
> Lead thro' perfect love to heaven.[13]

But this is also God's greatest gift as the Spirit enables the authentic child of God to grow into the full stature of Christ (Eph 4:13), and Wesley knew the dangers of limiting the power, efficacy, and immediacy of God's grace in the life of any person.

In a single-stanza hymn, published in his *Scripture Hymns* collection, Wesley reflects on the phrase from 1 Thessalonians 4:3: "For this is the will of God, your sanctification."

> He wills that I should holy be;
>   That holiness I long to feel,
> That full divine conformity
>   To all my Savior's righteous will.
> See, Lord, the travail of your soul
>   Accomplished in the change of mine,
> And plunge me, every whit made whole,
>   In all the depths of love divine.[14]

In this hymn, Charles claims that God's deep desire is for everyone to become loving, to be holy. All God's children exist for this very purpose. He infers that all people have a deep longing for this as well, whether they are willing to acknowledge it or not. Wesley's mysticism emerges in the closing lines. One can only say in the end that God's love is a mystery into which we plunge ourselves.

A confluence of many sources shaped this lofty vision of the Christian life in both Wesley brothers. Time precludes my exploring even the major influences, but suffice it to say that their native Anglicanism, and particularly the liturgy in which they immersed their lives, provided fertile soil in which this idea of Christian perfection could root and grow. Perhaps no single element of the 1662 Book of Common Prayer provided a more formative influence, with regard to both thought and language, than Cranmer's famous "Collect for Holy Communion":

---

13. C. Wesley, *Scripture Hymns*, 2:355–56.
14. C. Wesley, *Scripture Hymns*, 2:325; no. 631, "He wills that I should holy be."

ALMIGHTY God, unto whom all hearts be open, all desires known, and from whom no secrets are hid; cleanse the thoughts of our hearts by the inspiration of thy Holy Spirit, that we may perfectly love thee, and worthily magnify thy holy Name; through Christ our Lord. Amen.[15]

Charles most likely drew his inspiration for a hymn still sung by many today from this collect and its scriptural point of reference (Ps 51:10). This hymn provides one of the most mature expressions of Charles's vision of a life perfected in holiness and love, articulating several of its most critical elements:

> O for a heart to praise my God,
> > A heart from sin set free!
> A heart that always feels thy blood,
> > So freely spilt for me!
>
> A heart in every thought renewed
> > And full of love divine,
> Perfect and right and pure and good,
> > A copy, Lord, of thine.
>
> Thy nature, gracious Lord, impart;
> > Come quickly from above;
> Write thy new name upon my heart,
> > Thy new, best name of Love.[16]

In this hymn, Wesley maintains the intimate connection between holiness and the human heart. He assumes that whatever is written on the heart reflects the true character of the person. His hymn celebrates the heart of the believer—the heart upon which God has written the law of love. God writes on the heart, shapes the character, forms the disciple, restores the image of Christ in the child. While his poetic exposition of Psalm 51 addresses the aspiration of perfect love in the believer, Wesley focuses the singer on the idea of God's steadfast love. As in all aspects of his theology, God remains prevenient. As ST Kimbrough has observed with regard to this hymn, "it is through the *steadfast love of God* that we are granted

---

15. Book of Common Prayer, 238.

16. Wesley and Wesley, *Hymns and Sacred Poems* (1742), 30–31; "Hymn on Psalm 51," sts. 1, 4, and 8.

pure hearts. It is *God's love* that enables and sustains purity of heart. There is no way to purity and holiness without love!"[17] Charles never wavered from this conviction and celebrated the liberation that this process entails. Neither does he ever lose hope of feeling the efficacy of God's action on his behalf, both in justification and in sanctification. He longs to experience holiness not only as an intellectual affirmation, but as emotional vitality, to both know and feel the power of God's transforming love in the depth of his being. The concept of renewal occupies a central place in Wesley's articulation of the ideal. Through the refining process of sanctification God renews the image of Christ in the believer. God transcribes or copies the mind, perfection, righteousness, purity, and goodness of Jesus into the life of the apprentice. God imbues those open to the Holy Spirit with Christ's—with God's—own nature—"thy new, best name of Love."

It is not too much to say that once Wesley had experienced the unconditional love of God in Christ and developed a clear vision of his purpose in life as a child of God, he made the pursuit of this holiness his primary goal. "His subsequent spiritual life," as J. Ernest Rattenbury stated so succinctly, "might be summed up compendiously in one phrase: 'a quest for love.'"[18] Perhaps no verses he penned ever expressed his passion about this quest more than the concluding stanzas of a hymn written soon after his poignant experience of God's love in May 1738. John included the full hymn in the first joint collection of *Hymns and Sacred Poems* the following year.

> To love is all my wish,
>   I only live for this:
> Grant me, Lord, my heart's desire,
>   There by faith for ever dwell:
> This I always will require
>   Thee and only thee to feel.
>
> Thy pow'r I pant to prove
>   Rooted and fixt in love,
> Strengthen'd by thy Spirit's might,
>   Wise to fathom things divine,
> What the length and breadth and height,
>   What the depth of love like thine.

---

17. Kimbrough, *Heart to Praise*, 140. Italics added for emphasis.
18. Rattenbury, *Evangelical Doctrines*, 278.

> Ah! Give me this to know
> With all thy saints below.
>> Swells my soul to compass thee,
>> Gasps in thee to live and move,
>> Fill'd with all the deity,
>> All immerst and lost in love![19]

II. Restoration

For Charles Wesley, a restored loving spirit is "the one thing needful," and the famous sermon of this title provides a helpful outline for an exploration of holiness and sanctification from his perspective. Kenneth Newport has provided an extremely helpful introduction to this sermon, based on Luke 10:42, in his critical edition of Charles Wesley's sermons, so I have no need to belabor the various questions surrounding this text.[20] A few brief comments must suffice. Newport includes this sermon in the collection of Charles's sermons despite the fact that it was written by John.[21] Well-documented evidence demonstrates that Charles preached it on multiple occasions without significant disruption to the narrative or obvious interpolation of the text. Charles, in other words, made this sermon his own, and Newport, as well as others, believes that it has a legitimate place among Charles Wesley's works. The main point is that in this sermon written by John, but embraced and preached by Charles, "'the one thing needful' is none other than the 'renewal of our fallen nature,' that is, the restoration of the image of God."[22]

> To recover our first estate, from which we are thus fallen, is the one thing now needful—to re-exchange the image of Satan for the image of God, bondage for freedom, sickness for health. Our one business is to rase out of our souls the likeness of our destroyer, and to be born again, to be formed anew after the likeness of our Creator. It is our one concern to shake off this servile yoke and to regain our native freedom; to throw off every chain, every passion and desire that does not suit an angelical

---

19. Wesley and Wesley, *Hymns and Sacred Poems* (1739), 169; IId Hymn to Christ, "Saviour, the world's and mine," sts. 4, 5, and 6. Rattenbury makes the interesting point that Charles only uses the word "perfect" rarely in connection with love. "Generally he seems to have regarded the adjective as tautological" (*Evangelical Doctrines*, 280–81).

20. Newport, *Sermons of Charles Wesley*, 360–61.

21. See Outler, *Works*, 1:131–41 for an analysis of this sermon in the context of John Wesley's works.

22. Newport, *Sermons of Charles Wesley*, 360.

nature. The one work we have to do is to return from the gates of death to perfect soundness; to have our diseases cured, our wounds healed, and our uncleanness done away.[23]

In this statement, Charles Wesley proclaimed a vision of holiness that entails spiritual liberation, inner healing, and divine restoration.[24]

Spiritual Liberation and Inner Healing

In a lyrical exposition of Matthew 14:36: "and all who touched [the fringe of his robe] were healed," Wesley celebrates the spiritual liberation and inner healing that accompany the gift of perfect holiness and love.

> Come, Saviour, come, and make me whole,
>   Entirely all my sins remove,
> To perfect health restore my soul,
>   To perfect holiness and love.[25]

The glorious liberty that accompanies this work of the Spirit not only frees from sorrow, fear, and sin, but also liberates believers to love fully.[26]

> Lord, we believe; and wait the hour
>   That brings the promis'd grace,
> When born of God we sin no more,
>   But always see thy face.
>
> Since thou wouldst have us free from sin,
>   And pure as those above,
> Make haste to bring thy nature in,
>   And perfect us in love.[27]

---

23. Newport, *Sermons of Charles Wesley*, 364; ¶ I.5.

24. It is worthwhile to note that Don Saliers, who has spent a lifetime exploring the interface of music and faith, has described the way in which the practice of singing can liberate, heal, and transform human life. His deep roots in the Wesleyan tradition make this observation second nature, given the centrality of sacred song to the Methodist heritage. See Saliers, "Singing Our Lives."

25. C. Wesley, *Scripture Hymns*, 2:169–70 (no. 171, ls. 5–8). This one-stanza hymn was joined as stanza two to his one-stanza exposition of 1 Thess 4:3 to form the hymn, "He wills, that I should holy be."

26. The following exposition is based, in part, upon Chilcote, "Charles Wesley's Lyrical Credo."

27. C. Wesley, *Hymns and Sacred Poems* (1749), 2:189, sts. 5–6. Cf. Wesley and

When Charles prepared his two-volume collection of *Hymns and Sacred Poems* for publication in 1749, independent of his brother's editorial hand, he included a section in the second volume entitled "Hymns for Those that Wait for Full Redemption." He illustrates this element of the Christian goal in many of the thirty-seven hymns he included in this sub-unit of the volume. The Spirit consumes, blots out, erases, and drives out sins, emptying the disciple of all that separates him or her from God. With regard to this apophatic work, Charles proclaims, "I believe thou wilt remove, / thoroughly wash out all my stains."[28] The closing stanzas of the second hymn in this section express the confidence of the believer in God's ability to perform this spiritual surgery.

> Bounds I will not set to thee,
> > Shorten thine almighty hand:
> Save from all iniquity,
> > Let not sin's foundations stand,
> Every stone o'erturn, o'erthrow;
> I believe it *may* be so.
>
> Wilt thou lop the boughs of sin,
> > Leaving still the stock behind?
> No, thy love shall work within,
> > Quite expel the carnal mind,
> Root and branch destroy my foe;
> I believe it *shall* be so.[29]

In Wesleyan theology, however, God empties for the purpose of filling. The Spirit fills the follower of Christ with the Lord's mind and righteousness, restores the image of Christ, and teaches the disciple how to love. "Into sin I cannot fall," observes Wesley, "while hanging on thy love."[30] "I even I believe in him," he confesses, in order that "thou wilt form thy Son in me, / and

---

Wesley, *Hymns and Sacred Poems* (1742), 261–64, Wesley's 28 stanza hymn, "Pleading for the Promise of Sanctification," based on Ezek 36:23.

28. Wesley and Wesley, *Hymns and Sacred Poems* (1742), 211, st. 6, the concluding stanza.

29. C. Wesley, *Hymns and Sacred Poems* (1749), 2:149, sts. 3–4.

30. C. Wesley, *Scripture Hymns*, 2:410; a single-stanza hymn on Jude 24.

perfect me in him."[31] He underscores the kataphatic nature of perfection in one of his hymns on full redemption:

> Lord, we believe, and rest secure,
>> Thine utmost promises to prove,
> To rise restor'd, and throughly pure,
>> In all the image of thy love,
> Fill'd with the glorious life unknown,
> Forever sanctified in one.[32]

The believer experiences God's work of grace not only as liberation, but also as healing. The Great Physician comes with "healing in his wings" (Mal 4:2), a favorite expression of Charles sung in hymns such as, "Hark, the herald angels sing!"[33] But he maintains a dynamic interrelation of these two elements: freedom and health. The singer who proclaims "Rejoice in hope, rejoice with me / We shall from all our sins be free" prays simultaneously, "My inbred malady remove; / To perfect health restore my soul."[34] In his exposition of 2 Corinthians 3:17, Wesley proclaims:

> Come then, and dwell in me,
>> Spirit of power within,
> And bring the glorious liberty
>> From sorrow, fear, and sin:
> The seed of sin's disease,
>> Spirit of health, remove,
> Spirit of finish'd holiness,
>> Spirit of perfect love.[35]

In a reflection on Isaiah 40:31, "They that wait on the Lord shall renew their strength," Charles sings: "Faith to be healed, thou know'st, I have, / From sin to be made clean."[36] In a lesser-known stanza of the well-known

31. Wesley and Wesley, *Hymns and Sacred Poems* (1742), 254, st. 19; reflections on Rom 4:16.

32. C. Wesley, *Hymns and Sacred Poems* (1749), 2:187, st. 8.

33. Cf. his monumental hymn, "Wrestling Jacob," Wesley and Wesley, *Hymns and Sacred Poems* (1742), 118, st. 10; and Wesley and Wesley, *Hymns and Sacred Poems* (1740), 88, st. 8.

34. The first quoted text is the refrain of "Ye happy sinners, hear," Wesley and Wesley, *Hymns and Sacred Poems* (1742), 183–4; a hymn "Rejoicing in Hope," while the second comes from Wesley's lyrical paraphrase of Ps 103:3 in C. Wesley, *Scripture Hymns*, 1762, 1:271, st. 2.

35. C. Wesley, *Scripture Hymns*, 2:298.

36. Wesley and Wesley, *Hymns and Sacred Poems* (1742), 226, st. 10.

hymn, "Jesu, thy all-victorious love," he prays for the infilling of the "Spirit of health, and life, and power, / And perfect liberty."[37]

He also employs images drawn from the healing ministry of Jesus to illustrate the intimate connection between the disease of sin and the healing of the soul.

> Thou seest me wretched, and distress'd,
>   Feeble, and faint, and blind, and poor:
> Weary I come to thee for rest,
>   And sick of sin, implore a cure.
>
> My sin's incurable disease
>   Thou Jesus, thou alone canst heal,
> Inspire me with thy power, and peace,
>   And pardon on my conscience seal.
>
> A touch, a word, a look from thee
>   Can turn my heart, and make it clean,
> Purge the foul inbred leprosy,
>   And save me from my bosom sin.[38]

Charles rests secure in the promise that "A word, a gracious word of thine, / The most inveterate plague can cure."[39]

Restoration of the Image of Christ

The phrase "restoration of the image of Christ" reflects the heart of Charles Wesley's vision of "the one thing needful." Like other aspects of his soteriology, in addition to the preeminent witness of Scripture, he owed a debt to many spiritual forebears for this concept. For a number of years, ST Kimbrough has engaged scholars within the Orthodox tradition in an ongoing dialogue concerning the synergy of Wesleyanism and the doctrinal/spiritual legacy that traces its roots to patristic sources. While there is neither time nor space to examine all the influences upon Charles's vision, I do want to claim

---

37. Wesley and Wesley, *Hymns and Sacred Poems* (1740), 156, st. 3, of the Hymn, "My God! I know, I feel thee mine," the fourth stanza of which begins with the famous line, "Jesu, thine all victorious love."

38. C. Wesley, *Hymns and Sacred Poems* (1749), 1:89, sts. 3–5.

39. C. Wesley, *Hymns and Sacred Poems* (1749), 1:93, st. 4.

the particular influence of Orthodox thought and practice with regard to the image of restoration. As Kimbrough has acknowledged, "while one might labor to find numerous quotations of the Early Fathers in Charles Wesley's poetry, his theology exudes the spirit of much of their theology."[40]

In his article, "All Creation in United Thanksgiving," Peter Bouteneff finds resonance between Gregory of Nyssa and Charles Wesley, in particular, around the "themes of salvation as restoration, and as change and movement from glory to glory."[41] The concluding stanza of Wesley's signature hymn, "Love Divine, All Loves Excelling"—some of the most beloved lines in all his poetic production—celebrates this lofty goal.

> Finish then thy new creation,
>   Pure and sinless let us be,
> Let us see thy great salvation,
>   Perfectly restor'd in thee;
> Chang'd from glory into glory,
>   Till in heaven we take our place,
> Till we cast our crowns before thee,
>   Lost in wonder, love, and praise![42]

Kimbrough notes how the concern of *theosis* "surfaces time and again in Charles Wesley's poetry in concert with many of the Early Fathers of the Church."[43] He illustrates this connection with an example from Wesley's *Nativity Hymns* in which the twin themes of Incarnation and restoration find profound expression.

> Made flesh for our sake,
> That we might partake
> The nature divine,
> And again in his image, his holiness shine;
>
> And while we are here,
> Our King shall appear,
> His Spirit impart,

---

40. Kimbrough, *Lyrical Theology*, 88. The following paragraphs follow the analysis of Kimbrough in this work closely.

41. Bouteneff, "All Creation," 194.

42. C. Wesley, *Redemption Hymns*, 12 (no. 9.4).

43. Kimbrough, *Lyrical Theology*, 89.

And form his full image of love in our heart.[44]

It is dangerous to minimize the complexity of this concept of restoration, but three themes, in particular, find repeated expression in Wesley's verse: the claim that the Spirit restores the image of Christ in the believer, that transformed disciples of Jesus will be like him, and that this kind of transformation enables them to shine to the glory of God.

The Spirit Restores the Image of Christ in the Believer

Holiness means restoration. In a lyrical paraphrase of Genesis 1:3, Charles prays for the ultimate, divine gift.

> Father, Son, and Holy-Ghost,
> > In council join again
> To restore thine image, lost
> > By frail apostate man:
> O might I thy form express,
> > Thro' faith begotten from above,
> Stamped with real holiness,
> > And filled with perfect love![45]

While believers engage in a quest for holiness, Charles couches the restoration of the image of Christ in passive language. "Let us, to perfect love restored, / Thy image here receive."[46] We receive the image. "Diffuse thine image through my soul," Wesley pleads, "Shine to the perfect day."[47] God disseminates his love. Sometimes he employs the ancient concept of stamping an image in the same way the emperor's image, for example, was impressed upon a coin.

> Transform my nature into thine,
> > Let all my powers thine impress feel,
> Let all my soul become divine,
> > And stamp me with thy Spirit's seal.[48]

---

44. C. Wesley, *Nativity Hymns*, 12 (nos. 8.5 and 8).
45. C. Wesley, *Scripture Hymns*, 1:4 (no. 5).
46. C. Wesley, *Scripture Hymns*, 2:89 (no. 1376, on Micah 7:20).
47. Wesley and Wesley, *Hymns and Sacred Poems* (1740), 98; "Christ our Sanctification," st. 4.
48. Wesley and Wesley, *Hymns and Sacred Poems* (1742), 136; Wesley's exposition of Luke 12:50.

Elsewhere he prays: "And stamp thine image on my heart."[49] God stamps the image of Christ on the believer.

Wesley also employs a peculiar expression in defining the outcome of God's restorative process. He describes the fully restored disciple as a transcript of the Trinity. This is one of his most unique and powerful metaphors related to *theosis*. In the hymn he prepared for the funeral of an early Methodist saint, Mrs. Lefevre, he affords this inspirational portrait:

> She *was* (what words can never paint)
> A spotless soul, a sinless saint,
>> In perfect love renew'd,
> A mirror of the deity,
> A transcript of the One in Three,
>> A temple fill'd with God.[50]

In one of his Trinity hymns, Charles explains the way in which this therapeutic transcription serves to honor and bring praise to the Three-One God.

> Remember thy Creators, God
>> In Persons Three confest,
> Who rais'd thee up a breathing clod,
>> And with his name imprest:
> The Persons Three in council join'd
>> To make his earth-born son;
> And, stampt with his immortal mind,
>> He claims thee for his own.
>
> He challenges thy youthful days
>> Who did thy being give:
> Created for his only praise,
>> For him rejoice to live;
> Transcript of holiness divine,
>> The Tri-une God proclaim,
> And spirit, and soul, and flesh resign
>> To glorify his name.[51]

---

49. Wesley and Wesley, *Hymns and Sacred Poems* (1742), 91; a hymn on Matthew 11:28. Cf. C. Wesley, *Hymns and Sacred Poems* (1749), 1:89; a hymn on Hebrews 13:8.

50. C. Wesley, *Funeral Hymns*, 47 (no. 27.5).

51. C. Wesley, *Trinity Hymns*, 63 (no. 97, "Remember thy CREATOR (Heb., CREATORS) in the days of thy youth," Eccl xii. 1).

While "how one is transformed into the divine nature remains a mystery" to Charles, as Kimbrough avers, nevertheless the poet writes with fervent zeal about the transparent character of the transformed child of God.

Transformed Disciples of Jesus Will Be Like Him

Holiness means Christlikeness.[52] Those who bear the image of Christ conform to him in mind and life. In a journal entry dated November 4, 1737, Wesley records that he "heard an excellent sermon at St. Antholin's on holiness, or likeness to God."[53] Wesley enunciates this central theme in a unique formulation of Matthew 10:25, "it is enough for the disciple to be like the teacher," first expressed, perhaps, in his "Thanksgiving" hymn of 1742:

> My spirit meek, my will resigned,
> Lowly as thine shall be my mind—
> The servant shall be as his Lord.[54]

He explicitly connects this restoration with conformity to Christ:

> We rest on His word
> We shall here be restored
> To His image; the servant shall be as his Lord.[55]

For Charles, this call to conformity to Christ defines the disciple—it characterizes the Christian who is altogether God's—and it also reflects God's promise. In virtually every hymn in which this phrase appears, it implies both a demand and a gift. "I stay me on thy faithful word," cries the follower of Christ groaning for full redemption, "The servant shall be as his Lord."[56] In the powerful hymn, "Prisoners of hope," this statement of vocation and promise functions as the refrain for the concluding stanzas.

> Thou wilt perform thy faithful word:
> "The servant shall be as his Lord."
>
> We only hang upon thy word,

---

52. In this section I develop themes first explored in Chilcote, "Claim Me for Thy Service."
53. C. Wesley, *Manuscript Journal*, 1:93.
54. Wesley and Wesley, *Hymns and Sacred Poems* (1742), 170.
55. C. Wesley, *Hymns and Sacred Poems* (1749), 2:179.
56. Wesley and Wesley, *Hymns and Sacred Poems* (1742), 170.

"The servant shall be as his Lord."[57]

But what does it mean to be like Jesus, according to Wesley?

The central place that Wesley gives to the kenotic hymn of Philippians provides a clue.[58] In Charles's poetic exposition of Philippians 2:5, "Let this mind be in you, which was also in Christ Jesus," in successive stanzas he describes this mind in vivid detail as quiet, heavenly, humble, gentle, patient, noble, spotless, loving, thankful, and constant, and he concludes the hymn in confident affirmation of God's promise.

> I shall fully be restor'd
> To the image of my Lord,
> Witnessing to all mankind,
> Jesu's is a PERFECT mind.[59]

He takes this image a step further in a composite hymn, opening with a lyrical paraphrase of "Jesus and the woman at the well" (John 4:10–15). Here he conjoins the "mind" of Philippians 2 with the "action" of James 1.

> Thy mind throughout my life be shown,
>   While listening to the wretch's cry,
> The widow's and the orphan's groan,
>   On mercy's wings I swiftly fly
> The poor and helpless to relieve,
> My life, my all for them to give.[60]

Perhaps no hymn better expresses the character of the disciple whose mind is conformed to that of Christ than Charles's lyrical reflection on the Beatitudes. This text includes many of the images we have just explored:

> Come, thou holy God and true!
> Come, and my whole heart renew;
> Take me now, possess me whole,
> Form the Saviour in my soul.

---

57. Wesley and Wesley, *Hymns and Sacred Poems* (1742), 234, sts. 11 and 13.

58. In his examination of *kenosis* in "Ephrem and Charles Wesley," Kimbrough claims that both of these important theologians "view God's self-emptying, self-limitation, and self-effacement in the Incarnation of Jesus Christ as the foundational foci for Christian spirituality." See Kimbrough, "Kenosis," 265.

59. Wesley and Wesley, *Hymns and Sacred Poems* (1742), 221–23.

60. C. Wesley, *Scripture Hymns*, 2:380 (no. 738).

In my heart thy name reveal,
Stamp me with thy Spirit's seal,
Change my nature into thine,
In me thy whole image shine.

. . .

Happy soul, whose active love
Emulates the blest above,
In thy every action seen,
Sparkling from the soul within.
Thou to every sufferer nigh,
Hearest, not in vain, the cry
Of the widow in distress,
Of the poor and fatherless!
Rayment thou to all that need,
To the hungry deal'st thy bread,
To the sick thou giv'st relief,
Sooth'st the hapless prisoner's grief.
The weak hands thou liftest up,
Bid'st the helpless mourners hope,
Giv'st to those in darkness light,
Guid'st the weary wanderer right.

. . .

Only feel'st within thee move
Tenderness, compassion, love,
Love immense, and unconfin'd,
Love to all of humankind.
Love, which willeth all should live,
Love, which all to all would give,
Love, that over all prevails,
Love, that never, never fails.[61]

---

61. C. Wesley, *Hymns and Sacred Poems* (1749), 138–39 (no. 8, ls. 97–104, 129–44, and 111–18). This poem on the Beatitudes consists of 162 lines of rhyming couplets.

As this hymn proclaims, *those who are fully conformed to the image of Christ shine to God's glory.* Holiness means radiance.

> God of all sufficient grace,
> > My God in Christ thou art;
> Bid me walk before thy face,
> > 'Till I am pure in heart,
> 'Till transformed thro' faith divine
> > I gain that perfect love unknown,
> Bright in all thine image shine,
> > By putting on thy Son.[62]

The shining lives of God's restored children have a critical evangelistic role in the unfolding of God's reign. Light attracts; those who radiate the love of God draw others into the reign of God.

> Their seed by characters divine
> > Shall be among the Gentiles known,
> And in a land of darkness shine,
> > When all are perfected in one.
>
> Whoe'er behold their heavenly grace,
> > Their glory shining from within,
> Shall own them the peculiar race,
> > Whom God hath blest from all their sin.[63]

For Charles Wesley, Christ is the true and only light of the world whose radiance transcends all darkness, and when it floods the soul, all manner of darkness vanishes. He prays for the inbreaking of the glorious light of the One "whose glory fills the skies":

> Visit then this soul of mine,
> > Pierce the gloom of sin, and grief,
> Fill me, radiancy divine,
> > Scatter all my unbelief,
> More and more thyself display
> Shining to the perfect day.[64]

---

62. C. Wesley, *Scripture Hymns*, 1:194 (no. 55, on Gen. 27:1).
63. C. Wesley, *Hymns and Sacred Poems* (1749), 1:29, sts. 8–9.
64. Wesley and Wesley, *Hymns and Sacred Poems* (1740), 25, st. 3.

Holiness and Holy Communion

For Charles Wesley the sacrament of Holy Communion functions as a focal point for "the one thing needful." The Lord's Supper both presents a vision of holiness and, perhaps even more importantly, offers sanctifying grace to the faithful on their journey toward holiness of heart and life. Wesley's Eucharistic hymns provide a lyrical theology of holiness. In his incisive study of Wesley's *Hymns on the Lord's Supper*, entitled *The Altar's Fire*, Daniel Stevick examines the conjunction of forgiveness and holiness in this collection and affords this summative comment:

> In describing Wesley's understanding of redemption, it should be remarked that for him, salvation and holiness of life—justification and sanctification—are inseparable. If the sacrament conveys the very reality of Christ's atonement, it brings forgiveness of sins; but forgiveness necessarily inaugurates a new creation. If a life of holiness does not follow from faith, it is as though Christ had died in vain.[65]

In his view, the essential soteriological concerns regarding restoration, conformity to the image of Christ—of holiness as the end toward which the process of sanctification moves—come to clear focus in these hymns.

In several of the Eucharistic hymns, Wesley employs an interesting metaphor drawn from the highly evocative language of John 19:34: "one of the soldiers pierced his side with a spear, and at once blood and water came out." For Charles, the blood signifies atonement for sin—the power of God's forgiving love in Christ; the water refers to God's work of purification in which the Spirit sanctifies pardoned sinners and makes them holy. One hymn among several in the section on the sacrament "As it is a Sign and Means of Grace" suffices to illustrate this dual theme of "pardon and purity."

> O Rock of our salvation, see
> The souls that seek their rest in thee,
> Beneath thy cooling shadow hide,
> And keep us, Saviour, in thy side,
> By water and by blood redeem,
> And wash us in the mingled stream.
>
> The sin-atoning blood apply,
> And let the water sanctify,
> Pardon and holiness impart,

---

65. Stevick, *Altar's Fire*, 36.

> Sprinkle and purify our heart,
> Wash out the last remains of sin,
> And make our inmost nature clean.
>
> The double stream in pardons rolls,
> And brings thy love into our souls,
> Who dare the truth divine receive,
> And credence to thy witness give,
> We here thy utmost power shall prove
> Thy utmost power of perfect love.[66]

The pardon procured through the blood and the holiness provided through the water, while distinct, remain inseparably bound together.

Wesley's spiritualizing interpretation (while somewhat strained) was hardly new.[67] It appears in Ambrose's treatise *On the Sacraments* at the end of the fourth century. In answer to the questions, "Why water? Why blood?" he explains succinctly, "Water to cleanse, blood to redeem."[68] In one of Isaac Watts's communion hymns, he describes the "double flood" that poured from Jesus' side, "By water we are purify'd / And pardon'd by the blood."[69] Even more importantly, perhaps, Daniel Brevint (whose essay, *The Christian Sacrament and Sacrifice,* supplied the primary structure for Charles's *Hymns on the Lord's Supper*) provides an extended discussion of a "first irradiation of God's mercy" related to the blood and a second ablution with water that "washes and sanctifies the sinner."[70] In his journal, Wesley often notes the dynamic connection between pardon and purity, and the need to press on toward holiness. He strongly commended the preaching of his colleague, George Whitefield, because he "warned them everywhere against apostacy, and strongly insisted on the necessity of holiness after justification."[71] Preaching at Zennor in 1746, he "showed the twofold rest of pardon and holiness."[72]

Wesley draws on these various sources in his exploration of the link between forgiveness and holiness in the Christian journey. While holding

---

66. Wesley and Wesley, *Hymns on the Lord's Supper,* 24–25 (no. 31); cf. nos. 37, 38, 74, and 75.

67. I am indebted to Stevick, *Altar's Fire,* for this historical background. See Stevick, *Altar's Fire,* 101–03 from which I have drawn these references.

68. Ambrose, *Sacraments,* 96.

69. Watts, *Hymns and Spiritual Songs,* 291–92.

70. Brevint, *Christian Sacrament and Sacrifice,* III.8.

71. Watts, *Hymns and Spiritual Songs,* 642–43.

72. C. Wesley, *Manuscript Journal,* 2:466.

justification and sanctification together in this way in his use of the metaphor, he more fully explicates the goal of holiness in the opening three stanzas of a six-stanza hymn.

> Worthy the Lamb of endless praise,
>   Whose double life we here shall prove,
> The pard'ning and the hallowing grace,
>   The childish and the perfect love.
>
> We here shall gain our calling's prize,
>   The gift unspeakable receive,
> And higher still in death arise,
>   And all the life of glory live.
>
> To make our right and title sure,
>   Our dying Lord himself hath given,
> His sacrifice did all procure,
>   Pardon, and holiness, and heaven.[73]

The most interesting thing here is Charles's description of forgiveness as "childish love," in contrast to the perfect love that characterizes the truly holy life. In an account of his preaching on Romans 6:22 in 1756, he records that he "insisted largely on freedom from sin, as the lowest mark of faith, and the necessity of laboring after holiness."[74] His religious poetry and prose writings reflect a consistent concern about growth in grace, the restoration of the full image of God—of maturity in faith and love.

The Eucharistic hymns not only explicate Wesley's vision of holiness, they also reflect his understanding about how the Spirit conforms believers to the image of Christ through their participation in the sacrament.[75] "In Wesleyan Eucharistic spirituality," as Lorna Khoo observes, "Christ is the one who calls us, enabling us by his grace and through his Spirit to grow toward the goal: Christian perfection. The calling and the goal would form the character of the Methodists and also colour their perceptions of life."[76] Two particular dimensions of sanctifying grace in the sacrament surface in Charles's hymns. First, he simply affirms that participation in the Eucharist shapes the fullest possible love in the disciple of Jesus.

---

73. Wesley and Wesley, *Hymns on the Lord's Supper*, 28 (no. 38.1–3).
74. C. Wesley, *Manuscript Journal*, 2:627.
75. See Chilcote, "Eucharist and Formation," upon which this section depends.
76. Khoo, *Wesleyan Eucharistic Spirituality*, 179.

> O what a soul-transporting feast
> Doth this communion yield!
> Remembring here thy Passion past
> We with thy love are fill'd.[77]

Second, the fullest possible infilling of love ultimately means conformity to the cross as well. The "suffering servants" of God are called to take up their crosses daily in multifarious acts of self-sacrificial love. Nowhere do the images of self-emptying, service, and sacrifice—the signs of the cruciform life—converge more poignantly than in these hymns. Wesley repeatedly describes the full extent of solidarity with the crucified Lord.

> His servants shall be
> With Him on the tree,
> Where Jesus was slain
> His crucified servants shall always remain.[78]

To possess the mind of Christ, to be fully restored in love, means to be shaped in the form of the cross.

Through these hymns, Wesley also communicates a profound, corporate dimension with regard to his vision of holiness. The Eucharist shapes the followers of Jesus into a community that suffers with others for the sake of love. Lester Ruth has summarized this vision of Eucharistic formation well:

> The Wesleys did not intend a merely ritualized, formal concept of sacrifice in the Lord's Supper. They intended that the Lords' Supper would show how we actually live by taking up the cross daily, dying to sin, denying ourselves, and enduring suffering that we might do good in the world. The Lord's Supper reveals that we are both priests and sacrifices like Christ is. This is the essence of what it means to be God's people.[79]

The Eucharist "forms the Savior in the soul," to use Charles Wesley's own phrase, and that formation takes place not only in the individual heart of the believer, but in the heart of the church. Perhaps the most critical question in this regard, as David Lowes Watson once pointed out, is "how to permit God's grace to foster a maturity of constant obedience, so that sanctifying grace might work with an unimpeded love."[80]

---

77. Wesley and Wesley, *Hymns on the Lord's Supper*, 82 (no. 44:1–2).
78. Wesley and Wesley, *Hymns on the Lord's Supper*, 120 (no. 142:3).
79. Ruth, "Word and Table," 146.
80. Watson, *Accountable Discipleship*, 34.

Charles Wesley tuned his life to the keynote of perfect love. In his vision of the Christian life, God engages forgiven children in a process of sanctification leading to holiness of heart and life—a process the goal of which is the fully restored image of Christ. This process entails freeing those in bondage to sin and death, healing the broken and wounded, and filling the believer with a love that resembles the love of Jesus. Whenever we gather around the Table of the Lord, we open ourselves to the life-transforming power of the Spirit who makes all things new and transcribes the image of God on our hearts and in our lives. Wesley, like so many others, yearned for a world filled with such transcripts of the Trinity who reveal the true nature of our loving God, and the questions and affirmations of his hymn reverberate through the ages.

> Where is the glorious church below,
> > From every spot and wrinkle free!
> The trees that to perfection grow,
> > The saints that blameless walk with thee,
> Adorn'd in linnen white and clean,
> The born of God that cannot sin!
>
> Where are the spirits to Jesus join'd,
> > Freed from the law of death and sin?
> The Saviour's pure and spotless mind?
> > The endless righteousness brought in?
> The heavenly man, the heart renew'd,
> The living portraiture of God?
>
> Lord, we believe, and rest secure,
> > Thine utmost promises to prove,
> To rise restor'd, and throughly pure,
> > In all the image of thy love,
> Fill'd with the glorious life unknown,
> Forever sanctified in one.[81]

May we all pray for the one thing needful—to rise, restored in all the image of his love.

---

81. C. Wesley, *Hymns and Sacred Poems* (1749), 2:187, sts. 1, 3, and 5.

Part 2
John and Charles Wesley's Practical Divinity

Chapter 4

Rethinking the Wesleyan Quadrilateral

Source Note: Published in *Good News Magazine* 38.4 (January/February 2005) 22–23.

I WILL NEVER FORGET a conversation I had one August afternoon in 1982 at Oxford University with Professor Albert Outler. We were talking about the many terms he had coined over the years. He said rather abruptly, "There is one phrase I wish I had never used: the 'Wesleyan Quadrilateral.' It has created the wrong image in the minds of so many people and, I am sure, will lead to all kinds of controversy."

Without question, his words were prophetic. Over the past quarter century, few theological topics have created more debate within United Methodism. Concerns were raised almost immediately about both aspects of the term. Was this concept genuinely "Wesleyan"? Could it actually be traced back to Wesley himself? Does not the term "quadrilateral" infer an equilateral? Are the guidelines for theological formulation—namely, Scripture, tradition, reason, and experience—of equal value? Or does Scripture hold a preeminent place in the interrelationship of these sources or criteria for theological reflection?

The term first came into general United Methodist parlance by means of the 1972 *Book of Discipline*, despite the fact that the phrase "Wesleyan Quadrilateral" itself was never used in the official documents. The debate that ensued led to the serious revisions of 1988. In 1991, Tom Langford edited a volume of essays seeking to set the theological statements of these two disciplines in historical context and to encourage reflection and discussion on these important questions related to authority.[1] A number of church leaders and scholars, in fact, renewed the conversation vigorously. In 1997, a team of

---

1. Langford, *Doctrine and Theology*.

authors brought both clarity to and affirmation concerning this now-familiar term in a volume entitled *Wesley and the Quadrilateral*.[2]

But given the fact that the Wesleyan Quadrilateral seems to be here to stay, what image can be used to capture its meaning and value for us today? That question carries me back to 1982, because that is the very question my conversation with Albert Outler had stimulated at that time. What was the best way to present this dynamic conception of authority with regard to Christian faith and practice? After some period of struggle, an image came to mind as I stood, of all places, over the crib of my little daughter. Hanging over her pillow was a mobile. It consisted of a number of brightly colored figures, suspended from a rainbow arch that served as the mobile's base. Its purpose, of course, was to stimulate and excite as it was set in motion in moments of play and discovery.

As I played with this image in my mind, Scripture immediately became the base to which tradition, reason, and experience were attached. Here, I thought, was a dynamic image for the interrelationship of these four components as they interacted with each other in an inextricable way. For some years, this was the model I used to talk about the quadrilateral concept. At the conclusion of a course taught on the Wesleys one summer at Garrett-Evangelical Theological Seminary, however, one of my students observed, "You know, I love the image of the mobile, but there is a particular kind of mobile that I think works even better—a wind chime." As we talked about the wind chime together, a number of new (and I think powerful) images began to emerge.

In this wind chime image, Scripture, again, has central place. It is the foundation, the base, the primary source and criterion for Christian doctrine and life. But Scripture itself must be balanced by the counterweight of the chimes (tradition, reason, and experience), all of which are tied directly into the biblical witness. None of these functions independently of Scripture or separately from the other norms with which each interacts. Each has its own tone, its own voice, that needs to sound in order to create harmonious music. The Scriptures actually come to life in new historical settings and cultural contexts as they are "illumined by tradition, vivified in personal experience, and confirmed by reason."[3] Moreover, the music of these chimes is not produced by their collision with one another. Rather, in most wind chimes, a clapper or ball is suspended from the very center of the base—rooted, as it were, in the heart of Scripture—swinging back and forth among the chimes to strike the tones. This ball is, for me, the community of faith—the church—or the individual disciple who is involved in a dynamic way with each and all of these norms related to Christian praxis.

2. Gunther, *Wesley and the Quadrilateral*.
3. *Book of Discipline*, 82–88, ¶105.

One final touch. The purpose of the wind chime is to make music. If there is no wind, then the chimes stand stagnant, purposeless, and silent. But when the wind blows—when a dynamic force sets the wind chime in motion—then the music begins. The wind in this image is, of course, the Holy Spirit. It is the Spirit that, as the Wesleys would say, animates the whole. When the fresh wind of the Spirit blows, and the church struggles to deal with the issues, questions, and concerns of the day in this dynamic way, the consequence is a song. That music will sound differently, perhaps, in different times and different places because the chimes may be made of wood here, or metal there, or bamboo somewhere else. But the music comes nonetheless from our faithful interaction with God's Word.

The wind chime, I believe, is a powerful image that is both authentic to the dynamic concept of authority in our United Methodist theological statements and much more scintillating than the image of a square, or three-legged stool, or some other static model purportedly representing the Wesleyan Quadrilateral. Perhaps the best aspect of this image is the fact that, true to our Wesleyan heritage, it all ends in song. In our yearning to live authentic Christian lives in the community of faith and in very difficult times, our prayer might just be that of Charles Wesley's:

> Jesu, soft harmonious name,
> > Every faithful heart's desire,
> See thy followers, O Lamb,
> > All at once to thee aspire;
> Drawn by thy uniting grace,
> > After thee we swiftly run,
> Hand in hand we seek thy face,
> > Come, and perfect us in one.
>
> Mollify our harsher will,
> > Each to each our tempers suit
> By thy modulating skill,
> > Heart to heart, as lute to lute:
> Sweetly on our spirits move,
> > Gently touch the trembling strings,
> Make the harmony of love,
> > Music for the King of kings.[4]

---

4. C. Wesley, *Hymns and Sacred Poems* (1749), 2:329-30, sts. 1, 2, and 4.

——— Chapter 5 ———

"Practical Christology" in John and Charles Wesley

Source note: This essay was solicited as the lead chapter for *Methodist Christology: From the Wesleys to the Twenty-First Century*, edited by Jason Vickers, 1–35 (Nashville: Wesley's Foundery, 2020).

IN SPRING 1725, JOHN Wesley, a student at Oxford at that time, contemplated taking Holy Orders. He wrote to his father about his plans, but his mother's reply contained a statement that most certainly set the trajectory of his theological vision for years to come.

> I approve the disposition of your mind. I think this season of Lent the most proper for your preparation for Orders, and I think the sooner you are a deacon the better, because it may be an inducement to greater application in the study of practical divinity, which of all other I humbly conceive is the best study for candidates for Orders. Mr. Wesley differs from me, and would engage you, I believe, in critical learning (though I'm not sure), which though of use accidentally and by way of concomitance, yet is in no wise preferable to the other. Therefore I earnestly pray God to avert that great evil from you, of engaging in trifling studies to the neglect of such as are absolutely necessary.[1]

Susanna's appeal fixed a distinction in John's mind, and certainly in Charles's mind as well, between practical and speculative divinity. The brothers took their mother's advice seriously and committed themselves to the pursuit of a form of theological inquiry that would make a difference in the lives of real people in real time. In his preface to his first volume of

---

1. J. Wesley, *Works*, 25:160.

Sermons on Several Occasions, John revealed this approach in his typically terse style: "I design plain truth for plain people."[2]

It should be no surprise that neither John nor Charles devoted any energy to the production of treatises or poetic collections dedicated specifically to Christology—to an explication of the person and work of Jesus Christ. On the other hand, it would be a serious mistake to conclude that Christology does not pervade the corpus of both Anglican theologians. The sermons and treatises of John the preacher and the hymns of Charles the poet reflect their deep concern to understand who Jesus Christ was (is) and what he has done for the redemption of God's creation. Nothing, in fact, was more core to their theology. Any effort to categorize their Christological vision, therefore, requires a process of discernment, ferreting out their leading ideas from the extremely broad spectrum of material they produced. But this exercise, if it produced nothing but clear labels, would mitigate their own vision of the purpose of theology.

In my teaching of theology, I have often noticed the way the declarations of the Council of Constantinople (381) bring a sense of "closure" among my students with regard to the Christological debates of the early church. The first great ecumenical Council of Nicaea (325) essentially addressed the question of Jesus' divinity with a definitive statement about his being *homoousion* (of one substance) with the Father, over against movements (such as Arianism) that denied his divinity or overstressed his humanity. Later in the fourth century, Constantinople reasserted Jesus' full humanity over against those who overemphasize his divinity (primarily the Apollinarians, who drew a distinction between Jesus' humanity and our own). By the end of the fourth century, in other words, the church definitively answered the question, Who is Jesus Christ? "Jesus Christ," the Council declared, "is fully divine and fully human." The well-known formula, "Jesus is one person in two natures," later codified this conclusion.

I find that my students are happy with this resolution of the issue and feel little need to go beyond this. But, having answered the primary question about Jesus, two subsequent councils (Ephesus, 431) and (Chalcedon, 451) address a secondary question: If Jesus Christ is fully divine and fully human, then how do these two natures in Christ relate to one another? Instinctively, I think, my students generally sense a leap from the practical to the speculative at this point and view the subsequent debates accordingly. As they have engaged the intricacies and nuances of Nestorianism (which emphasized the distinction between the two natures) and Monophysitism (which emphasized the unity of the person of Jesus, blurring the distinction

---

2. J. Wesley, *Works*, 1:104.

between the natures), for example, I think they reflect something of the reticence of the Wesleys to plunge too deeply into these mysteries. Like the Wesleys, while affirming the later Chalcedonian formulas of *hypostatic union* and *communicatio idiomatum*, their preference is to reside at Constantinople rather than Ephesus or Chalcedon.

To state it rather bluntly, they can discern the practical "so what?" factor related to a disproportional emphasis on either Jesus' humanity or his divinity. But speculative attempts to explain the natures' interrelationship leave my students without clear practical guidance for their journey into the fullest possible love of God and neighbor. I sense a similar disposition of mind and heart in the Wesleys. Given this essay's leading position in this volume and in an effort to more fully understand the Wesley brothers' "practical Christology," I first offer a comprehensive examination of the literature related to the Wesleys' vision of Christ and the "Christological sources" in each brother's corpus.[3] Second, I address four key themes in their writings related to their vision of the person and work of Christ and identify the respective implications of their "practical Christology" as these relate to the quest for holiness of heart and life.

Studies and Sources Related to the Wesleys' Christology

"A study of Wesley's Christology is faced by one great difficulty," A. Raymond George once claimed, "namely that Wesley was interested primarily, not in Christology, but in soteriology."[4] While referring to the older brother John, this statement most certainly exemplifies the lyrical theology of Charles, as well. Given this fact, it is somewhat surprising that the vast majority of studies in this arena revolve around the question of whether John Wesley, in particular, maintains an "orthodox" view of the person of Christ. They address a fairly direct question: Does Wesley demonstrate a tendency toward Monophysitism? Does a purported emphasis on the divinity of Jesus lead to a diminution of his humanity in Wesley's teaching? Is Jesus' humanity lost in the sea of his divinity? Scholars have

---

3. This task was undertaken with regard to John Wesley by Richard M. Riss in 2010. His annotated bibliographical essay remains the most thorough survey of the literature on this topic: "John Wesley's Christology in Recent Literature." He examines the material in chronological order. Given this previous documentation, the scholarly review of John provided here follows but augments the analysis of Riss. Given that no such review has been provided previously for Charles Wesley in this regard, more space and greater detail are devoted to the study of his Christology.

4. George, "Review of 'Wesley's Christology,'" 382.

focused their attention more on the person, in other words, than the work of Christ with regard to John's Christology.

As regards Charles Wesley, much less effort has been expended on his Christology, to say nothing of his theology in general. Only in recent years—with a growing literature that has elevated the importance of "lyrical theology"—have scholars turned their attention to Charles's theological vision. Some have raised questions, however, of whether hymnody even affords a proper platform for a "first order" theological topic such as Christology.[5] Despite the more speculative nature of some of these questions, the debates of twentieth-century scholars are of "use accidentally and by way of concomitance" (to borrow Susanna Wesley's phrase) in an effort to more fully appreciate the Wesleys' practical theological perspective.

A Review of Studies on John Wesley's Christology

The question of John's "functional" or "practical Monophysitism" can be traced back to *Wesley's Christology: An Interpretation*, the fruit of John Deschner's doctoral studies at Basel under the direction of the neoorthodox theologian Karl Barth.[6] This study remains the most thorough, careful, and perceptive examination of this topic. A single sentence articulates his ultimate conclusion succinctly: "Wesley betrays a decided emphasis on the divine nature and a corresponding underemphasis on the human."[7] Despite Deschner's cogent arguments regarding Wesley's Monophysite tendency—following the viewpoints of David Lerch and Robin Scroggs before him[8]—Geoffrey Wainright's critique merits serious consideration. Attending to both Wesley's context and his wider corpus, he simply viewed Wesley's position "as a healthily Alexandrian view of Christ's Person."[9] Regardless, ever since the publication of Deschner's study in 1960, a host of other scholars have echoed his concerns or have sought to support them.

Among those who affirm this purported tendency of Wesley to overemphasize Jesus' divinity, Albert Outler stands out as one of the most significant scholars.[10] While Randy Maddox echoes some of the same concerns, he

5. See, for example, Langford, "Charles Wesley as Theologian."
6. Deschner, *Wesley's Christology*.
7. Deschner, *Wesley's Christology*, 6.
8. Lerch, *Heil und Heiligung*; and Scroggs, "John Wesley as Biblical Scholar."
9. Wainright, "Review of 'Wesley's Christology.'"
10. Outler advances his argument primarily in his editorial commentary on Wesley's sermons. In particular, see his introductory comments to "On Knowing Christ after the Flesh," one of the very few places in Wesley's corpus where he actually attacks a Christological heresy (J. Wesley, *Works*, 4:97–106).

does not embrace them fully.[11] More recently, Matthew Hambrick and Michael E. Lodahl, over against Maddox and because of his defense of Wesley's position, have pressed the claim of Wesley's aberrant Christological views even further.[12] In their efforts to confirm Deschner's earlier conclusion, all these scholars resorted primarily to Wesley's *Notes on the New Testament* and a number of his sermons: "The Lord Our Righteousness," "Sermon on the Mount I," "The End of Christ's Coming," "Spiritual Worship," and "On Knowing Christ after the Flesh," in particular.[13]

Interestingly, references to Wesley's redaction of the Thirty-Nine Articles of Religion, his *Notes on the New Testament*, and the sermon "Spiritual Worship" in particular, feature prominently as evidence on both sides of this debate. John R. Renshaw,[14] William R. Cannon,[15] Charles R. Wilson,[16] Kenneth J. Collins,[17] Thomas C. Oden,[18] Timothy L. Boyd,[19] John R. Tyson,[20] David A. Graham,[21] Rob DeGeorge,[22] and Edgardo Rosado[23] all used these sources to counter the Monophysite claim and to portray Wesley as an orthodox Anglican theologian. Jerome Van Kuiken provides the most up-to-date distillation of all the evidence surrounding the Monophysite controversy and demonstrates, in my view, the myth of Monophysitism, Docetism, or Apollinarianism in Wesley.[24] At the time

---

11. Maddox, *Responsible Grace*, 94–118; esp. 114–18.

12. Hambrick and Lodahl, "Responsible Grace in Christology."

13. J. Wesley's abridgment of the writings of Ignatius of Antioch in the *Christian Library* also figures in the argument.

14. Renshaw, "Atonement."

15. Cannon, *Theology of John Wesley*.

16. Wilson, "Christology."

17. Collins, *A Faithful Witness* and *Theology of John Wesley*.

18. Oden, *John Wesley's Scriptural Christianity*, 177–90.

19. Boyd, *John Wesley's Christology*.

20. Tyson, *Charles Wesley*. Tyson is one of the limited number of Wesley scholars who has sought to examine Wesleyan theology through the lens of both brothers. He depicts John Wesley's Christology as robust, orthodox, and Anglican; his discussion of Charles's lyrical Christology will be discussed later in the chapter.

21. Graham, "Chalcedonian Logic." One of the most significant defenders of Wesley's orthodox perspective, Graham gives particular attention to the way his antagonism to the deistic cultural context shaped his theology.

22. DeGeorge, "Rehabilitating John Wesley's Christology."

23. Rosado, *John Wesley's Christology*. A very recent publication, this English translation of the original Spanish work explores the implications of Wesley's Christology for social witness and action in the face of injustice and deprivation.

24. Van Kuiken, "Deschner's Wesley."

Deschner's claims first surfaced, A. Raymond George[25] and Geoffrey Wainright,[26] among others, both challenged his conclusions in formal responses to his work. Wesley's *Letter to a Roman Catholic*—a document Randy Maddox has described as "Wesley's most compact summary of his Christological commitments"—provides some of the most compelling evidence supporting his Chalcedonian perspective.[27]

A Review of Studies on Charles Wesley's Christology

Very little discussion, to say nothing of debate, has arisen with reference to Charles Wesley's Christology because so few studies have focused on his theology or this particular aspect of it. In general, most scholars who have addressed this topic in any way have depicted him as classically Anglican, embracing the robust Chalcedonian view of Jesus Christ articulated in the Articles of Religion, and describe his view of Christ's redemptive work through the broadest possible lens of biblical imagery. No scholar has attended exclusively to the topic of Christology in Charles Wesley's theology. As was the case with regard to John, given Charles's cultural context and the teleological orientation of his theology, he tends to emphasize the divinity of Christ without compromising his humanity.

J. Ernest Rattenbury, the most distinguished of the early twentieth-century students of Charles Wesley, addressed primary Christological themes in two chapters of his monumental *Evangelical Doctrines of Charles Wesley's Hymns*.[28] In a chapter titled "Our Lord Jesus Christ," he reflected particularly on Wesley's hymns related to the Lord's birth, resurrection, and ascension, and the Trinity. He detected a strong Lutheran element in this constellation of lyrical material, emphasizing God's unique self-revelation in the person of Jesus Christ. "Jesus Christ was to him God manifest in the flesh, the second person of the Trinity, 'our God contracted to a span,' 'Jehovah crucified.' . . . Not only is God seen through Him, but He is God."[29] In Rattenbury's examination of the Christological imagery of these hymns, he devoted more energy to Charles's articulation of Jesus' humanity than any other issue because of the following explicit concern:

25. DeGeorge, "Rehabilitating John Wesley's Christology," 382–84.
26. Wainwright, "Review of 'Wesley's Christology,'" 55–56.
27. Maddox, *Responsible Grace*, 303.
28. Rattenbury, *Evangelical Doctrines*, 152–72. In the absence of any review of the literature relating to this issue in Charles Wesley's theology, a fuller exploration of the primary sources that include a discussion of this topic is included herein.
29. Rattenbury, *Evangelical Doctrines*, 153–54.

> The problem of Charles Wesley's view of the Person of Christ is what he meant by His humanity. What he meant by His Deity is made clear by hundreds of allusions and by innumerable implications in his verses, but the humanity is so differently conceived from that of the human portraits of Jesus which are painted by modern students that some of them might wonder whether Wesley had any true view of the humanity at all.[30]

He argued that "no one has realized the true humanity of Jesus more literally than Charles Wesley."[31]

The hermeneutical key that unlocks these mysteries for Rattenbury was Charles's "kenotist" view of Jesus and his identification with "suffering humanity." He illustrates this theme with a hymn text drawn from the 1749 collection of *Hymns and Sacred Poems* titled "Desiring to Love":

> Quite from the manger to the cross
> Thy life one scene of sufferings was,
>   And all sustain'd for me:
> O strange excess of love divine!
> Jesus, was ever love like thine!
>   Answer me from that tree![32]

He noted the way all aspects of Wesley's Christology ultimately revolve around the central conception of love divine—a love that will go to such great lengths to redeem and restore. "Thus we learn how from the manger to the cross," Rattenbury concluded, "Charles Wesley saw in Christ God manifest in the flesh and realized never more than at the manger that the flesh with which God clad Himself was very human."[33]

Rattenbury also devoted an entire chapter in this work to "The Atonement."[34] He examined both the "finished" and the "unfinished" work with illustrations drawn primarily from what he describes as Wesley's three theological hymnbooks: *Hymns on God's Everlasting Love* (1741, 1742), *Hymns on the Lord's Supper* (1745), and *Hymns on the Trinity* (1767). "In the hymns on God's Everlasting Love the doctrine of the Atonement is relatively

---

30. Rattenbury, *Evangelical Doctrines*, 156.
31. Rattenbury, *Evangelical Doctrines*, 158.
32. C. Wesley, *Hymns and Sacred Poems* (1749), 1:61.
33. Rattenbury, *Evangelical Doctrines*, 172.
34. Rattenbury, *Evangelical Doctrines*, 188–203. Rattenbury also provides an analysis of "the Wesleys' doctrine of the atonement and the modern mind" in a subsequent chapter of that title (204–14), which carries the discussion beyond the scope of this present exploration.

incidental," he wrote. "The scope and extent of the Atonement are emphasized rather than its content. In the Eucharistic hymns, the Lord's Supper is incidental to the Atonement—an instrument for remembering and applying it."[35] After examining the various Christological images Wesley employed in these hymns—all of which reflect the full range of atonement theories—he concluded, "The fact to be most noted is that all these allusions to satisfaction, substitution, penal suffering, and the like are dominated by the central truth of God's love in the Cross; they are regarded as expressions of that love, and of the manner in which it acted. Love, however it is explained, is the central doctrine of the Cross."[36] All the various images of atonement coalesce in the stellar hymn "All Ye That Pass By," a hymn that actually displaced "O for a Thousand Tongues to Sing" as the opening selection in the 1785 Methodist pocket hymnbook.[37] It fully explicates Wesley's view of Christ's "finished work," demonstrated by a selection of lines:

> Your ransom and peace, / Your surety he is . . .
>
> For what you have done / His blood must atone . . .
>
> He dies to atone / For sins not his own . . .
>
> Your debt he hath paid, / and your work he hath done.
>
> Ye all may receive
>
> The peace he did leave,
>
> Who made intercession, "My Father, forgive!"

Charles's hymn "Arise, My Soul, Arise" perfectly illustrates the importance of the "unfinished work of Christ" in his Christology.

> Arise, my soul, arise,
>> Shake off thy guilty fears,
>
> The bleeding sacrifice
>> In my behalf appears;
>
> Before the throne my surety stands;
>
> My name is written on his hands.

---

35. Rattenbury, *Evangelical Doctrines*, 189.

36. Rattenbury, *Evangelical Doctrines*, 192.

37. First published in Wesley, *Hymns on Festivals*, 8–10, from which the selections that follow are drawn.

> He ever lives above
>> For me to interceed,
> His all-redeeming love,
>> His pretious blood to plead;
> His blood aton'd for all our race,
> And sprinkles now the throne of grace.[38]

"The 'unfinished' work of Christ's priestly intercession," wrote Franz Hildebrand and Oliver Beckerlegge, "the blood of sprinkling, the joint witness of Spirit and blood, the name written on his hands are central themes for Wesley."[39] In Rattenbury's estimation:

> The two hymns, "Arise, my soul, arise" and "All ye that pass by," taken together, condense in a few verses the substance of Wesley's teaching about the Atonement, about the finished and the unfinished work of Christ. In the latter the Atonement, once for all made for the human race, is the basis of the appeal to sinful men to come to Christ; in the former the work is conceived as unfinished, as being carried on in Heaven by Christ, so that individuals may receive the benefits for which He died.[40]

For Charles, Jesus' eternal intercession must also be considered a crucial aspect of his atoning work.

In his *Wesley Hymns as a Guide to Scriptural Teaching*, John Lawson provides limited commentary on the divine Son, the Incarnation, the two natures of Christ, the cross, Christ as victor and sacrifice vis-à-vis atonement, and Christ as high priest.[41] Wesley's hymn "We Know, by Faith," Lawson claimed, demonstrates Charles's view that in Jesus "God came not only to reveal something, but supremely to do something, to perform an historic divine saving act within our world, as a member of the human race, and on behalf of our race. By consequence our Lord is to be confessed as the eternal divine Son."[42] He argued that in Wesley's poetry the profound truth of the divine-human Person—the mystery of the Incarnation—is "set forth in the language of daring paradox, to be interpreted symbolically."[43] Lawson,

---

38. Wesley and Wesley, *Hymns and Sacred Poems* (1742), 264–65. Quoting here the first two stanzas of the hymn, see also Rattenbury's full explication of all five verses in *Evangelical Doctrines*, 198–200.

39. J. Wesley, *Works*, 7:324.

40. Rattenbury, *Evangelical Doctrines*, 198–99.

41. Lawson, *Wesley Hymns*.

42. Lawson, *Wesley Hymns*, 46.

43. Lawson, *Wesley Hymns*, 53.

like Rattenbury, illustrated Wesley's robust conception of atonement with Charles's two hymns, "Arise, My Soul, Arise" and "All Ye That Pass By." He identified more than a hundred scriptural allusions in these hymns, ranging from Leviticus to Revelation, all of which demonstrate Wesley's emphasis on the symbiosis of sacrifice and victory in the cross.[44] According to Lawson, Charles's hymn "Entered the Holy Place Above" demonstrates that "there is eternally within the nature of the God of glory One who knows what it is to be frail and tempted, and of whose sympathy we may be sure."[45]

John R. Tyson's several explorations of Christological themes in Charles Wesley's hymns, sermons, journals, and letters demonstrate his focus on the work of Christ within the larger matrix of soteriology. His two-volume doctoral dissertation, "Charles Wesley's Theology of the Cross," actually argues that Wesley's entire theological project revolves around the "atonement-redemption nexus."[46] He concluded that, while Wesley contributes nothing new to the standard theological content of the doctrine, he presented his conception of redemption in fresh and daring lyrical forms that are simultaneously biblical and balanced. He based this conclusion largely, though not exclusively, on an examination of Wesley's use of individual words. Tyson only alluded to Christology in his *Charles Wesley: A Reader*.[47] He described Wesley's view as "robust," employing the traditional devices for describing the person and work of Christ. But the fifty different Christological titles Tyson identified in Charles's hymn corpus also demonstrate his lyrical creativity and versatility in explicating the doctrine.[48] He identified the patristic conception of "recapitulation" (particularly as developed in Irenaeus) as a key that unlocks the mystery of Jesus' person and work in Wesley's Christological vision, the restoration of the image of Christ in the believer being "the one thing needful."

In a reflection on Wesley's *Hymns for our Lord's Resurrection*, Tyson returned to these themes, describing Charles's robust Christology and his doctrine of atonement/redemption as two of three persistent theological constants in this collection.[49] He explored all these themes further in *The Way of the Wesleys*, in which he devoted two chapters to Christological concerns, "Risen with Healing in His Wings: Jesus Christ" and "An

---

44. Lawson, *Wesley Hymns*, 62–63.

45. Lawson, *Wesley Hymns*, 71.

46. Tyson, "Charles Wesley's Theology of the Cross." His research supersedes the earlier work of Renshaw, "Atonement," primarily in terms of its scope and breadth. For a redacted form of this research, see Tyson, *Charles Wesley on Sanctification*.

47. Tyson, *Charles Wesley*, 40–43.

48. Tyson, *Charles Wesley*, 491.

49. Tyson, "Lord of Life."

Interest in My Savior's Blood: The Atonement."[50] He argued cogently that Wesleyan Christology can only be understood properly within the larger context of soteriology, that in the context of English deism an emphasis on the divinity of Christ was to be expected of anyone claiming to be a "Bible Christian," and that Charles's vision of the restoration of humanity to health and freedom followed a Christological pattern reminiscent of the ancient Eastern Church Fathers.[51]

No person has contributed more to an appreciation for and understanding of Charles Wesley's lyrical theology in the past quarter-century than ST Kimbrough Jr. In recent years, he has devoted much energy to a collaborative study of the ways Charles opened a window to the East.[52] His own contributions to these ongoing discussions reflect his keen concern for particular Christological themes in Wesley's corpus, particularly the issues of *kenosis* and *theosis*. In an exploration of the nativity hymns vis-à-vis Charles Wesley and Ephrem the Syrian, he argued that "both view God's self-emptying, self-limitation, and self-effacement in the Incarnation of Jesus Christ as the foundational foci for Christian spirituality."[53] The critical Christological themes emerging from this research—those elements that shaped Wesley's thought and expression—include the centrality of mystery (the unfathomable), paradox (the irreconcilable), and participation (the teleological).

In an article exploring the theme of *theosis*, primarily in Wesley's *Hymns for the Nativity of Our Lord*—hereinafter *Nativity Hymns*—and *Hymns on the Lord's Supper*, Kimbrough demonstrated an interrelatedness of the Incarnation and the Eucharist in Wesley's Christology.[54] "One may approach 'being made divine' only in the context of the ultimate Mystery,"

---

50. Tyson, *Way of the Wesleys*, 80–90, 105–17.

51. Charles Yrigoyen Jr. was commissioned to prepare a popular volume on Charles Wesley's theology for the use of the church on the occasion of the tercentenary of his birth—*Praising the God of Grace*. His chapter on "Jesus, God Incarnate" includes a discussion of classical Christological themes drawn from the Christmas hymn, "Hark! The Herald Angels Sing": Jesus as prophet, priest, and king; the concept of "veiled in flesh"; and the imagery of Christ as "Prince of Peace" (25–33).

52. See Kimbrough, "Charles Wesley and the East." Kimbrough edited three significant volumes devoted to this quest, *Orthodox and Wesleyan Spirituality, Orthodox and Wesleyan Scriptural Understanding and Practice*, and *Orthodox and Wesleyan Ecclesiology*, which consist of presentations from four consultations on "Orthodox and Wesleyan Spirituality" convened at St. Vladimir's Orthodox Theological Seminary and sponsored jointly by the seminary and the United Methodist General Board of Global Ministries under Kimbrough's leadership.

53. Kimbrough, "Kenosis," 265.

54. Kimbrough, "Theosis."

he averred, "which cannot be fully comprehended. How one is transformed into the divine nature remains a mystery for Wesley."[55] While he does not offer commentary in his *Lyrical Theology of Charles Wesley* on Christological questions per se, his careful selection of hymn texts on "The Grace of Jesus Christ" reflect these same concerns and even identify *kenosis* as a central theme.[56] *Partakers of the Life Divine* represents his most comprehensive treatment of the Incarnation and *theosis*.[57] In this work he demonstrates the inseparable connection between the person and work of Christ in Wesley's Christology—how the incarnation of God in the person of Jesus Christ enables salvation and how redemption culminates in a mystical participation in God.[58] Following the lead of Gordon Wakefield, Kimbrough finds the fullest expression of this interrelation in Charles's hymn on the Incarnation, "Let earth and heaven combine."

> He deigns in flesh t' appear,
> > Widest extremes to join,
> To bring our vileness near,
> > And make us all divine;
> And we the life of God shall know,
> > For God is manifest below.[59]

Incarnation conceived as *kenosis* and participation conceived as *theosis* constitute the primary elements of Wesley's Christology.[60]

Several other studies that include some discussion of Charles's Christology, either directly or tangentially, deserve at least brief mention here. Wesley's *Hymns on the Trinity* (1767) figure prominently, of course, in terms of his view of the person of Christ. He drew inspiration for these

---

55. Kimbrough, "Charles Wesley and the East," 166. In this article, Kimbrough provided an "Annotated Bibliography" (165–71) which, while not directly related to Christology, sheds light on important ancillary research. Of particular significance in this regard is the work of A.M. Allchin, Michael Christensen, Geoffrey Wainwright, and Kenneth Carveley on the doctrines of deification, Trinity, and Incarnation.

56. Kimbrough, *Lyrical Theology*, 130–37.

57. Kimbrough, *Partakers of the Life Divine*.

58. See Kimbrough, *Partakers of Life Divine*, 37–44, in particular.

59. C. Wesley, *Nativity Hymns*, 8.

60. I pursued this same line of argument in two chapters of *A Faith That Sings*: chapter 1, "Incarnation: The Word Became Flesh," and chapter 2, "Redemption: The Lamb That Was Slain." I touch indirectly on Christological issues, particularly *kenosis* and *theosis*, in several articles: "Claim Me for Thy Service"; "Charles Wesley's Vision of Servant Vocation," "God in Christ Reconciling"; "Charles Wesley's Lyrical Credo"; and "All the Image."

hymns from a prose work of William Jones, titled *The Catholic Doctrine of the Trinity*. This collection represents a lyrical exposition of Jones's work—following the structure and content rather compulsively—the purpose of which was to combat the neo-Arian tendencies of deism, which overemphasized Jesus' humanity. The collection includes an opening section of fifty-seven hymns (one-third of the volume) on "the divinity of Christ." In 1989, Wilma J. Quantrille provided a detailed analysis of this collection in which Christological concerns naturally emerged.[61] She concluded that, while Wesley sought to affirm orthodox teaching with regard to Christ throughout the collection, his primary concern was doxological and not theological; he was more interested in words sung *to* God in praise than words *about* God in the hymns. The hymns reflect a portrait of Christ as the One who embraces fallen humanity with divine love, effects the work of salvation, restores the believer to the original image of God, and indwells the faithful, bringing the joys and blessings of divine love to each through the body of Christ, the church.

Charles Wesley not only produced hymns, he preached. Kenneth G.C. Newport's definitive edition of his sermons, therefore, provides an important corpus of material frequently neglected in the articulation of Wesley's theology.[62] Having said this, however, it must be acknowledged that Newport's intention was not to provide theological analysis of these prose texts; rather, he purposed to provide definitive texts. Regardless, his limited theological reflection on these sermons can be summarized in a terse statement about the collection as a whole. "With all these texts," he observed, "the one overriding concern is salvation and how it is achieved, and the one consistent answer given is that it is by faith in Christ, who has paid the price of human sin."[63]

While the tercentenary volume that Newport coedited with Ted Campbell provides several points of entry with regard to theological discourse, attention to Christological concerns remains indirect. ST Kimbrough's essay, "Charles Wesley and a Window to the East" has already been discussed. Likewise, John Tyson's discussion of Charles Wesley and redemption rehearses his well-worn themes. Ted Campbell's portrait of "Charles Wesley, Theologos" infers throughout that he used precise language of historic Christian teaching with regard to his own doctrinal formulations. In his reflections on Charles's doctrine of the Trinity, Jason Vickers concludes that Wesley's view of the person of Christ can be understood as an aspect of economic

---

61. Quantrille, "The Triune God."
62. Newport, *Sermons of Charles Wesley*.
63. Newport, *Sermons of Charles Wesley*, 62.

trinitarian thinking, that in his hymns Charles captured the mystery and ineffability appropriate to divine transcendence, and that he "summons his readers to praise, adoration, thanksgiving and love for God."[64]

In his review of Deschner's study of John Wesley's Christology, Geoffrey Wainwright hinted at an arena begging for further exploration. "By deliberately limiting himself to the Standard Sermons, the Notes on the New Testament, and the Articles," he opined, "Deschner effectively minimized the attention given to an important dimension in Wesley, namely the sacramental."[65] Francis Frost advanced this agenda in two articles published in the *Proceedings of the Charles Wesley Society*.[66] Two of his insights related to the Wesleys' Eucharistic theology confirm earlier Christological perceptions. First, while confessional statements were critical for the Wesleys, the brothers were perennially reaching beyond them to the heart of Scripture, the gospel, and the community of living faith centered in Christ and the Eucharist. Second, Charles, in particular, showed that "intimate union with Jesus, in communion at the sacramental memorial of his Supper, is the deepest experience of our earth-bound existence and, as such, is not only the surest guarantee of the fullness to come, but also the most efficacious means of growing towards it." Frost described this as Wesley's "Christ-Mysticism." The sacrament, in other words, focuses the attention of the faithful on the supreme importance of the Incarnation—the "alpha event" related to Christ's being—and the "omega event"—the culmination of the process of participatory redemption in the restoration of Christlike love through union with Christ.

Christological Principles in the Wesleys' "Practical Theology"

Three principles related to the Wesleys' engagement with specifically Christological concerns or questions shaped their practical understanding of the person and work of Christ.

(1) The Wesleys employed a *"distinct, but not separate" principle* in two critical areas. First, in explicating the person of Christ, they viewed the divine and the human natures as distinct, but not separate. Second, they retained a dynamic understanding of the interrelationship of Christ's person and work as distinct, but inseparable as well. Who Jesus is affected their

---

64. Vickers, "Charles Wesley and Doctrine of the Trinity," 292.
65. Wainwright, "Review of 'Wesley's Christology,'" 56.
66. Frost, "Veiled Unveiling"; and "Christ-Mysticism."

understanding of what he does; Jesus' purpose and mission lived out in history shaped their vision of who he is.

(2) Given the soteriological focus of Wesleyan theology, in general, both brothers viewed Christology through the lens of redemption and thereby tended to place greater *emphasis on the redemptive work of Christ*. In this arena of Christological discourse—as opposed to that concerned more with the person of Christ—the existential "so what?" factor becomes all the more apparent. Despite the inseparability of the person and work of Christ, the brothers' theology revolves around God's ultimate mission of redemption and how Jesus Christ fits into the larger salvific mission of the triune God.

(3) Both John and Charles Wesley went to great lengths to exhibit the *full range of biblical imagery* related to the person and work of Christ, with only limited explication of these themes or discussion of nuances that would divert their attention from the primary themes of redemption. They employed the language, analogies, and iconography of Scripture to proclaim a more richly textured and robust view of Christ's redemptive work. They devoted less energy to the task of elucidating the more elusive aspects of Christ's person. A concern for transformation, rather than information, drove their theological vision and program.

The Wesleys on the Person of Christ

Four primary themes characterize the "practical Christology" of John and Charles Wesley. The first two reflect concerns related to the person of Christ; the third and fourth relate to their vision of Christ's redemptive work.[67]

John and Charles Wesley embraced a robust understanding of the person of Christ as articulated in the historic creeds of the church and affirmed in their Anglican tradition. Both brothers exhibited a keen interest in *kenosis* as a means of explicating the mystery of the Incarnation.

Christology within the Bounds of Nicene Orthodoxy

"God in the Person of his Son"[68]

"See in that Infant's face / The depths of Deity."[69]

---

67. In these summative statements I make no effort to survey or discuss the breadth of the Wesleys' discussion of these themes; rather, my intention is to illustrate conclusions drawn from their primary Christological sources and to illustrate these with clear statements from their works.

68. C. Wesley, *Trinity Hymns*, 5.

69. C. Wesley, *Nativity Hymns*, 7.

John and Charles Wesley explicitly affirmed a traditional Chalcedonian understanding of Jesus Christ. Thomas Oden, in *John Wesley's Scriptural Christianity*, declares that "Wesley effortlessly employed the language of Chalcedon in phrases such as 'Real God, as real man,' 'perfect, as God and as man.'"[70] In his sermon "Scriptural Worship," John ascribed to Jesus "all the attributes and all the works of God. So that we need not scruple to pronounce him God of God, Light of Light, very God of very God, in glory equal with the Father, in majesty coeternal."[71] John defended the humanity of Jesus, as well, particularly in his *Notes on the New Testament*, describing him as "real man, like other men," whose human existence culminates in death and burial.[72] In his redaction of Article 2 of the Articles of Religion—the primary standard of doctrine and practice that shaped his life and ministry as well as his theology—he declared that "two whole and perfect natures, that is to say, the Godhead and Manhood, were joined together in one Person, never to be divided, whereof is one Christ, very God, and very man."[73]

Charles Wesley composed literally hundreds of hymns on the Incarnation. In these lyrical articulations of his Christology, he described Jesus Christ, the second person of the Trinity, as the friend of humanity. In Jesus Christ, God enters human history, comes close, lives with us, and offers friendship through a human person to every person. Many of Charles's nativity hymns, as in the case of the following example, underscore this understanding of the person of Christ:

> Glory be to God on high,
>> And peace on earth descend;
> God comes down and bows the sky,
>> And shows himself our friend!
> God the invisible *appears*,
>> God the blest, the great I AM
> Sojourns in this vale of tears,
>> And Jesus is his name.[74]

He affirms Jesus as true God and true human, a commitment illustrated, as well, in a hymn on "The presence of the Lord," based on Matthew 1:23.

---

70. Oden, *John Wesley's Scriptural Christianity*, 177.

71. J. Wesley, *Works*, 3:91.

72. See Wesley, *Notes upon the New Testament*, Mark 6:6; Luke 2:40, 43, 52; John 4:6; Phil 2:7–8; and Heb 2:17 in particular.

73. J. Wesley, *Sunday Service*, 306.

74. C. Wesley, *Nativity Hymns*, 5–6.

> God is in our flesh revealed,
>> Earth and heaven in Jesus join,
> Mortal with Immortal filled,
>> And human with Divine.

> Fulness of the Deity
>> In Jesus's body dwells.[75]

The Wesleys were familiar with all the Christological debates in early church history. They adhere firmly to the orthodox view of the person of Christ defined at the Council of Nicaea (325), later refined in the Nicene Creed, and reiterated in the theology and doxology of their Anglican tradition. They carefully avoided all forms of Arianism that view Jesus as anything less than fully divine. Likewise, they avoided a gnostic or docetic understanding that denies Christ's full humanity. The practical implications are clear. If Jesus is not fully divine, then he simply provides guidance to those seeking recovery and restoration by means of his example. If Jesus is not fully human, then God does not truly enter into the realities of human life with redemptive power. On the other hand, in "Jesus our Savior" we encounter the true God—love incarnate. And in "Jesus our brother," we discover our true selves—agents of love in God's world.

Paradox, Mystery, and Kenosis

> "Being's source *begins to be*, / And God himself is BORN!"[76]

> "He emptied himself of all but love"[77]

John and Charles Wesley both framed their understanding of who Jesus is in terms of paradox and mystery. Rather than attempting to explain the Incarnation in philosophical terms as if to master the inexplicable, they simply described the lengths to which God's love will go to reach people wherever they are. In his sermon, "God's Love to Fallen Man," John proclaimed,

> "Beloved, what manner of love is this," wherewith God has loved us! So as to give God's only Son! In glory equal with the Father; in majesty coeternal! What manner of love is this wherewith the only-begotten Son of God has loved us! So as to "empty himself,"

---

75. C. Wesley, *MS Matthew*, 4.
76. C. Wesley, *Nativity Hymns*, 6.
77. C. Wesley, *MS Scripture Hymns*, 29.

as far as possible, of his eternal Godhead! As to divest himself of that glory which he had with the Father before the world began! As to "take upon him the form of a servant, being found in fashion as a man!" And then to humble himself still farther, "being obedient unto death, yea, the death of the cross!"[78]

Charles also used the concept of *kenosis* (self-emptying) as a metaphor to more fully understand the nature of God's mysterious act of Incarnation.[79] A lyrical medium, perhaps, provides a more appropriate form of discourse in which to express this great mystery, and Charles Wesley possessed unique gifts in this arena. He viewed God's self-emptying, self-limitation, and self-effacement in the incarnation of Jesus Christ—described in the hymn embedded in Philippians 2:5–11—as the primary building blocks of Christian theology and spirituality. His most profound exposition of the kenotic theme comes in a hymn exploring the titles of Christ.

> Equal with God, most high,
>
> He laid his glory by:
>
> He, th' eternal God was born,
>
> >   Man with men he deign'd t' appear,
>
> Object of his creature's scorn,
>
> >   Pleas'd a servant's form to wear.
>
> He left his throne above
>
> Emptied of all, but love:
>
> Whom the heav'ns cannot contain
>
> >   God vouchsaf'd a worm t' appear,
>
> Lord of glory, *Son of man*,
>
> >   Poor, and vile, and abject here.[80]

Two practical implications emerge from this kenotic paradigm related to humility and self-sacrifice in the Christian journey of discipleship. Both these practices figure prominently in the brothers' appeal to all followers of Jesus to "imitate Christ." The paragraph quoted above from John's sermon based on Romans 5:15 concludes with the following admonition:

---

78. J. Wesley, *Works*, 2:428.
79. See Kimbrough, "Kenosis."
80. Wesley and Wesley, *Hymns and Sacred Poems* (1739), 165, 167.

"If God so loved us, how ought we to love one another!"[81] The qualities of humility (obedience) and self-emptying love (service) shaped Wesley's portrait of Christ. Throughout Christian history, devout followers of Jesus have prayed intentionally and cooperated with God's grace in a quest to realize these lofty virtues in their lives. To imitate Christ—to have the same mind in you that was in Christ (Phil 2:5 NRSV), to grow to the measure of the full stature of Jesus (Eph 4:13 NRSV), to be a letter of Jesus written on the tablet of the human heart (2 Cor 3:3 NRSV)—meant to become like Jesus in his humility and self-sacrificial service.

The Wesleys on the Work of Christ

John and Charles Wesley display the full range of biblical imagery with regards to the work of Christ. Charles's hymn, "Desiring to Love," published jointly by the brothers in their 1742 collection *Hymns and Sacred Poems*, demonstrates the breadth of their vision.

> What shall I do my God to love,
>> My Saviour, and the world's to praise?
> Whose bowels of compassion move
>> To me, and all the fallen race;
> Whose mercy is divinely free
> For all the fallen race, and me.
>
> I long to know, and to make known
>> The heights and depths of love divine,
> The kindness thou to me hast shewn,
>> Whose every sin was counted thine:
> My God for me resign'd his breath,
> He died, to save my soul from death.
>
> All souls are thine: and thou for all
>> The ransom of thy life hast given,
> To raise the sinner from his fall,
>> And bring him back to God and heaven,
> Thou all the world hast died to save,
> And all may thy salvation have.

---

81. J. Wesley, *Works*, 2:428.

> How shall I thank thee for the grace,
> > On me, and all mankind bestow'd!
> O that my every breath were praise,
> > O that my heart were fill'd with God!
> My heart would then with love o'erflow,
> And all my life thy glory shew.[82]

In this hymn, the Wesleys directly tie the Incarnation to its primary purpose—the atonement of all and reconciliation with God. Their doctrine of the redemptive work of Christ is richly textured, reflecting all the classical theories of atonement drawn from various strands of the biblical witness. The reference to Christ taking the sin of humanity upon himself resonates with a *substitutionary* or *satisfaction theory*. Their conception of Christ's victory over death reflects a more ancient *Christus victor* theme, as does Charles's reference to the metaphor of ransom and release. They alluded to the *moral influence theory* of atonement in their explication of "love divine" and its implied power to transform. Given the full breadth of the biblical imagery they used, "one is tempted to describe this," avers Randy Maddox, "as a Penalty Satisfaction *explanation* of the Atonement which has a Moral Influence *purpose*, and a Ransom *effect*."[83]

While all these themes pervade their sermons and hymns, the Wesleys explicated the work of Christ primarily through reference to the threefold office of Christ as prophet, priest, and king. Both brothers exhibited a keen interest in *theosis* as a means of explicating redemption as the restoration of the image of God and the role of Eucharist in this process.

The Threefold Office of Christ

> "Jesus to you his fulness brings /
> Pardon, and holiness, and heaven."[84]

> "Make, O make my heart thy seat /
> Christ, be Lord, be King to me!"[85]

The breadth of their soteriological concerns "led the brothers to emphasize relating to Christ 'in all his offices,'" claims Maddox, "not just as the priest who atones for guilt, but also as the prophet who teaches the ways in which we are to live, and as the king who oversees the restoration of wholeness in

---

82. Wesley and Wesley, *Hymns and Sacred Poems* (1742), 24–25.
83. Maddox, *Responsible Grace*, 109.
84. C. Wesley, *Redemption Hymns*, 63.
85. Wesley and Wesley, *Hymns and Sacred Poems* (1739), 174.

our lives."[86] Likewise, Oden described John's focus on the offices of Christ as the crux of his Christology.[87] In John's *Letter to a Roman Catholic*, he summarized his teaching in this regard.

> I believe that Jesus of Nazareth was the Saviour of the world, the Messiah so long foretold; that, being anointed with the Holy Ghost, he was a *prophet*, revealing to us the whole will of God; that he was a *priest*, who gave himself a sacrifice for sin, and still makes intercession for transgressors; that he is a *king*, who has all power in heaven and in earth; and will reign till he has subdued all things to himself.[88]

This Christological formula figures prominently in his sermon, "The Law Established by Faith, II," as well, with a fuller explication of the meaning of each office.

> We must . . . proclaim Christ in all his offices. To preach Christ as a workman that needs not to be ashamed is to preach him, not only as our great *High Priest*, "taken from among men, and ordained for men, in things pertaining to God," as such, "reconciling us to God by his blood" and "ever living to make intercession for us."—but likewise as the *Prophet of the Lord*, "who of God is made unto us wisdom," who, by his word and his Spirit, is with us always, "guiding us into all truth";—yea, and as remaining a *King* forever, as giving laws to all whom he has bought with his blood, as restoring those to the image of God whom he had first re-instated in his favor, as reigning in all believing hearts until he has "subdued all things to himself,"—until he hath utterly cast out all sin and brought in everlasting righteousness.[89]

John drew here upon a long-standing tradition in Western theology (owing much to John Calvin) that conceived Jesus' work through the lens of these particular roles.[90] While Wesley was concerned about how to properly interpret the "past" or "finished" work of Christ—his redemptive work that made atonement possible—he emphasized with equal or even greater vigor the "present" work of Christ. Despite the foundational nature of "Christ dying for us," he was equally concerned about "Christ reigning in us." In other words, he did not view Christ's atoning death as the totality of his redemptive

---

86. Maddox, "Theology of John and Charles Wesley," 29.

87. See Oden, *John Wesley's Scriptural Christianity*, 187–90.

88. Outler, *John Wesley*, 404.

89. J. Wesley, *Works*, 2:37–38.

90. See the discussion of these concepts in Chilcote, *John and Charles Wesley*, 90–91; cf. Maddox, *Responsible Grace*, 109–14.

work; rather, he viewed the cross as the foundation of God's present and transforming work through Christ in the life of the believer. Following the order of the offices that Wesley seems to have preferred, Christ's role as priest—through which God mediates the experience of pardon—precedes his culminating work of restoration. As prophet, Christ reveals the moral image of God and initiates the renewal of Christlike character. The present work of Christ comes to fruition through the office of Christ as king (or physician).[91] Christ as Lord rules in all believing hearts and enables full conformity to his own image as the believer grows into the fullest possible love of God and neighbor. Christ as priest forgives (pardon); Christ as prophet guides (holiness); Christ as king restores (heaven).

Charles Wesley replicated this Christological paradigm in the concluding stanzas of a "Hymn to the Son."

> Prophet, to me reveal
> Thy Father's perfect will.
> Never mortal spake like thee,
>   Human prophet like divine;
> Loud and strong their voices be,
>   Small and still and inward thine!

> On thee my priest I call,
> Thy blood aton'd for all.
> Still the Lamb as slain appears,
>   Still thou stand'st before the throne,
> Ever off'ring up my pray'rs,
>   These presenting with thy own.

> Jesu! Thou art my King,
> From thee my strength I bring!
> Shadow'd by thy mighty hand,
>   Saviour, who shall pluck me thence?
> Faith supports, by faith I stand
>   Strong as thy omnipotence.[92]

---

91. See Maddox, *Responsible Grace*, 112–13.
92. Wesley and Wesley, *Hymns and Sacred Poems* (1739), 110.

In other hymns, Charles demonstrates his full alignment with his brother's understanding of the kingly role of Christ in terms of restoration—the recovery of God's image in the believer and the reign of love in all believing hearts. The supplicant cries,

> I pant to feel thy sway
> And only thee t' obey.
> Thee my spirit gasps to meet,
> > This my one, my ceaseless pray'r,
> Make, O make my heart thy seat,
> > O set up thy kingdom there![93]

One might easily expect three primary implications from this exposition of the offices of Christ. First, the priestly role of Christ reveals that God graciously forgives and reconciles those who have no claim to pardon. Our trust in the fact that God has already accepted us and loves us defines living faith. Christ came to demonstrate this amazing love to us. Second, salvation means more than forgiveness of sin. Christ as prophet reveals that the purpose of a life reclaimed by faith is the recovery of God's image. Faith is the means to love's end. In other words, the Christian life moves toward the goal of holiness of heart and life and ever greater conformity to the image of Christ. Third, the kingly rule of Christ reveals salvation as *therapeia*—divine therapy that heals the child of God. The goal of the way or process of salvation is the fullest possible restoration to health in those who put their trust in Christ. The Wesleys' concept of ultimate spiritual health is *theosis*—the fullest possible participation of the believer in God. The goal of the redemptive work of Christ is the fullest possible love of God and others.

Partaking of the Life Divine in the Eucharist

> "To rise restor'd, and throughly pure, /
> In all the image of thy love."[94]

> "That I thy nature might partake."[95]

Everything in John and Charles Wesley's concept of redemption aligns toward the goal of fully restored love. While affirming the forensic or juridical aspects of the work of Christ, they also understood the human need for

---

93. Wesley and Wesley, *Hymns and Sacred Poems* (1739), 174.
94. C. Wesley, *Hymns and Sacred Poems* (1749), 2:187.
95. Wesley and Wesley, *Hymns on the Lord's Supper*, 39.

divine *therapeia*; freedom from slavery to sin provides a foundation for the restoration of the living presence of God in the believer. For the Wesleys, the work of Christ culminates in the fullest possible recovery of the *imago Dei*. Whether influenced directly or indirectly by patristic sources, *theosis*—God became like us so that we might become like God—defines the primary purpose or *telos* of Christ's work.[96]

"Ye know that the great end of religion," John would repeat on a number of occasions, "is to renew our hearts in the image of God, to repair that total loss of righteousness and true holiness which we sustained by the sin of our first parents."[97] He defined this theotic goal as "Christian perfection."[98] In "The Scripture Way of Salvation," he provided one of his most succinct definitions of this vision: "The word [i.e., "perfection"] has various senses: here it means perfect love. It is love excluding sin; love filling the heart, taking up the whole capacity of the soul. It is love 'rejoicing evermore, praying without ceasing, in everything giving thanks.'"[99] "This great gift of God, the salvation of our souls," he averred in his *Plain Account of Christian Perfection*, "is no other than the image of God fresh stamped on our hearts. *It is a renewal of believers in the spirit of our minds, after the likeness of him that created them.*"[100] John articulated his vision of *theosis*—participation in the divine nature—in his translation of a Gerhardt hymn in which the singer pleads for love to fill one's whole being.

> O grant that nothing in my soul
>   May dwell, but thy pure love alone!
> O may thy love possess me whole,
>   My joy, my treasure, and my crown;
> Strange flames far from my heart remove—
> My every act, word, thought, be love.[101]

This concept of *theosis* also shaped Wesley's understanding of Eucharist, a connection exploited more fully by his younger brother.

---

96. In the foreword to his 1985 reprint edition of his original *Wesley's Christology*, Deschner acknowledged that it was important to take the Eastern theme of *theosis* more seriously in order to understand Wesley (ix).

97. J. Wesley, *Works*, 2:185.

98. For a full discussion of this Wesleyan concept, see the introduction to Wesley's Christian perfection corpus in *Works*, 13:3–25.

99. J. Wesley, *Works*, 2:160.

100. J. Wesley, *Works*, 13:150.

101. Wesley and Wesley, *Hymns and Sacred Poems* (1739), 156.

The concluding stanza of Charles Wesley's famous redemption hymn, "Love Divine, All Loves Excelling," celebrates redemption's lofty goal.

> Finish then thy new creation,
> > Pure and sinless let us be,
> Let us see thy great salvation,
> > Perfectly restor'd in thee;
> Chang'd from glory into glory,
> > Till in heaven we take our place,
> Till we cast our crowns before thee,
> > Lost in wonder, love, and praise![102]

Kimbrough noted how the concern of *theosis* "surfaces time and again in Charles Wesley's poetry in concert with many of the Early Fathers of the Church."[103] Wesley encapsulated this vision in a simple couplet from his hymn on Philippians 2:5: "I shall fully be restored / To the image of my Lord."[104] The twin themes of incarnation and restoration find profound expression in one of his nativity hymns.

> Made flesh for our sake,
> That we might partake
> The nature divine,
> And again in his image, his holiness shine;
>
> And while we are here,
> Our King shall appear,
> His Spirit impart,
> And form his full image of love in our heart.[105]

In his lyrical corpus, three corollaries of *theosis* receive repeated attention: the claim that the Spirit restores the image of Christ in the believer, that transformed disciples of Jesus will be like him, and that this kind of transformation enables them to radiate the glory of God.[106]

"The Eucharistic hymns especially exhibit a *participatory* understanding of our relation to Christ," observes Geoffrey Wainwright. "Charles

---

102. C. Wesley, *Redemption Hymns*, 12.

103. Kimbrough, *Lyrical Theology*, 89; cf. Kimbrough's most fully developed examination of this theme, *Partakers of the Life Divine*.

104. Wesley and Wesley, *Hymns and Sacred Poems* (1742), 223.

105. C. Wesley, *Nativity Hymns*, 12.

106. See the discussion of these themes in Chilcote, "All the Image," 21–40.

Wesley's Easter hymn expresses it exactly: 'Made like Him, like Him we rise! Ours the cross, the grave, the skies!'"[107] For Charles, the sacrament of Holy Communion functions as a focal point for "the one thing needful," namely, the restoration of the divine image in the believer. The Lord's Supper both presents a vision of holiness and, perhaps even more importantly, offers sanctifying grace to the faithful on their journey toward holiness of heart and life. In his incisive study of Wesley's *Hymns on the Lord's Supper*, Daniel Stevick examines the conjunction of forgiveness and holiness in this collection and affords this summative comment:

> In describing Wesley's understanding of redemption, it should be remarked that for him, salvation and holiness of life—justification and sanctification—are inseparable. If the sacrament conveys the very reality of Christ's atonement, it brings forgiveness of sins; but forgiveness necessarily inaugurates a new creation. If a life of holiness does not follow from faith, it is as though Christ had died in vain.[108]

The concept of "partaking in the life divine" comes into clear focus in these hymns.

Three particular insights related to this divine partaking surface in Charles's hymns. First, he simply affirmed that participation in the Eucharist shapes the fullest possible love in the disciple of Jesus.

> O what a soul-transporting feast
>
> Doth this communion yield!
>
> Remembering here thy Passion past
>
> We with thy love are fill'd.[109]

Second, the fullest possible infilling of love ultimately means conformity to the cross. The "suffering servants" of God are called to take up their crosses daily in multifarious acts of self-sacrificial love. Wesley repeatedly described the full extent of solidarity with the crucified Lord.

> His servants shall be
>
> With Him on the tree,
>
> Where Jesus was slain
>
> His crucified servants shall always remain.[110]

---

107. Wainwright, "Review of 'Wesley's Christology,'" 56.
108. Stevick, *Altar's Fire*, 36.
109. Wesley and Wesley, *Hymns on the Lord's Supper*, 82.
110. Wesley and Wesley, *Hymns on the Lord's Supper*, 120.

To possess the mind of Christ, to be fully restored in love, means to be shaped in the form of the cross.

Third, he also communicates a profound, corporate dimension with regard to his vision of conformity to the divine. The Eucharist shapes the followers of Jesus into a community that suffers with others for the sake of love. The Eucharist "forms the Savior in the soul," to use Charles's own phrase; that formation takes place not only in the individual heart of the believer, but in the heart of the church. Holy Communion enables the believer to realize participation in the divine.

> Saviour, thou didst the mystery give
> > That I thy nature might partake,
> Thou bidst me outward signs receive,
> > One with thyself my soul to make,
> My body, soul and spirit to join
> Inseparably one with thine.[111]

The singular, practical implication of John and Charles Wesley's vision of Christ's redemptive life and work in which God invites us to partake of the divine nature could not be any clearer. Christ is the true light of the world whose radiance transcends all darkness, and when it floods the soul, all manner of darkness vanishes. Living into this light and this love is the chief end of life. So, Charles prayed for the in-breaking of the glorious light of the One "whose glory fills the skies":

> Visit then this soul of mine,
> > Pierce the gloom of sin, and grief,
> Fill me, radiancy divine,
> > Scatter all my unbelief,
> More and more thyself display
> Shining to the perfect day.[112]

---

111. Wesley and Wesley, *Hymns on the Lord's Supper*, 39.
112. Wesley and Wesley, *Hymns and Sacred Poems* (1740), 25.

―――― Chapter 6 ――――

John and Charles Wesley on "God in Christ Reconciling"

Source note: Delivered as a plenary paper on the conference theme of "Reconciliation" before the World Methodist Historical Society Meeting in Seoul, South Korea, July 19, 2006, and published under this title in *Methodist History* 47.3 (April 2009) 132–45.

The Call to Reconciliation

THE TURN OF THE millennium birthed a renewal of concern about reconciliation. Given a world of destructive conflicts and the reality of personal lives characterized by alienation and fragmentation, this renewed interest is hardly surprising. Unfortunately, the Christian community is caught up frequently in the divisive spirit of this age and sometimes contributes to increased alienation by promoting a defective gospel, rather than living in and for God's vision of beloved community in this world. In a time such as this, those who designed this World Methodist Conference event have served us well by focusing our attention on the foundational Pauline theme of "God in Christ Reconciling." For this gathering of the Historical Society, I have been asked to address this theme from the perspective of John and Charles Wesley. Before examining the contribution they make to our understanding and application of this *missio Dei* (mission of God), however, I think it would be helpful to dwell on the conception of reconciliation itself for just a moment, in light of our contemporary circumstances.

I suppose it was the dismantling of apartheid in South Africa and the work of the Truth and Reconciliation Commission that reintroduced me, and many of us, to the agony and the ecstasy of reconciliation in dramatic ways.¹ That amazing process revealed the cost of true reconciliation.² It wrenched us from a foolish or dangerously naïve conception of reconciliation that made life all too simple. In that process, we could see again how genuine repentance and accountability, restorative justice and forgiveness, are indispensable elements in the quest for reconciliation. As Scott Appleby demonstrates, the complexity of it all has led some skeptics to abandon the "politics of forgiveness and reconciliation" as an empty promise that can hardly hope to deliver its goal in this world.³ And yet, people live in the hope and expectation of—and, in fact, do experience—reconciliation.

Drawn from another context of human brutality, suffering, and sin, the work of Miroslav Volf explores the dynamic of "exclusion and embrace."⁴ Volf reminds us of the centrality of solidarity in suffering to our Christian faith. He helps us rediscover how reconciliation and resurrection become possible for us under the sign of the cross. In his reflections upon similar concerns, another contemporary theologian, Walter Wink, emphasizes the distinction between forgiveness and reconciliation, concepts often blurred in popular Christianity. While forgiveness can be unilateral, true reconciliation requires mutuality.⁵ Forgiveness and reconciliation are distinct but not separate; forgiveness being the foundation upon which reconciliation is built. As the leaders of an emergent reconciliation movement remind us, "reconciliation is not forgetting the past . . . Christians are called to fearlessly seek and name the truth of what has happened, guided by repentance and forgiveness."⁶ John Paul Lederach, widely acclaimed Professor of International Peacebuilding in the Notre Dame Kroc Institute for International Peace Studies, defines reconciliation quite simply but profoundly as that place where truth, justice, mercy, and peace meet.⁷

---

1. According to Kevin Avruch and Beatriz Vejarano, between 1973 and 1995 when the South African commission was established, over twenty "truth commissions" for the purpose of peace-building and reconciliation have been established around the world, and the number has nearly doubled since the turn of the century (Avruch and Vejarano, "Truth and Reconciliation Commissions," 1).

2. For a discussion of the conditions under which genuine reconciliation becomes possible, see Battle, *Reconciliation*.

3. See Appleby, *Ambivalence*.

4. See Volf, *Exclusion and Embrace*.

5. Wink, *When the Powers Fall*, 14. Cf. Peterson and Helmick, *Forgiveness and Reconciliation*.

6. Rice, *Reconciliation*, 7.

7. See the important studies of Lederach, *Moral Imagination* and *Building Peace*, but particularly *Journey Toward Reconciliation*, in which he first develops this quadrilateral image.

These ancient-future lessons must inform our reflections on this theme of "God in Christ Reconciling." While stunningly contemporary, none of these concepts or ways of thinking about reconciliation is foreign to our Wesleyan heritage. Indeed, as we shall see, the personal dimension of reconciliation with God in Christ (that aspect most common in our way of thinking) is inextricably bound with God's larger vision for the human family and its history. But before we turn to John and Charles Wesley, we must also sojourn for a moment, as our forebears would have demanded, in the biblical text that frames our conversations.

The Biblical Vision

St. Paul writes to the embattled church in Corinth: "God was in Christ, reconciling the world unto himself, not imputing their trespasses unto them; and hath committed unto us the word of reconciliation" (2 Cor 5:19). This is the translation that would have been most familiar to John and Charles Wesley, and I really do want us to reflect on this entire verse and not simply the conference theme, which is a sound bite summation of the whole. This verse comes, of course, from a larger discourse in the letter (namely, 2 Cor 5:11–21) in which the apostle discusses the ministry of reconciliation. Many of Paul's most familiar themes resound in this fifth chapter: new creation (the theme explored at the most recent Oxford Institute of Methodist Theological Studies), imputation, the righteousness of God. Here we encounter St. Paul's great manifesto on reconciliation, a statement that should be laid alongside the other locus of this teaching, namely, Colossians 1:19–20: "For it pleased the Father that in him should all fullness dwell; And, having made peace through the blood of his cross, by him to reconcile all things unto himself; by him, I say, whether they be things in earth, or things in heaven" (using again the Authorized Version of the Wesleys' day).

In these summary statements, St. Paul captures God's total mission to which, he believes, the entirety of the scriptural witness bears testimony. Friendship with God characterizes this vision of life. Those drawn into this realm love both God and neighbor. Christ makes this kind of existence possible by breaking down all the barriers that divide people and disrupt God's intended harmony in the created order. Reconciliation itself is a sign of God's presence and the nearness of God's rule. "Amidst the world's profound brokenness," so claims the Reconciliation Network, "God's peace in the risen Christ is now powerfully at work, seeking to reconcile humanity to

God's intended purposes for union with God, one another, and the material creation, resulting in the flourishing of all."[8]

It is noteworthy, perhaps, that the image of Jesus as the agent of this reconciliation is somewhat unique to St. Paul.[9] Jesus' ministry and mission, in fact, point to a much larger reality than most tend to envisage when they consider the soteriological dimensions of this new creation. Older English translations of Second Corinthians 5 (v. 17, in particular) tended to obscure the more radical nature of St. Paul's vision. In his *Explanatory Notes upon the New Testament*, John Wesley actually deviates from the King James Version with regards to this pivotal verse. Over against the Authorized Version, in which we read, "Therefore if any man be in Christ, he is a *new creature*," Wesley suggests: "Therefore if anyone be in Christ, there is a new creation." His exposition of the verse explores the breadth of Paul's meaning:

> Only the power that makes a world can make a Christian. And when he is so created, *the old has passed away*—Of their own accord, even as snow in spring. Behold! the present, visible, undeniable change! *All things are become new*—he has new life, new senses, new faculties, new affections, new appetites, new ideas and conceptions. His whole tenor of action and conversation is new, and he lives, as it were, in a new world. God, men, the whole creation, heaven, earth, and all therein, appear in a new light, and stand related to him in a new manner, since he was created anew in Christ Jesus.[10]

Given the absence of a subject and verb in the original Greek, Richard Hays suggests a more literal rendering: "If anyone is in Christ—new creation." His interpretation of Paul moves in the same direction as that of Wesley.

> Paul is not merely talking about an individual's subjective experience of renewal through conversion; rather, for Paul *ktisis* ("creation") refers to the whole created order (cf. Rom. 8:18–25). He is proclaiming the apocalyptic message that through the cross God has nullified the *kosmos* of sin and death and brought a new *kosmos* into being.[11]

The implications that surround these biblical insights are profound. Again, Richard Hays' discussion is instructive.

---

8. Rice, *Reconciliation*, 11.
9. See Bruce, "Christ as Conqueror and Reconciler."
10. Wesley, *Notes upon the New Testament*, 2:457–58.
11. Hays, *Moral Vision*, 20.

> Once the church has caught the vision of living as a sign of the new creation in which racial and ethnic differences are bridged at the table of the Lord, how it is possible for the community of Christ's people to participate in animosity toward "outsiders"? If God is the creator of a whole world who wills ultimately to redeem the whole creation—if the death of Christ was the means whereby "God was pleased to reconcile to himself all things, whether on earth or in heaven, by making peace through the blood of his cross" (Col. 1:20)—then how can the church that is called to bear God's message of reconciliation in an unredeemed world (2 Cor. 5:17-20) scorn or reject people of any race or tongue, whether they are Christians or not? ... the church has the task of embodying "the ministry of reconciliation" in the world.[12]

While the reconciliation of the believer in Christ to God is an accomplished fact, the reconciliation of the cosmos is a continuing process into which the community of faith is invited as the representatives of God's alternative vision in the world. We are called to stand in the juncture, as it were, between the old world which is passing away and the new world that is being birthed in Christ, despite all appearances.[13]

How did these texts and this biblical vision shape the Wesleyan tradition? How did John and Charles Wesley proclaim and manifest this message of God in Christ reconciling in their own day? When we turn to the witness of John and Charles Wesley we discover a profound balance of the individual and the social, the personal and the cosmic, the joy of reconciliation and the claim of discipleship. Without having minimized the importance of personal conversion, they expanded the horizon of the early Methodist people to embrace the larger vision of God's shalom. After exploring the "reconciling Word" as the "true foundation" of the life of "faith," I will examine the Wesleyan concepts of "gratitude" and "benevolence" as the keynotes of a Wesleyan theology of reconciliation.

Laying the True Foundation: The Reconciling Word

Lutheran Pietists exerted a profound influence upon John Wesley in his quest for a proper foundation in life. During his sojourn among the Moravians at Herrnhut in the summer of 1738, he encountered a clear

---

12. Hays, *Moral Vision*, 441.

13. This image simply confirms the conclusions of Herman Ridderbos, namely, that in Paul, God is the Author and Initiator of reconciliation and that this reconciliation has a profoundly eschatological character. See Ridderbos, *Paul*, §32: "God's Reconciling Activity in Christ."

articulation of the "true foundation" in the preaching of Christian David, one of Count Zinzendorf's earliest collaborators. Wesley recounts from memory one of David's sermons.

> This is "the word of reconciliation" which we preach. This is the foundation which never can be moved. By faith we are built upon this foundation. And this faith also is the gift of God. It is his free gift, which he now and ever giveth to everyone that is willing to receive it . . . But this gift of God lives in the heart, not the head. The faith of the head, learned from men or books, is nothing worth. It brings neither remission of sins nor peace with God. Labour then to believe with your whole heart. So shall you have redemption through the blood of Christ. So shall you be cleansed from all sin. So shall ye go on from strength to strength, being renewed day by day in righteousness and all true holiness.[14]

In his later letter "To the Moravian Church," which opens the fourth published extract of his journal, Wesley identifies this foundational concept as the source of their common vision: "What united my heart to you is the excellency (in many respects) of the doctrine taught among you: your laying the true foundation, 'God was in Christ, reconciling the world to himself'; your declaring the free grace of God the cause, and faith the condition of justification."[15]

This vision of salvation by grace through faith, corroborated strongly by Wesley's own Anglican tradition, revolved around Christ's righteousness, God's grace, and the gift of faith. Wesley expounded these themes in his sermon on "The Righteousness of Faith," drawing heavily upon the Second Corinthians text. "The righteousness of faith," according to Wesley, "is that method of reconciliation with God which hath been chosen and established by God himself . . . it was of mere grace, of free love, of undeserved mercy, that God hath vouchsafed to sinful man any way of reconciliation with himself."[16] He subsequently pleads with his reader:

> Whosoever therefore thou art who desirest to be forgiven and reconciled to the favour of God, do not say in thy heart, "I must first do this: I must first conquer every sin, break off every evil word and work, and do all good to all men; or I must first go to Church, receive the Lord's Supper, hear more sermons, and say more prayers." Alas, my brother, thou art clean gone out of the

---

14. J. Wesley, *Works*, 18:272.
15. J. Wesley, *Works*, 19:117.
16. J. Wesley, *Works*, 1:213.

way. Thou art still "ignorant of the righteousness of God," and art "seeking to establish thy own righteousness" as the ground of thy reconciliation. Knowest thou not that thou canst do nothing but sin till thou art reconciled to God? Wherefore then dost thou say, I must do this and this first, and then I shall believe? Nay, but first believe. Believe in the Lord Jesus Christ, the propitiation for thy sins. Let this good foundation first be laid, and then thou shalt do all things well.[17]

In a verse inspired by 2 Corinthians 5:17, Charles Wesley celebrates the momentous change in the believer's life effected by trust in Christ.

> Thrice acceptable word,
>
> I long to prove it true!
>
> Take me into thyself, O Lord,
>
> By making me anew;
>
> Me for thy mercy sake
>
> Out of myself remove,
>
> Partaker of thy nature make,
>
> Thy holiness and love.[18]

The Wesleys also describe this profoundly personal dimension of God in Christ reconciling as justification by faith. In his introduction to the sermon corpus in *The Works of John Wesley*, Albert Outler actually uses the terms "reconciliation" and "justification" interchangeably.[19] When we talk about reconciliation in this sense, as it refers to the Wesleyan way of salvation, we are talking about nothing other than justification by grace through faith, and this is the true foundation of authentic Christian life.

It is no surprise, therefore, to discover that the Second Corinthians text figures quite prominently in many of John Wesley's discussions of this fundamental doctrine. Even his standard definition of "faith" makes explicit reference to St. Paul's words.

> Faith in general is a divine, supernatural *elegchos*, "evidence" or conviction "of things not seen," not discoverable by our bodily senses as being either past, future, or spiritual. Justifying faith implies, not only a divine evidence or conviction that "God was in Christ, reconciling the world unto himself," but a sure trust

---

17. J. Wesley, *Works*, 1:214.
18. C. Wesley, *Scripture Hymns*, 2:300.
19. J. Wesley, *Works*, 1:80.

and confidence that Christ died for my sins, that he loved me, and gave himself for me.[20]

In his sermon on "The Way to the Kingdom," the autobiographical allusions are obvious in Wesley's description of faith as "a sure trust in the mercy of God through Christ Jesus. It is a confidence in a pardoning God. It is a divine evidence or conviction that "God was in Christ, reconciling the world to himself, not imputing to them their former trespasses"; and in particular that "the son of God hath loved me and given himself for me; and that I, even I, am now reconciled to God by the blood of the cross."[21] Elsewhere, his prose achieves a poetic quality as he reflects on the foundation of life in Christ.

> Also it is a matter of daily experience that "by grace we are thus saved through faith." It is by faith that the eye of the mind is opened to see the light of the glorious love of God. And as long as it is steadily fixed thereon, on God in Christ, reconciling the world unto himself, we are more and more filled with the love of God and man, with meekness, gentleness, long-suffering; with all the fruits of holiness, which are, through Christ Jesus, to the glory of God the Father.[22]

We discover, essentially, our true identity as the children of God. "We then see, not by a chain of *reasoning*," claims Wesley, "but by a kind of *intuition*, by a direct view, that 'God was in Christ reconciling' . . . In that day 'we know that we are of God,' children of God by faith."[23] The love of God constrains the preacher, therefore, to admonish all hearers: "Rejoice to embrace every opportunity of hearing 'the word of reconciliation' declared by the 'ambassadors of Christ, the stewards of the mysteries of God.'"[24]

In his religious verse, Charles Wesley describes this true foundation of life with God as the "reconciling word":

> See me, Saviour, from above,
>   Nor suffer me to die!
> Life, and happiness, and love,
>   Drop from thy gracious eye;
> Speak the reconciling word,
>   And let thy mercy melt me down;

---

20. J. Wesley, *Works*, 1:194.
21. J. Wesley, *Works*, 1:230.
22. J. Wesley, *Works*, 1:614.
23. J. Wesley, *Works*, 2:481.
24. J. Wesley, *Works*, 1:570. For the numerous occasions upon which John Wesley preached on 2 Cor 5:19, see J. Wesley, *Works*, 20:277, 306, 312, 427; 21:318; 24:11, 35, 56, 106, 113, 142, and 152.

> Turn, and look upon me, Lord,
>> And break my heart of stone.[25]

This reconciling word of God illuminates the soul with the gift of faith. God restores sight to the blind and rescues those who dwell in darkness. Those who entrust their lives to God through Christ by faith pray for all the fullness of God in their lives.

> The gift unspeakable impart:
>> Command the light of faith to shine,
>
> To shine in my dark, drooping heart,
>> And fill me with the life divine;
>
> Now bid the new creation be!
> O God, let there be faith in me!
>
> Thee without faith I cannot please,
>> Faith without thee I cannot have;
>
> But thou hast sent the Prince of peace
>> To seek my wandering soul, and save;
>
> O Father, glorify thy Son,
> And save me for his sake alone!
>
> Save me through faith in Jesu's blood,
>> That blood which he for all did shed;
>
> For me, for me, thou know'st it flowed,
>> For me, for me, thou hear'st it plead;
>
> Assure me now my soul is thine,
>> And all thou art in Christ is mine![26]

For those who are "reconciled by grace," God justifies through faith alone, opens mercy's door, offers assurance of forgiveness, relieves burdens, and makes meet for heaven.[27] God's will is that all might be saved and the extent of God's love so great that we "tremble at the word / Of reconciling grace."[28] This reconciling word composes the weary breast and sinks us into

---

25. J. Wesley, *Works*, 7:209 (no. 103.4).

26. C. Wesley published the first verse cited here as v. 3 in the hymn as it appears in J. Wesley, *Works*, 7:259 (no. 142). The final two verses, restored here from the original *Redemption Hymns*, no. 14.4–5, are also reprinted in many of the subsequent hymnals.

27. J. Wesley, *Works*, 7:142 (no. 50.2).

28. J. Wesley, *Works*, 7:454 (no. 298.4).

visions of eternity, but also raises us to sing our Savior's praise, flows from our hearts, fills our tongues, permeates our life with purest love, and joins us to the communion of God's faithful throughout the ages.[29]

One of Charles Wesley's more familiar hymns, "Prisoners of hope, arise," celebrates God's offer of reconciliation, the true source of the hope of glory in our lives.

> Prisoners of hope, arise,
> > And see your Lord appear!
> Lo! on the wings of love he flies,
> > And brings redemption near.
> Redemption in his blood
> > He calls you to receive;
> Look unto me, the pard'ning God!
> > Believe, he cries, believe!
>
> The reconciling word
> > We thankfully embrace,
> Rejoice in our redeeming Lord,
> > A blood-besprinkled race.
> We yield to be set free,
> > Thy counsel we approve,
> Salvation, praise ascribe to thee,
> > And glory in thy love.[30]

Manifesting the True Christian Character: Gratitude and Benevolence

For John and Charles Wesley, God's own reconciling word is the true foundation of the abundant life, and "gratitude and benevolence" constitute the

---

29. J. Wesley, *Works*, 7:475 (no. 319.3–4).
30. J. Wesley, *Works*, 7:549 (no. 376.1–2).

faith-filled response to God's offer of reconciliation. John Wesley rings the changes on this theme in his sermon on "The Unity of the Divine Being." In characteristic fashion he describes the primary threats to genuine Christianity, namely, the false religions of right opinions (or orthodoxy), outward forms, and good works.[31] His fourth critique of what he describes as a "religion of atheism," however, strikes at the heart of our concerns here.

> [The religion of atheism is] every religion whereof God is not laid for the foundation. In a word, a religion wherein "God in Christ, reconciling the world unto himself," is not the Alpha and Omega, the beginning and the end, the first and the last point.
>
> True religion is right tempers towards God and man. It is, in two words, gratitude and benevolence: gratitude to our Creator and supreme Benefactor, and benevolence to our fellow-creatures. In other words, it is the loving God with all our heart, and our neighbour as ourselves.[32]

In his very last sermon, "On Faith," written in January 1791, John Wesley asks the all-important question about the goal of the Christian life: "How will [the faithful] advance in holiness, in the whole image of God wherein they were created!" He responds with reference to these dual foci of the Christian life: "In the love of God and man, gratitude to their Creator, and benevolence to all their fellow-creatures."[33] First, gratitude is the response of the creature to the Creator; the response of those who are reconciled to the Reconciler. God in Christ reconciling produces grateful hearts and lives characterized by thanksgiving. Second, benevolence or good will is the response of the disciple whose vision of life has been transformed by the God of love. Having discovered God's purpose for life and their place within God's unfolding story, disciples of Christ immerse themselves in and commit themselves to God's vision for a just and peace-filled world. In conclusion, I will dwell on each of these images only briefly.

---

31. See his similar depiction of false religion in the sermon, "Walking by Sight and Walking by Faith," in which he argues that true religion is neither harmlessness, morality, nor formality. Rather, true religion is "living in eternity, and walking in eternity; and hereby walking in the love of God and man, in lowliness, meekness, and resignation" (J. Wesley, *Works*, 4:57–58).

32. J. Wesley, *Works*, 4:66–67. In his sermon entitled "An Israelite Indeed," Wesley counters Francis Hutcheson's naturalistic theories articulated in a work entitled *The Original of our Ideas of Beauty and Virtue*. Wesley counters with his view of the impossibility of virtue apart for the God whose prevenient love is the foundation of all virtue (J. Wesley, *Works*, 4:278–89).

33. J. Wesley, *Works*, 4:196.

Gratitude

Grateful hearts testify to the blessedness of life in Christ. In John Wesley's sermon, "On Love," he describes the quality of happiness that characterizes the lives of those reconciled to God in Christ: "Without love nothing can so profit us as to make our lives happy. By happiness I mean, not a slight, trifling pleasure, that perhaps begins and ends in the same hour; but such a state of well-being as contents the soul, and gives it a steady, lasting satisfaction."[34] He directly connects one's experience of the Triune God with this most profound discovery:

> This is religion, and this is happiness, the happiness for which we were made. This begins when we begin to know God, by the teaching of his own Spirit. As soon as the Father of spirits reveals his Son in our hearts, and the Son reveals his Father, the love of God is shed abroad in our hearts; then, and not till then, we are happy.[35]

Gratitude characterized the lives of the early Methodist people who bore witness to the blessed nature of life. Isabella Wilson expressed this sentiment in her journal.

> This is love unspeakable! [God's] delight is to make us happy. O how does his love exceed all that fancy can form, or imagination paint. The favoured soul is ready to say, I have heard great and glorious things spoken of thee, but, oh, how little was said to what I find! O how unable are the tongues of mortals to set forth the pleasures of those who are united to this Jesus! We joy in his redeeming love.[36]

Charles Wesley captures this spirit of gratitude in one of his "family hymns."

> With singing we praise
> The original grace
> By our heavenly Father bestowed;
> Our being receive
> From his bounty, and live
> To the honour and glory of God.

---

34. J. Wesley, *Works*, 4:386.
35. J. Wesley, *Works*, 4:67.
36. Pipe, "Memoir of Isabella Wilson," 465.

> For thy glory we are,
> Created to share
> Both the nature and kingdom divine;
> Created again,
> That our souls may remain
> In time and eternity thine.
>
> Hallelujah we sing
> To our Father and King,
> And his rapturous praises repeat;
> To the Lamb that was slain
> Hallelujah again
> Sing all heaven, and fall at his feet![37]

He celebrates the rapture of the newfound child of God.

> Abba, Father! hear thy child,
> Late in Jesus reconciled;
> Hear, and all the graces shower,
> All the joy, and peace, and power,
> All my Saviour asks above,
> All the life and heaven of love.[38]

Benevolence

For most Methodist people, this kind of praise—this response and quality of gratitude—comes as no surprise as we contemplate the meaning of God in Christ reconciling. God's love in Christ elicits a reciprocal love in God's child. But, for the Wesleys, as important as this newly discovered relationship is, ultimately, salvation is not all about us! They are adamant in their claim that love of God must move the believer ineluctably toward love of neighbor. In his sermon on "The Case of Reason Impartially Considered," John Wesley demonstrates how the love of neighbor springs, in fact, from gratitude to God.

---

37. J. Wesley, *Works*, 7:663–64 (no. 478.3, 4, and 7).
38. J. Wesley, *Works*, 7:552.

> As reason cannot produce the love of God, so neither can it produce the love of our neighbour, a calm, generous, disinterested benevolence to every child of man. This earnest, steady goodwill to our fellow-creatures never flowed from any fountain but gratitude to our Creator. And if this be . . . the very essence of virtue, it follows that virtue can have no being unless it spring from the love of God.[39]

Elsewhere he proclaims: "And if any man truly love God he cannot but love his brother also. Gratitude to our Creator will surely produce benevolence to our fellow-creatures. If we love him, we cannot but love one another, as Christ loved us. We feel our souls enlarged in love toward every child of man."[40]

Benevolence means mission.[41] The Wesleys believed that God calls the community of faith to live for others. The ultimate goal of Wesleyanism is for those within the family of God to become God's partners in the redemption of the whole world. "The primary question for the Methodist," as I have written elsewhere, "is not, am I saved? The ultimate question is, for what purpose am I saved? For the Wesleys, the answer was clear. My neighbor is the goal of my redemption, just as the life, death and resurrection of Christ are oriented toward the salvation of all humanity."[42] "Benevolence," for the Wesleys, consisted in all efforts to realize God's shalom in the life of the world. This mission, this goodwill toward our fellow-creatures, this ministry of reconciliation, this benevolence manifests itself in particular ways in the Wesleyan tradition, but none more distinctive than outreach to the marginalized and resistance to injustice, both actions expressed through works of mercy that bear witness to God's rule over life.[43]

---

39. J. Wesley, *Works*, 2:598.

40. J. Wesley, *Works*, 3:336 (Sermon 94, "On Family Religion"). Cf. Wesley's discussion of St. Paul's conception of "neighbor love" in his exposition of 1 Cor 13:1–3 (J. Wesley, *Works*, 3:295).

41. See the exceptional study of Meistad, "Missiology of Charles Wesley: Introduction": "Because Wesleyan soteriology begins in the creation and ends in the new creation," he observes, "the transformation of the person becomes a part of the transformation of the entire cosmos (cf. Col 1:15–23; cf. Rom 8:33–39)" (49). In his examination of "The Messianic Kingdom and the Year of Jubilee," Meistad argues that the concept of "jubilee" shaped the common life of the early Christian community, leading them to share resources and care for the poor. The early Methodists modeled their lives after this pattern.

42. Chilcote, *Recapturing the Wesleys' Vision*, 101.

43. For a helpful discussion of "works of mercy," see Miles, "Works of Mercy." For the ethical implications of discipleship in the Wesleyan spirit, consult Hynson, *To Reform the Nation*; Long, *John Wesley's Moral Theology*; Marquardt, *John Wesley's Social Ethics*; and Stone, *Wesley's Life and Ethics*.

In his great family hymn, Charles Wesley bears witness to the eschatological vision of the peaceable kingdom, referring once again to the consequences of God in Christ reconciling.

> Jesu, Lord, we look to thee,
> Let us in thy name agree;
> Show thyself the Prince of peace,
> Bid our jars for ever cease.
>
> By thy reconciling love
> Every stumbling-block remove,
> Each to each unite, endear:
> Come, and spread thy banner here!
>
> Let us each for other care,
> Each the other's burden bear;
> To thy church the pattern give,
> Show how true believers live.[44]

"The first Methodists, who intended to revive the life of the original Christian church," as Tore Meistad attempted to demonstrate, "made a just distribution of economic, educational, and medical resources their top priority. This is evident in John Wesley's sermons as well as in Charles's hymns."[45]

Responding to the insanity of human strife and warfare, and using language just as relevant today as in his own age, Charles Wesley cries out in prayer for the healing of a broken world.

> Our earth we now lament to see
>   With floods of wickedness o'erflowed;
> With violence, wrong, and cruelty,
>   One wide-extended field of blood,
> Where men like fiends each other tear,
> In all the hellish rage of war.

---

44. J. Wesley, *Works*, 7:683–84 (no. 495:1–3).
45. Meistad, "Missiology of Charles Wesley: Introduction," 51.

> O might the universal Friend
> > This havoc of his creatures see!
> Bid our unnatural discord end;
> > Declare us reconciled in thee!
> Write kindness on our inward parts
> And chase the murderer from our hearts!⁴⁶

Gratitude and benevolence—love of God and love of neighbor—functioned as keynotes in the Wesleyan song of life. These are the marks of those who have been reconciled to God in Christ.

Permit me to leave you with a series of questions. It is one thing to discuss the Wesleyan understanding of "God in Christ Reconciling"; it is something quite different to permit God's reconciling love to penetrate our hearts and live right here, right now. These are the questions of John Wesley, actually, posed to his followers who had gathered for the laying of the foundation of the Methodist chapel in City Road, London. May they pierce our hearts!

> Are you a witness of the religion of love? Are you a lover of God and all mankind? Does your heart glow with gratitude to the Giver of every good and perfect gift? The Father of the spirits of all flesh, who giveth you life, and breath, and all things? Who hath given you his Son, his only Son, that you "might not perish, but have everlasting life"? Is your soul warm with benevolence to all mankind? Do you long to have all men virtuous and happy? And does the constant tenor of your life and conversation bear witness of this? Do you "love, not in word only, but in deed and in truth"? Do you persevere in the "work of faith, and the labour of love"? Do you "walk in love, as Christ also loved us, and gave himself for us"? Do you, as you have time, "do good unto all men"? And in as high a degree as you are able? "Whosoever" thus "doeth the will of my Father which is in heaven, the same is my brother, and sister, and mother." Whosoever thou art whose heart is herein as my heart, give me thine hand.⁴⁷

---

46. J. Wesley, *Works*, 7:607 (no. 430.1 and 3).
47. J. Wesley, *Works*, 3:592.

Part 3
Early Methodist Women

———————— Chapter 7 ————————

Biblical Equality and the Spirituality of Early Methodist Women

Source note: Commissioned by Christians for Biblical Equality, International, and published in *Priscilla Papers* 22.2 (Spring 2008) 11–16.

The Essential Role of Women in Early Methodism

O, blessed fountain of love! Fill my heart more with [Thy] Divine principle. Sink me lower in the depths of humility, and let me sit at the feet of Jesus, and learn of Him. Enlarge my soul, that I may better contemplate Thy glory. And may I prove myself Thy child, by bearing a resemblance to Thee, my heavenly Father![1]

THIS PRAYER OF MARY Hanson expresses the power and beauty of Christian spirituality among early Methodist women. Like Mary, most of these women remain unknown, not only to the larger Christian community, but even to contemporary Methodists. Their legacy is amazing. In an effort to introduce you to this neglected treasure and the witness of these women to biblical equality, I want to begin where they would most likely begin, in a narrative fashion. Theirs is a spirituality of biography and story. The equality of women and men in early Methodism begins in the simple fact that both had stories about their lives to tell, and all honored the testimony of their faith.

There is no question whatsoever that women played a major role within the life of the eighteenth century Wesleyan Revival, both historically and theologically.[2] The fact of female preponderance in the Methodist

---

1. Quoted in Clarke, *Memoirs of Mary Cooper*, 170–171.
2. See Chilcote, *Wesley and Women*; and *She Offered Them Christ*.

network of Societies only serves to illustrate a much larger reality.[3] Anecdotal evidence concerning the formative influence of women abounds in journals, diaries, and has been preserved in local history. Women were conspicuous as pioneers in the establishment and expansion of Methodism. They founded prayer groups and Societies, and in their attempts to bear witness to their newly discovered faith often ventured into arenas that were traditionally confined to men.

The story of Dorothy Fisher illustrates a typical missiological scenario of functional equality. Converted under John Wesley's preaching in London, Dorothy joined the Methodist Society there in 1779. She introduced Methodism to Great Gonerby in Lincolnshire in 1784 by inviting the itinerant preachers to hold services at her home after her move to the north. Two years later, she purchased a small stone building, which, after renovation, served as a Methodist chapel. Learning of Dorothy's pioneering work, Sarah Parrot (having been told by God to do so) invited her to help establish a Methodist Society in Lincoln. Discerning that this was indeed a call from God, Dorothy consented, settled her affairs, moved to Lincoln, procured a suitable residence, and commenced her pioneering labors once again in Pauline fashion. In 1788, a small Society was formed in an old lumber-room near Gowt's Bridge, consisting of four women, Dorothy Fisher, Sarah Parrot, Hannah Calder, and Elizabeth Keyley. Dorothy built yet another chapel with an adjoining residence, all of which was deeded to the Methodist Conference in later years. This story is consistent, in much of its tone and detail, with the many accounts of Methodist origins throughout the British Isles.

An excerpt from the journal of Grace Murray reveals an extensive ministry.

> Mr. Wesley fixed me in that part of the work, which he thought proper; and when the House was finished, I was appointed to be the Housekeeper. Soon also, the people were again divided into Bands, or small select Societies; women by themselves, and the men in like manner. I had full a hundred in Classes, whom I met in two separate meetings; and a Band for each day of the week. I likewise visited the Sick and Backsliders . . . We had also several Societies in the country, which I regularly visited; meeting the women in the daytime, and in the evening the whole society. And oh, what pourings out of the Spirit have I seen at those times![4]

---

3. For a full discussion of the evidence related to female initiative in the formation and establishment of Methodist Societies, see Chilcote, *Wesley and Women*, 49–54.

4. Bennet, *Memoirs of Grace Bennet*, 13–14. Cf. Chilcote, *Wesley and Women*, 74–75.

There is no question that women were preponderant in the movement, functioned as some of its most indefatigable pioneers, and even preached in the network of Methodist Societies that stretched the length and breadth of Britain. A little more than two years after the establishment of the Foundery Society in London, John Wesley drew up the first list of sixty-six leaders. Of this group of formative leaders within nascent Methodism, forty-seven were women. This example from the heart of the early movement is typical of the whole. Early records of the Society in Bristol afford similar evidence with a two-to-one ratio of women to men.[5] Such female presence and influence begs the question, What led them to this elevated status and made possible the roles that they assumed alongside the Methodist men of their day?

Factors that Opened Doors for Women

Certainly a wealth of factors combined both in the founder and the movement to create a climate conducive to the acceptance and empowerment of women. Three factors, however, seem to have been particularly significant.[6]

The Personal Influence of John Wesley

Firstly, the elevated status of women within the Wesleyan Revival cannot be understood apart from the person of John Wesley. Much of his appreciation for the place of women in the life of the church can be traced to his formative years in the Epworth rectory. Largely due to the influence of his mother, Susanna, Wesley seldom wavered from this fundamental principle: No one, including a woman, ought to be prohibited from doing God's work in obedience to the inner calling of her conscience. This conviction would later lead him not only to sanction but to encourage the controversial practice of women's preaching. Wesley was an outspoken advocate for the rights of women in an era of tremendous social upheaval. Many statements from his sermons and treatises reflect his desire to translate spiritual equality into day-to-day reality in the lives of women.

---

5. Exclusively female Societies were noteworthy in the early years of the revival and actually elicited some of Wesley's antagonists' most biting criticism concerning the founder and his intentions. There can be no doubt that women wielded tremendous influence during these critical years wherever Methodism was planted and flourished. See Chilcote, *Wesley and Women*, 60–61.

6. These three themes were first identified in Chilcote, "Empowerment of Women," 1–3.

The Liberating Environment of the Methodist Society

Secondly, the Methodist Societies, which were *ecclesiolae in ecclesia* (little churches within the church) functioning as catalysts of renewal inside the established church and composed of still smaller groups known as class and band meetings, provided a liberating environment for women.[7] One of the unique features of early Methodism was its capacity to create its own leadership from within. The early pioneers who were responsible for the initiation of new Societies naturally assumed positions of leadership. The large extent to which women functioned in this sphere was a major factor contributing to the inclusiveness and vitality of the movement. By allowing women to assume important positions of leadership within the structure of the Societies, Wesley gave concrete expression to the freedom he proclaimed in his preaching. The end result was that individuals who stood impotently on the periphery of British society were empowered and gifted for service in the world. Women, who were otherwise disenfranchised in a world dominated by men, began to develop a new sense of self-esteem and purpose.

The Egalitarian Impulse of Wesleyan Theology and "Concern for Biblical Equality"

While John and Charles Wesley and their followers never used the language of "biblical equality," nor would they have felt compelled to do so, their theology was founded upon an understanding of the New Testament community that bore witness to a radical new vision of life in Christ for all of God's children. This third element—a cohesive and dynamic matrix of biblical and theological principles—merits more thorough exploration because this egalitarian impulse was integral to the spirituality of the early Methodist women. Egalitarianism within the Methodist movement was not unique; rather, it was founded upon certain principles held in common with historic movements of Christian renewal. Included among these were the value of the individual soul, the possibility of direct communion with God, the emphasis on the present activity of the Holy Spirit in the life of the believer, the importance placed upon shared Christian experience, the rights of conscience, and the doctrine of the priesthood of all believers. These views all combined to create a theological environment conducive to the empowerment of women.

---

7. For a full account of the rise and development of the Methodist Societies, see J. Wesley, *Works*, 9:1–29. Cf. Baker, "People Called Methodists, 3. Polity."

John Wesley's goal was personal religious experience and its power to transform both individuals and society. His dynamic view of salvation and the Christian life, evoked by a gift of grace, tended to transcend gender and social differences. His stress on charismatic leadership fostered a leveling sentiment among the Methodists. The unity and equality of all believers in Christ became an inherent aspect of the evangelical preaching of Wesleyan itinerants. Not only was faith to be expressed in the works of all, but also individual talents were to be developed as a sacred trust from God. One of the Methodist preachers, William Bramwell, in his own preaching encouraged women to exercise their gifts. He observed in one sermon, "Why are there not more women preachers? Because they are not faithful to their call."[8] Women interpreted his rebuke as a clarion call to respond in faithfulness, and they received his strong support when they did. These attitudes undercut prevailing stereotypes about the status and role of women in society. Thus, the phenomenon of female leadership was a natural progression, a logical extension of the Wesleyan theology of religious experience.

Given the Opportunities, Women Exercised Leadership

The primary training ground for the women was the small group and primarily band and class meeting leadership. It was within this arena that women found the widest range of opportunity. These leaders stood nearest to the rank and file of the movement, and for this reason occupied a strategic position within the Societies. The primary function of these leaders was to assist their Methodist brothers and sisters in a common quest for holiness. Appointment to such an office was based primarily upon one's ability to empathize with the spiritual and temporal struggles of the members for whom they cared. Of the other offices in which women functioned as pioneers, the most important include those of housekeepers, visitors of the sick, preacher's wives, and local and traveling preachers.[9]

Of much greater significance than might be inferred from the title, housekeeper was an office within the Methodist institutional structure, which entailed serious managerial and spiritual responsibilities.[10] Sarah Ryan was one of the earliest housekeepers and viewed her provision of hospitality and the maintenance of order among her appointed "family" to be serious aspects of her Christian vocation and spirituality. Another office in which the early

---

8. See Chilcote, *Her Own Story*, 175.

9. See Brown, "Standing in the Shadow"; "Women of the Word"; and "Feminist Theology."

10. See Chilcote, *Wesley and Women*, 68, 74–75, 125.

Methodist women excelled was that of sick visitor. Wesley first developed this office in London in 1741, but described this important role in his *Plain Account of the People Called Methodists*: "It is the business of a Visitor of the sick, to see every sick person within his district thrice a week. To inquire into the state of their souls, and to advise them as occasion may require . . . What was Phebe the Deaconess, but such a Visitor of the sick?"[11]

Wesley also approved and promoted the preaching ministry of women in his evolving movement. He had come to the affirmation of women preachers over time, and not without some personal struggle; but once he was convinced that God was working through a whole host of women called to preach, he embraced their work on behalf of his movement wholeheartedly. A number of these women were key players in the amazing drama of female liberation and promotion. Primary among them are Sarah Crosby, the first authorized woman preacher; Margaret Davidson, blind evangelist and first woman preacher in Ireland; Hannah Harrison; Elizabeth Hurrell; Sarah Mallet; Dorothy Ripley; Mary Stokes; and Mary Taft, greatest female evangelist of the nineteenth century, among others. Whether a member of this illustrious band or a simple class leader in a local Society, however, in the multiplicity of the offices they assumed, early Methodist women functioned as co-workers, pastors, and partners in God's renewal of the church. They felt free to express themselves and exercise their gifts. They led the Methodist family in their simple acts of worship and service. They were the glue that held Wesleyanism together on the most practical levels of its existence. Men and women functioned as equals in the life of the movement, and this egalitarianism was built upon a solid biblical foundation.

Wesley's analysis of Matthew 25:36, "I was sick and you visited me," elicited one of his most radical statements, not only concerning the working equality of women in the life of the church, but of their legitimate and noble place within the order of creation, as well.

> "But may not *women* as well as men bear a part in this honourable service?" Undoubtedly they may; nay, they ought—it is meet, right, and their bounden duty. Herein there is no difference; "there is neither male nor female in Christ Jesus." Indeed it has long passed for a maxim with many that "women are only to be seen, not heard." And accordingly many of them are brought up in such a manner as if they were only designed for agreeable playthings! But is this doing honour to the sex? Or is it a real kindness to them? No; it is the deepest unkindness; it is horrid cruelty; it is mere Turkish barbarity. And I know not how any

---

11. J. Wesley, *Works*, 26:55–56.

woman of sense and spirit can submit to it. Let all you that have it in your power assert the right which the God of nature has given you. Yield not to that vile bondage any longer. You, as well as men, are rational creatures. You, like them, were made in the image of God: you are equally candidates for immortality. You too are called of God, as you have time, to "do good unto all men." Be "not disobedient to the heavenly calling." Whenever you have opportunity, do all the good you can, particularly to your poor sick neighbour. And every one of *you* likewise "shall receive *your* own reward according to your own labor."[12]

Despite the fact that this statement came late, published first in 1786, the practice itself was extremely early, and Wesley's sentiments on this practice were consistent throughout his lifetime.

Women Preachers

It was the venture of women into preaching more than anything else, however, that tested the egalitarian principle, and the Bible was brought to bear on both sides of the argument. St. Paul's purported prohibitions against such a practice, such as 1 Corinthians 14:34 and 1 Timothy 2:12, were marshaled against the first women preachers.[13] Wesley's initial recourse with regard to the women in these instances, as was the case with regard to his defense of lay preaching in general, was always to "an extraordinary impulse of the Spirit." He viewed these more "radical activities" as exceptions to the general rule; but over time, as more and more exceptions arose, the preaching ministry of women became a de facto rule, and no longer an exception, within the life of the Methodist Societies.

The first to really press the full equality of women in the preaching ministry of the church was Mary Bosanquet. During the summer of 1771, in a letter to John Wesley, she developed a lengthy defense of the practice, similar to the classic statement of Margaret Fell in *Womens Speaking Justified*.[14] She carefully considers the classic "prohibitions" and addresses six objections. Her first conclusion is that the so-called prohibitive passages refer to specific situations in which certain women were meddling with church discipline and do not apply, therefore, to women in general or preaching in particular. She points to the internal contradiction in Paul's own statements,

---

12. J. Wesley, *Works*, 3:395–96.

13. For a discussion of early exchanges on these texts, see Chilcote, *Wesley and Women*, 118–23.

14. See Chilcote, *Wesley and Women*, 141–45, and the full text of the letter, 299–304.

barring them from speaking at one point and admonishing them to cover their heads while prophesying at another (1 Cor 11:5). Limiting the speaking of women to times of "peculiar impulse" places too severe a limitation, she believes, on the gracious activity of God. She rejects the notion that women's preaching is "immodest," pointing to the examples of Mary, the woman of Samaria, the handmaid of Second Samuel 20, and Deborah, all of whom were characterized by purity and humility yet publicly declared the message of the Lord. To the claim that all these instances were extraordinary calls, she retorts: "If I did not believe so, I would not act in an extraordinary manner.—I praise my God, I feel him very near, and I prove his faithfulness every day." As a consequence, Wesley not only permitted such activities among the women, but encouraged them more and more.

Characteristics of Wesleyan Theology

Commitment to these biblical egalitarian principles shaped the spirituality of the early Methodist people. Before turning to several distinctive characteristics related to the spirituality of early Methodist women, it might prove helpful to survey some of the common, salient themes of Wesleyan spirituality, namely, the foundation of grace, spiritual autobiography and the narrative of liberation, accountable discipleship and the communal nature of spirituality, works of piety (including prayer and fasting, immersion in Scripture, worship and Eucharist), and works of mercy.

The Foundation of Grace

Christian discipleship—the arena of God's continuing activity in the life of the believer—is, first and foremost, a grace-filled response to God's all-sufficient grace. Since God's grace is available to all, it privileges none more than others. Grace, as it was experienced and understood among the Methodists, exerted a profound and universal leveling influence. All are equal in God's eyes, because God's grace is extended to all.[15]

Spiritual Autobiography and the Narrative of Spiritual Liberation

Wesley believed that all Christian faith is autobiographical.[16] Everyone, no one excluded, has a story to tell, and central to the narrative of the early

15. See J. Wesley, *Works*, 3:542–63.
16. I have discussed this important matter in Chilcote, *Her Own Story*, 14–18.

Methodists was the experience of conversion—a process involving a call to personal repentance, moral transformation, and concomitant freedom to love. Not only was this experience possible for both women and men alike; it was viewed as essential. The decisive conclusion to be drawn from the accounts of women in particular, however, is that salvation essentially meant liberation. This newfound freedom, more often than not, was rooted in the concept of "new creation," and this experienced liberation challenged all forms of bondage and discrimination.

Accountable Discipleship and the Communal Nature of Spirituality

Intimate circles of married and single women, the Wesleyan band meetings under the leadership of women, were the primary locus of spiritual accountability. Characterized by close fellowship and stricter obligations, the bands were potent in the empowerment of women and the development of their spiritual gifts. The primary purpose of these bands was intense personal introspection coupled with rigorous mutual confession for those who were "pressing on to perfection."[17] It was in these intimate groups that friendship and fellowship emerged as critical aspects of a developing Wesleyan spirituality. The Christian fellowship and intimacy provided through the class and band meetings, for the women in particular, were a potent means of grace. In the intimacy of these small groups, and particularly the bands, women learned what it meant and were given equal opportunity to grow in Christ. Together they plumbed the depths of God's love for them all.

Works of Piety

The "means of grace," namely, prayer and fasting, Bible study, Christian fellowship, and participation in the sacrament of Holy Communion, not only nurtured and sustained their growth in grace, but also provided the "energy" which fueled the Wesleyan movement as a powerful religious awakening.[18] No means of grace was as important to the Wesleys or the women as the sacrament of the Lord's Supper. The early Methodists sang, and the women bore witness to the testimony of the hymn,

> The prayer, the fast, the word conveys,
>
> When mix'd with faith, Thy life to me;

---

17. See Davies, *History of the Methodist Church*, 1:213–55.
18. The most important recent work on this topic is Knight, *Presence of God*.

> In all the channels of Thy grace
> I still have fellowship with Thee:
> But chiefly here my soul is fed
> With fulness of immortal bread.[19]

These "feasts of love," as the women often described them, shaped their understanding of God's love for them and their reciprocal love for God, all powerfully symbolized for them in the sharing of a meal.

Works of Mercy

Those who encountered the good news of the gospel and were subsequently drawn into Christian communities of love were also propelled into the world with a mission of witness and service. Again, none were excluded from this categorical imperative.

Wesleyan spirituality always demonstrates an essential concern for social justice and mission rooted in evangelical faith. The women of early Methodism were people of vision, and the image of the church they lived out was one of active social service, commitment to the poor, and advocacy for the spiritually, politically, and socially oppressed. For the women there could be no separation of their personal experience of God in Christ from their active role as agents of reconciliation and social transformation in the world. Their autobiographical portraits are bold images of people living in and for God's vision of shalom. The women had learned from the Wesleys that authentic Christianity is mission and sincere engagement in God's mission is true religion. The center of this missiological calling and identity, moreover, was simply their desire to share the good news they had experienced in Christ with others. In other words, in their view, the heart of mission was evangelism.

Implications for Women

Methodist women, therefore, sought out people in need—the poor, the hungry, the destitute and the neglected. They preached the Word, visited prisons, established orphanages and schools, and practiced their servant-oriented faith as devoted mothers who discerned the presence of God in

---

19. Wesley and Wesley, *Hymns on the Lord's Supper*, 39 (no. 54.4). Cf. Rattenbury, *Eucharistic Hymns*, 176–249. For a discussion of the sacrament as an "effective means of grace," see Borgen, *Wesley on the Sacraments*, 183–217.

the most menial of chores. Hardly passive Christians for whom ministry was performed; these women were active, ministering servants who cared for one another and extended their ministry into the communities they served. The advice of Wesley to a Methodist woman aspiring to "perfection" is a typical expression of this gospel alongside the poor: "Go and see the poor and sick in their own little hovels. Take up your cross, woman! Remember the faith! Jesus went before you, and will go with you. Put off the gentlewoman: You bear a higher character."[20]

In her preface to the life of Elizabeth Mortimer, Agnes Bulmer claims that the central thrust of early Methodist women's lives was "a renovated spirit, and a holy life."[21] She provides a simple definition of "spirituality" that helps frame the distinctive features of the spirituality lived out by women like the subject of her biography. Spirituality involves every aspect of life, she maintains, that demonstrates "there is a real, a delightful, a transforming intercourse to which the human spirit is admitted with the ever-blessed God."[22] In addition to the various aspects of spirituality held in common with many of the early Methodist men, the spirituality of early Methodist women is distinctive in its revolution around *pathos* (mystery in life), beauty (majesty in life), and love (miracle in life). The egalitarian impulse of the Wesleyan movement made it possible for the women to develop a spirituality that was real, blessed, and loving. Rather than being compelled to conform to a preconceived masculine mold, they were able to embrace their own unique giftedness as women within the life of the movement.

A Spirituality of Pathos—the Mystery in Life

Early Methodist women were masters at practicing the presence of God. They managed to find God in the common round of daily life. Because of this their writings reflect a healthy realism grounded in the ordinary, the tragedies and triumphs of real life. In her manuscript journal, Mary Entwisle reflects upon the death of her son. Her meditations are filled with *pathos*. She asks the deepest questions of her soul. She struggles. She expresses her anger. She lives in despair, but hope eventually breaks through. One line out of her extended narrative related to the birth of a child under extremely harrowing circumstances speaks volumes with regard to the

---

20. Jackson, *Letters of John Wesley*, 6:153–54, in a letter to Miss March (June 9, 1775). For an excellent discussion of Wesley's "preferential option for the poor," see Jennings, *Good News to the Poor*, 47–69.
21. Bulmer, *Memoirs of Elizabeth Mortimer*, 7.
22. Bulmer, *Memoirs of Elizabeth Mortimer*, 10.

experience of women and the nature of their spirituality: "[God] made me the living mother of a living child."[23]

A Spirituality of Beauty—the Majestic in Life

These amazing women were quick to make connections between life in the Spirit and the wonders of creation. Not so much a "creation-centered" spirituality, theirs was an aesthetic spirituality that valued beauty in all its variety. Mary Hanson writes in a letter to a friend:

> My garden begins to demand my renewed labours. When will you inhale the fragrance of my roses, and help me to admire the kindness of our God in providing so much innocent pleasure for the delight of the senses? The study of nature is still my favourite recreation; but to increase in the love and knowledge of God almost swallows up every other desire.[24]

She writes in her journal:

> How delightful is the contemplation of the works of God! My enraptured eye runs over the productions of the earth with a curiosity and interest that never leave me. The passing clouds, the opening flowers, the sweet river, whose constant changes give a variety to the scenes. How successively do these steal on my imagination, and oft-times how inexpressible is my gratitude for receiving from the hands of God so many outward blessings.[25]

A Spirituality of Love—the Miracle in Life

The language of spirituality that is more pervasive than any other in the writings of the early Methodist women is related to their overwhelming sense of God's presence. It is the language of the heart filled with love. Linked directly in the Methodist mind to holiness, this image often carries with it the overtones of humility, purification, and the miraculous wonder of in-filling love. Here is a spirituality of love. Holiness equals love; love equals holiness, and all is miracle as the faithful live out their lives on the

---

23. Entwisle, *Manuscript Journal.*
24. Clarke, *Memoirs of Mary Cooper*, 87.
25. Clarke, *Memoirs of Mary Cooper*, 123–24.

foundation of God's grace.[26] Mary Fletcher expresses it well in these words of admonition to her fellow disciples in Christ:

> that you would therefore do as Jacob did, be earnest with the Lord, that his love may fill your heart, as the Scripture expresses it, the love of God, shed abroad in your hearts by the Holy Ghost, given unto you. If you get your hearts full of the love of God, you will find that is the oil by which the lamp of faith will be ever kept burning . . . Pray, my friends, pray much for this love; and remember that word, "He that dwelleth in love dwelleth in God, and God in him!"[27]

Conclusion

In the Wesleyan tradition, a disciple with a living faith is the one whose whole heart has been renewed, who longs to radiate the whole image of God in his or her life and therefore hears the cry of the poor and wills, with God, that all should truly live! Those who are truly servants of Christ in the world empty themselves of all but love and find their greatest reward in the realization of God's dream of shalom for all. This is the living legacy of the early Methodist women for us today. The "Hymn, In Honour of Jesus," by the blind Irish preacher, Margaret Davidson, is an amazing vision of the final triumph of God's love in the world. It is also a fitting conclusion to this discussion of the spirituality of early Methodist women—a life lived, a ministry engaged, in equal partnership with all of God's children.

> Contrain'd by energy divine
>
> To call my Jesus ever mine,
>
> I languish to be all like thee,
>
> Till lost in thy immensity:
>
> Struggling into thy dear breast,
>
> Lord, I enter,
>
> And there center,
>
> Happy in thy glorious rest.

---

26. Elsewhere I have discussed the connection between holiness and happiness in the writings of early Methodist women. Their conception of the Christian life could equally be described as a spirituality of happiness or blessedness. See Chilcote, "Sanctification," 93–95.

27. Quoted in Tooth, *Letter to Madeley*, 17–18.

I wait till wafted up to thee,
O thou mysterious One in Three
By love's incircling arms caress'd,
And with a view of glory bless'd,
Now I Abba, Father, cry—
The same blessing,
Without ceasing,
Pour on all below the sky.

Then hallelujahs shall we raise
Superior to Angelic lays,
Whilst we adore a bleeding God,
Who bought, and cleans'd us with his blood—
Cast our crown before his feet,
Self-abasing—
Jesus praising—

Lost in transport, endless, sweet.[28]

---

28. Smyth, *Margaret Davidson*, 162–64, sts. 3, 4, and 6 of the original hymn.

Chapter 8

An Early Methodist Community of Women

Source note: Published in *Methodist History* 38.4 (July 2000) 219–30.

EARLY METHODISM WAS COMPRISED of many small communities of women. The preponderance of women in the Wesleyan Revival as a whole only illustrates quantitatively a much larger reality, yet to be fully explored. From time to time, these women drew themselves together into intentional communities in which the rhythms of mutual accountability and active social service modeled vital Christianity to the world around them. What is of particular interest were communities of women that involved a common life in the sense of actually living together and experiencing Christian community in a cenobitic or semi-monastic style of life. Mary Bosanquet was the center of one such community, the influence and legacy of which were critical to the history of early Methodism.[1]

In 1763, a property near her place of birth in Leytonstone, known locally as "The Cedars," became vacant. Mary and Sarah Ryan (the friend whom John Wesley would later describe as her "twin soul") moved there on March 24 with the intention of establishing an orphanage and school on the basis of Wesley's own prototype at Kingswood.[2] John Wesley kept this model Christian com-

---

1. The standard biographical account of Mary, without any question one of the most prominent figures in Wesley's Methodism, is that of Moore, *Life of Mary Fletcher*, which passed through numerous editions on both sides of the Atlantic during the nineteenth century. Perhaps no life was so well known to the women of early Methodism as that of Mary. A number of her publications, including her able defense of women's preaching, *Letter to the Rev. John Wesley* (1764), a catechetical writing entitled *An Aunt's Advice to Her Niece* (1780), and her *Thoughts on Communion with Happy Spirits* were widely circulated and extremely influential both during and after her lifetime.

2. A part of Sarah's responsibilities as housekeeper at the New Room in Bristol was the management of Wesley's school from 1757 to 1761. For background information

munity, combining vibrant personal piety and active social service, under his personal surveillance. On December 1, 1764, he expressed his optimism and great expectations concerning its progress. "M[ary] B[osanquet] gave me a further account of their affairs at Leytonstone. It is exactly *Pietas Hallensis* in miniature. What it will be does not yet appear."[3] The following year, on December 12, 1765, he reported, "I rode over to Leytonstone, and found *one truly Christian family*. This is what that at Kingswood *should be*—and *would*, if it had such governors."[4]

After much careful deliberation the women decided to take in none but the most destitute and hopeless. The children came, as Mary recalled, "naked, full of vermin, and some afflicted with distemper." At first, the family consisted of Mary, Sarah, a maid, and Sally Lawrence, Sarah Ryan's orphaned niece of about four years of age. With the addition of five more orphans and confronted with the problem of Sarah's declining health, Ann Tripp was secured as a governess for the children. They formed themselves into a tightly knit community, adopted a uniform dress of dark purple cotton, and ate together at a table five yards in length. Over the course of five years, they sheltered and cared for thirty-five children and thirty-four adults.

In Mary's account of this community, she observed that "the first Light Given Concerning outward things was that we should walk according to Rule in our family."[5] The children rose to dress in time for family prayers at 6:30. Breakfast followed at 7:00, with play until 8:00, when a full morning of educational activities commenced. An hour of free time preceded the midday meal at 1:00. Three hours of study and an hour devoted to household

---

concerning the design and implementation of this project, see Ives, *Kingswood School*, 7–51. Education, as we shall see, was a particular emphasis of Continental Pietism, and to this end, A.H. Francke's Orphan-school in Halle, shaped in part by the model of Duke Ernest the Pious of Gotha, gave classical expression to this aspiration.

3. J. Wesley, *Works*, 21:495. Cf. Schmidt, *John Wesley*, 2:175–86. This "further account" supplemented the pamphlet that she had published anonymously under Wesley's auspices in November, *Letter to the Rev. Mr. John Wesley. By a Gentlewoman*. Further research is required to determine the relationship between this document and an improperly identified manuscript in the Methodist Archives bearing the title, *An Account of the Rise and Progress of the Work of God in Latonstone, Essex, 1763*, which is in Mary Bosanquet's unmistakable hand. Elizabeth Ritchie was identified originally as the authoress, and the volume then catalogued under Sarah Ryan, whose authorship was uncritically accepted by Brown. See Brown, *Women of Mr. Wesley's Methodism*, 53–59. This small duodecimo volume includes the record of a diary in Mary Bosanquet's hand as well, the entries of which, concluding on January 11, 1765, are followed by fragments last dated August 24, 1768. From this account it is clear that Mary commenced her work in Hoxton Square in February 1761.

4. J. Wesley, *Works*, 22:26.

5. Bosanquet, *Account*.

duties filled the afternoon, with supper at 6:00. Family prayers followed at 7:30 with an early bedtime of 8:00. "Family meetings," which were held on Fridays at noon, provided an opportunity for the community to gather together, to discuss and make decisions concerning their rule of life. Decision-making apparently included all members of the community, adults and children alike. Mary's primary responsibilities, according to her own report, included planning and leading worship, caring for the sustenance of the community, teaching the children, meeting each member of the family alone each week at a set time to discuss personal and spiritual matters, superintending public meetings, and caring for the sick of the community.[6] For all intents and purposes, Mary functioned as an "abbess" of a religious community, whose influence in worship and religious life extended not simply to the "Leytonstone family," but to the surrounding community, as well.

It is not clear when Sarah Crosby became directly connected with the community of women and children at Leytonstone, but as early as September 1766, Wesley was sending letters to her at that address.[7] From that point on, it is clear that the lives of the three women, Mary and the two Sarahs, became inextricably interwoven. On February 12, 1767, Wesley was delighted by the effective ministry of the community and, after preaching at Leytonstone, exclaimed, "O what an house of God is here! Not only for decency and order, but for the life and power of religion! I am afraid there are very few such to be found in all the king's dominions."[8] Having established a definitive pattern of life together on a semi-monastic model of austere communal life, disciplined religious contemplation, and service to the needy, this community transplanted its ideals to a northern setting in Yorkshire in the year 1768.

Despite Sarah Ryan's death shortly after their resettlement at "Cross Hall," near Leeds, the family soon became a vital center of Methodist worship and witness, as it had been in London. The life of the community was disrupted in 1781, however, when Mary fell in love with and married John Fletcher, the saintly vicar of Madeley and Wesley's "designated successor." The property was sold and places were found for the remnant "women of Israel in Yorkshire," as they were affectionately known. Sarah Crosby and Ann Tripp seem to have taken up residence in Leeds with these changes, the community of women experiencing something of a metamorphosis in

---

6. Moore, *Fletcher*, 76.

7. See Telford, *Letters of John Wesley*, 5:25–26. It is interesting to note that the letters exchanged at this time between Wesley and the community often reflect a critical disposition of the women toward Wesley's spiritual experience. See in particular, his letter to Sarah Ryan (5:17–18).

8. J. Wesley, *Works*, 22:70.

the process. According to J.E. Hellier, they lived in a small house adjoining the parent chapel of the original Society in Leeds, known as the Old Boggard House. Ann and Sarah together assumed leadership of a strong and influential band of women preachers, known, with unconscious humor perhaps, as the "Female Brethren."[9]

Mary Fletcher lived out the remainder of her life in her beloved Madeley where she died in 1815, but had left behind a "rule" for the forming of good societies, both a legacy and a blueprint which must have guided Sarah and Ann, and those who joined them, in their life together.

1. Consider no one a member who is not steadily seeking after Christian perfection; that is a heart simplified by love divine.

2. Come together with a lively expectation our souls should be refreshed by our meeting, as our bodies should be refreshed by our food.

3. Bear with each other's mistakes or infirmities in love.

4. Be well aware of that deadly poison so frequent among professors, I mean evil-speaking.

5. Hold Fast the Truth.

6. Be always ready to give an account to those who ask you a reason of the hope that is in you. Here is the command to testify freely.

7. Keep your eyes fixed on Christ, your Head.

8. Consider yourselves as united by a holy covenant to God and to each other; aiming to advance the glory of God all you possibly can.[10]

John Wesley had already made an explicit connection between this unique community of women in its original setting and the so-called *Stiftungen* of August Hermann Francke in his observation that they were "exactly *Pietas Hallensis* in miniature."[11] The close connections between Continental

---

9. Hellier, "Mother Chapel of Leeds," 64. The insufficiency of records and the lack of reliable data make it difficult to determine the precise composition of this group or what their common life was like. It would seem likely, however, that Elizabeth Hurrell and Sarah Stevens participated in these new developments, and it would be surprising if, in later years, Mary Barritt did not play some part in the enterprise, as well.

10. Moore, *Fletcher*, 80–82.

11. Francke (1663–1727), German Pietist and educational pioneer, was a follower of Philipp Jakob Spener, Lutheran founder of the movement and author of the pietist manifesto, *Pia Desideria*. After study at Erfurt and Kiel, and a first teaching appointment as lecturer at Leipzig, he was appointed in 1692 to the new university at Halle, which thereafter became a center of Pietist influence. On Francke, see Sattler, *God's Glory, Neighbor's Good*. Cf. Erb, *Pietists*, 97–215, on Francke and the Halle School. The classic works on the movement remain Ritschl, *Geschichte des Pietismus*; Schmidt, *Pietismus*; and the two-volume work of Stoeffler, *Rise of Pietism*; and *German Pietism*.

Pietism and the Wesleyan movement, particularly through the relationship of the Wesleys to its Moravian expression, are well known and do not need to be rehearsed here.[12] What is of significance is the striking affinity, in both spirit and methodology, of the Leytonstone experiment and Francke's Halle/Glaucha enterprise. While the exact extent of Mary Bosanquet's knowledge of Francke's work is difficult to ascertain, it would appear that the Orphan-house *Stiftung* (Institute) founded by him in Halle in 1695 was a primary model for her own community, the major difference being its exclusively female character.

Francke's practical spirituality is tersely summarized in the title of Sattler's recent biographical study, *God's Glory, Neighbor's Good*. The characteristic foci of the Pietist program of church renewal are all present in his distinctive communities, but more important than anything else was his rediscovery of *tätige Liebe* (active love) as the most important aspect of the life of faith. This lofty ideal of "active love conjoined to faith" was most appropriately realized, he believed, in a Christian *koinonia* (community) that lived out its faith in service to the world. This is precisely what Wesley discerned in his visits to the Leytonstone family and what elicited his strong statements of support and hope. In both Glaucha and Halle, Francke had provided a redemptive alternative to the poorhouse, workhouse, and penal institution in one wholistic model. The Leytonstone family was nothing less than this, but certainly more.

While the parallelism between the Halle and Leytonstone Orphan-schools is striking, even more dramatic are the similarities with the Beguine communities of the medieval world. Leslie Church was the first to allude to this fascinating connection in his description of the Leytonstone community as "a school, an orphanage, a hospital and a kind of *beguinage* for poor widows."[13] The beguines have been described as the "first European women's movement."[14] Essentially, these were pious women who chose to lead communal lives of prayer and service, first founding their communities (known as beguinages) in the twelfth century in the Netherlands and Belgium. They lived a semi-monastic and somewhat austere communal life without vows. While free to maintain private property, to leave the community, and even to marry, they generally made an informal vow to remain celibate while

---

12. See in particular, Towlson, *Moravian and Methodist*; Schmidt, *John Wesley*; and Snyder, *Radical Wesley*.

13. Church, *More about Early Methodist People*, 189. No effort is made in this work, however, to expand the image or to identify critical points of convergence.

14. Bowie, *Beguine Spirituality*, 13. Cf. McDonnel, *Beguines and Beghards*; and Lerner, *Heresy of the Free Spirit*, 35–54.

living as beguines.[15] A host of factors gave rise to this movement, including major demographic and social disruptions, in addition to shifting currents of religious enthusiasm, in the late medieval world. The breadth and depth of the movement defy simplistic conclusions of any kind. While the intrinsic nature of the movement mitigated against the development of a single style or pattern of life, however, Colledge notes (in the form of a generalization) the unique contribution which the beguines made to the development of Christian community: "Free from monastic enclosure, observing the rules which they themselves devised to meet the needs of individual communities, following lives of intense activity which might be devoted to prayer, to teaching and study, to charitable works, or to all three," they afforded a new model of religious contemplation and service to the world.[16]

It was customary for each beguinage to appoint one or more "grand mistresses," whose responsibility it was to administer the community and order its life. Younger aspiring women were placed under the care of older, mature beguines who guided them through an informal novitiate of one or two years. "Taking the habit" marked an important turning point in the life of each candidate, as Fiona Bowie explains,

> The beguine habit evolved only slowly. In the early days beguines dressed much as other women, although more simply, avoiding expensive cloth and ornamentation, but eventually a grey or blue habit, which from the seventeenth century became black with a white head covering, was adopted. If the "novice mistress" and council considered the applicant suited to beguine life the candidate would make a simple promise to "offer themselves to Christ," to "live religiously all their lives" or "to serve the Lord Jesus Christ in the habit of a beguine."[17]

While life from one community to another could vary greatly, a number of common elements can be discerned. A monastic pattern of prayer and

---

15. Most noteworthy, perhaps, among the beguines were three thirteenth-century women, Mechthild of Magdeburg, Beatrice of Nazareth, and Hadewijch of Brabant, whose mystical writings have been rediscovered in our time.

16. Colledge, *Medieval Netherlands Religious Literature*, 8. For a particularly incisive discussion of "Group Life within the Beguinehouse" and a discussion of the distinction between "prebendal" (private interest) and "corporative" (common consciousness) communities, see Phillips, *Beguines*, 156–59. Their mystical tendencies and sympathies with heterodox movements of the same era eventually led to their dissolution. Following a century of persecution the beguines had become little more than charitable institutions by the fifteenth century and were nearly extinguished entirely at the time of the French Revolution.

17. Bowie, *Beguine Spirituality*, 23; quoting Southern, *Western Society*, 326.

devotion provided the "spiritual rhythm" of the house. The women were expected to attend mass daily, to set aside time for meditational reading and reflection, to say the Divine Office, and to observe the penitential and celebrative traditions of medieval Catholicism. Weaving, bleaching, carding, and spinning filled those hours of the day set apart from devotional practices and social services among the poor. In contrast to the convents of the day that catered to the needs of the gentry and nobility, teaching was reserved for those children who were marginalized and deprived of education. This led to large numbers of resident children and orphans in many of the homes. According to Bowie, a 1646 census of the Great Beguinage in Leuven revealed "a total of 272 children living in about sixty different houses (out of a total of around a hundred), the number of children exceeding that of beguines."[18]

The parallels are striking. This could just as easily be a description of the Leytonstone family of early Methodism. While there is no evidence that Mary had any direct knowledge of the beguine tradition, the kindredness of spirit is unmistakable. There is a connectedness here to the roots of a common inheritance, a practical spirituality in the Catholic tradition, a way of life that was exerting such a critical influence upon the Wesleys themselves during the early years of the revival.[19] In addition to the well-documented influence of Catholic devotional writers, such as Thomas á Kempis, Brother Lawrence, and Gregory Lopez, or the post-Tridentine Catholic works of Blaise Pascal and Madame Bourignon, the influence of two exemplars of the Catholic spiritual tradition is striking with regards to its potential connection to the women's communities via Wesley.

According to Butler, "in 1758 Wesley claimed that de Renty's *Life* was his favourite book; certainly it was the one that he quoted from most in his later life."[20] Among the reasons for Wesley's love of de Renty which Eamon Duffy has identified in his incisive study of "Wesley and the Counter Reformation," he includes the Marquis' charitable work for the poor, the simplicity and austerity of his style of life, and his promotion of religious societies in Paris and Toulouse.[21] Fenelon, famed Archbishop of Cambrai, exerted a second, powerful influence, especially in his concept of "true simplicity" in the Christian life, what Wesley would have described as "singleness of eye." In one of the Archbishop's letters to the Duke of Burgundy, reproduced by Wesley in his *Christian Library*, he speaks eloquently of the love of friends. "The love

---

18. Bowie, *Beguine Spirituality*, 26.

19. See Orcibal, "Theological Originality," 1:83–111; Butler, *Methodists and Papists*, 141–58; Massa, "Catholic Wesley"; and Tuttle, *Mysticism*.

20. Butler, *Methodists and Papists*, 143.

21. Duffy, "Wesley and Counter Reformation."

of God," which, according to Fenelon is resident in the heart of the believer, "loves its friends without views of self-interest, and so loves them patiently with all their faults; it seeks no more but what God has given them; it looks to nothing in them but God and his gifts."[22] Wesley and his Leytonstone women, with their dual imperative of love for God and love for neighbor, certainly resonated with the Catholic spirit of this practical mysticism.

All of these connections should make Mary Bosanquet's virtually unknown 1766 tract, entitled *Jesus, Altogether Lovely*, somewhat less of a surprise, but the form and nature of the spiritual direction she provides is truly astounding. Published in the same year as Wesley's *Plain Account of Christian Perfection*, this tract is actually a letter written from Hoxton on March 10, 1763, just two weeks prior to her settlement at Leytonstone with Sarah Ryan. When seen within the context of this critical development, on the very eve of their inauguration of a semi-monastic community for women, the document takes on heightened significance. "My desire and prayer to God for you," writes Mary to a group of unidentified single women, "is, that you may every moment behold Jesus, as *altogether lovely*! . . . That there is but one way of beholding him now, and that this way is by faith, we all know; but how to keep this eye of the soul always clear and unsullied, like the finest glass, free from every speck and flaw, is the point we want to be instructed in."[23] Essential to the task of keeping their "eye simply fix'd on Jesus," she explains, is the necessity for them to "take up their cross daily" and to "deny themselves." Concluding her prefatory comments on the nature of this self-denial, Mary makes her "spiritual program" explicit and outlines its central components.

> I was not a little blest the other day with the words of a good man, expressing his desire of being devoted to God, in a solemn observance of *chastity, poverty,* and *obedience*. The words struck me much, and appeared to contain the whole of a Christian life. The Lord was pleased to apply them close to my soul; and I will endeavour simply to relate what then occurred on each head.[24]

Mary begins her discussion of chastity, the first of the three traditional monastic vows, by quoting the familiar beatitude, "Blessed are the pure in heart, for they shall see God" (Matt 5:8). Here is the essence of chastity "in

---

22. J. Wesley, *Christian Library*, 38:5–7. It is interesting to note that the Pietist Francke was an ardent defender of Miguel de Molinos, a major proponent of this school of Spanish Quietism.

23. Bosanquet, *Jesus, Altogether Lovely*, 2.

24. Bosanquet, *Jesus, Altogether Lovely*, 2–3. The identity of Mary's source is yet to be determined. I would heartily welcome any speculations or formal identifications!

its [allegorical] first sense," namely, with reference to Jesus and the soul. Purity of heart enables the believer to reflect the "glorious image of Christ," the one who is "fairer than ten thousand, and altogether lovely," as in a clear mirror. In Wesleyan theology in general, so here in particular, holiness is the goal, the heart the center, and the health of the soul the key to happiness in God and life.[25] Mary expands the images which were "in a lively manner imprest on my mind," as she explains,

> We should consider our souls as the image of God, and our bodies as the temples of the Lord, both pure and consecrated to his service; and our hearts as an altar, on which the love of Jesus, as a pure flame, should continually burn, and that the fewel we are to cast into this fire, is every earthly object that presenteth itself, whether to the eye, the ear, or any other of our senses, casting them in, as soon as perceived, feeling the force of that expression, "All the vain things that charm me most, I sacrifice to Jesu's love"![26]

In her exposition of the second sense of chastity (the more earthy side), Mary applies herself directly to the single women she addresses, confessing that some who stand outside their circle may be offended by her sentiments on the subject. Convinced, however, that it is not her "business to please," she offers her advice to those who have chosen to live a single life.

> To *you*, who are able to receive this saying, I will speak the inmost sentiments of my heart. Whatever others are, *you* are called to the glorious privileges of a single life. O cast them not behind you; nor, having beheld the beauties of the lovely Jesus, now forget, that he is fairer than the sons of men. I shall not attempt to enumerate the particular advantages of your situation. I am not persuading you to it. I need not. All your soul stretches itself out, after that entire devotion to him, whom having *seen* you love.[27]

Mary then advises the women to guard against three dangerous snares. Firstly, avoid men, especially single ones. Secondly, do not succumb to the temptation of thinking that there are more advantages to another way of life. Rather, "stand all the day long on your watch-tower," she admonishes, "fixing it in your mind, I have given myself wholly unto thee; and 'will know

---

25. Mary even includes the classic text, "without holiness of heart, no man shall see the Lord," in the body of her narrative. See my discussion of "The goal of happiness in Christ" in Chilcote, "Sanctification," 93–95.

26. Bosanquet, *Jesus, Altogether Lovely*, 5. Mary quotes here from the second stanza of the famous hymn of Isaac Watts, "When I Survey the Wondrous Cross."

27. Bosanquet, *Jesus, Altogether Lovely*, 5–6.

no other love than thine.'"[28] Thirdly, pride and a judgmental spirit, especially toward those who have not embraced the same style of life to which you have been called, Mary claims, will bring everything to nothing.

> O beware of judging; for God is love, and every wound to love may therefore, in some sense be said, to be a wound to God. May he, who came, not to judge, but to save the world, preserve you from this most pernicious of all evils. Never then consider yourself as secure, but hang every moment on Jesus as if on the very brink of falling; and let your reading, meditation and prayer, turn as much as may be, on the advantages of a single life. And may a holy ambition, to know nothing but Jesus, fire your spirits, while you are made deeply sensible "*no* grace can be guarded but by humility."[29]

Mary's explication of *poverty* follows a similar line of argument. She examines it first with regard to "outward things," and then with reference to "the temper of the soul." In the first instance, she points immediately to the example of Christ. But she is quick to avoid a too literal "imitation of Christ" that would compromise our individual callings as Christians in the world. "I do not here mean," she clarifies, "that we are always bound, at once to dispose of all we have in this world, in order to become a Christian. By no means. We should in many cases, by so doing, put it out of our power to act in that sphere of life, God hath called us unto." The most important point with regard to poverty in this outward sense is to realize "that nothing of what we possess is properly *our own*." The key is proper stewardship over the resources with which we have been blessed, and a constant care never to consider something to be necessary which we know "in God's account is not so."[30]

Poverty in temporal things, however, is a symbolic, perhaps even superficial, representation of the deeper issue of "spiritual poverty," upon which subject Mary next expends considerable energy. In Wesleyan sermonic-essay fashion, she discusses what poverty of spirit is not, what it is, and what its fruits are. This poverty does not consist in denigrating the good things God has done in our lives. Neither does it involve the sacrifice of our own authenticity in an effort of become all things to all people.

---

28. Bosanquet, *Jesus, Altogether Lovely*, 6.

29. Bosanquet, *Jesus, Altogether Lovely*, 7. It is interesting that Mary makes no mention of celibacy in any of her discussions of chastity. It would be interesting as well to speculate about her reflections on this early tract after her marriage to John Fletcher in later life. To my knowledge, no references to this work appear in her journal or any of the accounts of her life.

30. Bosanquet, *Jesus, Altogether Lovely*, 8.

Rather, spiritual poverty consists in "the *true* knowledge of ourselves, from the light of God shining on our hearts, by faith."[31] And this knowledge is the ground and foundation of all religion.

Moreover, this spirit liberates the creature so as to enter into the fullest possible fellowship with the Creator, delighting both in God's justice and God's mercy and drinking deep into the spirit of humility. As to its fruits, spiritual poverty "will shew itself in various ways; but in none more than these four: unwearied patience, constant gentleness, entire resignation, and a perfect willingness to be accounted *nothing* in the esteem of man."[32] Concerning this last and most crucial quality, Mary simply adds: "I have some reason to fear there is too little of this spirit among us . . . It is your heart I pray the Lord to model; and then you will soon be convinced, nothing is little, that can either help or hinder your progress in holiness."[33]

Always the practical spiritual guide, Mary concludes her discussion of poverty with "three more little instances of self-denial, which you will find very conducive to the spirit I am speaking of." Do not push yourself forward. Avoid conspicuous places that draw attention to yourself. And above all, "beware of proud thoughts." Self-sufficiency and independency of spirit, the arrogant and reckless claim of our autonomy before God and our fellow creatures is the sure path to destruction. The watch-word is, "I am nothing; God is all."[34]

"To you who have kept the faith, it will not be grievous to say, study obedience as the rule of your life. Obedience to God, and to man, for his sake." While we owe God "absolute and entire" obedience in things both great and small, just as in her discourse on poverty, so too here, Mary focuses her attention on the little things in which "we are most apt to offend."

> In short, we should see God in every thing, and make it our sole business, inwardly to listen to that still small voice, which none but silent souls can hear; and outwardly, to meet him in the order of his providence, remembering we are all his own, and "lying before him as soft wax, ready to be formed into any shape he pleases." And this simple recollecting ourselves in the presence

---

31. Bosanquet, *Jesus, Altogether Lovely*, 9.
32. Bosanquet, *Jesus, Altogether Lovely*, 9.
33. Bosanquet, *Jesus, Altogether Lovely*, 9–10.
34. Bosanquet, *Jesus, Altogether Lovely*, 10. See my discussion of "the all sufficiency of God's grace" and "theonomy" related to the prayer of Hester Ann Rogers. "In their experience of this great paradox of grace, self-emptying, rather than leaving the believer with a hollow sense of loss, simply paved the way to God's filling . . . The acclamation, 'He is all!' immediately springs from the confession, 'I am nothing'" (Chilcote, "Sanctification," 91–93).

of God, receiving every occurrence as from him; and offering up every action to him, is the spirit and life of true religion.[35]

With regard to that *obedience* which we owe to those in authority, it does not consist merely in "affection" (I will obey because I love him.), or in "virtue" (I will obey because he is very spiritual.). Rather, we obey simply and purely out of love to God (I will obey because it is God I obey in him.). On this subject, Mary quotes her unknown source at length:

> We should be wholly given up to the conduct of him, whom God hath placed over us, in all things (where no sin lies) following his judgment not our own, except in very particular cases, where his commands actually wound our conscience, in which case we ought to say so, and lay it before two or three impartial persons. And if they all agree, and we still can't follow his advice, it argues not strength but weakness of grace.[36]

The same author describes "three degrees in this obedience." The first and lowest degree is when we willingly submit to those commands we are obliged to submit to. The second is complying to orders we are not obliged to comply with. The third and most perfect degree of obedience is "when knowing our superior's will, and not waiting for his orders, we prevent them by an antecedent conformity."[37]

Mary concludes her spiritual guidance with a plea for the cultivation of the primary Christian virtue:

> Cry for an obedient, humble, peaceable spirit. O were we all but penetrated with true humility . . . The earnest desire of my soul for you is, that you may abide in the faith, and indure unto the end. That you may covet to walk in the most excellent way, and be found continually standing on your guard and watching unto prayer. Then will the eternal God be your refuge, and underneath you, the everlasting arms. He will set your sins far from you; and cause you to dwell in purity of heart and in safety. You shall be a people saved of the Lord, who shall himself become your guide and your exceeding great reward.[38]

What are we to make of this amazing document? Of one thing we can be very clear, that on the eve of the Leytonstone experiment, Mary Bosanquet's mind was revolving around a model or models for living out the Christian

---

35. Bosanquet, *Jesus, Altogether Lovely*, 11.
36. Bosanquet, *Jesus, Altogether Lovely*, 12.
37. Bosanquet, *Jesus, Altogether Lovely*, 12.
38. Bosanquet, *Jesus, Altogether Lovely*, 12–13.

faith with integrity and in community with other women. At the center of this vision was a concern for holiness and happiness rooted in purity of heart or intention, one of the central pillars of her nascent Wesleyan heritage and a conception of the Christian life which permeates Wesley's *Plain Account* of the same year. One way forward in the journey toward this "altogether lovely vision" was through a solemn observance of chastity, poverty, and obedience, all of which, coming out of the rich monastic tradition of the West, points unmistakably to humility as the essence of the Christian faith. And all of this Mary would attempt to live out in a community which in its praxis conjoined serious religious contemplation and active social service.

This is the foundation upon which the Leytonstone women built a spirituality of active love. The confluence of beguine, Pietist, and Catholic monastic spirituality in the Christian praxis of this group is truly remarkable. The mystical writings of the beguines are filled with the images of God's inbreaking transformation of life, a divine presence that is personal and intimate, and of struggles that must be endured along the way toward holiness. "The journey," as Bowie writes, "may be perceived as hard, . . . but it is a way freely chosen and rewarding in this life, not merely in the life to come."[39] Contemplation *and* action was its key. For Francke and the Halle Pietists, the Christian life was a life of self-denial in the service of active love, of obedience to the law of love reflected in God's glory and neighbor's good, and of childlike faith and absolute trust in God. The consequence of obedient, active love was joy. The monastic heritage elevated the lofty vision of a Christian community in which one discovers the basis of relationship within the life of a family, in which harmony, wholeness, and balance are the consequence of obedient love and service to others, and in which humility liberates the self to love as Christ has loved.

All these elements are central to the life and witness of the women of early Methodism and the Leytonstone family, in particular. Their spirituality of active love rested on the solid foundation of humility, the acknowledgment of true self-knowledge as the path to hope in Christ and intimacy with God. Surrender to Christ, reliance upon him in all the vicissitudes of life, and a commitment to learning from him through obedience to the law of love were all important means toward the flying goal of the Christian life; to possess a heart that was "altogether lovely," like that of Jesus, because it was filled with the love of God.

---

39. Bowie, *Beguine Spirituality*, 42.

Chapter 9

Sanctification as Lived by Women in Early Methodism

Source note: Delivered as a plenary paper before a conference on "Sanctification in the Benedictine and Methodist Traditions" at the Franciscan Retreat Center in Rocca di Papa, Rome, in July 1994, and published in *Methodist History* 34.2 (January 1996) 90–103. A subsequent Italian translation was published as "La santificazione vissuta dalle donne del primometodismo," in *La santificazione nelle tradizioni Benedettina e Metodista*, edited by Febe C. Rossi, 299–319 (Verona: Il Segno dei Gabrielli editori, 1998). This essay was also later adapted and published as "The Blessed Way of Holiness," *Journal of Theology* 100 (Summer 1996) 29–51.

IN ADDITION TO BEING a close friend and correspondent of John Wesley, Hester Ann Rogers was noted for her life of prayer and holiness.[1] The following excerpt from a meditation in her diary serves not only to illustrate the spirituality of early Methodist women, but also provides the simple outline for my discussion of sanctification as they lived it.

1. Hester, born on January 31, 1756, was the only daughter of the Rev. James Roe of Macclesfield. In 1784, she married James Rogers, one of Wesley's preachers. She kept a diary from the time of becoming a Methodist and engaged in extensive correspondence about religious matters, including the doctrine of sanctification. Her *Experience* (1793), an autobiographical account drawn from her diary, and her *Spiritual Letters* (1796) were combined with her *Funeral Sermon* by Thomas Coke (1795) and an appendix prepared by her husband to form a volume entitled *The Experience and Spiritual Letters of Mrs. Hester Ann Rogers*. This work was extremely popular among Methodist women for over a century and went through many reprintings under several titles on both sides of the Atlantic. She was often pointed to as an example of holy living in the Methodist tradition. See Chilcote, "John Wesley as Revealed," 111–23.

> O how precious are Jesus' ways to my soul,
> suited to my weakness,
> worthy of a God!
> I am nothing! He is all!
> I live moment by moment upon his smiles,
> and desire nothing but to please him:
> To grow in inward conformity to his will,
> and sink deeper into humble love;
> to let the light
> of what his grace hath bestowed,
> shine on all around,
> and to live and die proclaiming,
> GOD IS LOVE![2]

This reflective meditation is profound and engaging. Hester's prayer reveals the heart of Methodist praxis. Here we see clearly how doctrine was translated into action by the early followers of Wesley. What they lived shaped in large measure the belief of the people called Methodist. I would like for Hester's prayer, therefore, to become an act of worship, something of a litany, punctuating some of the salient features of sanctification as lived by the women of early Methodism.

The All-Sufficiency of God's Grace

To turn now, more directly, to the issue of sanctification as lived by Methodist women, Hester's prayer begins: "O how precious are Jesus' ways to my soul, suited to my weakness, worthy of a God! I am nothing! He is all!" Here, she gives expression to a pervasive theme of the journals, letters, and memoirs of the Methodist women, and to the first of five aspects of sanctification, namely, *the all-sufficiency of God's grace.* Wesleyan soteriology, as has been widely noted, is rooted in grace. When Wesley defined "grace" in his *Instructions for Children,* he simply described it as "the power of the Holy Spirit, enabling us to believe and love and serve God."[3] Sanctification, therefore, is nothing other than the fruition of God's gracious activity in

---

2. Rogers, *Account,* 128–29.
3. Wesley, *Instructions for Children.* One of Wesley's few catechetical publications, this small tract was a revised English "extract" from an early eighteenth century French work by the prominent mystic, disciple, and biographer of Antoinette Bourignon, Pierre Poiret.

our lives, empowering us to believe, love, and serve "to the uttermost," an expression often used by the women. This is why Wesley, when pressed to articulate what he meant by "Christian Perfection," simply referred time and time again to the "great commandment" of Jesus. It means, he would say, "to love the Lord your God with all your heart, and with all your soul, and with all your mind, and with all your strength, . . . and to love your neighbor as yourself" (Mark 12:29–31). Here is the essence of religion; the heart of the Christian faith. This act of loving God and neighbor, in Wesley's view and that of his women followers, must always be understood in the Johannine sense of reciprocal love ("We love because He first loved us," 1 John 4:19). The responsive nature of our love, moreover, reflects the great "paradox of grace" articulated by St. Paul in his confession: "It is no longer I who live, but Christ who lives in me" (Gal 2:20). And so, Hester cries out, "I am nothing! He is all!" The end of faith, as well as its beginning, is true self knowledge, humility, and absolute trust in God. Christian discipleship—the arena of God's sanctifying activity in the life of the believer—is first and foremost a grace-filled response to God's all-sufficient grace.

We are often impressed by the constant reference to total dependence upon God in the women's effort to articulate their experience of salvation, and sanctification, in particular. Ann Gilbert, the first Methodist woman to preach in Cornwall and one noted for her "softening eloquence," expressed her experience in these terms:

> My soul is humbled to the dust at the feet of the Lord, and I am as a little child on its mother's breast, always depending on the bounty of Heaven. I live but a moment at a time, and that moment,—for eternity . . . I never wanted Christ more than I do now. My strength is perfect weakness.[4]

In their experience of this great paradox of grace, *self-emptying*, rather than leaving the believer with a hollow sense of loss, simply paved the way to *God's filling*. In one of her many letters to John Wesley touching upon the issue of sanctification and perfect love, Sarah Crosby observe,

> I find a Rest in the centre of my soul, which nothing doth, or can, interrupt. I feel no Pride, no Anger, no Unbelief, no desire of anything evil. I have but one desire which nothing can satisfy, but the full fruition of God. And what kind of rest this gives, they only that find it know. The light of faith shines clear; the love of God does melt and meeken [sic] my soul, and reduces me

---

4. Gilbert, "Experience," 45.

to nothing; so that I live not, but Christ liveth in me. I know not that I need anything more, but to increase herein.[5]

The acclamation, "He is all!" immediately springs from the confession, "I am nothing." Following a description of the fallen nature of humanity which she compares to the setting of the sun, Bathsheba Hall, therefore, immediately interjects, "[But] the face of creation animates my soul. When we have God we have every thing! As the natural sun cheers the drooping plants, so do thy beams gladden my every power."[6] All of this in the midst of a protracted discussion of holiness.

Perhaps no early Methodist woman was more widely acclaimed for her proclamation of grace than Grace Murray, the major prototype for female leadership within the movement. At the end of her life and many years of faithful service to the Methodist cause, she left this dying testimony:

> I would have no encomiums passed on me; I AM A SINNER, SAVED FREELY BY GRACE: Grace, divine grace, is worthy to have all the glory. Some people I have heard speak much of our being faithful to the grace of God; as if they rested much on their *own* faithfulness: I never could bear this; it is *GOD'S FAITH-FULNESS to his own word of promise*, that is my only security for salvation.[7]

Maturity in Christ—the whole purpose of sanctifying grace in the Wesleyan understanding—was as much a gift of God's grace as everything else in the life of the believer.

O HOW PRECIOUS ARE JESUS' WAYS TO MY SOUL,

SUITED TO MY WEAKNESS, WORTHY OF A GOD!

I AM NOTHING! HE IS ALL!

---

5. Hall, "Extract."

6. Hall, "Diary," 95. A conscientious member of the Methodist Society in Bristol, she gave vivid expression to the tension many women felt between the evangelical duty to communicate their faith with others and their reticence to engage in a public ministry.

7. Bennet, *Grace Bennet*, 83. A Methodist from the outset of the revival, Grace served as a band leader at the Foundery in London, as housekeeper of Wesley's Orphan House headquarters in the north, and as Wesley's traveling companion throughout England and Ireland. Betrothed to John Wesley by a contract *de praesenti*, brother Charles intervened, hastily arranging the marriage of Grace to one of Wesley's preachers, John Bennet. In spite of the fact that the various parties were reconciled in the end, Bennet left Wesleyan Methodism for Calvinism, and Grace found her new role in the Warburton Church, conducting weekly prayer meetings and fellowship groups. See Leger, *Wesley's Last Love*; Baker, "John Wesley's First Marriage"; and Baker and Maser, "John Wesley's Only Marriage."

The Goal of Happiness in Christ

Hannah Ball, a leading member of the Methodist Society in High Wycombe, was the pioneer of Sunday Schools in England, long before Robert Raikes (who got the credit) had even conceived of his experiments in Gloucester.[8] The connection which she drew between God's grace and human happiness provides an appropriate bridge to the second facet of sanctification, *the goal of happiness in Christ*. "There is no state of life but needs much grace, and no real happiness but what comes from God," she wrote. "One day, meditating on what would constitute a person's happiness that had escaped the incidental allurements of youth, it was powerfully applied to my mind, 'The grace of God, and nothing else.' I have ever found it true."[9] In his sermon on "The Righteousness of Faith," in which Wesley rings the changes on "God's mercy freely given," he also boldly proclaims: "Now the best end which any creature can pursue is happiness in God."[10] In my well-worn copy of Albert Outler's classic little book, *Theology in the Wesleyan Spirit*, one passage, perhaps more than any other, first grasped my attention and continues to allure: "This man was a *eudaemonist*, convinced and consistent all his life. All his emphases on duty and discipline are auxiliary to his main concern for human *happiness* (blessedness, etc.)."[11]

We should not be surprised, therefore, by Hester's serendipitous phrase: "I live moment by moment upon his smiles, and desire nothing but to please him." In spite of the controversy that continually surrounded Wesley's doctrine, I believe (with Outler) that his concept of "going on to perfection" had a consistent character and a clear end in view. Radical trust in the sufficiency of God's grace leads to love, both of God and neighbor, and to a quality of happiness in life that can only be attributed to the indwelling of the Spirit in the life of the believer. "To live joyously in the Spirit" is, perhaps, the simplest and best definition of "holiness." And it is not a monumental leap from this realization to the observation that a happy faith is a faith that sings. Let it

---

8. In fact, she founded a Sunday School in 1769 for the teaching of Scripture, reading, and other elementary subjects to neglected children, eleven years prior to the similar experiment of Raikes in his own parish in 1780. She met the children on Sundays and Mondays. See the account of her life and work based on her journals and correspondence, originally published in 1796 with many subsequent editions and reprintings: Cole, *Hannah Ball*.

9. Cole, *Hannah Ball*, 118.

10. J. Wesley, *Works*, 1:213. See the editor's note on "Wesley's eudaemonism" as reflected in this statement.

11. Outler, *Theology*, 81. He goes on to say that Wesley "believed (with Aquinas, Erasmus, and Richard Lucas before him) that all our truly human aspirations are oriented toward *happiness*."

not be forgotten that it was through the hymns of the Methodist tradition, the major collection of which Wesley described as "A Little Body of Experimental Divinity,"[12] that the singers were exposed to this contagious form of a happy faith. Methodism was born in song.

Perhaps the interesting expression concerning the "smiles of Jesus" in Hester's meditation was drawn from many similar allusions in the hymns of Charles Wesley. In his poetic exposition of the story of Mary and Martha we find these pertinent lines:

> Come let us arise,
> And press to the skies;
> The summons obey,
> My friends, my beloved, and hasten away!
> The Master doth call,
> And deigns to approve
> With smiles of acceptance our labour of love.[13]

Of even greater interest for my purposes here is the Wesleys' exchange of the word "holiness" for "happiness" in a number of the hymns.[14] For the Wesley brothers and their early Methodist followers, the words were simply interchangeable; "holiness is happiness."[15] Overwhelmed, on one occasion, by her reflections upon the "consolations of the Spirit" and the "blessed way of holiness," Isabella Wilson proclaims in wonder,

> This is love unspeakable! His delight is to make us happy. O how does his love exceed all that fancy can form, or imagination paint. The favoured soul is ready to say, I have heard great and glorious things spoken of thee, but, oh, how little was said to what I find! O how unable are the tongues of mortals to set forth

---

12. See J. Wesley, *Works*, 7:1–22.
13. J. Wesley, *Works*, 7:669. From the section "For the Society, giving Thanks."
14. In particular, see J. Wesley, *Works*, 7:194 (no. 92.4) and 395 (no. 254.2).
15. Perhaps Martin Schmidt was the first to draw major attention to this fundamental understanding of the Wesleys (see Schmidt, *John Wesley*, 1:96–105). He wrote: "The formula 'holiness is happiness' belongs to the fundamental data of Wesley's theological thinking and constitutes the root of his 'perfectionism'" (101). Elsewhere he traces the lineage of this eudaemonism back to Scougal via Susanna, the mother of the Wesleys. Indeed, a close study of her own prayers bears out the close relationship between holiness and happiness in her thinking. See Doughty, *Prayers of Susanna Wesley*, nos. 4, 6, 10, 16, and 23.

the pleasures of those who are united to this Jesus! We joy in his redeeming love. He is most precious, and altogether lovely.[16]

While their happiness was contagious, it had to be defended from time to time, perhaps the greatest testimony to the reality of the experience itself. The transparent happiness of Hester Rogers troubled a Calvinist friend who thought it not proper for a Christian to appear so full of joy.[17] Her happiness even drew a flurry of questions from her brother who was studying for the Anglican priesthood at Oxford at the time.

> Are you really possessed of the happiness you speak of? . . . Are you not deceived? Convince me that you are not . . . If it is real how did you attain it? . . . I would give up all the World to obtain the favor with God you speak of, but I know not which way to attain it.[18]

For the early Methodist women, "holiness is happiness." The life of holiness which they affirmed was life with a smile on its face, abundant life in Christ.

I LIVE MOMENT BY MOMENT UPON HIS SMILES,

AND DESIRE NOTHING BUT TO PLEASE HIM.

The Necessity of Growth into Deeper Love: Inward Holiness

Hardly a word in Hester's next statement is without significance, as we turn our attention to *the necessity of growth into deeper love, inward holiness* as a critical component of the evangelical piety of early Methodist women. "I desire," she writes, "to *grow* in *inward conformity* to his *will*, and *sink deeper* into *humble love*." Another classic statement of Albert Outler provides some guidance here. "The gospel is God's enacted promise in Christ," he wrote, "that we can live intentionally, following the inner leadings of the Holy Spirit, obedient to what we are given to know of God's will, growing ever into a deeper faith and a truer happiness than we could ever know, in and for and by ourselves."[19] The Wesleys always seemed to prefer the dynamic, biological, therapeutic images of new birth, growth, and recovery to the static, albeit biblical/traditional images of acquittal, imputation, and satisfaction.

16. Pipe, "Isabella Wilson," 465.

17. See the interesting account drawn from her manuscript journal in Brown, *Women of Methodism*, 206.

18. Rogers, *Manuscript Journal* (October 3, 1775).

19. Outler, *Theology*, 62–63.

Wesley found opportunity to speak at length about the necessity and reality of a relative change in one's forensic status before God. But this experience of justification by grace through faith was, for him, a means to the greater end of a real change, a regenerative act, the beginning of a process of recovery that restored the image of God in the heart of the believer. "Ye know that the great end of religion," he would repeat on a number of occasions, "is to renew our hearts in the image of God, to repair that total loss of righteousness and true holiness which we sustained by the sin of our first parents."[20] Wesley discovered, in the richness of Methodist religious experience, and particularly the experience of women, a spiritual development that was analogous to birth, growth, and ultimate maturity. "Perfect love," therefore, is the goal toward which the spiritual therapy of sanctifying grace must ever be directed.

Sarah Ryan, Wesley's faithful correspondent, had a vision one day of such growth and seized upon it as the directing principle of her life:

> [On Sunday] in Spitalfields Church, I saw the Lord Jesus standing, and a little child all in white before him: and he shewed me, he had made me as that child; but that I should grow up to the measure of his full stature. I came home full of light, joy, love, and holiness; and God daily confirmed what he had done for my soul. And, blessed be his name! I now know where my strength lieth, and my soul is continually sinking more and more into God.[21]

Perhaps the most critical question, as David Watson has pointed out, is "how to permit God's grace to foster a maturity of constant obedience, so that sanctifying grace might work with an unimpeded love."[22] In essence, the early Methodist women "sank deeper into humble love" by immersing themselves in the classic means of grace that were so central to the movement as a whole, what Wesley described simply as "works of piety." These "means" not only nurtured and sustained their growth in grace, but also provided the "energy" which fueled the movement as a powerful religious awakening. The emphasis which they placed upon mutual accountability and the strength drawn from intimate fellowship, their celebration of classic spiritual disciplines as important means of growth (as well as conversion), and their renewed interest in the sacramental life of the church were all part and parcel of growth in inward holiness.

---

20. J. Wesley, *Works*, 2:185 ("Original Sin," III.5). This and other Wesley sermons articulate his axial theme—the recovery of the defaced image of God.

21. Ryan, "Account," 309–10.

22. Watson, *Accountable Discipleship*, 34.

In a journal entry of February 18, 1775, Hannah Ball, in characteristic Wesleyan fashion, provides an outline of those means of grace she had found most helpful to her spiritual growth.

> I have received, I trust, an increase of patience: my soul rests in God. To the end that I may improve in the knowledge of Him, I read, write, and pray; hear the word preached; converse with the people of God; fast, or use abstinence; together with every prudential help, as channels only, for receiving the grace of God; but private prayer is in general the most strengthening means of all.[23]

There is no question that the class and band meetings, the marks of *ecclesiola in ecclesia*, were potent cells for the promotion of inward holiness or love of God. In the intimacy of these small groups, and particularly the bands, women learned what it meant to grow in Christ and, together, plumbed the depths of God's love for them all. Experiences in these groups often elicited the most eloquent testimonies of inward holiness, such as this statement of Isabella Wilson:

> All glory be to God for persevering grace and more conformity to him in all things. Oh! the unbounded love of Jesus to my soul. His promises are all precious. My peace flows as a river while he teaches me the lessons of his grace, of faith and holiness. My soul is athirst for all the mind that was in him.[24]

No means of grace, however, was as important to the Wesleys as the sacrament of the Lord's Supper. The early Methodists sang, and the women bore witness to the testimony of the hymn:

> The prayer, the fast, the word conveys,
>> When mix'd with faith, Thy life to me;
>
> In all the channels of Thy grace
>> I still have fellowship with Thee:
>
> But chiefly here my soul is fed
>> With fulness of immortal bread.[25]

---

23. Cole, *Hannah Ball*, 97–98. In general, for Wesley there are five chief means of grace: (1) prayer, (2) the Word (read, preached, and meditated upon), (3) fasting, (4) Christian conference (or what we would call "fellowship" or "religious conversation"), and (5) the Lord's Supper. See a concise discussion of this topic in Chilcote, *Wesley Speaks*, 33–48, which includes a modernized extract of Wesley's sermon on "The Means of Grace."

24. Pipe, "Isabella Wilson," 564.

25. Wesley and Wesley, *Hymns on the Lord's Supper*, 39 (no. 54.4).

These "feasts of love," as the women often described them, shaped their understanding of God's love for them and their reciprocal love for God—the source of "inward holiness" in their lives. This holiness was, in essence, founded upon a sense of communion with God through Christ, an abiding in Christ realized most fully in the context of a meal.

> I have been favoured this day with the means of grace, which were feasts of love to my soul. I have fed at the table of the Lord on rich grace with thanksgiving. Oh that I may be more united to Jesus, that I may see him in all things who is altogether lovely.[26]

Inward holiness, the necessity of growth into deeper levels of love for God, often came to fruition in the lives of the women as they remained faithful to these means of grace.

I DESIRE TO GROW IN INWARD CONFORMITY TO HIS WILL,

AND SINK DEEPER INTO HUMBLE LOVE.

The Witness of Loving Service to Others: Outward Holiness

Charles Wesley's hymn, "Come let us arise," quoted above for its smiles, describes the life of holiness in subsequent verses, drawing heavily upon the images of Matthew 25.

> His burden who bear,
> We alone can declare
> How easy his yoke:
> While to love and good works we each other provoke,
> By word and by deed,
> The bodies in need,
> The souls to relieve,
> And freely as Jesus hath given to give.
>
> Then let us attend
> Our heavenly friend
> In his members distressed,
> By want, or affliction, or sickness oppressed;
> The prisoner relieve,

---

26. Pipe, "Isabella Wilson," 564.

> The stranger receive,
>
> Supply all their wants,
>
> And spend and be spent in assisting his saints.[27]

For the women, holiness was essentially a practical matter. If in their articulation of the doctrine of sanctification they leaned heavily in the direction of mystical language, their mysticism was invariably a "practical mysticism." Works of piety found ultimate expression in works of mercy.

So Hester prays: "I desire to let the light of what his grace hath bestowed, shine on all around"; and this meant *loving service to other*, an *outward holiness* reflecting the love of God within.

Certainly, the Methodist women "offered the Christ" whom they had come to love and know in a variety of ways.[28] They sought out people in need—the poor, the hungry, the destitute, and the neglected. They preached the Word, visited prisons, established orphanages and schools, and practiced their servant-oriented faith as devoted mothers who discerned the presence of God in the most menial of chores. Hardly passive Christians for whom ministry was performed; these women were active, ministering servants who cared for one another and extended their ministry into the communities they served. The prison ministry of Sarah Peters, known to all in her day through the publications of John Wesley, is exemplary. This is the same woman who often said, "I must be always moving. I cannot rest, day or night."[29]

In a letter of May 8, 1774, Wesley admonished Elizabeth Ritchie, one of his most trusted friends, to a ministry like his own.

> I am not content that you should be pinned down to any one place. That is not your calling. Methinks I want you to be (like me) here and there and everywhere. Oh what a deal of work has our Lord to do on the earth! And may we be workers together with him![30]

And here, there, and everywhere they were. A glimpse into the diary of Sarah Crosby, the first woman preacher of Methodism, reveals the extent of her manifold activities during the year 1777.

---

27. J. Wesley, *Works*, 7:669 (no. 482.2–3).

28. An analysis of the many activities of women directed toward the needs of others is provided in Chilcote, *She Offered Them Christ*; cf. Brown, *Women of Methodism*, 50–74, in particular.

29. Wesley, "Sarah Peters," 128.

30. Telford, *Letters of John Wesley*, 6:84.

> Thou hast enabled me, from the first of last January to the fourth of this month (December), to ride 960 miles, to keep 220 public meetings, at many of which some hundreds of precious souls were present, about 600 private meetings, and to write an 116 letters, many of them long ones; besides many, many conversations with souls in private, the effect of which will, I trust, be "as bread cast on the waters." All glory be unto him, who has strengthened his poor worm.[31]

Contented to live a somewhat more settled existence, Hannah Ball was no less indefatigable in her efforts to extend her love to others. Nearly one year into her Sunday School experiment in High Wycombe, she recorded the following resolution in her diary:

> I desire to spend the remaining part of my life in a closer walking with God, and in labours of love to my fellow-creatures,—feeding the hungry, clothing the naked, instructing a few of the rising generation in the principles of religion, and, in every possible way I am capable, ministering to them that shall be heirs of salvation.[32]

The advice of Wesley to a Methodist woman aspiring to "perfection" is a typical expression of his gospel to the poor: "Go and see the poor and sick in their own little hovels. Take up your cross, woman! Remember the faith! Jesus went before you, and will go with you. Put off the gentlewoman: You bear a higher character."[33]

Elizabeth Dickinson, one of Mary Fletcher's "Female Brethren" preachers, fully embraced the motto "holiness to the Lord." One of her statements simply expresses the tradition of outward holiness that so many of the women represented: "We must not only preach the gospel, but live the gospel, or we shall do more harm than good."[34]

I DESIRE TO LET THE LIGHT OF WHAT HIS GRACE HATH BESTOWED, SHINE ON ALL AROUND

---

31. Crosby, "Account," 567. Cf. Chilcote, *Wesley and Women*, 53.
32. Cole, *Hannah Ball*, 57 (June 3, 1770).
33. Telford, *Letters of John Wesley*, 6:153 (June 9, 1775). For an excellent discussion of Wesley's "preferential option for the poor," see Jennings, *Good News*, 47–69.
34. Quoted in Bramwell, "Ann Cutler," 32.

The Proclamation of God's Love

Hester concludes her meditation with the most simple, the most profound affirmation, "I desire to live and die proclaiming, GOD IS LOVE." This was the message of the early Methodist women as they lived it out in their lives. Here we come full circle to where we began. The foundation of their praxis of sanctification was a profound optimism in God's grace linked with holiness of heart and life. For the women, holiness meant offering signposts for the pilgrim journey to those who were lost. It meant proclaiming a message of hope, through word and deed, to those considered to be the least among them. It meant living in and for a new order in God's love that elevated those who came last. This was an understanding of sanctification rooted in the all-sufficiency of God's grace, the goal of which was happiness in Christ. It was a view of Christian maturity that equally stressed the need of inward holiness, or love of God, and outward holiness, or love of neighbor. And so the necessity of growth into deeper levels of love could never be separated from the mandate to bear witness to that love in service to the world.

No woman of early Methodism, I believe, more fully embodied this Wesleyan principle of faith working by love leading to holiness of heart and life than Mary Fletcher. Her life's sermon was a message of urgency, of renewal, and of love. On one occasion late in her life, when she was unable to fulfill a preaching obligation due to an illness, she summed up her evangel—her call to scriptural holiness—in a brief letter to be read in her absence at the meeting of the Society:

> O that you would therefore do as Jacob did, be earnest with the Lord, that his love may fill your heart, as the Scripture expresses it, the love of God, shed abroad in your hearts by the Holy Ghost, given unto you. If you get your hearts full of the love of God, you will find that is the oil by which the lamp of faith will be ever kept burning; love makes all our duty easy; a soul united as one spirit to the Lord, if temptation presents, has a ready answer; such a one instantly cries out, How shall I do this great wickedness, and sin against God? against Him in whom my soul delighteth? Pray, my friends, pray much for this love; and remember that word, "He that dwelleth in love dwelleth in God, and God in him!"[35]

The goal of the dynamic, relational process of sanctification—the whole purpose of God's gracious activity in our lives—is to "get our hearts full of the love of God." May the prayer of our sisters, Mary and Hester, be our own.

---

35. Quoted in Tooth, *Letter to Madeley*, 17–18.

Part 4
Wesleyan Spiritual Practices

Chapter 10

Spirituality in the Wesleyan Tradition

Source note: Unpublished keynote address delivered *in absentia* before the Charles Wesley Society Meeting at Freudenstadt, Germany, September 30, 2005.

I HAVE BEEN ASKED to address the theme of spirituality in the Wesleyan tradition. This will strike you immediately as an unusually broad topic for a conference on issues of inculturation in Wesleyan mission and witness. The purpose, however, as we have already seen illustrated in the work of my colleague, Professor Maddox, is to provide a helpful foundation upon which to build our common work from our different cultural perspectives. So, while not focused directly upon the life and witness of Charles Wesley, my hope is that my reflections on this theme will draw our attention to the more critical aspects of the movement and simultaneously provide some direction for the future. I will say a word about sources, describe the broad contours of early Methodist spirituality, and conclude by identifying salient themes of continuing significance within the Wesleyan tradition.

Since "spirituality" is such a problematic and elusive term, it is important for me to be clear about how I am using it. In historical usage within the heritage of Christian faith, it covers a breadth of religious experience and a wide range of values, practices, and virtues.[1] I am employing this concept with a fairly broad connotation in mind, and in the same sense as two significant Methodist scholars. According to Gordon Wakefield, "spirituality concerns the way in which prayer influences conduct, our behaviour and manner of life, our attitudes to other people."[2] Similarly, Geoffrey Wain-

---

1. See Sheldrake, *Spirituality and History*, for a description of the range of meaning accruing to the term "spirituality" in the Christian context.

2. Wakefield, *Dictionary of Christian Spirituality*, v. Wakefield has also written a helpful introduction to the spirituality of British Methodists, entitled *Methodist Spirituality*.

wright suggests more simply that spirituality is "the combination of praying and living."[3] The simple fact that the Wesleys viewed the evangelical revival as a movement of God's Spirit within the life of the church shaped the way in which the early Methodists prayed and lived. Their "life of prayer" took on many forms and the "way they lived" reflected their souls. Their peculiar context—and the value that their leaders placed upon spiritual rediscoveries rooted in the apostolic witness of Scripture and the Anglican heritage—defined the Methodists. The spirituality of this movement of renewal, to put it in slightly different terms, may be the most distinctive contribution of the Wesleyan tradition to the life of the church today.

With regard to the spirituality of the eighteenth-century English church, "the private piety in this period," according to Henry Rack, "remains an unstudied area."[4] It is abundantly clear that, after the Bible, no single source shaped the Wesley family more than the Book of Common Prayer.[5] This reservoir of Anglican devotion established the rhythms and gave direction to the essential ethos of the Wesleyan Revival. Beyond this, however, two dominant streams of influence within English Christianity continued to shape the spirituality of the Church of England during this period: the High Church (or Anglo-Catholic) and the Puritan traditions.[6]

Within the High Church wing of the church, perhaps no group had more continuing influence than the Caroline Divines of the previous century, including renowned devotional writers such as Lancelot Andrewes, William Laud, Thomas Ken, George Herbert, and Jeremy Taylor.[7] John and Charles Wesley owed much to the latter two figures, both important interpreters of the Anglican heritage in which they stood. George Herbert is considered to be one of the most authentic representatives of the Anglican *via media* (the middle way) in both its spirit and teaching.[8] *A Priest to the Temple; or the Country Parson*, published posthumously in 1652, is his most famous prose work. It portrays the model priest as sober, learned, temperate, and devout; ideals he sought to emulate in his own brief ministry at Bremerton, near Salisbury. His collection of poems, entitled *The Temple* (1633), reveals his own personal struggles of faith, emphasizing the possibility of intimacy with

---

3. Wainwright, "Types of Spirituality," 592.

4. Rack, *Reasonable Enthusiast*, 21.

5. See Lawson, "Charles Wesley."

6. On the development of English traditions of spirituality, see Thornton, *English Spirituality*; Stranks, *Anglican Devotion*; and McAdoo, *Spirit of Anglicanism*.

7. See Thornton, "Caroline Divines," for an excellent overview of their spirituality.

8. See Summer, *George Herbert*; Bottrall, *George Herbert*; and Wall, *George Herbert*.

God, the priority of prayer to preaching, the integration of inward grace and outward expression, the exercise of Christian virtue in the supreme act of putting on Christ, and the resolution of life's contradictions in an abiding faith that leads to God. In the significant collection of *Hymns and Sacred Poems*, published jointly by the Wesley brothers in 1739, nearly one third of the selections are drawn from Herbert's greatest poetic work.

Jeremy Taylor was best known for his twin works, *The Rule and Exercise of Holy Living* (1650) and *The Rule and Exercise of Holy Dying* (1651).[9] They are characteristic expressions of Anglican spirituality in their balanced sobriety, disciplined piety, and emphasis on moderation in all things. The central theme of the Christian life, in Taylor's view, is God's requirement for believers to live holy lives. Such a life includes temperance and justice as well as godliness. The life of holiness demands a severe regimen and will include the ultimate crucible of suffering and death. His spirituality is oriented around the central Caroline ideal of true piety and sound learning.

The Non-juror, William Law, a contemporary and close friend of the Wesleys, also stood in this High Church tradition.[10] Inspired in part by the teachings of Thomas à Kempis, he published *A Serious Call to a Devout and Holy Life* in 1728, by far his most influential devotional work. In the midst of the Age of Reason, he developed a profound, rational argument for a life of devotion, demanding that serious Christians dedicate the whole and not just a part of their lives to God. He recommends the exercise of the moral virtues, meditation, and ascetical practices. But for him, such religious exercises represent only a small part of the spiritual life. He insists on the practice of the virtues in everyday life, temperance, humility, and self-denial, all being animated by the intention to glorify God.

The heart of Puritan spirituality was personal religion.[11] While the label itself is fraught with difficulties and clouded by later prejudicial images, the central tenets of Puritan devotion can be illustrated by several of its greatest proponents. First, John Bunyon, in his great autobiographical work, *Grace Abounding to the Chief of Sinners*, emphasizes the necessity of conversion, not an experience achieved nor followed without agony or struggle, but the fruition of the overwhelming call of God. His more famous classic, *The Pilgrim's Progress*, bears witness to the fact that the Christian life is a journey that requires a covenant community of support and encouragement. Richard Baxter's *The Saints' Everlasting Rest*, composed following an

---

9. See Hughes, *Piety of Jeremy Taylor*; and Carroll, *Jeremy Taylor*.

10. See Stanwood, *William Law*, for one of the best modern editions of the *Serious Call* and *The Spirit of Love*.

11. On the Puritan tradition of spirituality in England, see Wakefield, "Puritans."

extended illness in 1646, demonstrates the centrality of meditation to Puritan prayer. It was through hymns, however, that one of the greatest Puritans, Isaac Watts, influenced English devotional life in general and Charles Wesley in particular.[12] The spirituality of his hymns is characterized by a sense of divine transcendence, the glory and majesty of God, and the sweep of God's action in human history, focusing particularly on the gracious manifestation of God's love through the cross of Christ.

There were other formative influences, of course, that shaped the spirituality of the Wesleys and influenced the lives of their followers, as well. Two spiritual classics, both of which appear to have been among Susanna Wesley's favorites, were Henry Scougal's *The Life of God in the Soul of Man*[13] and Lorenzo Scupoli's *The Spiritual Combat*.[14] "True religion," according to Scougal, "is a union of the soul with God, a real participation of the divine nature, the very image of God drawn upon the soul."[15] Scupoli represents a Catholic tradition of "will mysticism," the goal of which is total resignation to God. The primary insight that John Wesley took away from his study of these classical works was the simple fact that the Christian life is a *via devotio* (a way of devotion) that finds its richest and fullest completion in God's love. Charles seems to have had a particular interest in the Catholic devotional writer, François Fénelon, a portion of whose writings he meticulously transcribed from the original French.[16] Perhaps he was drawn to the mystic's doctrine of pure love and his aspiration of union with God.[17]

Two other critical figures exerted a strong influence on John, who described them, together with Thomas à Kempis, as "real, inward Christians."[18] He apparently discovered the first, a Spanish mystic, through

---

12. See Davies, *Isaac Watts*; and Bishop, *Hymns of Isaac Watts*. Watts' *Guide to Prayer* is a sober and rigorous examination of the classic "parts of prayer." In this judicious work he describes eight aspects of prayer: (1) Invocation, (2) Adoration, (3) Confession, (4) Petition, (5) Pleading, (6) Self-dedication, (7) Thanksgiving, and (8) Blessing God.

13. Henry Scougal (1650–1678), Scottish theologian and mystic. Albert Outler includes him among Wesley's four great mentors in piety (Outler, *John Wesley*, viii).

14. A Spanish Benedictine monk (cf. 1536–99), whose highly esteemed devotional treatise, *De pugna spiritualis*, was falsely attributed to Juan de Castaniza in Wesley's day.

15. Scougal, *Life of God*, 30.

16. See Newport, *Sermons of Charles Wesley*, 277, 347.

17. For John Wesley, the influence of the Quietist mystic tradition of France and Spain, most notably the writings of Francis de Sales, Miguel de Molinos, Madame Guyon, and Fénelon, was more negative than positive. His appreciation for their profound insight into the nature of God was eclipsed by the fact that he absolutely detested what he considered to be their strong bias in the direction of antinomianism.

18. See J. Wesley, *Works*, 2:374–75. On both figures, cf. Butler, *Methodists and Papists*, 137–54.

the seventeenth-century translation of his biography, *The Holy Life of Gregory Lopez*.[19] The spirituality of Lopez revolves around the concept of holy living as a lifelong quest characterized by self-denial and contempt for the world, tranquillity of soul, identification with the poor, purity of intention in this life, and the equation of holiness and happiness. Gaston de Renty was John's primary exemplar of the "perfect Christian" outside the Methodist movement.[20] What was so appealing to Wesley about his life was the synthesis of spiritual devotion and practical service.[21] In 1758, he claimed that de Renty's *Life* was his favorite book, and it certainly was one from which he quoted frequently in his later life.[22]

Much further removed by time, but equally important in the larger context of Anglican spirituality, was the rediscovery of patristic writers and texts. Pseudo-Macarius stands first and foremost among these sources for the Methodists.[23] John Wesley knew and loved his *Fifty Spiritual Homilies*, quoting from one of them in his landmark sermon, "The Scripture Way of Salvation," and publishing twenty-two of them in the first volume of his *Christian Library*. Macarius' spirituality of the heart is concerned primarily with unceasing prayer and the idea of progress toward love in the Christian life. He views the ethical virtues as stages in the soul's development, until, through God's transforming grace, the fruits of the Spirit become second nature in the perfect child of God. John Wesley frequently mentions Ephraem Syrus, another early church figure, in conjunction with Macarius.[24]

---

19. Gregory Lopez (1542–96), an obscure Spanish mystic. J. Wesley, who abridged and published his life in the *Christian Library* (vol. 50), must have been impressed by his conversion account, his missionary exploits in the New World, and his attainment to such a high degree of virtue in life. There were also many striking parallels in their personal lives. Cf. J. Wesley, *Works*, 2:375.

20. Gaston Jean Baptiste de Renty (1611–49), an affluent French Catholic turned ascetic, had been converted while reading the *Imitation of Christ* and devoted himself exclusively to piety and charity. In 1741, J. Wesley published an extract of his life, which he later included in his *Christian Library* (vol. 29).

21. See Duffy, "Wesley and Counter Reformation."

22. As reported by Butler, *Methodists and Papists*, 143.

23. Pseudo-Macarius (4th cent.), monk and spiritual writer, was the author of *Fifty Spiritual Homilies*. J. Wesley extracted twenty-two of the homilies and published them in the very first volume of the *Christian Library* in 1749.

24. Ephraem Syrus (c. 306–73) was an obscure Syrian biblical exegete and controversial writer. Most of his voluminous exegetical, theological, controversial, and ascetic works are poetic in form. For a modern edition of his hymns, see McVey, *Ephrem the Syrian*. The influence of Clement of Alexandria is also significant. He taught that all believers are to go on to a perfection characterized by harmony of purpose and desire as well as the fullness of love.

The singular theme of Ephraem's voluminous writings is the full restoration of the lost *imago Dei* (image of God) in each human being. In a fascinating volume on *Orthodox and Wesleyan Spirituality*, the late Tore Meistad demonstrated the links between Charles Wesley's missiology and that of the Eastern Church, and Kathleen McVey and ST Kimbrough Jr. both explore the spiritual resonance of Charles with Ephraem.[25] But the work has only just begun in this essentially unexplored terrain.

From this diverse group of influential sources came such varying emphases as the importance of spiritual disciplines, the primacy of pure intentions, the role of the affections, and the necessity of participation in God in the quest for holiness of heart and life. The lasting legacy of this spiritual heritage was an emphasis upon the potential triumph of God's grace and the power of a wholehearted love of God and neighbor to displace all lesser loves. The Wesleys' quest was for Christian wholeness, for holiness of heart and life, and for faith working by love. Their driving passion was to bring balance and vitality to the Christian life and to restore it to the church they loved. All of these discoveries played a part in the birth of the Wesleyan Revival.

The Broad Contours of Wesleyan Spirituality

Given the fact that the Wesleys viewed the Christian life as a *via devotio*,[26] it is actually surprising that so little has been written about Wesleyan spirituality, *per se*. Literally, only a handful of authors' names come immediately to mind. Perhaps first among them is British Methodist Gordon Wakefield, already noted. In two classic studies, *Methodist Devotion* and *Fire of Love*, he points to balance and discipline as the keys to a better understanding of this dynamic movement and its founders. According to Wakefield, an emphasis on frequent Communion, study of Scripture, mutual encouragement related to ethical conduct, and service to the poor characterize the Wesleys and their followers. In his more recent publication, *Methodist Spirituality*, Wakefield highlights the importance of the means of grace, perfect love, the social gospel, and the rapture and order of the movement reflected in Charles Wesley's hymns and Methodist discipline.

Frank Whaling, in his introduction to the volume of *The Classics of Western Spirituality* devoted to the Wesley brothers, provides one of the

---

25. See Section 4 of the volume, in particular, Kimbrough, "Other Eastern Sources," 205–85.

26. See Chilcote, *Praying in the Wesleyan Spirit*; and *Wesley Speaks*.

most wide-ranging analyses of Wesleyan spirituality. He identifies the "key deposits" that the Wesleys have handed on to their spiritual progeny.

> Charles Wesley's hymns, the Covenant Service, faith as living reality rather than belief per se, perfect love, mission based on the conviction that "for all, for all, my Savior died," the importance of laymen, fellowship as *koinonia*, the spiritual importance of organization, a creative tolerance based on the notion that true religion is inward and social rather than merely doctrinal, and a pragmatic openness to developing situations.[27]

Beyond all of this detail, however, Whaling more simply concludes that the Wesleys "were unique for the integral nature of their spirituality. They were able to hold together what most Christian groups, even today, tend to keep apart."[28] In similar fashion, in his discussion of "The Methodist Synthesis" in *English Spirituality*, David Jeffrey elevates Wesley's ability to hold the "meditative tradition" and the "missionary tradition" of spirituality in dynamic balance.[29]

David Lowes Watson has also made important contributions in this area. In addition to his multiple works on Christian discipleship and the use of small groups in early Methodism, he contributed a lesser-known essay to Frank Senn's *Protestant Spiritual Traditions* in 1986, simply entitled "Methodist Spirituality."[30] It is a jewel, in my view, one of the most succinct and incisive statements about this crucial theme. Watson describes Methodist spirituality as a synthesis of an Anglican holiness of intent and a Puritan interior assurance. The spirituality of the early Methodist people, he argues, was shaped by a vital sense of mutual accountability (centered in the Methodist class meeting), the cultivation of a catholicity of grace, the quest for Christian perfection in this life, the constant use of the means of grace, and the celebration of God's pervasive presence through the singing of hymns.[31] Similar to the work of Watson, in her study entitled *Making Disciples*, Sondra Matthaei has interfaced Methodist spirituality with spiritual formation in a most helpful way.[32] Her essential argument is that formation for holiness of

---

27. Whaling, *John and Charles Wesley*, 62.
28. Whaling, *John and Charles Wesley*, 63.
29. Jeffrey, *English Spirituality*, 28–35.
30. Watson, "Methodist Spirituality," 217–73.
31. Also noteworthy is the chapter on the Wesleys in Gordon, *Evangelical Spirituality*, 11–40, which elevates the themes of salvation, poetry, Christian perfection, love, and the means of grace. See also Harper, *Devotional Life*; Knight, *Presence of God*; Clapper, *As if the Heart Mattered*; and Newton, *Faith Working by Love*.
32. Matthaei, *Making Disciples*.

heart and life served as the central thrust of the Wesleyan tradition. The three central themes in this "discipleship spirituality" are the search for living faith, the freedom of God's grace in and for all, and the importance of community in the formation of Christian disciples.

The empirical studies of Tom Albin also afford some important insights with regard to the spirituality of the early Methodist movement. After working through hundreds of accounts of religious experience, he concluded "that the primary force in the Evangelical Revival was laity rather than clergy."[33] The role of the laity in the communication of their spirituality was crucial, as well. "The breadth and depth of the revival," Albin observes, "had something to do with the ability of the laity to understand and experience God for themselves and then to enable others to enter into a personal relationship with God as well."[34] It was ordinary persons in community, rather than the high-profile leader, that exerted the most influence both inside and outside the movement as they attempted to put their faith into practice in the daily round of life. Albin's ultimate conclusion is "that early Methodist spirituality could be characterized as a positive process in which lay leadership and direction played a key role along with that of the local community rather than sudden experiences related to a fear of death or hell."[35]

It is obvious from these various interpretations of early Methodist spirituality that the vision of the Christian life for the Wesleys and their followers was that of breadth and wholeness. Their principal insight was that no spirituality is complete until God's love—experienced both personally and in the context of community—is carried into the world in concrete acts of compassion and justice.

Salient Themes

The salient themes of spirituality in the Wesleyan tradition include the foundations of the Christian life in grace, spiritual autobiography and the importance of Christian narrative, accountable discipleship and the communal nature of spirituality, works of piety (including prayer and fasting, immersion in Scripture, fellowship, and Eucharist), works of mercy, and the gift of song.

---

33. Albin, "Early Methodist Spirituality," 277.
34. Albin, "Early Methodist Spirituality," 278.
35. Albin, "Early Methodist Spirituality," 279.

Foundations in Grace

Wesleyan spirituality is built upon the foundation of grace.[36] In his sermon, "On Working Out Our Own Salvation," John Wesley talks about two grand heads of doctrine upon which the Christian life is built.[37] The first is grace as it pertains to the work of God *for* us in Jesus Christ; the second is grace as it pertains to the work of God *in* us through the power of the Holy Spirit. Grace is God's unmerited love, restoring our relationship to God and renewing God's own image in our lives. Nothing was more critical to the Wesleys than this understanding of spiritual restoration founded upon God's unconditional love. John most frequently defined "grace" in relation to the way of salvation in which the energy of God's love became manifest more fully in the life of the believer. He simply describes it as the power of the Holy Spirit, enabling us to believe and love and serve God. Christian discipleship—the arena of God's continuing activity in the life of the believer—is, first and foremost, a grace-filled response to God's all-sufficient grace.

While grace is essentially God's offer of relationship and restoration, the Wesleys describe it as prevenient, convincing, justifying, sanctifying, or sacramental, in order to describe the way in which Christians experience God's extension of love at various points in the spiritual journey. Charles Wesley illustrates all these aspects of grace in his hymns. In one particular hymn, however, he sings about the dimensions of grace, building upon a favorite text from Ephesians 3.

> What shall I do my god to love?
>   My loving God to praise
> The length, and breadth, and height to prove,
>   And depth of sovereign grace?
>
> Thy sovereign grace to all extends,
>   Immense and unconfined;
> From age to age it never ends;
>   It reaches all mankind.[38]

---

36. See Langford, *Practical Divinity*, 24–48.
37. See J. Wesley, *Works*, 3:199–209.
38. C. Wesley, *Hymns and Sacred Poems* (1749), 1:163 (no. 92.11).

This grace is a free gift.[39] It elicits the most amazing images and sublime expressions of gratitude among the early Methodist people. Hetty Roe, in a flight of spiritual ecstasy in a letter to her friend, exclaims,

> Great things, indeed, my dear sister, has the Lord done for you, and for your unworthy friend. And yet, O stupendous grace! we have only received a drop from the ocean of his love. An endless prospect, and a maze of bliss, lie yet before us! opening beauties, and such lengths, and breadths, and depths, and heights, as thought cannot reach or mind of man conceive! It is, my friend, the fulness of the triune God, in which we may bathe, and plunge, and sink, till lost and swallowed up in the ever-increasing, overflowing ocean of delights.[40]

Spiritual Narratives

Charles Wesley had a particular interest in spiritual narratives. In the early years of the revival, he solicited reflective materials of this nature from the rank and file of the movement on a regular basis. Only recently have scholars begun to bring this corpus together.[41] These narratives confirm that in the Wesleyan heritage the life of faith is by its very nature autobiographical. Whenever the Christian faith becomes *my* faith, there lies behind that transformation a story that begs to be told, a narrative that unfolds something of the mystery of life. Methodist spirituality is by definition, therefore, a narrative spirituality.[42] One of the characteristic emphases in the accounts solicited by Charles Wesley, therefore, is the experience of conversion—a process involving a call to personal repentance, moral transformation, and concomitant freedom to love. The decisive conclusion to be drawn from these accounts is that salvation means liberation.

The Wesleyan way of salvation, a topic explored thoroughly in our time, consisted essentially in three dynamic movements: repentance, justification by grace through faith, and holiness. John Wesley defines repentance as a

---

39. See Wesley's sermon, "On Free Grace," in which he describes God's grace as a free gift, in all, and for all. Cf. J. Wesley, *Works*, 3:544–63.

40. Rogers, *Account*, 223.

41. See the collection of transcribed manuscript materials in Barry and Morgan, *Reformation and Revival*, 75–104; similar collections in Hindmarsh, *Evangelical Conversion Narrative*; and Chilcote, *Her Own Story*. Cf. Kent, *Wesley and the Wesleyans*, for an interesting but overly provocative analysis of some of this material.

42. Ward and Heitzenrater observe that "the sheer bulk of the surviving evangelical self-representation and confession is a broad hint of the huge volume of class-meeting testimony and the like which never moved from oral to literary form" (J. Wesley, *Works*, 18:24; cf. Hindmarsh, "My chains fell off").

true self-understanding akin to that experienced by the prodigal son who came to himself in the realization that he was far from his true home. While it involves remorse and contrition, it carries a strong relational connotation, the initial turning of the heart and life homeward. Faith is the gift of trust in those things we cannot see, especially "Christ's love for me." But the word "faith" often functions as a shorthand symbol among the Wesleyan writers for the more specific concept of "justification by grace through faith," which refers to the experience of having been accepted and pardoned by God through faith in Christ alone. Holiness is another shorthand term that refers to the whole process of becoming Christlike in our lives. It includes both the idea of sanctification, the process of growing in grace and love, and Christian perfection, perhaps the most important of all Wesleyan concepts, which simply refers to the love of God and neighbor filling one's heart and life.

Repentance

The essence of repentance is to place oneself before God, to experience the gaping chasm that separates the sinful creature from the Creator, but to find in God the One who is also close at hand and truly loves. Because God is a God who seeks to restore all things and is a God of mercy and love, the movement from repentance to faith, the Wesleys believed, is but a step. Contemplation of this merciful God, who responds to the repentant sinner with such grace and mercy, set Mary Stokes' heart to music through a composition of her own.

> What wonderous grace! what boundless love!
>   What soft compassion this,
> That calls my rebel heart to prove
>   A never fading bliss!
>
> 'Tis mercy bids me seek the Lord;
>   'Tis mercy bids me fly;
> 'Tis mercy speaks the balmy word,
>   "Repent, thy God is nigh."
>
> 'Tis mercy fills my trembling heart,
>   With agonizing pain,
> With keen distress and poignant smart,
>   Nor heave these sighs in vain.

> The tears that now in torrents flow,
>> This mercy will repress;
> Remove the load, a pardon show,
>> And speak a healing peace.[43]

Faith

Drawing upon the teachings of his Anglican heritage, Charles Wesley defines saving faith as "a true trust and confidence of the mercy of God through our Lord Jesus Christ and a steadfast hope of all good things to be received at God's hand. This is the true, lively, and unfeigned Christian faith, and is not in the mouth and outward profession only, but it liveth and stirreth inwardly in the heart."[44] Likewise, he describes this faith in a lyrical mode.

> By faith we know thee strong to save
>> (Save us, a present Saviour thou!)
> Whate'er we hope, by faith we have,
>> Future and past subsisting now.

> To him that in thy name believes
>> Eternal life with thee is given;
> Into himself he all receives—
>> Pardon, and holiness, and heaven.[45]

The center around which all else revolved for the Methodists was the shared experience of faith-as-trust and salvation by grace. The more John preached and Charles sang this gospel through his hymns, the more people experienced spiritual liberation in their lives. The Spirit of God was alive and at work in the hearts and minds of many people, especially poor people, who had never experienced God as Someone real in their lives before.

---

43. Zechariah Taft quotes the entirety of her hymn in *Biographical Sketches*, 2:152–53.

44. Newport, *Charles Wesley's Sermons*, 155, from Sermon 5 on Titus 3:8. His quotation is from the homily of the Church of England, entitled "Of True Christian Faith."

45. J. Wesley, *Works*, 7:194 (no. 92.3–4).

Holiness

While justification by grace through faith is the foundation of the Christian life, holiness of heart and life, or sanctification, is the process that leads to the ultimate goal of perfect love in this life. The Wesleyan concept of salvation is that of faith made effective through love. Charles Wesley's writings are filled with a sense of longing for this ultimate gift of God's grace and with descriptions of such a life. The doctrine of Christian perfection is central to the spirituality of the early Methodist people, and while Charles's views differ in important ways from the doctrine of his brother, John, the following propositions characterize the areas of agreement:[46]

1. *Love.* Christian perfection is the fullest possible love of God and neighbor—no less but also no more.
2. *Purity of Intention.* The essence of Christian perfection is purity of intention, i.e., seeking to please God in all thought, word, and action.
3. *Dynamism.* Perfection in the Christian life is dynamic, and not static, in nature. Growth in holiness should continue within Christian perfection and not just before it.
4. *Restoration.* The understanding of salvation as the restoration of the image of God and of Christian perfection as the fullest possible restoration, is deeply rooted in the teachings of the early church. Perfection is essentially conformity to Christ in all things, the believer perennially dependent upon God for whatever level of restoration is made possible through the gracious power of the Holy Spirit.
5. *Happiness.* Holiness is happiness. The fullest expression of holiness in life is the truest form of happiness. The goal of the Christian life, therefore, is essentially "a blessed abiding" in God.

Accountable Discipleship

In defense of their expanding network of Methodist Societies, the Wesley brothers identified small groups as the distinguishing mark of the movement. In addition to organizing a network of itinerant preacher/evangelists, they built up a structure to sustain that ministry and in which their followers were encouraged to "watch over one another in love." The band and

---

46. See my introduction to the Christian Perfection corpus in J. Wesley, *Works*, 13:1–25.

class meetings—early Methodist hallmarks of mutual encouragement and genuine care—are celebrated in the hymn of Charles Wesley.

> Help us to help each other, Lord,
> > Each other's cross to bear;
> Let each his friendly aid afford,
> > And feel his brother's care.
>
> Help us to build each other up,
> > Our little stock improve;
> Increase our faith, confirm our hope,
> > And perfect us in love.[47]

Life in these accountability structures nurtured qualities such as self-denial, transparency, simplicity, sincerity, faithfulness, and immersion in the means of grace. In the intimacy of these small groups, early Methodist people learned what it meant to grow in Christ and, together, plumbed the depths of God's love for them all.

Works of Piety

Fellowship in small groups was just one "means of grace" in a constellation of spiritual practices or disciplines, the purpose of which was richer communion with God through Christ. In addition to Christian fellowship, or conference, the Wesleys also included prayer and fasting, Bible study, and participation in the sacrament of Holy Communion among the "instituted means of grace." He also called these "works of piety."[48] These activities nurtured and sustained the spiritual growth of the Methodists. They also fueled the Wesleyan movement as a powerful religious awakening which was both "evangelical" (a rediscovery of God's word of grace) and "Eucharistic" (a rediscovery of the sacrament of Holy Communion as a way to experience that grace).[49]

---

47. J. Wesley, *Works*, 7:677 (no. 489.3–4).

48. See Harper, "Works of Piety."

49. John Wesley's sermon on *Means of Grace* was an effort to clarify the difference between the proper use and possible abuse of prayer (and fasting), Bible study, Christian fellowship, and the sacrament of Holy Communion in faithful discipleship. These "means" were, in fact, the very foundation of Wesleyan spirituality and their rediscovery a powerful appropriation of ancient Christian practice. Cf. J. Wesley, *Works*, 1:376–97, and the most important recent work on this topic, Knight, *Presence of God*.

The Wesleys viewed sacramental grace and evangelical experience as necessary counterparts of an authentically Christian spirituality. The early Methodists sang and bore witness to the testimony of this Charles Wesley hymn stanza:

> The prayer, the fast, the word conveys,
> > When mix'd with faith, Thy life to me;
> In all the channels of Thy grace
> > I still have fellowship with Thee:
> But chiefly here my soul is fed
> > With fulness of immortal bread.[50]

Not only does the sacred meal enable the community to remember the past event of the cross and Christ's redemptive work for all (memorial), but it celebrates the presence of the living Lord in a feast of thanksgiving (sign and means of grace) and orients the community in hope toward the future consummation of all things in the great heavenly banquet to come (a pledge of heaven). The Wesleys illustrated these aspects of the sacrament in the 1745 *Hymns on the Lord's Supper*, a collection of 166 Eucharistic hymns consisting primarily in Charles's compositions.

Works of Mercy

The early Methodists found it impossible to separate their personal experience of God and devotion to Christ from their active role as agents of reconciliation and social transformation in the world. Their spirituality was truly incarnational. Their lives consisted of active social service, commitment to the poor, and advocacy for the oppressed.[51] Authentic Christianity, they had learned, is mission and sincere engagement in God's mission is true religion. The primary means by which they lived out this holistic understanding of the Christian faith was through "works of mercy" that paralleled the more interior works of piety.[52] Evangelism was the heart of this missionary vision, simply fueled by the desire to share the good news they had experienced in Christ with others in both word and deed.

John Wesley mandated that his followers engage in works of mercy, defined in the second of his "General Rules" in the most expansive way

---

50. Wesley and Wesley, *Hymns on the Lord's Supper*, 39 (no. 54.4).

51. For a contemporary Methodist expression of this theme, see Keller, *Spirituality and Social Responsibility*.

52. See Miles, "Works of Mercy."

possible—"do good." Methodist people were simply encouraged to do good, "by being in every kind merciful after their power, as they have opportunity doing good of every possible sort and as far as possible to all men."[53] In their effort to adhere to this spiritual instruction, Methodists sought out people in need—the poor, the hungry, the destitute, and the neglected. They visited prisons, established orphanages and schools, and practiced their servant-oriented faith in their own particular contexts, thereby extending the ministry of Methodism into the communities they served.

Charles Wesley memorialized this spirituality of action in an elegy to Mrs. Mary Naylor, whose life so powerfully illustrates the witness of Methodist commitment to the poor.

> Affliction, poverty, disease,
> Drew out her soul in soft distress,
> > The wretched to relieve:
> In all the works of love employed,
> Her sympatizing soul enjoyed
> > The blessedness to give.
>
> Her Savior in his members seen,
> A stranger she received him in,
> > An hungry Jesus fed,
> Tended her sick, imprisoned Lord,
> And flew in all his wants to afford
> > Her ministerial aid.
>
> A nursing-mother to the poor,
> For them she husbanded her store,
> > Her life, her all, bestowed;
> For them she labored day and night,
> In doing good her whole delight,
> > In copying after God.[54]

---

53. J. Wesley, *Works*, 9:70.
54. Kimbrough, *Songs for the Poor*, 12.

The Gift of Song

"Before we reached the place," writes Grace Murray, "we heard the people singing hymns. The very sound set all my passions afloat, though I did not know one word they uttered, which plainly shows how the affections may be greatly moved while the understanding is quite dark."[55] This reference to the important role that hymns played in the Wesleyan tradition is typical. The Wesleys revolutionized Anglican worship with the rediscovery of congregational singing. "The eighteenth-century revival," Richard Heitzenrater observes, "was to a great extent borne on the wings of Charles's poetry. Charles's hymns not only helped form the texture of the Methodist mind but also, perhaps more importantly, set the temper of the Methodist spirit."[56] The hymns themselves were a powerful tool in the Spirit's work of revival and shaped the spirituality of the Methodist people, perhaps more than any other single force besides the Bible. The hymns of the Wesleyan tradition have served consistently as catalysts for religious awakening and as acts of prayer. They express the language of the heart. Isabella Wilson's diary affords a glimpse into the nature of a spirituality that bursts inevitably into song:

> Oh! the unbounded love of Jesus to my soul. His promises are all precious. My peace flows as a river while he teaches me the lessons of his grace, of faith and holiness. My soul is athirst for all the mind that was in him.
>
> Lord, take my heart and let it be
> For ever clos'd to all but thee:
> Seal thou my breast, and let me wear
> That pledge of love for ever there.[57]

It should be no surprise that the hymns of Charles Wesley reflect the essence and provide a language for spirituality in the Wesleyan tradition. None expresses the holism and dynamism of life in Christ better than this text:

> O thou who camest from above
>   The pure celestial fire t'impart,
> Kindle a flame of sacred love
>   On the mean altar of my heart!

---

55. Bennet, *Memoirs of Mrs. Grace Bennet*, 6.
56. Quoted in Kimbrough, *Lost in Wonder*, 11–12.
57. Pipe, "Isabella Wilson," 597. The hymn reference is to *Hymns and Sacred Poems* (1740), 1:265.

There let it for thy glory burn
    With inextinguishable blaze,
And trembling to its source return
    In humble love, and fervent praise.

Jesu, confirm my heart's desire
    To work, and speak, and think for thee;
Still let me guard the holy fire,
    And still stir up thy gift in me;

Ready for all thy perfect will,
    My acts of faith and love repeat,
Till death thy endless mercies seal,
    And make the sacrifice complete.[58]

---

58. J. Wesley, *Works*, 7:473–74 (no. 318).

Chapter 11

Charles Wesley and Christian Practices

> Source note: Delivered as the keynote address at the Charles Wesley Tercentenary Conference, "A Charge to Keep: Charles Wesley at 300," at Duke Divinity School, June 22, 2007, and published in *Proceedings of the Charles Wesley Society* 12 (2008) 35–47.

OVER THE PAST COUPLE decades, two questions dominate the focused attention given to Christian practices: "What does it mean to live the Christian life faithfully and well?" and, "How can we help one another to do so?"[1] The concept of practices linked with specific communities of faith, of course, is nothing new, but contemporary students of ecclesial practices are discovering much about how these activities both shape people and reflect their values and senses of meaning. Perhaps no movement has exerted greater influence in these rediscoveries than the Valparaiso Project on the Education and Formation of People in Faith, directed by Dorothy Bass.[2] In their essay on "A Theological Understanding of Christian Practices," Craig Dykstra and Dorothy Bass define Christian practices precisely as "things Christian people do together over time to address fundamental human needs in response to and in the light of God's active presence for the life of the world."[3] Elsewhere Dykstra describes these practices in a somewhat more conversational style.

---

1. See Dorothy Bass's discussion of these questions in her forward to Dykstra, *Growing in the Life of Faith*, xii–xiv.

2. See the inaugural volume in the Practices of Faith Series, edited by Bass, *Practicing our Faith*. Since its inception, scholars have explored a number of Christian practices, such as honoring the body, testimony, song, and the gift of time, in this publishing project. The Valparaiso Project website (www.practicingourfaith.org) invites the reader to "explore a way of life shaped by practices that respond to God's grace and reflect God's love for you, for others, and for all creation."

3. Dykstra and Bass, "Theological Understanding of Christian Practices," 18.

> Christian practices are not, finally, activities we do to make something spiritual happen in our lives. Nor are they duties we undertake to be obedient to God. Rather, they are patterns of communal action that create openings in our lives where the grace, mercy, and presence of God may be made known to us. They are places where the power of God is experienced. In the end, these are not ultimately our practices but forms of participation in the practice of God.[4]

Charles Wesley's life and ministry revolved around the same concerns that have fueled the revival of Christian practices in our own time. His primary questions were those with which I began this presentation. His driving passion was to live faithfully in Christ and to establish communities in which others claimed this as their primary vocation, as well. Despite the fact that Christian practices were central to early Methodism, little has been written about the way in which spiritual disciplines shaped the lives of the Methodist people. Among scholars interested in such questions, Hal Knight undoubtedly stands out among them in the work he has done on the "means of grace." In a fairly recent book, he identifies some of the Christian practices that continue to enrich the heirs of the Wesleyan tradition. He explores eight "life-enriching practices," as he calls them, under the four rubrics of personal devotion, worshiping together, letting go, and reaching out.[5] While reclaiming these important aspects of the Wesleyan heritage, he actually gives very little attention to Charles Wesley and fails to give even passing mention to the formative role that sacred song has played as faithful practice in this "singing church." Kenneth Carter, in a more recent study, entitled *A Way of Life in the World*, discusses the six practices of searching the Scriptures, generosity with the poor, testimony, singing, Holy Communion, and life together, but also fails to describe Charles's role in inculcating these practices in any way.[6]

I would like to look with you at four themes that are pervasive in a collection of hymns Charles wrote to memorialize the lives of nine early Methodist women.[7] My contention is that in these hymns on the death of the

---

4. Bass, *Practicing Our Faith*, 5.
5. Knight, *Eight Life-Enriching Practices*.
6. Carter, *Way of Life*.
7. Wesley originally published epitaphs for Grace Bowen, Mrs. Lefevre, Mary Naylor, and Anne Wigginton in C. Wesley, *Funeral Hymns*. Funeral hymns for Elizabeth Blackwell, Hannah Butts, Hannah Dewal, and Lady Hotham were published posthumously and only existed in manuscript during Wesley's lifetime (C. Wesley, *MS Funeral Hymns*, 1756–82). Subsequently, all these texts were published together in the appendix of a nineteenth-century edition of Charles Wesley's journal, entitled "Selections from the Poetry of the Rev. Charles Wesley, Illustrative of His Journal and Correspondence" (Jackson, *Journal*, 2:287–431).

faithful departed, we encounter a composite portrait of Christian practice at its best—at least, at its best as conceived by Charles Wesley—an idealized vision held up before the Methodist people for their emulation.

The nine women included in this survey all died between the years 1755 and 1786, but most of them in the sixth decade of the eighteenth century. Their names are Grace Bowen, Lady Hotham, Mrs. Lefevre, Mary Naylor, Anne Wigginton, Hannah Dewal, Elizabeth Blackwell, Hannah Butts, and Mary Horton. Some of the women were well-known in their day; others were virtually unknown beyond the limited circle of the Methodist Society in which they thrived. The most lengthy hymn extends to forty-one stanzas in five parts. The shortest memorials—two examples in this sample—are hymns of only fifteen verses each. The more lengthy elegies follow a fairly consistent pattern involving several parts. The opening section, while acknowledging the reality of death, celebrates God's victory over death and the triumph of a faithful life. Subsequent segments often provide some of the biographical detail related to the subject, particularly elevating her experience of salvation by grace, or even outlining the way of salvation. The hymns almost always conclude with something approaching a vision of heaven—a description of the joys and ecstasies of life eternal with God.

Of greatest importance for our purposes here are those portions of these hymns that develop a portrait of the subject's faithful practice, generally, as one might well expect, in the biographical sections. To illustrate, Wesley devotes almost the entirety of Part III in his hymn "On the Death of Mrs. Mary Naylor" to the development of such an idealized portrait.

> Mercy that heaven-descending guest,
> Resided in her gentle breast,
>   And full possession kept;
> While listening to the orphan's moan,
> And echoing back the widow's groan,
>   She wept with them that wept.
>
> Affliction, poverty, disease,
> Drew out her soul in soft distress
>   The wretched to relieve:
> In all the works of love employ'd,
> Her sympathizing soul enjoy'd
>   The blessedness to give.

> Her Saviour in his members seen,
> A stranger she receiv'd him in,
> > An hungry Jesus fed,
> Tended her sick imprison'd Lord,
> And flew in all His wants t' afford
> > Her ministerial aid.
>
> A nursing-mother to the poor,
> For them she husbanded her store,
> > Her life, her all, bestow'd:
> For them she labour'd day and night,
> In doing good her whole delight,
> > In copying after God.[8]

These hymns, as you can immediately discern just from four stanzas of one particular hymn, reflect a wide range of practices, including hospitality, testimony, forgiveness, healing, social service, sick visitation, prison ministry, and generosity, but four practices stand out by virtue of their pervasiveness. I will call them gracious imitation, active faith, holy friendship, and generous inclusivity.

Gracious Imitation

All of these hymns, first and perhaps foremost, reflect lives lived in "gracious imitation" of Christ. The women memorialized by Charles practiced to be like Jesus in virtually everything they did. Two of the women featured here, Hannah Dewal and Elizabeth Blackwell were relatives and frequently hosted Wesley on his many visits to Lewisham, just southeast of London. Hannah's passion to be more like Jesus impressed him deeply. He describes the character-shaping value of her imitative practice. She was "transparent as the crystal stream." There were "no sudden fits of transient love" in her demeanor. Attributing every act of kindness to God's grace, she "waited all [Christ's] mind to gain." She was "careful to be, and not to seem, whate'er she was." Wesley identifies the guiding principle of her life in stanza four of the hymn.

---

8. C. Wesley, *Funeral Hymns*, 52–53. For the complete poem of sixty-three stanzas, see 49–61. ST Kimbrough Jr. included three of these stanzas in *Songs for the Poor* (23–24).

> On Him she fix'd her single eye,
>> And steady in His steps went on,
>
> Studious by works to testify
>> The power of God in weakness shown.
>
> A quiet follower of the Lamb,
>> She walk'd in Him she had received,
>
> And more and more declar'd his name,
>> And more and more like Jesus lived.[9]

Quite a number of the sub-themes under this general heading could be drawn directly from the opening chapters of Thomas à Kempis's *Imitation of Christ*, particularly from Thomas's discussion of the centrality of truth and justice in the desire to imitate the Lord.[10] "Justice composed her upright soul," claims Wesley of Mary Naylor, "Justice did all her thoughts controul, And form'd her character."[11] In her efforts to practice the life of Christ, she never put darkness for light, "Evil for good, or wrong for right, Or fraud for piety." "The truth she lov'd," he celebrates, "And spoke it from her heart."[12] Lady Hotham reflected all these values in a life oriented around "the love of truth, the dread of sin, the hunger after God."[13] The gracious imitation of Christ leads to spiritual renewal—the restoration of the capacity to love as God loves—and, in Charles's estimation, Mrs. Lefevre exemplified the fullest possible realization of this lofty ideal.

> She *was* (what words can never paint)
>> A spotless soul, a sinless saint,
>
>> In perfect love renew'd,
>
> A mirror of the deity,
>
> A transcript of the One in Three,
>> A temple fill'd with God.[14]

---

9. C. Wesley, *MS Funeral Hymns*, 43.

10. The formative influence of Thomas à Kempis's *The Imitation of Christ* on both brothers requires no extended discussion here. They undoubtedly encountered this devotional classic originally in the translation of George Stanhope (London, 1699). Beginning in 1735, John Wesley published several editions of *The Christian's Pattern*, as he titled it, based upon the earlier translation of John Worthington.

11. C. Wesley, *Funeral Hymns*, 51.

12. C. Wesley, *Funeral Hymns*, 52.

13. C. Wesley, *MS Funeral Hymns*, 3.

14. C. Wesley, *Funeral Hymns*, 47.

Active Faith

A second practice relates directly to the Wesleyan conception of "faith working by love" drawn from Galatians 5:6, namely, active faith. Both Wesleys referred perennially to the need to translate faith into action. When Charles uses expressions like "practical faith" or the "full assurance of faith," or admonishes the believer to press on toward the "obedience," "triumph," or "righteousness of faith," he refers to the process by which faith is made effective in love. Standing squarely in his Anglican heritage, he affirms that faith—God's restoration of the capacity to entrust one's life to God—is the foundation of the abundant life, but also claims that faith is but a means to love's end. The practice of this "active faith" dominated the life of the Methodist Society.[15]

Elizabeth Blackwell exemplified this practice: "Her living faith by works was shown," claims Wesley. Moreover, her cultivation of the ability to "[make] the sufferer's griefs her own, And [weep] sincere with those that [weep]"—her habituated pattern of empathetic concern, in other words—authenticated God's gift of faith in her life.[16] Four of the nine hymns under our inspection refer explicitly to the story of Mary and Martha in Luke 10, with specific reference to this concern about the practice of active faith. In every instance, Charles avoids the typical elevation of Mary and the concomitant spiritualization of the text; rather, he applauds both hands and heart and celebrates the conjunction of both in the life of the faithful disciple of Christ. Describing the character of Hannah Butts, he sings,

> Walking in her house with God,
>> Portion'd with the better part,
> She her faith by actions show'd,
>> Martha's hand and Mary's heart.[17]

Mary Horton, he observed, chose "to sit delighted at the Master's feet, And listening to His word," but she also "ran the way of His commands, And minister'd, with Martha's hands."[18] Lady Hotham "toil'd with Martha's hands," Charles reminds the would-be disciple of Jesus, but she also possessed Mary's part by "list'ning for her Lord's commands."[19] According to Charles,

---

15. See a discussion of this understanding of faith in Chilcote, "Charles Wesley and the Language of Faith."
16. C. Wesley, *MS Funeral Hymns*, 52–3.
17. C. Wesley, *MS Funeral Hymns*, 37.
18. Jackson, *Journal*, 2:414.
19. C. Wesley, *MS Funeral Hymns*, 4.

Anne Wigginton provided "a pattern to believers" because she was "Possesst of Mary's better part, and Martha's hands."[20] He points to the importance of Martha's and Mary's spirit both co-habiting the believer so that heart, head, and hands are fully conformed to the image of Christ.

Holy Friendship

The third practice reflected in these hymns is holy friendship. The early Methodist people lived in ever-widening circles of holy friendship. Certainly, one of the most important aspects of this practice for the women, in particular, was the way in which friendships created space for them. As Janice Raymond has described it, friendship helped "to create the world as women imagine it could be."[21] It is not surprising to find early Methodist women describing their friendships as precious, invaluable, blessed, and the delight of their hearts.[22] The establishment of these relationships, however, depended to a large degree on the practice of befriending the "other." On a very practical level, friendship mirrored the theological concern for accountable discipleship. Given the fact that the Wesleys viewed the Christian life as a journey, companionship—sharing bread with one another—bound the pilgrims together inextricably and promoted the kind of spiritual growth that is only possible in community. These women provided spiritual guidance to one another, often directing their companions through the difficult terrain of the journey. "Can you her artless warmth forget," asked Charles concerning Grace Bowen, "Her eager haste to turn your feet Into the narrow road . . . When'er ye stray'd from God!" No one could ever forget her "kind counsels," "fearful warnings," "loud protests," and "silent tears"—all of these efforts at spiritual direction being expressions of holy friendship.[23]

We should be careful not to underestimate the importance or value of these friendships, so powerfully exemplified in the life of Hannah Dewal.

> For friendship form'd, her swelling heart
> With pure, intense affection glow'd;
> She could not give her friend a part,
> Because she gave the whole to God.

---

20. C. Wesley, *Funeral Hymns*, 32.

21. Raymond, *Passion for Friends*, 205. Cf. Hunt, *Fierce Tenderness*; and Robert, *Faithful Friendships*.

22. See Chilcote, *Early Methodist Spirituality*, 54–55.

23. C. Wesley, *Funeral Hymns*, 26.

> Her friend she clasp'd with love entire,
> > Enkindled at the Saviour's throne,
> A spark of that celestial fire,
> > A ray of that eternal Sun.[24]

The practice of friendship, however, extended far beyond the circle of the loveable and lovely. In fact, the early Methodists acted in the spirit of Charles's injunction to "make the poor their bosom friends," and the way in which they established lasting friendships with the forgotten and marginal of their own day remains one of their most compelling testimonies.[25]

In this regard, Charles's frequent reference to Matthew 25 in the elegies should be no surprise. The women practiced discerning Christ in "the distressing disguise of the poor," to use the words of Mother Teresa.[26] Wesley provides the following portrait of Elizabeth Blackwell's character, shaped by her practice of befriending the least in her community:

> Nursing the poor with constant care,
> > Affection soft, and heart-esteem,
> She saw her Saviour's image there,
> > And gladly minister'd to Him.[27]

In similar fashion, he describes Mary Naylor as "a nursing mother to the poor," as we sang together earlier. Grace Bowen rejoiced "an hungry Christ to feed" and "to visit him in pain." To the poor, Wesley sings, she gave her all.[28]

Generous Inclusivity

This third practice of holy friendship leads seamlessly into the fourth and final practice I would like to explore with you today, namely, generous inclusivity. Charles Wesley actually develops some of his most powerful lyrical images around this theme. None is more potent, perhaps, than the expansion of the heart by means of faith's influence in the direction of greater love—the ultimate goal of all Christian practices, of course. A single stanza reflection on Psalm 81:10 captures the essence of this image.

24. C. Wesley, *MS Funeral Hymns*, 44.

25. This is a line from a poem of Charles Wesley which remained unpublished until 1990.

26. Mother Teresa, *In the Heart of the World*, 21.

27. C. Wesley, *MS Funeral Hymns*, 53.

28. C. Wesley, *Funeral Hymns*, 25.

> Give me the enlarged desire,
> 	And open, Lord, my soul,
> Thy own fullness to require,
> 	And comprehend the whole;
> Stretch my faith's capacity
> 	Wider and yet wider still;
> Then, with all that is in thee,
> 	My soul forever fill![29]

"Fill'd with purity of love," Hannah Dewal embraced the world with widespread arms. Particularly in her death, Wesley observes that her soul was drawn out to all humankind. Earlier in his hymn he describes the foundation of this expansive vision:

> Celestial charity expands
> 	The heart to all the ransom'd race;
> Though knit to one in closest bands,
> 	Her soul doth every soul embrace.
> She no unkind exception makes,
> 	A childlike follower of her God;
> The world into her heart she takes,
> 	The purchase dear of Jesu's blood.[30]

Elizabeth Blackwell sought to discern the image of God in every fellow creature and this practice shaped her into a person "whose love," in Wesley's words, "did the whole world embrace!"[31] Struggling to find the words to express the depth of this love restored in the life of Mary Naylor, Charles creates this magnificent image: "[She] stretch'd her arms of charity, / Ingrasping all mankind."[32]

All of these practices shaped the women of whom Charles Wesley sang, and his own range of practices, rooted in the tradition of his beloved Anglican church, formed him into a faithful witness to the love that would not let him go. The evangelistic import of the believer shaped by the practices of the faith was not lost on Charles Wesley, nor should it be lost on us.

---

29. C. Wesley, *Scripture Hymns* 1762, 1:268 (no. 841, on Psalm 81:10). See also J. Wesley, *Works*, 7:529 (no. 361).

30. C. Wesley, *MS Funeral Hymns*, 45.

31. C. Wesley, *MS Funeral Hymns*, 54.

32. C. Wesley, *Funeral Hymns*, 56.

Several stanzas from his hymn "On the Death of Mrs. Elizabeth Blackwell" bear witness to the larger significance of the God-shaped character formed in those who apprentice themselves to the Christ:

> Her living faith by works was shown:
>   Through faith to full salvation kept,
> She made the sufferer's griefs her own,
>   And wept sincere with those that wept:
> Nursing the poor with constant care,
>   Affection soft, and heart-esteem,
> She saw her Saviour's image there,
>   And gladly minister'd to Him.
>
> By wisdom pure and peaceable,
>   By the meek Spirit of her Lord,
> She knows the stoutest to compel,
>   And sinners wins without the word:
> They see the tempers of the Lamb,
>   They feel the wisdom from above,
> And bow, subdued, to Jesu's name,
>   As captive of resistless love.[33]

---

33. C. Wesley, *MS Funeral Hymns*, 51–3, sts. 7 and 4.

— Chapter 12 —

A Faith That Sings

The Renewing Power
of Lyrical Theology

Source note: This essay was published in *The Wesleyan Tradition: A Paradigm for Renewal*, edited by Paul W. Chilcote, 148–62 (Nashville: Abingdon, 2002).

THE WESLEYAN TRADITION WAS born in song. Early Methodist people found their true identity as the children of God through singing, and the hymns of Charles Wesley, in particular, shaped their self-understanding and praxis. Certainly, the spiritual rediscoveries of the Wesleys put a song in the hearts of their followers who were liberated by the good news of God's love in Jesus Christ. But this lyrical heritage was not rooted in the simple joy of song; rather, the leaders of the nascent revival recognized the potency of congregational singing as a legitimate medium of theology. The Wesleys understood, as an ancient writer once observed, that to sing is to pray twice, and as an African proverb maintains, if you can talk, you can sing. The singing of Christians is both prayer to God and speech about God. Hymns function both as a communal confession of faith and a common catechism for the faith.

This heritage of lyrical theology is to the Wesleyan tradition, therefore, what the *Institutes* of Calvin are to the Reformed, the Mass to a Roman Catholic, or the writings of the great patristic theologians to the Christian of Eastern Orthodoxy. The hymns constituted, as John would suggest in his preface to the 1780 *Collection of Hymns for the Use of the People Called Methodists*, "A Little Body of Experimental and Practical Divinity." So Methodists learned and practiced their theology by singing it. They were both formed and transformed by these texts of the faith put to music. When they sang the songs of Charles, in particular, they were singing Scripture. The hymns, packed with the "oracles of God," as the Wesleys would say, exposed the singer and the community unconsciously to the widest possible range of biblical image and story.

The singing of hymns was a characteristic practice of Wesleyan Christians at the outset of the revival, and it has continued to be a hallmark of the tradition. The Methodist denomination is still known in many places around the world as the "singing church." While Charles Wesley stands out as the first and most formative of Methodism's lyrical theologians (and of the historic Christian community, for that matter), hymn writers have articulated faithfully and have continued to shape the tradition today. In this chapter, we will examine the role played by Charles Wesley's hymns in the renewal of Christianity during the age of the Wesleyan Revival. We will also explore the contributions of contemporary Methodist lyrical theologians, a global chorus of voices in a Methodist world parish. Finally, we will see how the singing of the Christian community can lead to the rediscovery of vital faith and abundant life in Christ.

The Lyrical Theology of Charles Wesley

Charles Wesley has finally come out from under the shadow of his older brother, John.[1] Increasing attention is being given to the amazing contribution that Charles made to the birth, growth, and maturation of the Evangelical Revival. There is no question today that Methodism was co-founded. It took both brothers, the preacher and the poet, as well as many others, to launch this great work of God, to give it direction, and to maintain its spiritual vitality over the course of the eighteenth century. Charles's hymns—not all nine thousand, but many of them—played a major role in this endeavor. His lyrical theology pointed to the centrality of grace in the Wesleyan understanding of salvation, encouraged accountable discipleship in such a way as to promote holiness of heart and life, and proclaimed the ultimate foundation of all things in the unconditional love of God for us all in Christ Jesus. In relation to these primary themes, the early Methodist people sang and discovered their essential identity as children of God, learned how to integrate Christian faith and practice, and experienced the inclusivity of the community of faith through the very act of singing together. These salient rediscoveries are integral to renewal in any age.

1. See the work of ST Kimbrough Jr., founder of the Charles Wesley Society, who has devoted considerable energy to the rediscovery of the younger brother; in particular, his edited volume, *Charles Wesley,* and *Heart to Praise*; cf. Berger, *Theology in Hymns?*; and Tyson, *Charles Wesley.*

The All-Sufficiency of God's Grace and Our Identification as the Children of God

In his great hymn, "Jesus, Lover of My Soul," Charles proclaims of Jesus: "Thou art full of truth and grace. / Plenteous grace with thee is found." Grace was the keynote of John's preaching and, for Charles, the "perfect pitch" around which everything else in life must be tuned. Both understood grace in a relational way as God's unexplained lovingkindness. It would be easy to characterize Charles's hymns using his own phrase, "so free, so infinite God's grace." His hymns are in many ways the poetic expression of his brother's sermon on "Free Grace," in which John describes grace as God's free gift in all and for all.[2] John appended his brother's hymn, "Universal Redemption," to that sermon, which includes the lines, "The glory of thy boundless grace, / Thy universal love," "Be justified by faith alone, / And freely saved by grace," and "Grace will I sing, through Jesus's name, / On all mankind bestowed." At the conclusion of no less than thirty-six stanzas extolling the grace of God, Charles pleads: "Come quickly, Lord, we wait thy grace, / We long to meet thee now."

The Wesleys had discovered the all-sufficiency of God's grace in their own lives. The God they had come to know in Jesus Christ was a God of grace and mercy and love. God's grace—the free, unmerited love and mercy of God flowing out to them at all times as an offer of restored relationship—was the central message that had changed their lives, led to their own spiritual rebirth, and generated their movement of renewal in the life of the church. Charles had been particularly influenced by Matthew Henry's vision, described so vividly in his biblical commentary: "The springs of mercy are always full, the streams of mercy always flowing. There is mercy enough in God, enough for all, enough for each, enough for ever."[3] In his hymn on "The Woman of Canaan," he ends the last several stanzas with the repeated "Thy grace is free for all," and then concludes the hymn:

> If thy grace for all is free,
>
> > Thy call now let me hear;
>
> Show this token upon me,
>
> > And bring salvation near.
>
> Now the gracious word repeat,
>
> > The word of healing to my soul:
>
> Canaanite, thy faith is great!
>
> > Thy faith hath made thee whole.[4]

---

2. See J. Wesley, *Works*, 3:542–63.
3. J. Wesley, *Works*, 7:383.
4. J. Wesley, *Works*, 7:278–79.

Each of the four stanzas of one of Charles's "Recovery" hymns ends with the plea: "Keep me, keep me, gracious Lord, / And never let me go."[5] Here is the bedrock of the Wesleyan tradition, namely, the discovery that God is characterized by grace and by promise and will not let us go. The early Methodist singers understood themselves to be God's children, therefore, saved by grace and embraced by God. They viewed the Christian life as a life of gratitude founded upon the kind of transformation that is possible only through grace. In the hymn that Charles most likely penned when he was in the throes of his own evangelical conversion in May of 1738, "Where shall my wond'ring soul begin?" he sings,

> O how shall I thy goodness tell,
>> Father, which thou to me hast showed?
> That I, a child of wrath and hell,
>> I should be called a child of God!
> Should know, should feel my sins forgiven,
> Blest with this antepast of heaven![6]

Methodism was a profound movement of spiritual renewal because it pointed to the all-sufficiency of God's grace and gave to its followers a new identity, that of the children of God.

It should be no surprise that nearly every hymnal of the Methodist tradition opens with the most famous four lines that Charles Wesley ever wrote.

> O for a thousand tongues to sing,
>> My great Redeemer's praise;
> The glories of my God and king,
>> The triumphs of his grace!

Holiness of Heart and Life and Our Integration of Christian Faith with Practice

There is no question that the Wesley brothers believed salvation by grace through faith is the only proper foundation for the whole of the Christian life, if in fact, grace is the key to all of life itself. In other words, faith is the essential response to God's prior offer of unconditional, loving

---

5. J. Wesley, *Works*, 7:305–6.
6. J. Wesley, *Works*, 7:116.

relationship. But they also maintained that the purpose of a life reclaimed by faith alone is the restoration of God's image, namely, love, in the life of the believer. In other words, holiness of heart and life is the goal toward which the Christian life moves. Faith is a means to love's end. Faith working by love leading to holiness of heart and life is the very essence of the gospel proclamation of free grace. Faith without activated love, on the one hand, and works founded upon anything other than God's grace, on the other, are equally deficient visions of the Christian life.

This integral theology of faith and works, heart and life, found potent expression in Charles's hymns. One of the most explicit statements about these syntheses he articulates in one of the love-feast hymns.

> Let us join ('tis God commands),
> Let us join our hearts and hands;
> Help to gain our calling's hope,
> Build we each the other up.
> God his blessing shall dispense,
> God shall crown his ordinance,
> Meet in his appointed ways,
> Nourish us with social grace.
>
> Plead we thus for faith alone,
> Faith which by our works is shown;
> God it is who justifies,
> Only faith the grace applies,
> Active faith that lives within,
> Conquers earth, and hell, and sin,
> Sanctifies, and makes us whole,
> Forms the Saviour in the soul.
>
> Let us for this faith contend,
> Sure salvation is its end;
> Heaven already is begun,
> Everlasting life is won.
> Only let us persevere
> Till we see our Lord appear;

> Never from the rock remove,
>
> Saved by faith which works by love.[7]

The Wesleys were not only concerned that people experience forgiveness for the brokenness in their lives, they wanted them to move toward wholeness and healing, as well. The goal of spiritual maturity is love of God (a vertical dimension) and love of neighbor (a horizontal dimension). The important thing to the Wesleys was the simple fact that in this concept of the Christian life, faith leads to love, and to be loving or holy is to be truly happy. Holiness as happiness is a key to the renewal of the church.

The Proclamation of God's Love and the Inclusivity of Christian Community

One of Charles's most popular hymns, "Love divine, all loves excelling," reveals God's unconditional love. "Jesu, thou art all compassion," he sings, "Pure, unbounded love thou art." There is most certainly a mystical spirit in many of these texts, a concept of the Christian life that could be encapsulated in the closing line of this same hymn, "Lost in wonder, love, and praise."[8] For the Wesleys, love is the goal toward which everything else in life moves. Nothing fueled the Wesleyan Revival more than the simple discovery of God's essential nature revealed in Jesus Christ, namely, love. Charles fervently and eloquently expresses this fundamental understanding in a definitive hymn, "O for a heart to praise my God," which concludes:

> Thy nature, gracious Lord, impart;
>
> > Come quickly from above;
>
> Write thy new name upon my heart,
>
> > Thy new, best name of love![9]

It was amazing, indeed, to discover that God's "name is love," but all the more critical to come to the conclusion that this love is universal. Not only is love the nature and name of God, it is the very life of God offered to everyone, without exception. It is, perhaps, for this very reason that Isaac Watts once described Charles's hymn, "Wrestling Jacob," as the single poem worth all the verse he himself had ever written. Wesley uses the ancient narrative of Jacob at Peniel to illustrate his own life struggle

---

7. J. Wesley, *Works*, 7:698–99.
8. J. Wesley, *Works*, 7:545, 547.
9. J. Wesley, *Works*, 7:490–491.

to find God. But this hymn is not only autobiographical, it in fact reflects the quest of every soul. In one of the most powerful descriptions of the Christian experience of God in English literature, the light breaks through, the most important discovery of life is made.

> Yield to me now—for I am weak,
> > But confident in self-despair!
> Speak to my heart, in blessings speak,
> > Be conquered by my instant prayer:
> Speak, or thou never hence shalt move,
> And tell me if thy name is LOVE.
>
> 'Tis Love! 'Tis Love! Thou diedst for me;
> > I hear thy whisper in my heart.
> The morning breaks, the shadows flee,
> > Pure Universal Love thou art:
> To me, to all, thy mercies move—
> Thy nature, and thy name is LOVE.[10]

"Without the use of the ordinary technique of the theologian," Rattenbury observed in his reflections on this hymn, "it tells how sinful man, self-condemned, when his pride is broken and when in the presence of God he despairs utterly of himself, can achieve the vision and receive the power of God. Thus faith is born and faith penetrates into the mystery of God and discovers the secret that He is: PURE UNIVERSAL LOVE."[11]

The result of this discovery in the Wesleyan Revival was the creation of inclusive communities of people that shared this experience of the good news and sought to live it out in their lives with the help of small groups, in which they were held accountable to one another. These communities were the substance of which true renewal is made.

Charles Wesley was so prolific that the sound of his hymns, and his alone, filled the Methodist chapels of the next century. Before turning our attention to the contemporary scene, it will be worth remembering two important voices and hymn writers. It was not until the close of the nineteenth century and the birth of the "gospel hymn" that a new, and equally prolific, voice was heard within the tradition. Fanny Crosby is the only other hymn writer in the history of the church to challenge Charles

10. J. Wesley, *Works*, 7:251.
11. Rattenbury, *Evangelical Doctrines*, 98–99.

Wesley's nine-thousand hymns.[12] She probably wrote just as many. Written in a popular style that spoke to the emotions, the hymn that epitomizes her lyrical ethos is, without question, "Blessed Assurance" (1873).

> Blessed assurance, Jesus is mine,
> O what a foretaste of glory divine,
> Heir of salvation, purchase of God,
> Born of his spirit, washed in his blood.

This was her story and her song.

The other great hymn writer of the tradition who stands between Wesley and the contemporary church is Charles A. Tindley.[13] Born of slave parents in Maryland, this self-educated preacher attracted so many people to his Philadelphia church by means of street preaching and community activities that a new sanctuary seating three thousand had to be constructed. He preached to packed congregations in this church, later named Tindley Temple in his honor. And at one point, he boasted the largest Methodist church in the world, with over twelve-thousand members. Tindley also wrote hymns. His lyrical theology revolved around his experiences as an African American and the way God had sustained him through difficult times. No single hymn characterizes his life and work better than "Stand By Me" (1906).

> When the storms of life are raging, stand by me.
> When the storms of life are raging, stand by me.
> When the world is tossing me, like a ship upon the sea,
> Thou who rulest wind and water, stand by me.

Other hymn writers have emerged from time to time, such as Frank Mason North, who promoted the social gospel through his hymns, and Georgia Harkness, who renewed a global vision for the Methodist family. But no era has witnessed the rebirth of Christian song quite like our own.

The Contemporary Global Chorus of Voices

There is today a global chorus of voices that is giving renewed expression to the Wesleyan vision of the Christian life through song. In 1739, John Wesley

---

12. See Ruffin, *Fanny Crosby*.
13. See Jones, *Charles Albert Tindley*.

proclaimed prophetically, "I look upon all the world as my parish."[14] He could never have imagined in his own day just how far-reaching his movement of renewal would become one day. One of the most encouraging aspects of the renewal of the Wesleyan tradition in our own time is the amazing diversity of forms and expressions of the faith that we share. Several Methodist hymn writers, in particular, help us to appreciate the central themes of jubilation, journey, justice, and joy that are part and parcel of the renewing influence of Christian song in the Wesleyan spirit.

Jubilation

Erik Routley, an important historian of the Christian hymn, described Fred Pratt Green as the greatest Methodist hymn writer since Charles Wesley. There is no doubt that Green now reigns without rival as the most significant pastor/poet of the twentieth century. His contribution to the writing of hymns has been immense and unique, and decidedly Wesleyan.[15] In 1975, he offered this patently Methodist vision of his craft as a hymn writer.

> He is a servant of the church. It is the Church which asks him to write hymns and provides opportunities—such glorious opportunities—for them to be sung. The hymn writer exists to enrich the Church's worship, to express the wide range of Christian devotion, to offer salvation, to teach doctrine, and to guide our feet into the way of scriptural holiness.[16]

No single word, I think, better characterizes his hymns than jubilation.

The Christian community is jubilant in its adoration of God, jubilant in accepting redemption through Christ, jubilant in asking the Spirit to lead, jubilant in addressing the needs of the poor, jubilant in answering God's call to mission in the world. The jubilant band of Christ's followers we encounter in Green's hymns is thankful and thoughtful, hope-filled and helpful. The hymns are uplifting and inspiring. One hymn in particular, "The Caring Church," actually addresses the central theme of this volume, the renewal of the church.

> The church of Christ in every age
> Beset by change but Spirit led,

---

14. J. Wesley, *Works*, 19:67.

15. See the two-volume collection of his works, Pratt Green, *Hymns and Ballads* and *Later Hymns and Ballads*.

16. Green, "Poet and Hymn Writer," 192–93.

> Must claim and test its heritage
> And keep on rising from the dead.
>
> Then let the servant Church arise,
> A caring church that longs to be
> A partner in Christ's sacrifice,
> And clothed in Christ's humanity.[17]

Fred Pratt Green's signature hymn, "Let the People Sing," closes with this exultant stanza:

> Let every instrument be tuned for praise!
> Let all rejoice who have a voice to raise!
> And may God give us faith to sing always:
> Alleluia![18]

Journey

Simei Monteiro taught at the Methodist School of Theology (Faculdade de Teologia de Igreja Metodista) in São Paulo, Brazil. Showing her fascination of the relationship between liturgical song and theology, a theme which she explores in *O Cântico da Vida* ("The Song of Life," 1991), her compositions appear in collections throughout the Latin world. A consistent theme, drawn from both her native Guarani culture and her Christian experience, is that of pilgrimage or journey.

In her hymn, "Tua Palavra na vida" (Your Word in Our Lives), having described the Word of God, for example, as the "seed of the Kingdom," "food for the least," and "the mirror where we see," she concludes this powerful litany by singing,

> Your word in our lives, eternal,
>   Is light that shines on the long road,
> That leads us to the horizon,
>   And the bright Kingdom of God.[19]

---

17. Green, *Hymns and Ballads*, 17.
18. Green, *Hymns and Ballads*, 52.
19. Kimbrough, *Global Praise 1*, no. 65.

At a conference on mission evangelism in 1995, Monteiro described in vivid detail how her people walk, or journey. "We see our peoples moving from one place to another," she explained, "going and coming from one part of the country to another, looking for jobs, a better life, dignity, food, nurture . . . Their song sounds in the way, telling us about the long, long journey."[20] Her hymn, "Canção da caminhada" (If Walking Is Our Vocation), reminds us of this central Wesleyan theme. We are renewed when we journey together!

> If the journey is what is needful, we shall take to the road together,
>> and our feet, our arms, will sustain our steps.
> We will be no more a mob without choice, nor voice, nor history
>> but a church that moves out in a hope that unites.
>
> If the journey is what awaits us, we shall walk with all eyes on one vision,
>> and the Kingdom of God shall we have, as horizon for our life.
> We'll share the pains, and the sufferings and hardships,
>> as we are spreading the power of love in this hope that unites.
>
> If the journey is what is given us, we shall walk, pilgrims, together,
>> and our voice in the desert will make to spring forth new fountains.
> And the new life on earth will be foreseen in our frolics and joy.
>> . . . God, who is among us in the hope that forever unites.[21]

These hymns reveal the important truth that the Christian life is a journey, often characterized by struggle, but moving toward God's vision of shalom.

---

20. Monteiro, "Evangelization," 134.

21. English translation from the original Portuguese has been provided by J. Parke Renshaw.

Justice

I-to Loh has become well known in the Western world through his editorial work on Asian and ecumenical collections of hymns. A musician and specialist in the tribal melodies of his native Taiwan, he has edited hymn collections that carry titles such as *Christ the Light to Bali* and *The Love of God Sets Us Free*. While noted primarily for his own musical compositions, for his artful paraphrasing of the Psalms, and for his masterful translation of other Asian hymn writers, and some of his most impressive work can be found in the Christian Conference of Asia Hymnal (1990), entitled *Sound the Bamboo*. In this amazing collection, his particular contributions, as in his other publications, sound the note of justice.

To a particularly powerful Malasian hymn, "God of All Gods," he adds a characteristic verse: "Good news for poor folk, light in the darkness, / See, the redeemer lives. / Pardon for hatred, new life to sinners, / Freedom from chains he gives."[22] The gifts of Japanese poet, Ko Yuki, and I-to Loh, the musician/translator, combine in "On the Shore of Galilee."

> Through the days of pain and trial,
>   And the nights of fearful cries,
> Christ our Savior's ever near;
>   He shall overcome our fears.
> Lord, when will you hear our prayers,
>   Bring your kingdom down to earth?
> When shall oppression, hate disappear,
>   Peace and love forever prevail?[23]

In "Lord, We Thank You for This Food," one of the few hymns in which he composes both the musical and lyrical texts, I-to sings: "Lord, we thank you for this food, / Help us share with all in need; / Body, soul refresh anew to live the Gospel, / Serve your people, give your people love."[24] His hymns remind us of the Wesleyan call to be God's agents of justice in the world.

Joy

To be in the presence of Patrick Matsikenyiri, Zimbabwean composer and choral director, is to find oneself caught up in joy. He has been instrumental

---

22. *Sound the Bamboo*, no. 139.
23. Underwood, *Banquet of Praise*, no. 205.
24. *Sound the Bamboo*, no. 163.

in the introduction and growth of African church music within the global community, and the amazing body of African song that he has composed and arranged is now receiving widespread attention. Perhaps none of his compositions is more widely known than "Jesu, Tawa Pano" (Jesus, We Are Here), which has now been sung on every continent. He has been particularly concerned to adapt traditional Shona music for use in the church, and he has often given credit to women within the life of the church for the indigenization of Christian song. He explains exactly how this actually happened.

> Africans were forced to live two lives at once. When they were in church they had to sing like missionaries and when they got home they were free to sing with liberty of movement in the accompaniment of the drum, the shaker, and the rattle . . . Innovative women in the church, and in the United Methodist Church in particular, started to improvise tunes for some of the translated texts which were in the hymn books . . . they would start to sing *Ndindindi ndindi, ndindi vanamai imi* ("Oh, oh, oh you mothers") with movement and ululation in the process. The women's faces would light up with joy and expression.[25]

The keynote of this African Methodist contribution to global Wesleyan praise is joy. In virtually every one of Patrick's compositions, the rhythmic melodies and dancing schemes communicate a contagious spirit of rejoicing. From "Tino tenda Jesu" (Thank you Jesus, amen! Alleluia, amen!) and "Sana, Sananina" (Praise God) to "The Dream," which he composed for the official opening of Africa University, his hymns plant joy in the hearts of all who sing and hear. Joyous Christians renew the church.

Singing Our Way into a New Millennium

What can we learn about the renewal of the church today from the lyrical theology of our tradition as Wesleyan Christians? First, Christian song is a powerful tool in God's process of reviving the community of faith. From the very beginning, Methodist people have learned and practiced their faith by singing it. Christian hymns and songs have the amazing capacity to engage the whole person—thinking, feeling, and acting—and thereby form and transform in lasting ways. Moreover, since hymns are written for singing congregations, they draw us immediately into community and enable us to experience the power of solidarity in Christ. Nothing could be more Wesleyan.

---

25. Chilcote et al., "Singing and Dancing Church," 243.

Second, the hymn as theology is important. We have seen how the Wesleys communicated a theology rooted in grace and love to their followers and their spiritual progeny through the hymns they created. These lyrical creations exhibit a theology that is deep and broad, richly textured, and thoroughly biblical in its orientation. In an age that is essentially biblically illiterate and bereft of the images and stories that have shaped God's people throughout history, the sung story may be one of the most appealing means of communicating God's love in our many cultures today. We need to make sure, therefore, that the theology we sing is sound and that the singing in which we engage is Wesleyan, that is to say, rooted in God's unexplained lovingkindness.

Third, lyrical theology brings together the text and the context in such a way as to make the story of God's love come alive with relevance and potency. This is perhaps the most important quality of the Christian hymn. In our multi-cultural world today, we have much to learn from the global Methodist family. Perhaps a crucial aspect of our renewal will be related to the rediscovery of the Wesleyan message of God's unconditional love as it is filtered through the life and experience of those from outside our own culture and set to the rhythms and tones of worlds distant from our own. Perhaps we have something to learn from songs that speak a word of hope even though hammered out on the anvil of oppression, or from the exuberant melodies of Methodists who have learned to dance as they sing in the face of poverty and AIDS. Certainly, the renewal of our global family will come only through the sharing of our giftedness with one another. Rest assured, global praise has within it every potential to revive a global people of God.

It is most fitting, certainly, to close this discussion of lyrical theology and renewal with one of Charles Wesley's hymns.

> Since the Son hath made me free,
> Let me taste my liberty;
> Thee behold with open face,
> Triumph in thy saving grace,
> Thy great will delight to prove,
> Glory in thy perfect love.
>
> Abba, Father! Hear thy child,
> Late in Jesus reconciled;
> Hear, and all the graces shower,
> All the joy, and peace, and power,

> All my Saviour asks above,
> All the life and heaven of love.[26]

Could anyone devise a more potent catalyst for renewal in the life of the church than this portrait of a true child of God? And when children who have been renewed by God begin to sing, God is surely there.

---

26. J. Wesley, *Works*, 7:552.

Part 5

Worship, Sacraments, and Leadership

Chapter 13

John and Charles Wesley's Theology of the Sacraments

Source note: This commissioned essay was published simply as "John and Charles Wesley," in *Christian Theologies of the Sacraments: A Comparative Introduction*, edited by Justin S. Holcomb and David A. Johnson, 272–94 (New York: New York University Press, 2017).

JOHN AND CHARLES WESLEY directed a movement of spiritual renewal within the Church of England during the eighteenth century best described as an evangelical and sacramental revival.[1] While this revival entailed a rediscovery of the Christian life as a way of devotion—a life empowered by the Spirit and rooted in God's grace experienced in Jesus Christ—it also reclaimed the central place of the sacraments in this spiritual journey. At a time when sacramental devotion was at a low ebb in the life of their church, the Wesleys resituated their movement around the life-giving and grace-offering sacraments. Through the sacrament of baptism, God initiates the work of grace, they believed, and through the sacrament of Holy Communion, God sustains believers in their grace-filled pilgrimage of faith. John and Charles Wesley's theology and practice of sacraments emerged out of their larger vision of the Christian life as an act of worship—a life to be sung to the glory of God. Their theology maintained a vital synthesis of sacramental grace and evangelical experience.

---

1. Some of the more recent works that touch upon this theme include Chilcote, *Wesleyan Tradition*; Hynson, *To Reform the Nation*; and Snyder, *Signs of the Spirit* and *Radical Wesley*.

Sacraments within the Context of the Worship of God

The Wesleyan Revival, like nearly all other movements of renewal in the history of the church, was characterized by liturgical revolution. Worship shapes theology and theology shapes worship. The Wesleys conceived worship as the grateful surrender of all one is and all one has, a living sacrifice of praise and thanksgiving to the God of love who created all things and bears witness with one's spirit that he or she is a child of God. Once this essential discovery is made, all of life becomes an act of genuine worship, and all can sing with Charles Wesley:

> Thee I shall then forever praise,
>
> In spirit and in truth adore,
>
> While all I am declares thy grace,
>
> And born of God I sin no more,
>
> The pure and heavenly treasure share,
>
> And fruit into perfection bear.[2]

Baptism signals this new birth; Holy Communion provides the nourishment that leads to a life of perfect love. Worship in general and the sacraments in particular orient one's life around the pillars of authentic discipleship, a way of redemption characterized by faith, love, and holiness.[3] Orthodoxy (literally, "the proper praise of God") means quite simply (1) to believe in God by faith, (2) to desire nothing but God's love, and (3) to glorify God by following in the path of righteousness. It is interesting that John Wesley's first definition of Methodism revolved around the life of a worshiping community. A society, he wrote, is no other than "a company of men [and women] 'having the form and seeking the power of godliness,' united in order to pray together, to receive the word of exhortation, and to watch over one another in love, that they may help each other to work out their salvation."[4] Authentic Christian worship is worship in spirit and truth that enables the Christ follower to believe and love and serve God. In the context of a worshiping community, the sacraments anchor all who have been called to follow Jesus in this way of life.

---

2. Wesley and Wesley, *Hymns and Sacred Poems* (1742), 79–80.

3. See J. Wesley, *Works*, 1:531–49; sermon, "Upon the Lord's Sermon on the Mount IV."

4. J. Wesley, *Works*, 9:69, quoted from Wesley's *The Nature, Design, and General Rules of the United Societies*.

The Wesleys constructed their theology of the sacraments, therefore, around several critical doxological premises drawn from the worship of God.[5]

1. *God is more important than the way God is worshipped.* If the authenticity of worship is rooted in a relationship, then the object of faith, love, and holiness is much more important than the individual, peculiar, and culturally shaped means of entering into relationship with God. In their own age, and particularly under the shadow of the generations that immediately preceded them, the Wesleys lamented the way in which concerns about sacramental practice fractured the community of faith. Questions as to whether one stood or knelt when receiving Communion and were sprinkled or immersed in baptism led to deep divisions in the life of the church. For the Wesleys, God was more important than the methods or means of engaging God's presence.

2. *God reveals Godself through means as well as apart from them.* God can be known immediately (literally, "without any means"). But God also uses material, physical things to reveal the divine. Through the Incarnation, for example, God entered the physical world in the person of Jesus Christ. "The Word," as John's Gospel declares, "became flesh and made his home among us" (John 1:14 CEB). Building on this fundamental reality, in a Wesleyan perspective, the sacraments reveal that a bit of common bread can be the medium of the presence of God and that water can be the instrument of God's life-giving grace. Through the sacramental elements of water, bread, and wine, God uses material or physical things to reveal the spiritual. God transforms common, ordinary elements into sacred instruments of love.

3. *God not only offers grace to individuals but locates grace within the church.* The Wesley brothers built a religious revival upon this simple foundation—the personal and transforming experience of the love of God in Christ. The church (the body of Christ or fellowship of believers), they claimed, is composed of those persons who share this experience. Christians are, by the very nature of their faith, drawn into community; their faith is social as well as personal, and the sacraments amplify this dynamic reality. John Wesley spent much of his ministry redressing the neglect of this social dimension. "Holy solitaries," he exclaimed on one occasion, "is a phrase no more consistent with the gospel than holy adulterers. The gospel of Christ knows of no religion, but social [religion]."[6] The sacraments, therefore, are not only means of grace for individuals; they are also important social symbols.

5. On the Wesleys' general sacramentology, see Borgen, *Wesley on the Sacraments*; Parris, *Wesley's Doctrine of the Sacraments*; Staples, *Outward Sign and Inward Grace*; and Wainwright, "Sacraments in Wesleyan Perspective."

6. Wesley and Wesley, *Hymns and Sacred Poems* (1739), preface.

4. *God uses actions in addition to words to communicate the gospel.* It was impossible for the Wesleys to think about the spoken word (preaching) apart from the word made visible (Holy Communion). Both brothers frequently mention Word and sacramanet together. "The Lord gave us, under the word, to know the power of his resurrection"; Charles wrote on Easter 1747, "but in the Sacrament he carried us quite above ourselves and all earthly things."[7] Actions do speak louder than words, a principle the Wesleys had learned early in their lives. So, in similar fashion, the act of baptism declares the need for all to die to self in order to be born anew in ways more powerful than words alone. The sacraments proclaim God's claim upon every life and the Lord's death until he comes. They proclaim the nature of authentic existence as a rhythm that moves ineluctably from death to life—dying to self the believer is raised with Christ—and of one's perennial need of spiritual sustenance as the believer "feeds on him by faith with thanksgiving." The sacraments faithfully proclaim the Word through sign-acts of love. The purpose of worship, according to the Wesleys, was to cultivate personal, religious experience in the context of a supportive community of love. They assumed that God's love was potent enough to transform both individual lives and the life of the world. They held the individual and the community together, concerned equally about the parts as for the whole of God's design. The sacraments in the context of authentic worship became a powerful means in their effort to renew the church. As Ole Borgen concluded, "Baptism is *initiatory*; its function is to commence what the Lord's Supper (with other means of grace as well) are basically ordained to *preserve* and *develop*: a life in faith and holiness."[8]

The Wesleys' Definition of "Sacrament"

As devout Anglican priests, the Wesleys defined a sacrament on the basis of the Church of England *Catechism* as "an outward sign of inward *grace*, and a *means* whereby we receive the same."[9] Historians of doctrine trace this classic definition to St. Augustine. This definition included the philosophical distinction between *signum* (sign) and *res* (the thing signified). While the sign is outward and visible, the thing signified is inward and spiritual. In the sacraments, water, bread, and wine, the outward washing and the meal, signify respectively the inward cleansing and the spiritual

---

7. C. Wesley, *Manuscript Journal*, 2:499.

8. Borgen, *Wesley on the Sacraments*, 122.

9. J. Wesley, *Works*, 1:381, from Wesley's sermon "The Means of Grace (II.1)." The classic statement is "an outward and visible sign of an inward and spiritual grace."

nourishment of the soul. For the Wesleys, the sign and thing signified are distinct, but never separate. While the one is outward, visible, and material, the other is inward, invisible, and spiritual; but both must always be held together. The one goes inextricably with the other.

The Church of England also provided a more extended definition of the sacraments in the 39 Articles of Religion. When John Wesley edited these Articles and published his twenty-four revisions in *The Sunday Service* in 1784, he left the article pertaining generically to the sacraments virtually unaltered. In conformity to standard Protestant practice, the original article and Wesley's redaction omitted confirmation, penance, orders, matrimony, and extreme unction from the status of sacraments, counseled against an unbiblical veneration of any sacrament, and commended a worthy reception of the sacraments. The opening paragraphs of the article identify and describe the two dominical ordinances.

> Article XVI—Of the Sacraments
>
> Sacraments ordained of Christ, are not only badges or tokens of Christian Men's Profession; but rather they are certain Signs of Grace, and God's good Will toward us, by the which he doth work invisibly in us, and doth not only quicken, but also strengthen and confirm our faith in him.
>
> There are two Sacraments ordained of Christ our Lord in the Gospel; that is to say, Baptism, and the Supper of the Lord.[10]

The Wesleys' Theology of Baptism

Baptism, unlike Holy Communion, was not a subject of primary concern for either of the Wesley brothers. Because of the dearth of material on the topic in their corpus, the Wesleys' theology of baptism is one of the most difficult doctrines to assess fully in their theological program.[11] Robert Cushman lamented the "large elements of uncertainty and, perhaps, ambiguity in the express utterances as well as exasperating silences of John

---

10. J. Wesley, *Sunday Service*, 311. He reproduced Article XXV of the 39 Articles of Religion from the Book of Common Prayer (1662) nearly verbatim. Of the six articles that deal with the sacraments, Wesley omitted Articles XXVI, "Of the Unworthiness of the Ministers, Which Hinders Not the Effect of the Sacrament," and XXIX, "Of the Wicked Which Eat Not the Body of Christ in the Use of the Lord's Supper."

11. On the Wesleys' theology of baptism, see Felton, *This Gift of* Water; Holland, *Baptism in Early Methodism*; Galliers, "Theology of Baptism"; and Sanders, "Wesley and Baptismal Regeneration."

Wesley himself regarding the means of baptism and its significance."[12] But John Wesley did edit and publish two small tracts on baptism, both highly dependent on their original authors. In 1751, he anonymously published a twenty-one page redaction of William Wall's four-volume tome, *Thoughts on Infant-Baptism*. John Wesley's *Treatise on Baptism*, an abridgement of his father's work of 1710, provides greater insight into his views. It also included an earlier publication, *Serious Thoughts Concerning Godfathers and Godmothers* (1752), with the obvious connections to baptismal theology.[13] His article on baptism (XVII), while reducing Article XXVII of the Book of Common Prayer somewhat substantially, retained the essence of the Anglican view. "Baptism is not only a sign of profession, and mark of difference, whereby Christians are distinguished from others that are not baptized; but it is also a sign of regeneration, or the new birth. The baptism of young children is to be retained in the church."[14] While Charles Wesley left behind no definitive statement concerning his views on or practice related to baptism in his prose works, he produced many hymns specifically for use at both infant and adult rites.

Despite some twists and turns in John Wesley's early practice of baptism, once the Wesleyan Revival was in full swing, an earlier dogmatic spirit seems to have given way to moderation, especially with regard to the mode of baptism. His *Thoughts upon Infant-Baptism* reveal what might be considered his mature thinking relating to this particular issue.

> With regard to the mode of baptizing, I would only add, Christ no where, as far as I can find, requires *dipping*, but only *baptizing*; which word, many most eminent for learning and piety have declared, signifies to *pour on*, or *sprinkle*, as well as to *dip*. As our Lord has graciously given us a word of such extensive meaning, doubtless the parent, or the person to be baptized, if he be adult, ought to choose which way he best approves. What God has left *indifferent*, it becomes not *man* to make necessary.[15]

---

12. Cushman, "Baptism," 82.

13. In addition, J. Wesley's *Sunday Service* contains liturgical texts for both sacraments, but this work provides little additional guidance in these matters.

14. The full text of the original Anglican Article XXVII, "Of Baptism," reads: "Baptism is not only a sign of profession, and mark of difference, whereby Christians are discerned from others that are not christened, but it is also a sign of regeneration, or the new birth, whereby, as by an instrument, they that receive Baptism rightly are grafted into the Church; the promises of the forgiveness of sin, and of our adoption to be the sons of God by the Holy Ghost, are visibly signed and sealed; Faith is confirmed, and Grace increased by virtue of prayer unto God. The Baptism of young children is in any wise to be retained in the church, as most agreeable with the institution of Christ."

15. Quoted in Felton, *This Gift of Water*, 19.

This trend away from rigid conformity to formal ecclesiastical standards and toward a more flexible pattern of practice seems to have typified the mature view of both brothers.[16] With regard to two particular issues, they reflected a fairly conventional Anglican view of the sacrament: the proper recipients and the benefits of baptism

Throughout the course of his ministry, John Wesley endorsed infant baptism. The concluding sections of his *Treatise on Baptism* and the entirety of *Thoughts upon Infant-Baptism* provide arguments supporting this practice. He based his arguments on (1) the infant's need, (2) the desirability of the child's incorporation into the church, (3) the practice of the historic church, and primarily (4) the parallelism between circumcision in the old and baptism in the new covenant. Charles Wesley's lyrical paraphrase of Matthew 19:13 identifies at least two primary functions of infant baptism: blessing and incorporation.

> Jesus, in earth and heaven the same,
>   Accept a parent's vow,
> To Thee, baptiz'd into thy name,
>   I bring my children now;
> Thy love permits, invites, commands,
>   My offspring to be blesst:
> Lay on them Lord, thy gracious hands,
> And hide them in thy breast.
>
> To each the hallowing Spirit give
>   Ev'n from their infancy,
> And pure into thy church receive
>   Whom I devote to Thee;
> Committed to thy faithful care,
>   Protected by thy blood,
> Preserved by thine unceasing prayer,
>   And bring them all to God.[17]

According to Gayle Felton,

---

16. See Felton's discussion of Wesleyan baptismal practice in *This Gift of Water*, 13–25.

17. C. Wesley, MS Matthew, 221.

infant baptism is the ordinary vehicle of regeneration; adult baptism is accompanied by rebirth only under certain circumstances and, instead, functions as a more general means of grace. The person who has been converted should receive baptism as a testimony to the faith experience and as a rite of admission into the church.[18]

But the baptism of an adult can convey regenerating grace as well, as can be seen in a Charles Wesley text:

> Father, Son, and Holy Ghost,
>> In solemn power come down!
> Present with thy heavenly host,
>> Thine ordinance to crown.
> See a sinful worm of earth!
>> Bless to him the cleansing flood!
> Plunge him, by a second birth,
>> Into the depths of God.
>
> Let the promised inward grace
>> Accompany the sign;
> On his new-born soul impress
>> The character divine!
> Father, all thy love reveal!
>> Jesus, all thy name impart!
> Holy Ghost, renew, and dwell
>> For ever in her heart![19]

The Wesleys conceived both infants and adults as the proper recipients of baptism because both needed to be born again. They denied the false polarities of sacramental grace and evangelical experience, affirming the validity and necessity of both. Attempting to adjudicate the tension between baptism and subsequent conversion in the thought of the Wesleys, Albert Outler concluded in his prefatory comments to Wesley's *Treatise on Baptism*,

> The obvious purpose of this "extract" was to re-enforce the wavering convictions of some of the Methodist people as to the

---

18. Felton, *This Gift of Water*, 44–45.
19. C. Wesley, *Hymns and Sacred Poems* (1749), 2:246 (no. 418).

validity of infant baptism and to re-emphasize the objectivity of divine grace in this sacrament. One ought, however, to compare this essay on baptism . . . with the sermon on "The New Birth" . . . where the stress falls heavily on conversion as a conscious adult experience of regeneration. The point is that Wesley held to both ideas.[20]

In his *Treatise on Baptism* John Wesley identified five benefits of the sacrament: (1) removal of the guilt of original sin, (2) entrance into covenant with God, (3) incorporation into the church, (4) restoration as children of God, and (5) initiation into to the kingdom of God. Brian Galliers identified four additional benefits from other sources within the Wesleyan corpus: (6) solidarity in the death of Christ, (7) admission to the Lord's Table, (8) reception of the gift of the Holy Spirit, and (9) physical healing.[21]

In addition to these sources, the journals, sermons, and hymns of the brothers clarify their theology of baptism. First, the Wesleys refused to accept a reductionism which makes baptism a purely symbolic act. Second, they viewed baptism as initiatory. Third, they conceived this sacrament as the ordinary means to salvation within the community of faith. God "makes Christians" through baptism. Fourth, baptism situates the child of God on a trajectory, the goal of which is genuine living faith and holiness. The means cannot be separated from the goal, but the Wesleys focused attention on the end rather than the means. Fifth, all grace may be lost; but while possible, this loss is never inevitable. Their keen observation of Christian living taught the Wesleys that an experience of conversion subsequent to baptism was necessary in the lives of most, if not all, people. But such life-changing experiences did not negate the act of infant baptism. Neither did they empty baptism of its meaning. Rather, subsequent new birth simply culminated the work of the Spirit begun in baptism itself.

Many of these themes find poignant expression in one of Charles Wesley's hymns, "At the Baptism of a Child," from his *Family Hymns* collection.

> God of eternal truth and love,
>> Vouchsafe the promis'd grace we claim,
>
> Thine own great ordinance approve,
>> The child baptis'd into thy name
>
> Partaker of thy nature make,
> And give her all thine image back.

---

20. Outler, *John Wesley*, 318.
21. Galliers, "Theology of Baptism," 123.

Born in the dregs of sin and time,
> These darkest, last, apostate days,
Burthen'd with *Adam's* curse and crime
> Thou in thy mercy's arms embrace,
And wash out all her guilty load,
And quench the brand in Jesus' blood.

Father, if such thy sovereign will,
> If Jesus *did* the rite injoin,
Annex thy hallowing Spirit's seal,
> And let the grace attend the sign;
The seed of endless life impart,
Seize for thy own our infant's heart.

Answer on her thy wisdom's end
> In present and eternal good;
Whate'er thou didst for man intend,
> Whate'er thou hast on man bestow'd,
Now to this favour'd babe be given,
Pardon, and holiness, and heaven.

In presence of thy heavenly host
> Thyself we faithfully require;
Come, Father, Son, and Holy Ghost
> By blood, by water, and by fire,
And fill up all thy human shrine,
And seal our souls for ever Thine.[22]

The Wesleys' Holy Communion Theology

Charles Wesley described the sacrament of Holy Communion as the "richest legacy" that Jesus left the community of faith.[23]

22. C. Wesley, *Family Hymns*, 63–64 (no. 62).
23. On the Wesleys' Eucharistic theology, see Bowmer, *Lord's Supper in Early*

Fasting he doth and hearing bless,
And prayer can much avail,
Good vessels all to draw the grace
Out of salvation's well.

But none like this mysterious rite
Which dying mercy gave
Can draw forth all God's promised might
And all God's will to save.

This is the richest legacy
Thou hast on us bestowed,
Here chiefly, Lord, we feed on thee,
And drink thy precious blood.

Here all thy blessings we receive,
Here all thy gifts are given;
To those that would in thee believe,
Pardon, and grace, and heaven.

Thus may we still in thee be blessed
'Till all from earth remove,
And share with thee the marriage feast,
And drink the wine above.[24]

Scholars have documented the general neglect of the Eucharist in the Church of England during the Wesleys' day. In stark contrast to the norms of his age, John Wesley communed on average about once every four days throughout his lifetime and put the sacrament back at the very center of Christian spirituality and discipleship. When he sent his *Sunday Service* to the fledgling Methodist communities in North America, he advised them "to administer the Supper of the Lord on every Lord's day."[25] Both brothers viewed the

---

Methodism; Grislis, "Wesleyan Doctrine of Last Supper"; Rattenbury, *Eucharistic Hymns*; and Sanders, "Wesley's Eucharistic Faith and Practice."

24. Wesley and Wesley, *Hymns on the Lord's Supper*, 31 (no. 42:2–6).

25. J. Wesley, *Sunday Service*, ii.

Lord's Supper as the "chief means of grace."[26] Early Methodists flocked to the celebration of Holy Communion because they encountered God there. They received spiritual nourishment around the table. Locating the sacrament among other means of grace, Charles Wesley sang,

> The prayer, the fast, the word conveys,
> > When mixt with faith, thy life to me,
> In all the channels of thy grace,
> > I still have fellowship with thee,
> But chiefly here my soul is fed
> > With fullness of immortal bread.[27]

These "feasts of love," as the early Methodists often described them, shaped their understanding of God's love for them and their reciprocal love for God.

In his journal, John Wesley recorded every celebration of the sacrament in which he was involved and frequently commented on his sacramental theology. From a detailed comparison of Wesley's early and later diaries, John Bowmer came to two clear conclusions: (1) Throughout the course of his life, Wesley's frequent participation in the sacrament and his practice, in general, remained remarkably consistency, and (2) he either celebrated or participated in Eucharist whenever the opportunity presented itself.[28] With regard to the place of the sacrament among the Methodist people under the Wesleys' direction, Bowmer drew similar conclusions:

> There can be little doubt that the high place which the Sacrament occupied in early Methodism was due to the precept and the example of the Wesleys, for it is not too much to say that, for them it was the highest form of devotion and the most comprehensive act of worship the Church could offer. As necessary as preaching was—and it would be unjust to attempt to minimize its place in the Methodist revival—a preaching service was not, to the Wesleys, the supreme spiritual exercise. On the other hand, the Lord's Supper was completely satisfying.[29]

Of the many sources from which to construct John Wesley's theology of Holy Communion, his sermon on "The Duty of Constant Communion," published late in his life, provides the most succinct statement of his Eucharistic

---

26. See J. Wesley, *Works*, 1:376–97; sermon, "On the Means of Grace."
27. Wesley and Wesley, *Hymns on the Lord's Supper*, 39 (no. 54.4).
28. See Bowmer, *Lord's Supper in Early Methodism*, 55–61.
29. Bowmer, *Lord's Supper in Early Methodism*, 188–89.

doctrine and practice.[30] The primary purpose of this exposition of Luke 22:19 was to demonstrate the duty of every Christian to receive Holy Communion as often as possible. The primary reasons supporting this constancy included the fact that it is a plain command of Christ and that it is a blessing of God through which we receive the benefits of Christ's passion and love. In the sermon, Wesley identified and answered five common objections to the practice of constant Communion.

First, against those who lamented that their unworthiness disqualified their participation, he claimed that the root of this common attitude rests in a misinterpretation of St. Paul's purported prohibitions. Christ particularly welcomed the unworthy (i.e., all people) to the table. Second, whereas some claimed that an elevated esteem for the sacrament might unrealistically exaggerate their expectations concerning holiness in life, Wesley maintained that anything else would be a denial of their baptismal covenant. Third, Wesley argued that reverence for the command of proper preparation should never become a pretense for disobedience. Fourth, against those who expressed concern about the numbing effect of repetition, he argued that practices habituated within the community of faith need never lessen true religious reverence. Fifth, he bore testimony to the imperceptible strengthening often associated with the sacrament in response to those who "felt nothing" at the table. "No man can have any pretense to Christian piety," Wesley concluded, "who does not receive it (not once a month, but) as often as he can."[31]

While the Wesley brothers jointly published *Hymns on the Lord's Supper*, Charles wrote virtually all of the 166 hymns in this unique volume. This collection of religious verse comprises his fullest possible expression of Eucharistic spirituality—a theology in hymns. "The eighteenth-century revival," Richard Heitzenrater has observed, "was to a great extent borne on the wings of Charles's poetry. Charles's hymns not only helped form the texture of the Methodist mind but also, perhaps more importantly, set the temper of the Methodist spirit."[32] This collection of Eucharistic hymns included John's abridged version of Daniel Brevint's *The Christian Sacrament and Sacrifice*, which functioned as a preface to the volume.[33] John, most

---

30. J. Wesley, *Works*, 3:427–39. This sermon was a distillation of at least two earlier tracts on the sacrament, published by the Anglican divines, Robert Nelson ("The Great Duty of Frequenting the Christian Sacrifice") and Arthur Bury ("The Constant Communicant") in the seventeenth century, but extensively edited, expanded, and adapted by Wesley to make them his own.

31. J. Wesley, *Works*, 3:439 (II.21).

32. Quoted in Kimbrough, *Lost in Wonder*, 11–12.

33. This collection of hymns, properly described as a liturgical classic, went through nine editions during the lifetime of the brothers and was one of their primary means

likely, arranged the hymns under primary headings, closely following the pattern laid out by Brevint in his treatise.

1. As It Is a Memorial of the Sufferings and Death of Christ.
2. As It Is a Sign and a Means of Grace.
3. The Sacrament a Pledge of Heaven.
4. The Holy Eucharist as It Implies a Sacrifice.
5. Concerning the Sacrifice of Our Persons.
6. After the Sacrament.

The first three sections closely parallel the dimensions of time and provide the outline for Charles's lyrical theological reflections on the sacrament as a memorial, a sign and means of grace, and a pledge of heaven.

First, *the Lord's Supper is a memorial of the passion of Christ*.[34] The opening hymn of Wesley's collection sets the somber tone of this section.

> In that sad memorable night,
>> When Jesus was for us betray'd,
> He left his death-recording rite.[35]

The sacrament proclaims "the Lord's death until he comes," St. Paul reminded the Corinthian community (1 Cor 11:26). Charles's death imagery in these "past dimension hymns," therefore, should be no surprise. The fact that the redemptive suffering of Jesus procures eternal life for the believer, however, startles those who experience the power of this redemptive act of love.

> The grace which I to all bequeath
>> In this divine memorial take,
> And mindful of your Saviour's death,

---

to revive the Eucharistic life of the Church of England. In addition to the full reprinting of the hymns in Rattenbury, *Eucharistic Hymns*, 195–249. Daniel Brevint, Dean of Lincoln Cathedral during the Restoration, emphasized a high view of the sacramental presence of Christ, the sacrificial (albeit anti-Catholic) character of the sacrament, and the benefits of Holy Communion.

34. Wesley's Article XVI, drawn with only minimal changes from the Book of Common Prayer, maintained that "the Supper of the Lord is not only a sign of the love that Christians ought to have among themselves one to another, but rather is a sacrament of our redemption by Christ's death; insomuch, that to such as rightly, worthily, and with faith receive the same, the bread which we break is a partaking of the body of Christ; and likewise the cup of blessing is a partaking of the blood of Christ" (J. Wesley, *Sunday Service*, 311).

35. Wesley and Wesley, *Hymns on the Lord's Supper*, 1 (no. 1:1).

> Do this, my followers, for my sake,
> Whose dying love hath left behind
> Eternal life for all mankind.[36]

As critical as this memorial aspect is for the Wesleys, they recoil from a "bare memorialism" in their view of the sacrament. Rather, sacramental remembrance connotes *anamnesis*, i.e., calling an event to mind in such a way as to make it real in the present. Memory functioned in this way for the Jewish community in the annual remembrance of Passover. The Hebrew people celebrated the Passover meal, not simply to recall God's deliverance of the people of Israel from bondage in Egypt, but to experience liberation in the present moment, as well. Charles's masterful use of imagery created what J. Ernest Rattenbury called a "Protestant Crucifix," poetry that continues to bring the event of the cross to the forefront of our consciousness and into our experience.

> Endless scenes of wonder rise
>   With that mysterious tree,
> Crucified before our eyes
>   Where we our Maker see:
> Jesus, Lord, what hast thou done!
>   Publish we the death divine,
> Stop, and gaze, and fall, and own
>   Was never love like thine!
>
> Never love nor sorrow was
>   Like that my Jesus show'd;
> See him stretch'd on yonder cross
>   And crush'd beneath the load!
> Now discern the deity,
>   Now his heavenly birth declare!
> Faith cries out, 'Tis he, 'tis he,
>   My God that suffers there![37]

---

36. Wesley and Wesley, *Hymns on the Lord's Supper*, 2 (no. 1:5).
37. Wesley and Wesley, *Hymns on the Lord's Supper*, 16 (no. 21:2–3).

Excursus on Sacrifice

The sacrificial metaphors applied by the Wesleys to the Lord's Supper are those which the writers of Hebrews and Revelation employ most frequently; the slaughtered Lamb who was also the Great High Priest. This Priest-Victim imagery brings out with unequivocal force their sense of the continuing power of sacrifice on the part of the ascended Christ. The earthly symbol represents this ongoing sacrifice of Christ on behalf of all. The Priest-Victim pleads the cause of sinful children for whom he died. The sacrifice on which God is asked to look is not our own but the one oblation for the sins of the world—the sacrifice of God's beloved Son. But the oblation offered in the sacrament also belongs to the faithful who join their sacrifice to Christ's. The sacrament refers not only to the dynamic sacrifice of Christ, but reminds the community of faith—the church—of its obligation to engage in self-sacrificing acts of love in imitation of Christ. The followers of Jesus offer up to God all their thoughts, words, and actions, "through the Son of his love, as a sacrifice of praise and thanksgiving."[38] Participation in the sacrament mandates that all take up the cross, thereby permitting God to form them into cruciform followers of the Lamb through the power of the Spirit.

Charles describes this sacrificial character of the Christian life, in which the worshiper participates repeatedly at the table of the Lord, and clarifies its relationship to the sacrifice of Christ.

> While faith th' atoning blood applies,
> Ourselves a living sacrifice
>   We freely offer up to God:
> And none but those his glory share
> Who crucified with Jesus are,
>   And follow where their Saviour trod.

> Saviour, to thee our lives we give,
> Our meanest sacrifice receive,
>   And to thy own oblation join,
> Our suffering and triumphant head,
> Thro' all thy states thy members lead,
>   And seat us on the throne divine.[39]

---

38. J. Wesley, *Works*, 3:76; from Wesley's sermon "On Perfection (I.11)."
39. Wesley and Wesley, *Hymns on the Lord's Supper*, 110 (no. 128:3).

Second, *Holy Communion is a celebration of the presence of the living Christ.* The Wesleys associated this present dimension most closely with the sacrament as a "sign and means" of grace. Without any question, the earliest Eucharistic feasts of the Christian community, at which the disciples of Jesus "ate their food with glad and generous hearts" (Acts 2:46), were characterized by joy and thanksgiving. Charles Wesley captured that primitive spirit of *eucharistia* or thanksgiving:

> JESU, WE THUS OBEY
> > Thy last and kindest word,
> > Here in thine own appointed way
> > We come to meet our Lord;
> > The way thou hast injoin'd
> > Thou wilt therein appear:
> We come with confidence to find
> > Thy special presence here.
>
> OUR HEARTS WE OPEN WIDE
> > To make the Saviour room:
> > And lo! the Lamb, the crucified,
> > The sinner's friend, is come!
> > His presence makes the feast,
> > And now our bosoms feel
> > The glory not to be exprest,
> > The joy unspeakable.[40]

Through faith, the Wesleys believed, the outward sign transmits the signified. Those who believe meet Jesus at the table, and the heights to which faith can move them are immeasurable.

> The joy is more unspeakable,
> > And yields me larger draughts of God,
> 'Till nature faints beneath the power,
> > And faith fill'd up can hold no more.[41]

---

40. Wesley and Wesley, *Hymns on the Lord's Supper*, 69 (no. 81:1–2).
41. Wesley and Wesley, *Hymns on the Lord's Supper*, 39 (no. 54:5).

Excursus on Presence

The sacrament, according to the Wesleys, effects what it represents. According to Rattenbury, "an examination of the hymns will result quite frequently in the discovery of allusions to the 'real Presence' of Christ, but it is always a *personal* Presence."[42] One of Charles's hymns illustrates this well.

> O thou who this mysterious bread
> Didst in Emmaus break,
> Return herewith our souls to feed,
> And to thy followers speak.
>
> Unseal the volume of thy grace,
> Apply the gospel-word;
> Open our eyes to see thy face,
> Our hearts to know the Lord.
>
> Of thee communing still, we mourn
> Till thou the veil remove;
> Talk with us, and our hearts shall burn
> With flames of fervent love.
>
> Inkindle now the heavenly zeal,
> And make thy mercy known,
> And give our pardon'd souls to feel
> That God and love are one.[43]

While advocating what could be described with integrity as a "real presence," the Wesleys denied any position approaching "transubstantiation."[44] Ole Borgen described this Wesleyan concept of real presence as a "dynamic"

---

42. Rattenbury, *Eucharistic Hymns*, 59.

43. Wesley and Wesley, *Hymns on the Lord's Supper*, 22–23 (no. 29).

44. John Wesley left the statement on this issue untouched in his edited Articles of Religion from the Book of Common Prayer: "Transubstantiation, or the change of the substance of bread and wine in the Supper of our Lord, cannot be proved by Holy Writ, but is repugnant to the plain words of Scripture, overthroweth the nature of a sacrament, and hath given occasion to many superstitions" (Article XVIII, in J. Wesley, *Sunday Service*, 311).

or "living presence," affirming that "wherever God acts, there God is."[45] Essentially beyond the possibility of rational explanation, Charles declared the depths of this holy mystery.

> O the depth of love divine,
>> Th' unfathomable grace!
> Who shall say how bread and wine
>> God into man conveys?
> *How* the bread his flesh imparts,
>> *How* the wine transmits his blood,
> Fills his faithful people's hearts
>> With all the life of God!
>
> Let the wisest mortal shew
>> How we the grace receive:
> Feeble elements bestow
>> A power not theirs to give:
> Who explains the wondrous way?
>> How thro' these the virtue came?
> These the virtue did convey,
>> Yet still remain the same.
>
> Sure and real is the grace,
>> The manner be unknown;
> Only meet us in thy ways
>> And perfect us in one,
> Let us taste the heavenly powers,
>> Lord, we ask for nothing more;
> Thine to bless, 'tis only ours
>> To wonder, and adore.[46]

Third, *Holy Communion is a pledge of the heavenly banquet to come.* The holy meal anticipates the glorious reunion of the faithful at the heavenly feast. As the writer to the Hebrews claimed, "we are surrounded by a great cloud of

---

45. See Borgen, *Wesley on the Sacraments*, 58–69.
46. Wesley and Wesley, *Hymns on the Lord's Supper*, 41 (no. 57:1–2, 4).

witnesses" (Heb 12:1), and at no time does the reality of this communion of saints forcefully impress itself upon the present church as in the celebration of Holy Communion. The Wesleys spoke often of the sacrament as a foretaste of this banquet, an earnest, or pledge, of things to come. Their rediscovery of "the communion of the saints" in relationship to this Holy Communion was a significant contribution they made to the sacramental theology of their own day. Hope became the keynote of this future dimension of the sacrament in John's preaching and Charles's poetry.

"By faith and hope already there," sings Charles, "Ev'n now the marriage-feast we share."[47] This is a "soul-transporting feast," that "bears us now on eagles' wings" and "seals our eternal bliss."[48] The amazing imagery in Charles's lyrical theology reflects his vision of the church as a community of hope.

> How glorious is the life above
>> Which in this ordinance we *taste*;
> That fulness of celestial love,
>> That joy which shall for ever last!
>
> The light of life eternal darts
>> Into our souls a dazling ray,
> A drop of heav'n o'erflows our hearts,
>> And deluges the house of clay.
>
> Sure pledge of extacies unknown
>> Shall this divine communion be,
> The ray shall rise into a sun,
>> The drop shall swell into a sea.[49]

The Wesleys employ these various dimensions in an effort to communicate the depth and breadth of meaning in the sacrament and to enrich the experience of the participants. In this sign-act of love, the past, present, and future—faith, hope, and love—are compressed, as it were, into a timeless, communal act of praise. The fullness of the Christian faith is celebrated in the mystery of a holy meal and the people of God are empowered to faithful ministry and service. As faithful disciples repeatedly participate

---

47. Wesley and Wesley, *Hymns on the Lord's Supper*, 82 (no. 93:4).
48. Wesley and Wesley, *Hymns on the Lord's Supper*, 82–83 (no. 94:1, 3, 4).
49. Wesley and Wesley, *Hymns on the Lord's Supper*, 87 (no. 101:1, 3, 4).

in the Eucharistic actions of taking, blessing, breaking, and giving—the constitutive aspects of an authentic, sacrificial life—God conforms them to the image of Christ.

Conclusion

John Wesley's published letter of January 6, 1756, to William Law enunciated the central principle upon which the founders of Methodism constructed their theology of the sacraments.

> All the externals of religion are in order to the renewal of our soul in righteousness and true holiness. But it is not true that the external way is one and the internal way another. There is but one scriptural way wherein we receive inward grace—through the outward means which God hath appointed.[50]

While the Wesleys wrote little about baptism, assuming both its centrality and importance for the Christian life, they affirmed the initiatory role of this sacrament. They viewed this sign-act of grace as the initial step in a process that shapes a beloved child into a disciple of Jesus. The Wesleyan movement of renewal was both an evangelical and a Eucharistic revival. Methodist spirituality revolved around the sacrament of the Lord's Supper. The Wesleys believed that, in this sign-act of love, the Spirit meets disciples at their point of need and enables them to grow into the fullest possible love of God and others in this life.

---

50. Telford, *Letters of John Wesley*, 3:366–67.

Chapter 14

The Integral Nature of Worship and Evangelism

Insights from the Wesleyan Tradition

> Source note: Delivered as the 2005 Annual Wallace Chappell Lecture in Evangelism at the annual meeting of the Academy of Evangelism in Theological Education, held at Wesley Theological Seminary on October 6, and first published in the *Asbury Theological Journal* 61.1 (Spring 2006) 7–23; reprinted in *The Study of Evangelism: Exploring a Missional Practice of the Church*, edited by Paul W. Chilcote and Laceye C. Warner, 246–63 (Grand Rapids: Eerdmans, 2008).

WHEN MY FAMILY AND I first arrived in Mutare in August 1992, the entire southern region of Africa was experiencing one of the worst droughts of the century. In spite of the fact that our formal work was at Africa University and the Old Mutare Centre, Janet and I both felt called to do something to help the many hungry people that surrounded us. It did not take us long to discover that widows and children were starving within ten miles of the university. Through our contacts with the church, we met Rev. Elisha Kabungaidze, pastor of the Mundenda Circuit, with responsibility for some seven churches in one of the hard hit areas. With the help of Elisha and a devoted circle of lay leaders within his congregations, we began to identify the "poorest of the poor" within the bounds of his wide-ranging parish. Some were members of his churches; most were not. We traveled throughout the area with Elisha, delivering food and other items basic to life. It was a humbling experience, but through it all I rejoiced in the holistic vision of evangelism and its integral connection with worship embodied in this hardworking servant of God.

Each morning of worship/evangelism/mission began with our group standing together in a circle. We greeted one another with the name of Christ. We prayed. One of our members read the Word for the day. We sang. We prayed some more, and then we set out. We had the privilege of walking from hut to hut with Elisha and his parishioners, repeating the same, basic sign-act of love with him. Every day was truly sacramental. As we approached a homestead, Elisha would call out the names of the family in his deep, resonant voice and exchange the traditional greetings.

"Marara ere?" (Did you sleep well through the night?)

"Tarara marara o." (Yes. I slept well if you slept well.)

Elisha would explain to the families why we had come, for they were usually unaware of our plans to visit. He would tell them we knew that they had no food and that the love of Jesus had moved us to do whatever we could to help them in their need. Often the women would fall to the ground and weep, and then spring to their feet, dancing and singing the praises of God. The Shona of Zimbabwe have a saying: "If you can talk, you can sing. If you can walk, you can dance." And we had many opportunities to witness and to practice both. We always prayed together, and we almost always sang a song as we departed. It was a joyful song, a song of hope within the midst of suffering. More often than not it was *Makanaka Mambo Jesu, makanaka Mambo Jesu*; "Oh how good is our great chief, Jesus."

Elisha lived out a model of evangelism—a way of being in mission in the world—that struck me very deeply. His participation in God's mission reflects with integrity, I believe, what Albert Outler once described as the trio of dominical imperatives regarding evangelism, namely, heralding, martyrdom, and servanthood.[1] Before Elisha did anything, he acknowledged God's presence and adored the Triune One. Wherever he went, he announced the gospel, the good news. He boldly proclaimed the love of God for all people and pointed to the Creator, Savior, and Sustainer he had come to know through Jesus Christ. He provided witness in the sense of living out his life in solidarity with God's people. He lived the life of a servant, a life characterized by the ungrudging outpouring of himself. When I asked him on one occasion where he had learned this winsome way of life, he responded by saying, "I think it is simply in my Methodist blood."

Far from a partisan cry (hardly something I intend here), I think Elisha was directing us to an essential principle, for surely, as the Wesleys argued repeatedly, their effort was simply to rediscover "primitive Christianity." While never using the language of "evangelism," their primary project was to emulate a pattern of life in community that reflected the presence of a

---

1. Outler, *Evangelism*, 99–104.

living Lord and a liberating/healing Spirit.[2] Implicit in my narration of life in the shadow of Elisha is the integral nature of worship and evangelism in the community of faith. I don't know if Elisha could have distinguished worship from evangelism in any sophisticated or nuanced manner. In fact, I would submit to you that the fullest possible integration of doxology and disciple-making was the key to his contagious faith. He lived what many are beginning to rediscover in post-Christian Western cultures at this very time. In the past decade or so, a growing number of church leaders and scholars have begun to address the connection between evangelism and worship, that perennial question in all ages of renewal in the life of the church.[3] In such times as these, spiritual fruit has always been abundant.

In relation to these monumental questions, therefore, my proposal here is rather modest. As we meet together here in this seminary named for the founder of Methodism, I simply desire to explore the fundamental relationship between worship and evangelism, using the hymns and writings of Charles Wesley (the neglected brother) as a vehicle for discovery.

I.

The terms *worship* and *evangelism* suffer from a common malady. They both defy simple definition. Both can be defined so narrowly that the profound nature of their significance is lost; they can be defined so broadly that they come to mean nothing. In common discourse within the life of the church today, worship can mean anything from the entirety of the Christian life to a set of praise music in the context of the Christian assembly. Likewise, evangelism can range in meaning from the specific act of preaching the gospel to a group of unchurched homeless men in an inner city soup kitchen to the entirety of the Christian faith. Despite the importance of precision, I am actually quite happy, at this point, to leave us in a state of "happy ambiguity" with regard to definition, because a part of this exercise is to discern the interface of these practices in the life of the church. Defining these terms in too narrow a fashion may blind us to their

---

2. I first narrated this account at a conference on "Evangelization, the Heart of Mission: A Wesleyan Imperative," sponsored by the General Board of Global Ministries of The United Methodist Church and its Mission Evangelism Committee, in January 1995.

3. This conversation actually goes much further back within the *oecumene* of the church to the Second Vatican Council. But for the discussions within Protestant circles, and reflective of much more recent dialogue, consult Morgethaler, *Worship Evangelism*; Webber, *Worship Is a Verb*; Kiefert, *Welcoming the Stranger*; Benedict and Miller, *Contemporary Worship*; Keck, *Church Confident*; Langford and Langford, *Worship and Evangelism*.

broad-ranging application; applying only broad strokes may obliterate the fascinating detail that actually constitutes real life. While it will be important for me to establish some basic parameters shortly—which I hope to do more descriptively than prescriptively—I think we do well to start where Charles Wesley would have begun, namely, in Scripture.

There are many biblical texts that leap immediately to mind as we contemplate the meaning of worship or the meaning of evangelism, but one text jumps out at me as I reflect upon the integral dynamic that links the two: Acts 2:46–47.

> Day by day, as they spent much time together in the temple, they broke bread at home and ate their food with glad and generous hearts, praising God and having the goodwill of all the people. And day by day the Lord added to their number those who were being saved.

However brief this description might be, it is a fairly definitive portrait of life in Christ—a life that directly linked worship and evangelism. True spiritual worship, as St. Paul made so abundantly clear in Romans 12, has to do, in fact, with every aspect of life. There can be no separation of worship or liturgy from the totality of life as we really know it. Worship, in this broad sense then, is the grateful surrender of all we are and all we have, a "living sacrifice" of praise and thanksgiving to the God of love who has created all things and bears witness with our spirits that we are the children of God. It is living in and for God and God's way in human history in all things. The ministry of evangelism in this earliest Christian community, the consequence of which was "the Lord adding to their number day by day," consisted of spending time in the communal worship and praise of God, sharing together the sacred gift of food, and offering kindness and hospitality to others. Just a few verses earlier in this chapter, of course, Luke provides a little more detail. "They devoted themselves to the apostles' teaching and fellowship, to the breaking of bread and the prayers" (Acts 2:42). There was a certain specificity with regard to the foundation of this evangelistic community in Word and sacramanet. There was a peculiar nature to the worship of God that they practiced. But all of this life together—including the sharing of personal possessions so that no one lacked the basic necessities of life—was aimed at living in and manifesting the reign of God.

It is a cliché to describe worship, and more precisely liturgy, as "the work of the people" and to think of evangelism in similar fashion, not as the work of a single individual, but of "the whole people of God." The purpose of this corporate service—this shared labor of love—is to form us in praise and engage us in God's mission. Charles Wesley seems to have learned early in life that worship/evangelism is *paideia*—life-shaping instruction or formation through action. For the earliest Christians—like those we see in the Acts of the Apostles—this classical Greek understanding of discipline must have entailed all those things that are done in the community of faith that shape the whole person in their journey toward maturity in Christ. In this process, however, nothing was more critical than the words and actions of the liturgical assembly that spilled over naturally into lifestyles of good news in the world. True worship springs from the heart, but worship (defined here in the more narrow sense as the liturgy) also has the potential to shape Christ-like people who become evangel-bearers for others.

The writer to the Hebrews uses the language of *paideia* to describe a vision of the Christian life: "We had human parents to discipline us, and we respected them . . . But [God] disciplines us for our good, in order that we may share his holiness" (Heb 12:9–10). The concept of a discipline that frees the human spirit and leads the emancipated child of God into a life characterized by holiness of heart and life clearly inspired the Wesleys. Charles bears witness to the potency of the vision.

> Loose me from the chains of sense,
> > Set me from the body free;
> Draw with stronger influence
> > My unfettered soul to thee!
> In me, Lord, thyself reveal,
> > Fill me with a sweet surprise;
> Let me thee when waking feel,
> > Let me in thine image rise.
>
> Let me of thy life partake,
> > Thy own holiness impart;
> O that I might sweetly wake
> > With my Saviour in my heart!
> O that I might know thee mine!
> > O that I might thee receive!
> Only live the life divine!
> > Only to thy glory live![4]

---

4. J. Wesley, *Works*, 7:428 (no. 278.4, 5).

Authentic evangelism both reflects and creates an "O that I might..." *modus operandi* in life and a desire to praise God in all things. So orthodoxy—the right praise of God—involves a joyful obedience and a daring surrender. It is not too much to say that the evangelistic ministry of the community of faith and the worship of the assembly—and specifically the liturgy—shape us in such a way that we believe in God (faith), desire nothing but God (love), and glorify God by offering our lives fully to Christ (holiness).

St. Paul places this concept at the center of his admonition to Christian parents in Ephesians 6:4, where he commands them to bring up their children "in the discipline and instruction of the Lord." Charles picks up this theme in one of his "family hymns" and refers to this process—in a profoundly evangelistic turn of phrase—as a means to "draw their souls to God."[5] In a hymn written for the opening of the Methodist School in Kingwood, he expands the image.

> Come, Father, Son, and Holy Ghost,
> > To whom we for our children cry!
> The good desired and wanted most
> > Out of thy richest grace supply–
> The sacred discipline be given
> To train and bring them up for heaven.
>
> Answer on them the end of all
> > Our cares, and pains, and studies here;
> On them, recovered from their fall,
> > Stamped with the humble character,
> Raised by the nurture of the Lord,
> To all their paradise restored.[6]

The more famous fifth stanza of the hymn articulates the holistic nature of this integrative, formational process.

> Unite the pair so long disjoined,
> > Knowledge and vital piety:
> Learning and holiness combined,
> > And truth and love, let all men see

---

5. J. Wesley, *Works*, 7:637 (no. 456.8).
6. J. Wesley, *Works*, 7:643 (no. 461.1, 2).

In those whom up to thee we give,

Thine, wholly thine, to die and live.

My contention here is quite simple. I believe that the Wesleys viewed the liturgy of the church—doxological evangelism, if you will—as the primary matrix in which this nurture raised and restored the children of God, both those inside and potentially those outside the household of faith. Through Word and sacramanet, God sets us on our journey of faith, offers us spiritual nourishment, and provides the necessary guidance for us to find our way home, especially when we require the perennial reminder that home is wherever God's reign is realized in the life of the world.

II.

Another biblical text, I believe, affords a provisional lens through which to explore the integral nature of evangelism and worship.[7] In an effort to flesh out the foundational concepts of worship/evangelism as doxology and discipline, I want to import a motif that is not without some dangers; but I find it helpful in exegeting the Wesleyan tradition nonetheless. I refer to the so-called "Isaiah Motif" drawn from the call of the prophet in Isaiah 6:1–8, a pattern one time fashionable for ordering the various acts of Christian worship and also explicating the evangelistic call to mission. A reminder of the text might prove helpful.

> In the year that King Uzziah died, I saw the Lord sitting on a throne, high and lofty; and the hem of his robe filled the temple. Seraphs were in attendance above him; each had six wings: with two they covered their faces, and with two they covered their feet, and with two they flew. And one called to another and said:
>
> "Holy, holy, holy is the Lord of hosts:
> the whole earth is full of his glory."
>
> The pivots on the thresholds shook at the voices of those who called, and the house filled with smoke. And I said: "Woe is me! I am lost, for I am a man of unclean lips, and I live among a people of unclean lips; yet my eyes have seen the King, the Lord of hosts!" Then one of the seraphs flew to me, holding a live coal that had been taken from the altar with a pair of tongs. The seraph touched my mouth with it and said: "Now that this

---

7. The analysis of Isa 6:2–8 which follows relies heavily upon my Presidential Address to The Charles Wesley Society at Point Loma Nazarene University, October 2004; see Chilcote, "Preliminary Explorations."

has touched your lips, your guilt has departed and your sin is blotted out." Then I heard the voice of the Lord saying, "Whom shall I send, and who will go for us?" And I said, "Here am I; send me!"

The paradigm embedded in this narrative involves, at least, a fivefold progression:

1. Adoration, "Holy, holy, holy is the Lord of hosts," moves the worshiper to
2. Confession, "Woe is me!" to
3. Forgiveness, "your guilt has departed and your sin is blotted out," and through
4. Proclamation, "Then I heard the voice of the Lord saying," to final
5. Dedication, "Here am I; send me!"

While there is an abiding truth in this sequence of devotion, it is dangerous to transpose it mechanically either into worship or the practice of evangelism.[8] It is always important to remember that the inbreaking Word gives and sustains life. At times, God acts unpredictably. There is also a potential danger, I want to admit, in mechanically imposing this structure upon the Wesleys. But while it is artificial to choreograph God's presence and movement or to plot these serially in a service of worship or in a strategy of evangelism, much less to squeeze Wesley into this mold, there is a certain "evangelical" logic in the Isaiah motif that resonates with a Wesleyan understanding of the divine-human encounter. I think this is well worth exploring. So permit me to examine briefly these specific dimensions of Isaiah's theophany.

Adoration

The Isaiah narrative opens with an overwhelming sense of awe, majesty, and wonder. Our first response to God is an acknowledgment of whom it is we worship.[9] The good news about God only becomes intelligible in this posture. Virtually every day of Charles Wesley's life began with morning prayer, including the words of the ancient prayer of praise, the *Te Deum*:

> We praise thee, O God: we acknowledge thee to be the Lord.
> All the earth doth worship thee, the Father everlasting. To thee

---

8. See, in particular, the critique of the threefold pattern of vision, contrition, and commission drawn from the Isaiah text in Hoon, *Integrity of Worship*, 51, 287.

9. See Cushman, "Worship as Acknowledgment."

all Angels cry aloud: the Heavens, and all the powers therein. To thee Cherubim and Seraphim continually do cry, Holy, holy, holy, Lord God of Sabaoth; Heaven and Earth are full of the Majesty of thy Glory.

In the 1780 *Collection of Hymns for the Use of the People Called Methodists*, Wesley alludes to the Isaian *Sanctus* in at least four hymns.

> Meet and right it is to sing,
> > In every time and place,
> Glory to our heavenly King,
> > The God of truth and grace.
> > All in one thanksgiving join:
> Holy, holy, holy, Lord,
> > Eternal praise be thine![10]

Selections drawn from his earlier collection of *Hymns on the Trinity* emphasize the awe with which one should approach God and the glory of God's tremendous and mysterious majesty.

> Holy, holy, holy Lord,
> God the Father and the Word,
> God the Comforter, receive
> Blessing more than we can give!
>
> Thee while dust and ashes sings,
> Angels shrink within their wings;
> Prostrate Seraphim above
> Breathe unutterable love.
>
> Fain with them our souls would vie,
> Sink as low, and mount as high;
> Fall, o'erwhelmed with love, or soar,
> Shout, or silently adore!

---

10. J. Wesley, *Works*, 7:346 (no. 212.1). Note the explicit reference to the Communion Service of the Book of Common Prayer in the opening line.

"All honour and glory to Jesus alone!" Charles cries, as he stands in beatific rapture *coram Deo*—before a "universe filled with the glory of God."[11] It is the radiance of God's nature, revealed most fully in the dual graces of creation and redemption, that overtakes the awestruck child.

> Th'o'erwhelming power of saving grace,
> The sight that veils the seraph's face,
> The speechless awe that dares not move,
> And all the silent heaven of love![12]

Little wonder that one of the most memorable lines in all of Charles Wesley's verse concludes his great hymn to love: "Lost in wonder, love, and praise." Is this not where true worship, where faithful evangelism, must always begin; in this posture?

Repentance and Forgiveness

The prophet can only respond: "Woe is me! I am lost, for I am a man of unclean lips, and I live among a people of unclean lips!" When we contemplate our own lives in relation to this God—or compare them with the life of Jesus—we are overwhelmed, as well, by our inadequacy, our brokenness, our fallen condition. In the Wesleyan tradition, repentance is a paramount concern because it strikes at the very heart of salvation. Confession and forgiveness are central to the Christian view of what it is we need to be saved *from* and what it is we need to be saved *into*. For Charles, no less than for his brother, salvation is both legal and therapeutic; it is related both to Christ's redemptive work *for* us and the Spirit's transforming work *in* us; it revolves around freedom from sin and freedom to love. Repentance is like the threshold of a door that opens the way to our spiritual healing. It is like the first step in a journey that leads us home.

Nowhere in Scripture is repentance and forgiveness more poignantly expressed than in Jesus' parable of the lost child in Luke 15. Stripped of dignity, value, and identity, the critical turning point for the estranged son in the story comes with these important words, "But when he came to himself . . ." Both John and Charles define repentance as "true self-understanding." The prodigal "came to himself." In the depth of his despair, he remembered who he was and to whom he belonged. Charles plays with

---

11. J. Wesley, *Works*, 7:342, 344, the closing lines of no. 210.1, 7.
12. J. Wesley, *Works*, 7:92 (no. 9.10).

this image in his sermon on Ephesians 5:14. As he turns directly to the text itself, he admonishes,

> Wherefore, "Awake thou that sleepest, and arise from the dead." God calleth thee by my mouth; and bids thee know thyself, thou fallen spirit, thy true state and only concern below: "what meanest thou, O sleeper? Arise! Call upon thy god . . . that thou perish not."[13]

For Charles, repentance signifies a true self-knowledge that leads to contrition and total reliance upon God's pardoning mercy in Christ.

He employs this image in a hymn celebrating God's universal grace as it is made manifest in the context of the worshiping community of God's people:

> Sinners, obey the gospel word!
>
> Haste to the supper of my Lord;
>
> Be wise to know your gracious day!
>
> All things are ready; come away!
>
> Ready the Father is to own
>
> And kiss his late-returning son;
>
> Ready your loving Saviour stands,
>
> And spreads for you his bleeding hands.
>
> The Father, Son, and Holy Ghost
>
> Is ready with their shining host;
>
> All heaven is ready to resound:
>
> "The dead's alive! The lost is found."[14]

In the successive stanzas, Charles layers the imagery of spiritual emotion elicited from the struggle to know God and to entrust one's life to God: pardon, favor, peace; the seeing eye, the feeling sense, the mystic joys; godly

---

13. Newport, *Sermons of Charles Wesley*, 216. Cf. John Wesley's sermon on "The Way to the Kingdom (II.1)": "This is the way: walk ye in it. And first, repent, that is, know yourselves. This is the first repentance, previous to faith, even conviction, or self-knowledge. Awake, then, thou that sleepest. Know thyself to be a sinner, and what manner of sinner thou art. Know that corruption of thy inmost nature, whereby thou art very far gone from original righteousness . . ." (J. Wesley, *Works*, 1:225).

14. J. Wesley, *Works*, 7:90 (no. 9.1, 2, 5).

grief, pleasing smart; meltings, tears, sighs; guiltless shame, sweet distress, unutterable tenderness; genuine meek humility, wonder.

A full paragraph from another of Charles Wesley's sermons is well worth quoting in its entirety at this point. It is taken from his sermon on 1 John 3:14, which Charles preached at least twenty-one times during 1738 and 1739, just at the outset of the revival and as a consequence of the brothers' shared reawakening to living faith. The sermon itself is a depiction of the three states of humanity, describing those who do not know and do not seek God, those who do not know but seek God, and those who know God. It is a compelling appeal to come to one's self so as to know God fully. Charles pleads,

> "Therefore also now, saith the Lord, turn ye even to me with all your heart, and with fasting and with weeping, and with mourning. And rend your hearts and not your garments, and turn unto the Lord your God; for he is gracious and merciful, slow to anger and of great kindness, and repenteth him of the evil." Oh that this infinite goodness of God might lead you to repentance! Oh that any one of you would even now arise and go to his Father and say unto him, "Father, I have sinned against heaven and before thee, and am no more worthy to be called thy son!" He sees you now, while you are a great way off, and has compassion, and only awaits your turning towards him, that he may run and fall on your neck and kiss you. Then will he say, "Bring forth the best robe (even the robe of Christ's righteousness) and put it upon him, for this my son was dead and is alive again; he was lost and is found."[15]

Charles Wesley understood that worship, in all of its various dimensions, but particularly in the liturgy of the people of God, has the power to bring us into an awareness of the Holy. He also understood, it would seem, with Henri Nouwen, that forgiveness is the name of love in a wounded world. Acknowledgment and confession bring healing. Forgiveness liberates people from enslavement to sin through the power of God's love in Jesus Christ. Liturgy offers the gift of this divine forgiveness as God comes to us in Christ with "healing in his wings."[16] Wesley realized that reconciliation and restoration are only possible through the intervention of God's grace. That grace is offered, first and foremost, he believed, in the context

---

15. Newport, *Sermons of Charles Wesley*, 142.

16. For Charles's multiple references to this Mal 4:2 image, see J. Wesley, *Works*, 7:157, 252, 270, 385, 420, 530, 608, 611, and 630, in addition to "Hark, the Herald Angels Sing."

of a worshiping community that manifests the hospitality of God and proclaims boldly to all:

> His bleeding heart shall make *you* room,
>> His open side shall take *you* in.
> He calls you now, invites *you* home–
> Come, O my guilty brethren, come![17]

Proclamation

"Then I heard the voice of the Lord, saying . . ." Charles Wesley celebrated the presence of the Word of God and trusted in its power. It is not too much to claim that the Wesleyan Revival was nothing other than a rediscovery of the sacred Christian Scriptures. "The Bible, the whole Bible, nothing but the Bible," one Wesleyan scholar observed, "this is the theme of John Wesley's preaching and the glory of Charles's hymns."[18] It is not without value to remember that the most critical works related to Wesleyan doctrine—John's *Standard Sermons* and *Notes on the New Testament* and Charles's *Hymns* (particularly the 1780 *Collection*)—all revolve primarily around the community of God's people in worship. The proclamation of God's Word in corporate worship and the rediscovery of the "living Word" among the early Methodist people was the life force of the movement. The essential content of Charles Wesley's preaching was the inclusive love of God revealed to us in Jesus Christ. Nowhere in the Wesleyan corpus is the living encounter with this good news summarized more poignantly than in the familiar lines of his great hymn, "Wrestling Jacob":

> 'Tis Love! 'Tis Love! Thou diedst for me;
>> I hear thy whisper in my heart.
> The morning breaks, the shadows flee,
>> Pure Universal Love thou art:
> To me, to all, thy bowels move–
> Thy nature, and thy name, is LOVE.[19]

This inclusive, unconditional love is made known to us through the Word and the Spirit. For Wesley, the Word (Jesus Christ and the story of God's love in Scripture) is distinct, but can never be separated, from the Spirit of God.

---

17. J. Wesley, *Works*, 7:117 (no. 29.6.3–6). Emphasis added.
18. J. Wesley, *Works*, 7:3.
19. J. Wesley, *Works*, 7:251 (no. 136.7).

Three hymns that Charles intended for use "Before reading the Scriptures"[20] and one of his most noteworthy hymns of petition that precedes them[21] demonstrate this essential connection. He identifies the Holy Spirit as the "key" to the sacred book, the active force that opens to us the treasure of God's message of grace and love: "Come, Holy Ghost," he implores, "Unlock the truth, thyself the key, / Unseal the sacred book."[22] "Now the revealing Spirit send," he prays, "And give us ears to hear."[23] Only the Spirit is able to "Reveal the things of God" by removing the barrier to our spiritual sight.

> No man can truly say
>> That Jesus is the Lord
> Unless thou take the veil away,
>> And breathe the living word.[24]

Or again:

> While in thy Word we search for thee
>> (We search with trembling awe!)
> Open our eyes, and let us see
>> The wonders of thy law.[25]

"Come, Holy Ghost, *our* hearts inspire," pleads Wesley, "for you are the 'Source of the old prophetic fire.'"[26] His concern throughout is for a dynamic, relational, vibrant encounter with God through the Spirit, who can

> Inspire the living faith
>> (Which whosoe'er receives,
> The witness in himself he hath,
>> And consciously believes),
> The faith that conquers all,
>> And doth the mountain move,
> And saves whoe'er on Jesus call,
>> And perfects them in love.[27]

---

20. J. Wesley, *Works*, 7:185–87 (nos. 85–87).
21. J. Wesley, *Works*, 7:182–83 (no. 83).
22. J. Wesley, *Works*, 7:185 (no. 85.2.1, 3–4).
23. J. Wesley, *Works*, 7:186 (no. 86.3.3–4).
24. J. Wesley, *Works*, 7:182–3 (no. 83:1.1; 2.1–4).
25. J. Wesley, *Works*, 7:186 (no. 86.2).
26. J. Wesley, *Works*, 7:185 (no. 85.1.1, 3). Emphasis added.
27. J. Wesley, *Works*, 7:183 (no. 83.4).

Dedication

On the most basic level, all worship is response to God's prevenient action, and response is the goal of all evangelistic practice. In answer to the Lord's question, "Whom shall I send, and who will go for us?" Isaiah responds by saying, "Here am I; send me!" In Charles's vision of the worshiping community, and certainly in the evangelistic practice of the early Methodist communities, God commissions the faithful as ambassadors of Christ and graciously enables each disciple to reaffirm his or her true vocation. Charles's hymns reflect a myriad of potential responses to God's call, both individual and corporate. While each deserves full attention in its own right, I will simply hint at two interrelated aspects of dedicatory response in Wesley, namely, mission and Eucharist. The former aspect, related to Wesley's missiological ecclesiology, is, most likely, immediately obvious to most; the latter, reflecting the absolute centrality of Charles's sacramental vision of life, affords, I believe, some of Wesley's most important insights and contributions to contemporary conversations about worship and evangelism.

The Imperative of Mission. Charles's hymns frequently reflect an understanding of the Christian life in which the most appropriate response to God's transforming grace is Christian outreach to the world and participation in God's mission to restore justice, peace, and love to all.[28] In one of Wesley's greatest missionary hymns, as ST Kimbrough has observed,

> . . . there is an intermingling of praise and mission, for to follow means faithful service. How does one *know* and *feel* sins forgiven, *anticipate* heaven on earth and *own* that love, even in this world, is heaven? Through service to God and others—*by breaking out of the world of self and reaching out to others!*[29]

In Charles Wesley's vision of the church—and particularly the authentic community of faith in continuous praise of God—mission and evangelism flow directly out of our encounter with God's Word in worship. Evangelism, like worship, as we have seen, is an essential activity of the whole people of God. In imitation of Christ, and through our encounter with the living Word, we learn to woo others into the loving embrace of God and then help them to see that their mission in life, in partnership with Christ, is to be the signposts of God's reign in this world.

---

28. See, in particular, the analysis of "Glory to God, and praise and love" in Kimbrough, *Heart to Praise*, 17–27, where he discusses response in terms of "Outreach to the Marginalized," "Universal Outreach to All," and "Outreach to Each Individual." Cf. Meistad, "Missiology of Wesley and the Eastern Church," 214–18.

29 Kimbrough, *Heart to Praise*, 23.

In his hymn, "For a preacher of the gospel," Charles Wesley reminds us of this transforming, evangelistic call of God upon our lives.

> I would the precious time redeem,
>   And longer live for this alone,
> To spend and to be spent for them
>   Who have not yet my Saviour known;
> Fully on these my mission prove,
> And only breathe to breathe thy love.
>
> My talents, gifts, and graces, Lord,
>   Into thy blessed hands receive;
> And let me live to preach thy word;
>   And let me to thy glory live:
> My every sacred moment spend
> In publishing the sinner's friend.
>
> Enlarge, inflame, and fill my heart
>   With boundless charity divine!
> So shall I all my strength exert,
>   And love them with a zeal like thine;
> And lead them to thy open side,
> The sheep, for whom their Shepherd died.[30]

The imperative of Eucharist. The connection between evangelism and Eucharist is extremely intimate for Wesley, and can be discerned most clearly, I believe, in his concept of Eucharistic sacrifice. In Charles's sermon on Acts 20:7 (more properly what might be described as an introductory "treatise" to a larger, unfinished work on the sacrament) we encounter a concept of sacrifice consonant with the view he espouses in his *Hymns on the Lord's Supper* devoted to this theme. Charles views the sacrament as a "re-presentation" of the sacrifice of Christ.[31] As J. Ernest Rattenbury has demonstrated, his stress is persistently on the twofold oblation of the church in the sacrament; the body of Christ offered is not merely a sacred

---

30. J. Wesley, *Works*, 7:597 (no. 421.3-5).
31. Newsome, *Sermons of Charles Wesley*, 277-86. Cf. Bowmer, *Lord's Supper in Early Methodism*, 223-32.

symbol of Christ's "once-for-all" act of redemption, but is also the living sacrifice of the people of God.[32]

The sacrificial character of the Christian life, in which the worshiper participates repeatedly at the table of the Lord, and its relationship to the sacrifice of Christ is clarified in Charles's hymns. In this regard, he follows the language of Daniel Brevint's *The Christian Sacrament and Sacrifice* very closely; namely, "The main intention of Christ herein was not the bare *remembrance* of His Passion; but over and above, to invite us to His Sacrifice."[33]

> While faith th'atoning blood applies,
> Ourselves a living sacrifice
>   We freely offer up to God;
> And none but those His glory share,
> Who crucified with Jesus are,
>   And follow where their Saviour trod.
>
> Saviour, to Thee our lives we give,
> Our meanest sacrifice receive,
>   And to Thine own oblation join,
> Our suffering and triumphant Head,
> Through all Thy states Thy members lead,
>   And seat us on the throne Divine.[34]

Worship is recapitulation, and as we repeatedly participate in the Eucharistic actions of offering and thanking and breaking and giving—the constitutive aspects of an authentic, sacrificial life—God conforms us into the image of Christ—our lives become truly Eucharistic as faith working by love leading to holiness of heart and life.

---

32 See Rattenbury, *Eucharistic Hymns*, 123–47.
33 Rattenbury, *Eucharistic Hymns*, 178.
34 Rattenbury, *Eucharistic Hymns*, 236.

Chapter 15

"Claim Me for Thy Service"

Charles Wesley's Vision of Servant Vocation

> Source note: A workshop paper delivered before the Wesley Studies Group of the Oxford Institute of Methodist Theological Studies at Christ Church, Oxford, on August 28, 2007, and published in *Proceedings of the Charles Wesley Society* 11 (2006–2007) 69–85.

IN ONE OF THE great Trinitarian hymns included in John and Charles Wesley's *Hymns on the Lord's Supper*, the singer beseeches God,

> Claim me, for thy Service, claim
> All I have and all I am.
>
> Take my Soul and Body's Powers,
>   Take my Mem'ry, Mind, and Will,
> All my Goods, and all my Hours,
>   All I know, and all I feel,
> All I think, and speak, and do;
> Take my Heart—but make it new.[1]

The disciple of Christ asks the Three-One God to claim every aspect of his or her life in an oblation that can only be described as covenantal. In typical Wesleyan fashion, a series of "alls" characterizes the plea. All I have, all I am, all my goods, all my hours, all I know, feel, think, speak, and do. The

---

1. Wesley and Wesley, *Hymns on the Lord's Supper*, 129–30 (no. 155:3–4).

all-encompassing sacrifice of self—the offer of one's whole being in service to God—rests secure, as Charles makes abundantly clear throughout, on the foundation of a heart transformed by God's prevenient action. In hymns like this one, Charles Wesley cultivates a profound vision of servant vocation, a missional conception of Christian discipleship summarized tersely in the simple phrase: "Claim me for Thy service."

One can hear echoes of the baptismal covenant, perhaps, in Charles's use of language. The sacrament of baptism, of course, is that place where discipleship begins, that event in which God claims each person as God's own. It also signals the commitment of the individual and the community to God's mission. The ambiance of many Wesley hymns elicits a profoundly missiological vision of Christian community and engagement with the dominion of God in the world. Despite the centrality of this missional ecclesiology to the Wesleyan movement, few scholars have examined the missiology of Charles Wesley and the contribution of his hymns to the concept of servant vocation in the early Methodist heritage. Before his untimely death, Tore Meistad explored this theme in a preliminary way and even sought to link the Wesleyan concept of mission with the Eastern church.[2] In this brief essay I hope to build upon his insights as we examine Charles Wesley's understanding of service or self-sacrifice as the orienting principle of his missiological vision of Christian vocation.

Of course, Jesus functions as the primary exemplar and mentor in Charles's development of this vision. His frequent use of the ancient kenotic hymn (Phil 2:5-11, particularly v. 7) elevates self-sacrificial love in Jesus' own character and mission in the world. After an examination of this foundational portrait, I turn my attention to Charles's conception of conformity to the mind of Christ in light of the kenotic imagery of his hymns. In several signature hymn texts from the "For Believers Working" section of the 1780 *A Collection of Hymns for the Use of the People Called Methodists*, he develops something approaching a "theology of servant ministry" along these lines. I conclude with an examination of Wesley's concept of self-sacrifice as it relates to the sacrament, particularly as developed in the final section of the brothers' *Hymns on the Lord's Supper*, and demonstrate how this sacramental paradigm of sacrificial servanthood both shapes and reflects Charles's understanding of Christian vocation.

---

2. See Meistad, "Missiology of Wesley and Eastern Church." ST Kimbrough Jr. has also given attention to this theme, an implicit concern of much of his scholarship on Charles.

I. The Servant-Mind of Christ

Charles Wesley's Lyrical Settings of Philippians 2:5–11

In his examination of "'Kenosis' in the Nativity Hymns of Ephrem the Syrian and Charles Wesley," ST Kimbrough Jr. claims that both of these important theologians "view God's self-emptying, self-limitation, and self-effacement in the Incarnation of Jesus Christ as the foundational foci for Christian spirituality."[3] They drew these images, of course, from St. Paul's Letter to the Philippians, in which he reminds the community to imitate the Christ of whom they sing in one of the earliest hymns of the church.

> Let the same mind be in you that was in Christ Jesus, who, though he was in the form of God, did not regard equality with God as something to be exploited, but emptied himself, taking the form of a slave, being born in human likeness. And being found in human form, he humbled himself and became obedient to death—even death on a cross. Therefore God also highly exalted him and gave him the name that is above every name, so that at the name of Jesus every knee should bend, in heaven and on earth and under the earth, and every tongue should confess that Jesus Christ is Lord, to the glory of God the Father. (5–11)

This so-called *kenotic* hymn figures prominently in the sacred poetry of Charles Wesley. Owing perhaps to the influence of Nicolas von Zinzendorf, the concept of *kenosis*—or self-emptying—was taken up and elaborated theologically as a theory of the Incarnation.[4] It is not my purpose here to speculate about possible Pietistic influence upon Charles through the Zinzendorf connection or to discuss the Christological implications of this concept; rather, I am interested in how the *kenotic* imagery associated with Jesus functions as a paradigm for faithful Christian discipleship in the hymns of Charles.

Although Wesley provides no lyrical paraphrase of this Philippians hymn in his *Short Hymns on Select Passages of the Holy Scriptures* of 1762, allusions to the hymn can be found widely in his other collections.[5] In the Wesleys' *Hymns and Sacred Poems* of 1742, Charles reflects on St. Paul's

---

3. Kimbrough, "Kenosis," 265.

4. For a discussion and critique of this Christological theory, see Baillie, *God Was in Christ*, 94–98.

5. Space only permits the examination of the most pertinent texts here. For an example of Wesley's pervasive use of the Philippians text in the major Wesleyan hymn collection, see J. Wesley, *Works*, 7:101, 108, 118, 193, 197, 246, 265, 315–16, 421, 476, 507, 508, 520, 522, 524, 527, 531, 534, 577, 626, 644, 678, 697, and 710.

introduction to the ancient hymn in a twenty stanza lyrical paraphrase of "Let this mind be in you, which was also in Christ Jesus" (Phil 2:5).[6] The brothers published thirteen of these stanzas in their 1780 *Collection*, verses describing Christ's mind in turn as quiet, gentle, patient, noble, spotless, loving, thankful, constant, and perfect.[7] One of Wesley's most effective paraphrases of the *kenotic* hymn itself, however, comes in a four stanza hymn entitled "to be sung at Work," beginning "Son of the Carpenter, receive," published in *Hymns and Sacred Poems* (1739).[8] Attribution of this hymn to Charles remains uncertain, but the brothers published the last three verses of the hymn in the 1780 *Collection* as one of the lead selections in the section "For Believers Working."[9] Since this hymn focuses on the believer's quest to conform to the mind of Christ, rather than on the character of Jesus *per se*, I will examine the text in greater detail in the second section of the paper dealing with the *kenotic* paradigm of Christian discipleship.

In another extremely significant hymn of *Hymns and Sacred Poems* (1739) collection—not to be confused with the famous "atonement hymn" with the same first line—Wesley explores the titles of Christ. Four verses of the fifteen afford what may be his most profound exposition of the *kenotic* theme.

> Arise, my soul, arise,
>   Thy Saviour's sacrifice!
> All the names that love could find,
>   All the forms that love could take,
> Jesus in himself has joined,
>   Thee, my soul, his own to make.
>
> Equal with God most high,
>   He laid his glory by:
> He, th'eternal God was born,
>   Man with men he deigned t'appear,
> Object of his creature's scorn,
>   Pleas'd a servant's form to wear.

---

6. Wesley and Wesley, *Hymns and Sacred Poems* (1742), 221–23.

7. J. Wesley, *Works*, 7:507–509 (no. 345.1–2, 7, 9–10, 13–20; original in *Hymns and Sacred Poems* (1742), 221–23.

8. Wesley and Wesley, *Hymns and Sacred Poems* (1739), 193–94.

9. J. Wesley, *Works*, 7:468 (no. 313).

High above ev'ry name,
 Jesus, the great I AM!
Bows to Jesus ev'ry knee,
 Things in heav'n, and earth, and hell;
Saints adore him, demons flee,
 Fiends, and men and angels feel.

He left his throne above,
 Emptied of all, but love:
Whom the heav'ns cannot contain,
 God vouchsaf'd a worm t' appear,
Lord of glory, *Son of Man*,
 Poor, and vile, and abject here.[10]

Self-emptying: The Kenotic Paradigm

Three primary themes of a *kenotic* paradigm emerge from this hymn, namely, humility, estrangement, and self-emptying. The God revealed in the Incarnation is a self-humbling God. The *Nativity Hymns*, as Kimbrough has pointed out, provide some of the most powerful imagery related to a God "humbled to the dust."[11] Wesley's paraphrase of the *Gloria in excelsis* elevates the paradoxical connection between Christ's humiliation with his exaltation; the hymn writer binds humility and glory together as one.

See th' eternal Son of God,
 A mortal son of man,
Dwelling in the earthly clod,
 Whom heaven cannot contain![12]

---

10. Wesley and Wesley, *Hymns and Sacred Poems* (1739), 165–68, sts. 1–2, 9–10. The Wesleys published versions of this hymn in three other collections: Wesley and Wesley, *Hymns and Spiritual Songs*, no. 40, and J. Wesley, *Select Hymns*, no. 97, both hymns consisting of fifteen verses, as well, with one from 1739 omitted and another added. The hymn is reduced to nine verses in J. Wesley, *Works*, 7:315–317 (no. 187.1-4, 8–12).
11. Kimbrough, "Kenosis," 271, quoting C. Wesley, *Nativity Hymns*, 6 (no. 4.3).
12. C. Wesley, *Nativity Hymns*, 6 (no. 4:3).

This paradox extends to the concept of estrangement as well. Again, Kimbrough observes, "Charles Wesley comprehends well this dimension of *kenosis*, when he writes,

> Wrapped in swathes the immortal stranger,
> > Man with men,
> > We have seen
> > Lying in a manger.[13]

Father Francis Frost explored the same dynamic understanding of estrangement in Wesley's religious verse in an exceptionally incisive essay entitled "The Veiled Unveiling of the Glory of God in the Eucharistic Hymns of Charles Wesley: The Self-Emptying Glory of God."[14] Frost appropriates the language of the well-known line of "Hark, the herald angels sing," "Veiled in flesh, the Godhead see," in an effort to articulate the central mystery of the Incarnation.[15] All the *kenotic* themes converge as we "sound the depths" of the incarnate God of love. Frost attempts to articulate the central paradox.

> The self-emptying is also a veiling of the Godhead. Why? Jesus did not cease to be God in the self-emptying. Precisely because the very love which *is* God is in the self-emptying, the self-emptying is a manifestation of the Godhead. But it is an unveiling of it in veiling. The love unveils itself in the veiling of self-emptying.[16]

The essence of the *kenotic* paradigm, therefore, and the key to the mystery of love, is self-emptying. The concept is everywhere in Charles's poetry. In his *Hymns on the Lord's Supper*, we sing, "He came self-emptied from above, / That we might live through him."[17] "Jesus, Thou art the' Anointed One," Wesley confesses, "Who camest self-emptied from the sky."[18] Pondering with Mary the miraculous nature of Jesus' birth, Charles observes,

> O may I always bear in mind
> The Saviour's pity for mankind,
> > Which brought him from his throne,

---

13. Kimbrough, "Kenosis," 270, quoting C. Wesley, *Nativity Hymns*, 4 (no. 6:3).
14. Frost, "Veiled Unveiling."
15. Wesley and Wesley, *Hymns and Sacred Poems* (1739), 207.
16. Frost, "Veiled Unveiling," 88. Frost also quotes the famous statement of Charles de Foucauld in this context: "Self-lowering is of the essence of love."
17. Wesley and Wesley, *Hymns on the Lord's Supper*, 60 (no. 60).
18. C. Wesley, *MS Matthew*, 129.

> Emptied of all His majesty,
>
> A Man of griefs to comfort me,
>
> > And make my heart his own.[19]

In his famous hymn entitled "Free Grace," published in Wesley and Wesley, *Hymns and* SACRED *Poems* (1739) and more popularly known by the opening line, "And can it be, that I should gain," Wesley condenses the whole *kenotic* doctrine into a single line.

> He left his Father's throne above,
>
> > (So free, so infinite his grace!),
>
> *Emptied himself of all but love,*
>
> > And bled for Adam's helpless race:
>
> 'Tis mercy all, immense and free!
>
> For, O my God! it found out me![20]

No image of self-emptying impresses itself on our minds with greater veracity than the pervasive and distinctive phrase, "Emptied himself of all but love." It is there in his *Nativity Hymns*.

> All-wise, all-good, almighty Lord,
>
> Jesus, by highest heaven adored,
>
> > E'er time its course began,
>
> How did thy glorious mercy stoop
>
> To take thy fallen nature up,
>
> > When thou thyself wert man?
>
> The eternal God from heav'n came down,
>
> The King of glory dropped his crown,
>
> > And veiled his majesty,
>
> Emptied of all but love he came;
>
> Jesus, I call thee by the name
>
> > Thy pity bore for me.[21]

We find it in Wesley's paraphrase of Job 23:3.

---

19. C. Wesley, *MS Luke*, 28.
20. Wesley and Wesley, *Hymns and Sacred Poems* (1739), 118, st. 3. Emphasis added.
21. C. Wesley, *Nativity Hymns*, 19 (no. 15:1–2).

> O that I knew the way to find
> That Saviour of our sinful kind,
> > That Friend of misery!
> Who left His blissful realms above,
> Emptied Himself of all but love,
> > And died to ransom me![22]

Although found in his hymns as early as 1739, a close examination of this phrase in *A Collection of Psalms and Hymns* (1741) may even provide some clue to its origin—perhaps the editorial work of John rather than the creative mind of Charles.

> He left true bliss and joy above,
> Emptied himself of all but love;
> For me He freely did forsake
> More than from me He e'er can take:
> A mortal life for a divine
> He took, and did even that resign.[23]

This hymn is actually a very careful redaction (improvement?) of one verse from "The Resignation," a religious poem by the Cambridge Platonist, John Norris, published in his *A Collection of Miscellanies* in 1692, the original of which reads,

> He left true Bliss and Joys above,
> Himself he *emptied* of all good, but *love*:
> For me he freely did forsake
> More good, than he *from* me *can* ever *take*.
> A *mortal* life for a *Divine*
> He took, and did at last even *that* resign.[24]

In a brilliant essay on "'Experimental and Practical Divinity': Charles Wesley and John Norris," Dick Watson suggests the many ways in which Norris may have influenced the younger poet, but makes no mention of this particular connection to the Wesleyan corpus.[25] Regardless, whether originally John's or Charles's in its original form, the younger brother

---

22. C. Wesley, *MS Scripture Hymns*, 29; based on Job 23:3.
23. Wesley, *Psalms and Hymns*, 31.
24. Norris, *Collection of Miscellanies*, 107; "The Resignation," st. 5.
25. Watson, "Experimental and Practical Divinity."

takes ownership of the idea and, as Father Frost has observed, "'Emptied of all but love He came.' That is a poetic way of intimating, not so much that Jesus manifests his love for us in the absence of all else, as that the love is in the very self emptying."[26]

Footwashing: The Servant Character of Christ

In Jesus' life among his followers, nowhere was this self-emptying love manifest more poignantly than in the Upper Room. Here, among his closest friends, Jesus translates humility, estrangement, and self-emptying into a profound sign-act in his washing of the disciples' feet (John 13:1–20). Jesus acts out the meaning of the Incarnation. He demonstrates the paradoxical lesson that greatness in the community of his disciples is to be measured in terms of willingness to serve.[27] Jesus left no doubt that he is the chief of all servants who invites all into the ministry of self-emptying love. In Charles Wesley's lyrical exposition of John 13, all of the *kenotic* themes converge into a compelling portrait of life in a self-emptied Lord whose example compels others into the path of *kenotic* service for others.

> Jesu, by highest heavens adored,
>   The church's glorious Head;
> With humble joy I call Thee, Lord,
>   And in Thy footsteps tread.
>
> Emptied of all Thy greatness here
>   While in the body seen,
> Thou wouldst the least of all appear,
>   And minister to men.
>
> A servant to thy servants Thou
>   In thy debased estate,
> How meekly did thy goodness bow
>   To wash thy followers' feet!

---

26. Frost, "Veiled Unveiling," 87.

27. See the treatment of the *diakonia* theme in Wesleyan theology in Chilcote, *Recapturing the Wesleys' Vision*, 91–118.

> And shall a worm refuse to stoop,
>> His fellow-worms disdain?
> I give my vain distinctions up,
>> Since God did wait on man.
>
> At charity's almighty call
>> I lay my greatness by,
> The least of saints, I wait on all,
>> The chief of sinners I.
>
> Happy, if I their grief may cheer,
>> And mitigate their pain,
> And wait upon the servants here,
>> 'Till with the Lord I reign.[28]

II. Conformity to the Mind of Christ

> "The servant shall be as his Lord."

In his hymns, Charles Wesley relentlessly articulates God's invitation to allow the Spirit to conform the mind, the life, the "image" of the disciple to that of Christ. He enunciates this central theme in a unique formulation of Matthew 10:25, "it is enough for the disciple to be like the teacher," first expressed, perhaps, in his "Thanksgiving" hymn of 1742.

> My spirit meek, my will resigned,
> Lowly as thine shall be my mind—
> The servant shall be as his Lord.[29]

For Charles, this call to conformity to Christ defines the disciple—it characterizes the Christian who is altogether God's—but it is also a promise. In virtually every hymn in which this phrase appears, it implies both a demand and a gift. "I stay me on thy faithful word," cries the follower of Christ "Groaning for Redemption," "The servant shall be as his Lord."[30] In the

---

28. C. Wesley, *Hymns and Sacred Poems* (1749), 1:213–14.
29. Wesley and Wesley, *Hymns and Sacred Poems* (1742), 169.
30. Wesley and Wesley, *Hymns and Sacred Poems* (1742), 169.

powerful hymn, "Prisoners of hope," this statement of vocation and promise functions as the refrain for the concluding stanzas.

> Thou wilt perform thy faithful word:
> "The servant shall be as his Lord."
> . . .
> We only hang upon thy word,
> "The servant shall be as his Lord."[31]

Called to service, the service itself becomes God's greatest gift.

The fifth section of Part 4 of the Wesleys' *Collection* (1780) includes eight selections "For Believers Working." In these hymns Wesley elevates this call to servant ministry in conformity to Christ. I return here, therefore, to the hymn mentioned earlier, "Son of the Carpenter, receive," as it deals with the *kenotic* paradigm of Christian discipleship and the disciple's imitation of the Master.

> Servant of all, to toil for man
>   Thou wouldst not, Lord, refuse;
> Thy Majesty did not disdain
>   To be employed for us!
>
> Thy bright example I pursue,
>   To Thee in all things rise;
> And all I think, or speak, or do,
>   Is one great sacrifice.
>
> Careless thro' outward cares I go,
>   From all distraction free;
> My hands are but engaged below,
>   My heart is still with thee.[32]

Wesley presents at least three critical insights in this brief hymn. First, Christ takes upon himself the form of a servant because this is the nature of God's love. Second, imitation of Christ requires the sacrifice of one's whole

---

31. Wesley and Wesley, *Hymns and Sacred Poems* (1742), 234; cf. C. Wesley, *Hymns and Sacred Poems* (1749), 2:179 (no. 25:7).

32. Wesley and Wesley, *Hymns and Sacred Poems* (1739), 193–94, sts. 2–4.

self to God. Finally, only those who bind themselves to Christ and work the works of God are truly free in life.

The hymns of this section enunciate some of the other primary themes of servant ministry as well. Wesley links the significance of the disciple's service to the sacrifice of Christ.

> "Jesu, this mean oblation join
> > To thy great sacrifice.
> ...
> Stampt with an infinite desert
> > My work he then shall own."[33]

The servant of God pursues his or her "daily labor" in order to walk in a closer fellowship with God: "In all my works thy presence find."[34] Service is its own reward.

> Joyful thus my faith to show,
> > I find his service my reward;
> Every work I do below
> > I do it to the Lord.[35]

In what might be called the "signature hymn" of this section of the Wesleys' *Collection*, "O thou who camest from above," Charles articulates one of his most critical insights related to Christian servanthood: "Increase in us the kindled fire, / In us the work of faith fulfil." Reflecting upon this couplet, Oliver Beckerlegge observed: "It should not be forgotten that the early Methodist Conferences were "Conversations about the work *of* God, not the work of man for God! The flame of faith can be lit only from outside and above—it is the gift of the Holy Spirit. Christ is the subject and agent."[36] But what is the character of this graciously enabled labor of love?

The Practice of Christian Service

Charles Wesley goes to great lengths to specify the character of Christian service. First, the servant simply offers to others what he or she has freely

---

33. J. Wesley, *Works*, 7:468 (no. 312:3–4); the first two lines of st. 3 and the first two lines of st. 4; original in Wesley and Wesley, *Hymns and Sacred Poems* (1739), 165.

34. J. Wesley, *Works*, 7:470 (no. 315:2), from "Forth in thy name, O Lord, I go"; original in C. Wesley, *Hymns and Sacred Poems* (1749), 1:246.

35. J. Wesley, *Works*, 7:471 (no. 316:2); original in C. Wesley, *Redemption Hymns*, 8.

36. J. Wesley, *Works*, 7:474 (footnote).

received from God. Harkening back to the episode in which Jesus washes his disciples' feet in the Upper Room, Wesley reveals the heart of the "primitive Christian."

> O might my lot be cast with these,
> The least of Jesu's witnesses!
> O that my Lord would count me meet
> To wash his dear disciples' feet!
>
> This only thing do I require:
> Thou know'st 'tis all my heart's desire
> Freely what I receive to give,
> The servant of thy church to live.[37]

Servants, in other words, engage in evangelism—offering God's grace to all in word and in deed. After preaching on one occasion at Gwennap Pit in Cornwall, Charles celebrated this aspect of service to God.

> All thanks be to God,
> Who scatters abroad
> Throughout every place,
> By the least of his servants his savour of grace!"[38]

The unique feature of Wesley's vision, however, is the way in which he connects the sharing of grace with the restoration of the mind of Christ in the believer. In a composite hymn, opening with a lyrical paraphrase of "Jesus and the woman at the well" (John 4:10–15), Wesley conjoins the "mind" of Philippians 2 with the "action" of James 1:

> Thy mind throughout my life be shown,
>   While listening to the wretch's cry,
> The widow's and the orphan's groan,
>   On mercy's wings I swiftly fly
> The poor and helpless to relieve,
> My life, my all for them to give.[39]

---

37. J. Wesley, *Works*, 7:101 (no. 17:7–8); original in C. Wesley, *Hymns and Sacred Poems* (1749), 2:336.

38. C. Wesley, *Redemption Hymns*, 3 (no. 3:1).

39. C. Wesley, *Scripture Hymns*, 2:380 (no. 738).

To have the mind of Christ, in other words, is to care for the poor.

It is not surprising, therefore, that Jesus' words concerning the judgment of the nations in Matthew 25 should figure prominently in his depiction of authentic discipleship and Christian service. Wesley's lyrical formulation of the pertinent text comes, of all places, in a hymn written for Charles's bride, Sarah Gwynn, on the occasion of their wedding.

> Come let us arise,
> And press to the skies;
> The summons obey,
> My friend, my beloved, and hasten away!
> The Master of all
> For our service doth call,
> And deigns to approve
> With smiles of acceptance our labour of love.
>
> His burden who bear,
> We alone can declare
> How easy his yoke;
> While to love and good works we each other provoke,
> By word and by deed,
> The bodies in need,
> The souls to relieve,
> And freely as Jesus hath given to give.
>
> Then let us attend
> Our heavenly friend
> In his members distressed,
> By want, or affliction, or sickness oppressed;
> The prisoner relieve,
> The stranger receive,
> Supply all their wants,
> And spend and be spent in assisting his saints.[40]

---

40. C. Wesley, *Hymns and Sacred Poems* (1749), 2:280, sts. 1–3 of a four-stanza poem.

The early Methodist people, like their leaders, took this "call to serve the present age" with utmost seriousness. They lived out their lives in solidarity with those people who were shut out, neglected, and thrown away. Charles admonished his followers to befriend the poor and needy. In his *Songs for the Poor*, ST Kimbrough Jr. rediscovers some of Wesley's most profound expressions of this servant spirit, including this composite hymn drawn from his manuscript poems on Luke and Acts.

> The poor as Jesus' bosom-friends,
> > the poor he makes his latest care,
> to all his followers commends,
> > and wills us on our hands to bear;
> the poor our dearest care we make,
> > and love them for our Savior's sake.[41]

Charles was quick to point out those persons in whom this lofty ideal of gracious condescension was realized. He provides the following portrait of an early Methodist woman, Elizabeth Blackwell, whose character was shaped by her practice of befriending the least in her community.

> Nursing the poor with constant care,
> > Affection soft, and heart-esteem,
> She saw her Saviour's image there,
> > And gladly minister'd to Him.[42]

Grace Bowen rejoiced "an hungry Christ to feed" and "to visit Him in pain." To the poor, Wesley observes, this servant gave her all.[43]

III. Eucharist and Self-Sacrifice

The Cross-shaped Life

Conformity to the mind of Christ—to live and serve in this world after the model of Jesus—ultimately means conformity to the cross, as well. "When Christ calls a man," as Dietrich Bonhoeffer observed in *The Cost of Discipleship*, "he bids him come and die."[44] Personal sacrifice characterizes the

---

41. Kimbrough, *Song for the Poor*, 20–21.
42. Jackson, *Journal of Charles Wesley*, 2:386.
43. Jackson, *Journal of Charles Wesley*, 2:324.
44. Bonhoeffer, *Cost of Discipleship*, 7.

authentic Christian life. As my own theological mentor, Dr. Robert Cushman, said on many occasions, "The cross-shaped life is the only authentic Christian existence." The "suffering servants" of God take up their crosses daily in multifarious acts of self-sacrificial love.

> Thy every suffering servant, Lord,
>
> Shall as his perfect Master be;
>
> To all thy inward life restored,
>
> And outwardly conformed to thee.[45]

"And lo!" cries the faithful disciple, "I come thy cross to share, / Echo thy sacrificial prayer, / And with my Saviour die."[46] Nowhere do the images of self-emptying, service, and sacrifice—the signs of the cruciform life—converge more poignantly than in the *Hymns on the Lord's Supper*.

The Wesleys divided the 166 hymns of this 1745 collection into six sections, the fourth and fifth of which deal specifically with the issue of sacrifice. In Charles Wesley's sermon on Acts 20:7 (more properly what might be described as an introductory "treatise" to a larger, unfinished work on the sacrament) we encounter a concept of sacrifice consonant with the view he espouses in his *Hymns on the Lord's Supper* devoted to this theme. Charles views the Lord's Supper as a "re-presentation" of the sacrifice of Christ.[47] As J. Ernest Rattenbury demonstrated, his stress is persistently on the twofold oblation of the church in the sacrament; the body of Christ offered is not merely a sacred symbol of Christ's "once-for-all" act of redemption, but is also the living sacrifice of the people of God.[48]

The thirty hymns of Section Five in this collection, "Concerning the Sacrifice of our Persons," focus upon this living oblation of the church and all who seek to be faithful disciples of their Lord. The desire to "be all like Thee," inevitably leads to the heartfelt prayer, "Grant us full conformity, / Plunge us deep into thy death."[49] Wesley describes the full extent of solidarity with the crucified Lord,

> His servants shall be
>
> With Him on the tree,
>
> Where Jesus was slain
>
> His crucified servants shall always remain.[50]

---

45. J. Wesley, *Works*, 7:477 (no. 321:5).

46. C. Wesley, *Family Hymns*, 21, st. 6.

47. Newport, *Sermons of Charles Wesley*, 277–286. Cf. Bowmer, *Lord's Supper in Early Methodism*, 223–32.

48. See Rattenbury, *Eucharistic Hymns*, 123–47.

49. Wesley and Wesley, *Hymns on the Lord's Supper*, 129.

50. Wesley and Wesley, *Hymns on the Lord's Supper*, 120 (no. 142:3).

Suffering for the sake of love identifies those who are truly bound to Christ. In a profoundly anamnetic hymn placing the believer at the foot of the cross, Wesley asks the rhetorical question, "Would the Saviour of mankind / Without His people die?" The question elicits one of the most powerful images in the Eucharistic hymns: "No, to Him we all are join'd / As more than standers by." Given the fact that Christ took the suffering of the world freely upon himself, even to the point of death on a cross, "We attend the slaughter'd Lamb, / And suffer for His cause."[51] Hardly a mission for the faint of heart, the path of discipleship requires all one has and all one is.

In the Eucharistic hymns, Wesley develops what might be called a *sursum corda* principle. In the Prayer of Great Thanksgiving used in contemporary United Methodist congregations and drawn from the ancient practice of the church, the faithful "lift up their hearts" to the Lord, and this "up-lifting" provides a paradigm of the oblation of life offered up to God in Christ. In this act or gesture of self-oblation, the Christian confirms to God, "I offer my whole self to you anew." In the language of Charles's poetry, "Ourselves we offer up to God, / Implunged in His atoning blood." Despite the limited or partial nature of our self-sacrificial acts, God accepts them and joins them to Christ's oblation.

> Mean are our noblest offerings,
> Poor feeble unsubstantial things;
> But when to Him our souls we lift,
> The altar sanctifies the gift.[52]

Another sacrificial hymn makes these connections even more explicit.

> Thou art with all Thy members here,
>   In this tremendous mystery
> We jointly before God appear,
>   To offer up ourselves with Thee.
>
> True followers of our bleeding Lamb,
>   Now on thy daily cross we die,
> And, mingled in a common flame,
>   Ascend triumphant to the sky.[53]

The sacrificial character of the Christian life, in which the worshiper participates repeatedly at the table of the Lord, and its relationship to the

---

51. Wesley and Wesley, *Hymns on the Lord's Supper*, 112 (no. 131:1).
52. Wesley and Wesley, *Hymns on the Lord's Supper*, 117 (no. 137:4–5).
53. Wesley and Wesley, *Hymns on the Lord's Supper*, 120 (no. 141:7–8).

sacrifice of Christ is clarified in Charles's hymns. In this regard, Wesley adheres very closely to the position articulated in Daniel Brevint's *The Christian Sacrament and Sacrifice*, an important theological treatise he reprinted in abridged form as a "preface" to his hymns. "The main intention of Christ herein was not the bare *remembrance* of His Passion," claims Brevint, "but over and above, to invite us to His Sacrifice."[54]

> While faith th' atoning blood applies,
> Ourselves a living sacrifice
>   We freely offer up to God;
> And none but those his glory share,
> Who crucified with Jesus are,
>   And follow where their Saviour trod.
>
> Saviour, to thee our lives we give,
> Our meanest sacrifice receive,
>   And to thine own oblation join,
> Our suffering and triumphant Head,
> Through all thy states thy members lead,
>   And seat us on the throne Divine.[55]

The Living Sacrifice of Romans 12

St. Paul's word to the Roman Christians, "to present your bodies as a living sacrifice" (12:1), clearly alluded to in the hymn just cited, provides the foundation upon which the disciple builds this *kenotic*, self-sacrificial vision of life. With regard to the offering, Wesley clarifies several important points in the hymns. First, the Spirit makes our self-sacrifice possible. To live as Christ lived means to be filled with the Holy Spirit. "Yes, Lord, we are Thine," confesses Wesley, "And gladly resign / Our souls to be fill'd with the fulness Divine."[56] Second, the offering is holistic, involving both soul and body; Wesley guards against any false separation of the spiritual from the physical in the life of the believer. "Our souls and bodies we resign," claims Wesley, "With joy we render Thee / Our all, no longer ours, but

---

54. Rattenbury, *Eucharistic Hymns*, 178.
55. Wesley and Wesley, *Hymns on the Lord's Supper*, 110 (no. 128:3–4).
56. Wesley and Wesley, *Hymns on the Lord's Supper*, 131 (no. 156:4).

Thine / Through all eternity!"[57] Third, we restore to God what God has already freely given. "Now, O God, Thine own I am," affirms the servant of the Lord, "Now I give Thee back Thy own."[58] Fourth, self-sacrifice, while an act of obedience and compliance, roots us in love; self-giving love and God are one. Wesley expresses all of these themes eloquently in a hymn of supplication echoing the words of the prayer after Communion in the liturgy of the Book of Common Prayer.

> Father, on us the Spirit bestow,
> > Through which Thine everlasting Son
> Offer'd Himself for man below,
> > That *we*, even *we*, before Thy throne
> Our souls and bodies may present,
> And pay Thee all Thy grace hath lent.
>
> O let Thy Spirit sanctify
> > Whate'er to Thee we now restore,
> And make us with Thy will comply;
> > With all our mind, and soul, and power
> Obey Thee, as Thy saints above,
> In perfect innocence and love.[59]

In those hymns in which Philippians 2:5–11 figures prominently, Charles Wesley develops a *kenotic* paradigm of servant ministry—a vision of servant vocation—Jesus himself being the primary exemplar as the One who seeks to serve others in life. Wesley demonstrates how conformity to this servant-mind characterizes all who seek to be faithful disciples and practice Christian service. In his hymns on the Eucharist, he emphasizes the centrality of the cross-shaped life. The sacrament functions both to exemplify the living sacrifice of Romans 12 and to form the followers of Christ into those who sacrifice self for the sake of the world—those God claims for service for the sake of love. ST Kimbrough Jr. expresses it succinctly:

57. Wesley and Wesley, *Hymns on the Lord's Supper*, 131 (no. 157:4).
58. Wesley and Wesley, *Hymns on the Lord's Supper*, 130 (no. 155:5).
59. Wesley and Wesley, *Hymns on the Lord's Supper*, 126 (no. 150). Following the rubrics of the 1662 Book of Common Prayer, after the congregation has received the sacrament, the priest prays: "O Lord and heavenly Father, we thy humble servants desire thy Fatherly goodness mercifully to accept this our sacrifice of praise and thanksgiving ... And here we offer and present unto thee, O Lord, ourselves, our souls and bodies, to be a reasonable, holy, and lively sacrifice unto thee," etc.

"to be emptied of everything but love is what it means to serve a God who in Christ was emptied of all but love."[60]

We conclude, therefore, where we began, with lines from the hymn described by J. Ernest Rattenbury as "perhaps the greatest hymn of personal consecration in our language."[61]

> *Claim me, for thy service,* claim
> All I have and all I am.
>
> Take my soul and body's powers,
>   Take my memory, mind, and will,
> All my goods, and all my hours,
>   All I know, and all I feel,
> All I think, and speak, and do;
> Take my heart—but make it new.
>
> Father, Son, and Holy Ghost,
>   One in Three, and Three in One,
> As by the celestial host
>   Let Thy will on earth be done;
> Praise by all to Thee be given,
> Glorious Lord of earth and heaven.[62]

Worship is recapitulation, and as we repeatedly participate in the Eucharistic actions of offering aristic actions of offering, and thanking, and breaking, and giving—the constitutive aspects of an authentic, sacrificial life—God conforms us into the image of Christ—our lives become truly Eucharistic as faith working by love leading to holiness of heart and life.

---

60. Kimbrough, "Kenosis," 283.
61. Rattenbury, *Eucharistic Hymns*, 26.
62. Wesley and Wesley, *Hymns on the Lord's Supper*, 129–30 (no. 155:3–4).

Part 6
Missional Ecclesiology and God's Rule

Chapter 16

The Mission-Church Paradigm of the Wesleyan Revival

Source note: A commissioned essay published in *World Mission in the Wesleyan Spirit*, edited by Darrell L. Whiteman and Gerald H. Anderson, 151–64 (Franklin: Providence, 2009).

JOHN AND CHARLES WESLEY's rediscovery of a "mission-church paradigm" in eighteenth-century England fueled the renewal of the church and offers a model of enduring significance for global Christianity today.[1] This paradigm, drawing committed Christian disciples perennially to Jesus and to one another in community (centripetal movement) and spinning them out into the world in mission and service (centrifugal movement), reflected an apostolic vision of the people of God in their view. This essay examines those aspects of Wesleyan theology that provided the foundation for this vision and the hymns of Charles Wesley that inculcated missional praxis.

Theological Foundations of a Mission-Church Paradigm

A robust theological foundation undergirded the missional vision that gave birth to a dynamic movement of spiritual renewal under the leadership of the Wesleys. In the mind of these Anglican reformers, mission began with God and not with them.[2] They conceived a "missionary God"

---

1. I have discussed the centrality of this "mission-church" theme in Wesleyan theology and practice elsewhere. See Chilcote, *Recapturing the Wesleys' Vision*, 93–106; *Wesleyan Tradition*, 34–37; "Evangelistic Practices of the Wesleyan Revival"; "Servants of Shalom in the World"; "Wesleyan and Emergent Christians"; and "Claim Me for Thy Service."

2. This vision is consonant with a contemporary missiological consensus

because the God they had come to know in Jesus Christ was a God of love who was always reaching out from self to others—an expression of God's love and grace they described as God's prevenient action.³ The missional practices of the Wesleys and of the Methodist Societies they founded mirrored this understanding of God's nature and character. Moreover, they firmly believed that God was active and at work in the world to save and restore all creation. These primary convictions led the Wesleys to reclaim mission as the church's reason for being and evangelism as the heart of that mission in the world.⁴ They developed a holistic vision of mission and evangelism that refused to separate faith and works, personal salvation and social justice, physical and spiritual needs.

The Wesleys anchored this missional vision in the fundamental affirmations of the Christian faith, namely, in the doctrines of Creation and Redemption, Incarnation, and Trinity, all of which point to the "centrifugal nature" of God's activity. They understood God's creation of all things out of nothing, for example, as a sheer act of grace, an extension God's love motivated by nothing but God's loving character.⁵ The Incarnation—God taking on human flesh in the person of Jesus of Nazareth—demonstrated the same missional quality. In the fullness of time, God entered human history and reached out to the beloved through Jesus Christ in order to re-create and restore all things in Christ. God's mission—God's evangelistic activity—God's proclamation and embodiment of Good News—in their view, began in creation, continues through redemption, and stretches out toward

---

summarized in the term *missio Dei*, or the "mission of God." As Darrell Guder has argued, "mission is the result of God's initiative, rooted in God's purposes to restore and heal creation" (Guder, *Missional Church*, 4).

3. See the discussion of John Wesley's understanding of prevenient grace in Maddox, *Responsible Grace*, 83–84. Of particular interest is Wesley's sermon, "The Promise of Understanding," in which he expounds how "we cannot know till hereafter how God works [graciously] in many cases which are daily before our eyes" (J. Wesley, *Works*, 4:281–91).

4. It is important to note that the Wesleys made this discovery without ever using this more contemporary language concerning it. The words "mission" and "evangelism" hardly ever appear in the Wesleyan corpus, but the Wesleyan Revival was at once profoundly missional and evangelistic in nature. David Bebbington has argued that one of the "striking symptoms of discontinuity" between the Evangelical Revival under the Wesleys and the previous two centuries was "a new emphasis on mission." The impetus for this development, in some measure, was the triumph of Wesleyan Arminian theology over entrenched Calvinism by the end of the eighteenth century. See Bebbington, *Evangelicalism*, 40.

5. See "Thoughts Upon God's Sovereignty," in J. Wesley, *Works*, 13:547–50.

the consummation. This description of God's missionary character, in fact, even reflects God's Triune nature.[6]

The Wesleys built their theology of mission upon the understanding of a Three-One God postured in perpetual, grace-filled, outward movement—Father, Son, and Holy Spirit in perennial interaction with one another and the world in a great dance of love. While mission belongs to God, the Wesleys believed that all people have the privilege of participating in God's mission through their own proclamation and embodiment of the Good News of God's love in Christ. In the same way that God entered human history and took on flesh in the person of Jesus, the Wesleys sought to live incarnationally by investing themselves in the lives of God's children wherever they found them. Charles Wesley used a powerful image to communicate this understanding of mission and God's call to be "Gospel-bearers." He described the Christian as a "transcript of the Trinity." That means essentially that God writes God's self into our very being so that when other people "read" our lives, they perceive God in us.

> Cloath'd with Christ, aspire to shine,
>
> Radiance He of Light Divine;
>
> Beam of the Eternal Beam,
>
> He in God, and God in Him!
>
> Strive we Him in Us to see,
>
> Transcript of the Deity.[7]

The theological method of the Wesleys reinforced this foundational vision. Instead of setting aspects of the Christian faith over against each other—for example, forcing a choice between *either* personal salvation *or* social action—the Wesleys tended to see matters of faith from a *both/and* perspective.[8] Personal salvation, they would argue, must be held together with social action, works of piety with works of mercy, in Christian discipleship. This approach to Christian thought and praxis shaped their understanding of mission and evangelism—and their doctrine of the church, as

---

6. For an interesting discussion of the interface of God's mission and God's Triune being, see "On the Discoveries of Faith," in J. Wesley, *Works*, 4:29–38.

7. Wesley and Wesley, *Hymns and Sacred Poems* (1739), 178.

8. I explore this "conjunctive methodology" in *Recapturing the Wesleys' Vision* where I identify eight primary syntheses, including faith and works, Word and Spirit, personal and social, form and power, heart and head, pulpit and table, Christ and culture, and piety and mercy. Cf. Collins, *Theology of John Wesley*, where the author employs essentially the same interpretive framework.

we shall see momentarily—in profound ways. Several excerpted couplets from a hymn by Charles Wesley illustrate this synthetic method.

> Let us join ('tis God commands),
> Let us join our hearts and hands
>
> Still forget the things behind,
> Follow Christ in heart and mind
>
> Plead we thus for faith alone,
> Faith which by our works is shown.[9]

Note the intimate connection of hearts and hands, heart and mind, faith and works. The words of brother John reveal the direct application of this principle to the missional vocation of all Christians:

> By experience [the genuine Christian] knows that *social love* (if it mean the love of our neighbour) is absolutely, essentially different from *self-love*, even of the most allowable kind, just as different as the objects at which they point. And yet it is sure that, if they are under due regulations, each will give additional force to the other, "till they mix together never to be divided."[10]

Genuine love of self, rooted in God's affirmation—God's prior love—must find expression in love of others. The two must always be held together. One of the most important legacies left by the Wesleys is this effort to hold faith and love, the form and power of godliness, love for God and love of neighbor together in a growing, dynamic, vital expression of the Christian faith.

This conjunctive method informed the Wesleys' conception of the church and the relation of the Methodist Societies to that larger body, while the cultural and ecclesial context in which they lived helped them to clarify their peculiar vision and mission. Rupert Davies has provided the most incisive analysis of this dynamic tension and identifies, perhaps, the most unique quality of early Methodism.

> A "society" acknowledges the truths proclaimed by the universal church and has no wish to separate from it, but claims to cultivate, by means of sacrament and fellowship, the type of inward holiness, which too great an objectivity can easily neglect and

---

9. J. Wesley, *Works*, 7:698.
10. Quoted in Chilcote, *Recapturing the Wesleys' Vision*, 47; from J. Wesley, *Plain Account of Genuine Christianity*, 6.1.6.

of which the church needs constantly to be reminded. A society does not unchurch the members of either church or sect . . . it calls its own members within the larger church to a special personal commitment which respects the commitment of others.[11]

The Wesleys designed the Methodist Societies, in other words, to function like catalysts of renewal within the life of the larger church. Having rediscovered a mission-church paradigm within the life of their own *ecclesiolae in ecclesia* (little churches within the church"), their hope was that the leavening action of these small groups of committed missioners would re-awaken the Church of England to its primary vocation in the world, namely, the *missio Dei*. The Methodist Societies were like little dynamos, spinning inside the church and building momentum in order to re-establish a centrifugal force in the church itself, spinning it out in turn in mission. There can be no doubt that the cell structure of the Methodist organism accounts for the dynamism and growth of the movement and its influence.[12]

It is not too much to claim that three concepts taken together—church, evangelism, and mission—defined early Methodism. A missional ecclesiology emanated directly from the Wesleys' theological vision and method. God forms gospel-bearers in and through the community of faith which is itself a manifestation—imperfect though it may be—of the gospel in the world. The Wesleys concluded that the central purpose of the church is mission—God's mission. They attempted to replicate the model of the church they discovered in the pages of the New Testament. The church, they believed, is not called to live for itself, but for others. It is called, like Christ, to give itself for the life of the world. It is not so much that the church has a mission or ministries; rather, the church is mission. The church of Wesley's England had exchanged its true vocation (mission) for maintenance, a confusion that often slips into the life of the church in every age. It desperately needed to reclaim its true identity as God's agent of love and shalom in the world. The Wesleys firmly believed that God raised up the Methodists specifically for the task of resuscitating a mission-church.

11. J. Wesley, *Works*, 9:3.

12. Mike Henderson has identified eight major principles that led to the success of Wesley's system, all of which have missiological import: (1) Human nature is perfectible by God's grace. (2) Learning comes by doing the will of God. (3) Mankind's nature is perfected by participation in groups, not by acting as isolated individuals. (4) The spirit and practice of primitive Christianity can and must be recaptured. (5) Human progress will occur if people will participate in "the means of grace." (6) The gospel must be presented to the poor. (7) Social evil is not to be "resisted," but overcome by good. (8) The primary function of spiritual/educational leadership is to equip others to lead and minister, not to perform the ministry personally. See Henderson, *John Wesley's Class Meeting*, 127–60.

This vision, as you might well expect, was deeply rooted in Scripture. When John Wesley adapted the Puritan Covenant Renewal Service for use in his own communities, he linked this annual event with one of Jesus' most poignant images for the church, namely, the vine and branches of John 15. In this passage, Jesus presents a picture of the church. As we abide in Christ, who is the true vine, we take nourishment from him as the source of all life. We are constantly drawn into the center, to the core, to the source. There is something similar here to the centripetal force of the wheel, something that persistently draws us closer to Christ and closer to one another. But the purpose of the vine is not simply to be drawn in, to revel in our connectedness and fellowship. The vine does not exist for its own benefit, but for the benefit of others through its fruit. What continues to give vitality to the church is the centrifugal force that spins us out into the world with the fruit of the Spirit. As we share this fruit with others, they are enabled to taste and see that God is good. The Wesleys came to believe that a church turned in on itself (that is only centripetal) will surely die, for it has lost its reason for being. But a church spun out in loving service into the world (that is also centrifugal) rediscovers itself day by day. "Offering Christ," to use Wesley's own terminology for the work of mission, involves both word and deed, both proclamation and action; it connects the gospel to the world. Jesus' mission was characterized by healing those who were sick, liberating those who were oppressed, empowering those who stood on the margins of life, and caring for the poor. In all of these actions he incarnated shalom, God's vision of peace, justice, and well-being for all, and his disciples, the Wesleys taught, are called to do nothing less.

In this dynamic conception of a mission-church, the Wesleyan genius was to hold mission and evangelism together without pitting personal salvation against social justice. Mission for the Wesleys meant partnering with God in the realization of shalom in the world. Such a task is necessarily rooted in Christ, for we cannot speak of God's reign apart from Christ, or of Jesus without God's reign. The way in which the Wesleys envisaged this essential connection between evangelism and mission is, perhaps, one of their greatest contributions to the life of the church today.

In her attempt to present an authentic Wesleyan perspective on this relationship, Dana Robert has made recourse to St. Paul's image of the church as a body.[13] In this paradigm, an organic relationship obtains between these two crucial practices of the church; while evangelism is the heart, mission is the body itself. The body moves in different contexts, interacting, engaging, constantly at work. But the heart sends the life-giving blood throughout the

---

13. See Robert, *Evangelism as the Heart of Mission*.

whole. Without the heart—without Jesus at the center—there is no vitality, no abundant life. But the body lives to continue the mission of Jesus in the world, namely, to announce and demonstrate the reign of God. The heart and the body, evangelism and mission, Christ and culture, are interdependent and interconnected, and this is the essence of the Wesleyan synthesis—the dynamism of the mission-church paradigm.

In his very last sermon, "On Faith," written in January 1791, John Wesley asked the all-important question about the goal of the Christian life: "How will [the faithful] advance in holiness, in the whole image of God wherein they were created!" He responded with reference to the dual foci of the Christian life and afforded a different language to contemplate the interface of evangelical piety and mission: "In the love of God and man, *gratitude* to their Creator, and *benevolence* to all their fellow-creatures."[14] Benevolence, here, is Wesley's term for mission. But in his sermon, "On Family Religion," he demonstrated how the family of God must build this mission upon the foundation of gratitude—the two being distinct but not separate. "And if any man truly love God he cannot but love his brother also," Wesley maintains. "*Gratitude* to our Creator will surely produce *benevolence* to our fellow-creatures. If we love him, we cannot but love one another, as Christ loved us. We feel our souls enlarged in love toward every child of man."[15]

The Wesleys believed that God calls the community of faith to live for others. The primary method of mission in the Wesleyan tradition is for those within the family of God to become God's partners in the redemption of the whole world. As I have written elsewhere,

> The primary question for the Methodist is not, am I saved? The ultimate question is, for what purpose am I saved? For the Wesleys, the answer was clear. My neighbor is the goal of my redemption, just as the life, death and resurrection of Christ are oriented toward the salvation of all humanity.[16]

"Benevolence," for the Wesleys, consisted in all efforts to realize God's shalom in the life of the world. This mission, this goodwill toward our fellow-creatures, this ministry of reconciliation, this benevolence manifests itself in particular ways in the Wesleyan tradition, but none more distinctive than outreach to the marginalized and resistance to injustice, both actions expressed through works of mercy that bear witness to God's rule over life.[17]

14. J. Wesley, *Works*, 4:196. Emphasis added.
15. J. Wesley, *Works*, 3:336. Emphasis added.
16 Chilcote, *Recapturing the Wesleys' Vision*, 101.
17 For a helpful discussion of "works of mercy" and their intimate connection to mission, see Miles, "Works of Mercy," 98–110.

"The first Methodists, who intended to revive the life of the original Christian church," as Tore Meistad attempted to demonstrate, "made a just distribution of economic, educational, and medical resources their top priority. This is evident in John Wesley's sermons as well as in Charles's hymns."[18]

The Mission-Church Paradigm Reflected in Charles Wesley's Hymns

Methodism was born in song, and the followers of the Wesleys learned their theology—that is to say, they discovered their missional vocation—by singing it.[19] Mission-church images pervade the hymn corpus of Charles Wesley. Even the most famous of all the hymns, "O for a thousand tongues to sing," is nothing other than a mission manifesto, calling all believers "To spread through all the earth abroad / The honors of thy name."[20] Another favorite hymn reminds all singers of their responsibility before God.

> A charge to keep I have,
> A God to glorify,
> A never-dying soul to save,
> And fit it for the sky;
> To serve the present age,
> My calling to fulfil;
> O may it all my powers engage
> To do my Master's will.[21]

These words communicate an extremely important principle: God has chosen the faithful for service, not to privilege, and the primary vocation of

---

18 Meistad, "Missiology of Charles Wesley," 51.

19. See J. Wesley, *Works*, 7:1. Not enough research has been devoted to the topic of how Christian hymnody shapes, or misshapes, mission theology. Certainly, there have been periods in the history of the church in which "mission hymns" have encouraged a triumphalist model of Christian mission. How choral traditions, from "praise songs" to "classic hymns," form the attitudes of believers today with regard to mission remains a major area of concern. It is a part of my argument that the Wesley hymns helped to form a missional vision among the early Methodist people and inculcated healthy practices that balanced evangelism and mission, physical and spiritual concern, warm-hearted faith and compassionate engagement for justice in the world.

20. See Meistad, "Missiology of Charles Wesley," 52–55. ST Kimbrough Jr. observes that stanzas often omitted from contemporary hymnals "fuse praise with mission and remind us of the inclusiveness of the gospel" (Kimbrough, *Heart to Praise*, 143).

21. J. Wesley, *Works*, 7:465.

Jesus' disciples is "to serve the present age" by bearing the gospel in word and deed to everyone, everywhere. Jesus' disciples are called to use all their gifts, all their powers, to declare the amazing love of God to all.

In one of the great Trinitarian hymns included in John and Charles Wesley's *Hymns on the Lord's Supper*, the singer beseeches God,

> Claim me for Thy service, claim
> All I have and all I am.
>
> Take my soul and body's powers,
> Take my memory, mind, and will,
> All my goods, and all my hours,
> All I know, and all I feel,
> All I think, and speak, and do;
> Take my heart—but make it new.[22]

The disciple of Christ asks the Three-One God to claim every aspect of his or her life in an oblation that can only be described as covenantal. In typical Wesleyan fashion, a series of "alls" characterizes the plea. All I have, all I am, all my goods, all my hours, all I know, feel, think, speak, and do. The all-encompassing sacrifice of self—the offer of one's whole being in service to God—rests secure, as Charles makes abundantly clear throughout, on the foundation of a heart transformed by God's prevenient action. One can hear echoes of the baptismal covenant, perhaps, in Charles's use of language. The sacrament of baptism, of course, is that place where discipleship begins, that event in which God claims each person as God's own. It also signals the commitment of the individual and the community to God's mission. Baptism establishes the mission-church and the sacrament of Holy Communion sustains it. The ambiance of many Wesley hymns elicits a profoundly missiological vision of Christian community and engagement with the dominion of God in the world. In hymns like these, Charles Wesley cultivated a profound vision of servant vocation modeled after that of Jesus—a missional conception of Christian discipleship summarized tersely in the simple phrase, "Claim me for Thy service."

Charles Wesley goes to great lengths to specify the character of this Christian service. In the practice of mission, the servant simply offers to others what he or she has freely received from God. "This only thing do I require," sings Christ's co-missioned disciple, "Freely what I receive to

---

22. Wesley and Wesley, *Hymns on the Lord's Supper*, 3–4 (no. 155).

give, / The servant of thy church to live."²³ Servants, in other words, engage in an evangelistic mission in life—offering God's grace to all in word and deed. The unique feature of Wesley's vision, however, is the way in which he connects the sharing of grace with the restoration of the mind of Christ in the believer. In a composite hymn, opening with a lyrical paraphrase of "Jesus and the woman at the well" (John 4:10–15), Wesley conjoins the "mind" of Philippians 2 with the "action" of James 1, yet another important conjunction in his missional vision.

> Thy mind throughout my life be shown,
> While listening to the wretch's cry,
> The widow's and the orphan's groan,
> On mercy's wings I swiftly fly
> The poor and helpless to relieve,
> My life, my all for them to give.²⁴

To have the mind of Christ, in other words, is to care for the poor.

> Happy soul, whose active love
> emulates the Blessed above,
> in thy every action seen,
> sparkling from the soul within:
>
> Thou to every sufferer nigh,
> hearest, not in vain, the cry
> of widow in distress,
> of the poor, the shelterless:
>
> Raiment thou to all that need,
> to the hungry dealest bread,
> to the sick givest relief,
> soothest hapless prisoner's grief:
>
> Love, which willest all should live,
> Love, which all to all would give,

---

23. J. Wesley, *Works*, 7:101.
24. J. Wesley, *Works*, 7:522.

Love, that over all prevails,
Love, that never, never fails.
Love immense, and unconfined,
Love to all of humankind.[25]

Notice in particular Wesley's language of "active love." A disciple with a living faith is the one whose whole heart has been renewed, who longs to radiate the whole image of God in his or her life *and therefore* hears the cry of the poor and wills, with God, that all should truly live! The Wesleyan vision of mission, thus understood, is *a life*, not just an act, that unites piety and mercy, worship and compassion, prayer and justice. It involves a humble walk with the Lord that is lived out daily in kindness and justice. Healing those who were sick, liberating those who were oppressed, empowering those who stood on the margins of life, and caring for the poor, it must always be remembered, characterized Jesus' mission and models that mission to which all are called in his name.

ST Kimbrough Jr. articulates the essence of this missional vision succinctly: "to be emptied of everything but love is what it means to serve a God who in Christ was emptied of all but love."[26] Those who are truly servants of Christ in the world, and those communities that rediscover what it means to be a mission-church, empty themselves, like Jesus, and find their greatest reward in the realization of God's dream of shalom for all. Certainly, the fundamental vision of Christian mission is being sent to continue and participate in that movement of God towards humanity which began with the mission or sending of Christ and the Holy Spirit. The Wesleys and their followers realized that this is a mission of global proportions.

This Wesleyan vision of a "mission-church paradigm" offers much to a church needing to rediscover the central place of evangelism and mission as constitutive practices of the whole people of God. While evangelism includes all of those activities that draw others in, mission reaches out to all, and particularly to those dear to God's heart who are most vulnerable and in need. In imitation of Christ, a mission-church woos others into the loving embrace of God and then helps them to see that their mission in life, in partnership with Christ, is to be the signposts of God's reign in this world. In his hymn, "For a preacher of the gospel," Charles Wesley reminds us of this transforming call of God upon our lives.

---

25. Kimbrough, *Songs for the Poor*, no. 1.
26. Kimbrough, "Kenosis," 283.

I would the precious time redeem
And longer live for this alone,
To spend and to be spent for them
Who have not yet my Saviour known:
Fully on these my mission prove,
And only breathe to breathe thy love.[27]

---

27. J. Wesley, *Works*, 7;597.

Chapter 17

Lessons from the "Society Planting" Paradigm of Early Methodist Women

> Source note: Delivered as the presidential address before the Academy for Evangelism in Theological Education, meeting at Techny Towers, Illinois, June 15, 2012, and published in *Witness: Journal of the Academy for Evangelism in Theological Education* 27 (2013) 5–30.

JOHN AND CHARLES WESLEY rediscovered a missional church model of the community of faith in eighteenth-century Britain. Their biblical paradigm, drawing committed Christian disciples perennially to Jesus and to one another in community (centripetal movement) and spinning them out into the world in mission and service (centrifugal movement), reflected an apostolic vision of the people of God in their view. Women played a major role in the practice and multiplication of this model. They functioned as pioneers of Methodist Societies within the Church of England and planted these catalysts of renewal across the British Isles. Their Society-planting paradigm offers valuable insights for those who seek to rediscover a missional vision and a church planting ethos today. In this brief address, I will seek to locate the efforts of these women in the larger context of church planting, examine the unique vision that fueled their work, describe two particular scenarios common to their practice, and articulate lessons that we can learn from their engagement with God's mission in the world.

An examination of the contemporary literature on church planting reveals a bewildering array of models, strategies, and paradigms, most of these aspects of the Christian practice couched in the framework of "how-to" manuals and practical guides.[1] It is not my purpose here to survey

---

1. Required reading lists in contemporary syllabi for church planting courses reveal

this material; I have neither the space in this brief essay nor the personal competence to provide such an overview. Rather, my primary interest is to provide a broad historical and theological framework within which to locate the early Methodist women Society-planters whose perspectives and methods may have value for us today. Before I lay out that framework, however, reference to several more recent studies provides something of a generic portrait of the particular interests today related to the planting of Christian communities.

I turn first to two widely acclaimed texts (both now in their second editions) because of their pervasive use across the spectrum of Christian traditions. Nearly twenty years ago now, Daniel Sanchez described Aubrey Malphurs's *Planting Growing Churches for the 21st Century: A Comprehensive Guide for New Churches and Those Desiring Renewal* as "one of the most comprehensive, instructive, and inspiring books on the subject of American church planting written to date."[2] In great alliterative fashion, he articulates a vision of preparation, personnel, principles, and processes for church planting that takes the unique identity, location, and community with utmost seriousness. "Not only are we to sow new works to reach the various people groups here on the North American mission field," Malphurs concludes, "but these, in turn, can sow churches on the mission fields of other countries."[3] In *Planting Churches Cross-Culturally: North America and Beyond*, David Hesselgrave attends closely to what he describes as the "Pauline Cycle."[4] Carefully avoiding the viewpoint that St. Paul had no strategic vision (Michael Green), on one hand, and that the Apostle developed a highly nuanced strategy on the other (Donald McGavran), he articulates a mediating position based primarily on the work of Herbert Kane in an effort to get back to the missionary methods of the early church.[5] He identifies ten phases of cross-cultural church planting based on St. Paul's missionary example, to which we will return at a later point.

In *Global Church Planting: Biblical Principles and Best Practices for Multiplication*, Craig Ott and Gene Wilson seek to answer the more theological/ecclesiological question, What kind of church is to be planted? Their response is unequivocal.

---

the practical orientation of many of these texts: Bird, *Starting a New Church*; Brock, *Indigenous Church Planting*; Cheyney, *Seven Steps for Planting Churches*; Payne, *Whats, Whys, and Hows of Global Church Planting*; and Schaller, *Forty-four Questions for Church Planters*.

2. Sanchez, "Review of 'Planting Growing Churches,'" 359.
3. Malphurs, *Planting Growing Churches*, 393–94.
4. Hesselgrave, *Planting Churches Cross-Culturally*, 41–53, in particular.
5. See Kane, *Christian Missions*, for a synthetic perspective on this debate.

Unfortunately many books on church planting or growth give little attention to the kind of church that is to be planted. However, if churches are to be planted as we have attempted to biblically define them, they must adhere to more than some minimal definition or denominational standard. They must be *kingdom communities, healthy congregations, reproducing organisms, indigenous churches,* and *interdependent fellowships.*[6]

According to Ott and Wilson, movements that have sought to emulate this vision throughout the history of the church tend to be works of the Holy Spirit, gospel-centered, lay grassroots movements, have a multiplication DNA, and are influenced by external factors.[7] They distinguish three types of church planters.[8] The "pastoral church planter" simply begins a new church and pastors it until appropriate new leadership assumes responsibility for the community. Ott and Wilson consider this to be the most common method in church planting. The "catalytic church planter" intends to remain in pastoral leadership of a newly created community that will birth many other churches, thereby launching a movement. The "Apostolic church planter" represents a radically different perspective. "This church planter," they explain, "seeks to follow the model of the apostle Paul, who as far as we know never became the pastor of a church he planted. Instead, after initial evangelism, he focused on empowering the local believers, primarily laypersons, to carry on and expand the work after his departure."[9]

In each of these popular texts, the authors place great importance on reclaiming a biblical model of church planting—one in which the ministry of the apostle Paul looms large. They also emphasize the importance of context and genuinely incarnational models of life and work. They seek, in other words, to carefully balance the text and the context. Some church planting authors provide some historical background to this practice, but very little has been written, actually, on the history of church planting. One exception is *Church Planting: Laying Foundations*, in which Anabaptist scholar Stuart Murray provides a very brief but helpful analysis along historical lines. He identifies four main kinds of church planting in the history of the church.[10]

---

6. Ott and Wilson, *Global Church Planting*, 13.
7. Ott and Wilson, *Global Church Planting*, 73–77.
8. Ott and Wilson, *Global Church Planting*, 90–100.
9. Ott and Wilson, *Global Church Planting*, 96.
10. Murray, *Church Planting*, 87–105. Scholars offer historical analysis related to mission, evangelism, and church growth, of course, but the relatively nascent status of "church planting" as a discipline explains the dearth of historical material.

Pioneer planting refers to the practice of establishing churches in areas previously unreached by the gospel.

Replacement planting has to do with the practice of establishing churches in areas where churches had previously been planted, but no longer exist.

Sectarian planting refers to the practice of establishing more churches in areas where churches already exist, to express and embody distinctive doctrinal or ecclesiological convictions.

Saturation planting refers to the practice of establishing more churches in areas where churches already exist, to enhance the ability of these churches to engage in mission within these areas.[11]

While the creation of new churches across two millennia of church history has happened primarily in areas previously unreached by the gospel, Murray argues that "contemporary church planting does not fall within the category of pioneer planting."[12] The two mediating models—replacement and sectarian planting—while reflective of particular periods of decline in the history of the church, do not have a dynamic presence today, either. Rather, saturation planting dominates, the purpose of which "is not to impact new areas, nor to recover lost ground, nor to develop new kinds of churches, but to plant more churches in already churched areas."[13] Murray's historical analysis is helpful, enabling contemporary church planters to locate themselves in the larger context of God's mission in the world, but the practices of the early Methodist women do not fit neatly into any of these categories. In order to find a place for them in a taxonomy of church planting, we must take a closer look at the holistic approach of Wesleyan ecclesiology.

A Holistic Model of Church and Mission

In an effort to embrace the perennial tensions between maintenance and mission, modalities and sodalities, church and sect in the life of the Christian community, the Wesleys developed a holistic model of church and mission. Early Methodist women exhibited this paradigm in their Society-planting practices. An examination of these polarities and the way in which these women sought to hold them together may be instructive for us today.

---

11. Murray, *Church Planting*, 88–89.
12. Murray, *Church Planting*, 90–91.
13. Murray, *Church Planting*, 97.

Maintenance and Mission

Given the fact that the church is both a community of faith and an agent of God's mission in the world—both an institution and a movement—it should be no surprise that these two realities represent something of a natural tension. In the history of the church, context has often played a major role in the "tipping of the scales" one direction or the other with regard to these two constitutive elements of church. History demonstrates that balance is not easy to maintain with regard to this particular tension. Rather than functioning as a means to a spiritual end, the institution, with its structures and forms, can easily become an end in itself. On the other hand, unless properly channeled and directed with intentionality, Spirit-led mission may have no clear trajectory—much wind and fury without any healthy impact. Quoting Robert Warren's *Building Missionary Congregations*, Stuart Murray observes,

> "A church wholly given to 'mission work' is not a sustainable model." The result is exhausting activism and a "sales-addicted organization." This is not what becoming a missionary congregation implies. But when maintenance becomes central or all-consuming, as it frequently has in European church history ... mission has been marginalized, and the church has forgotten its *raison d'être*.[14]

Years ago, George Peters advanced the argument that the history of Protestant missions exacerbated the bifurcation of maintenance and mission in Western, European Christianity. As a consequence, what he considered to be an abnormal historical development "produced autonomous, missionless churches on the one hand and autonomous churchless missionary societies on the other hand."[15]

John and Charles Wesley sought to tackle this issue head on in their own day. As I have written elsewhere,

> The church of Wesley's England had exchanged its true vocation—mission—for maintenance. (This is a confusion that slips into the life of the church in every age.) It had become distant from and irrelevant to the world it was called to serve.

---

14. Murray, *Church Planting*, 106; cf. Warren, *Building Missionary Congregations*, 26.

15. Peters, *Biblical Theology of Mission*, 214. It might be argued in parallel fashion that similar forces led to the bifurcation of church and evangelism. Parachurch organizations took up the practice of evangelism (on behalf of the church) while those very organizations disengaged evangelism from the church, leading to "evangelism-less churches" and "churchless evangelism."

It needed desperately to reclaim its true identity as God's agent of love in the world. The Wesleys firmly believed that God was raising up the Methodists for the task of resuscitating a missional church.[16]

The Wesleys drew this holistic vision primarily from Jesus' poignant vine and branches image of the church in John 15. The church maintains faith as believers abide in Christ, drawn into the center, to the core, to the source through the means of grace. But the vine does not exist for its own benefit. Rather, it exists for the benefit of others through its fruit. The Spirit spins the church into the world, therefore, in loving service and witness. The Wesleys fervently believed that a church turned in on itself would surely die, for it would lose sight of its reason for being. But a church rooted in Christ and spun out in loving service into the world rediscovers itself day by day. They held maintenance and mission together in dynamic tension.

Modalities and Sodalities

Nearly a half century ago now, Ralph Winter associated these polarities with the sociological terms "modality" and "sodality," developing a theory of their normative character in the life of the church.[17] These concepts have now made their way into the common parlance of the mission and church planting disciplines. Winter used these terms to distinguish between the larger church or congregation (the modality) and distinct, smaller sub-communities that had a strong missional orientation (the sodalities). He traced these structures back to the Apostolic community and throughout the history of the church. While the modality comprises all believers and revolved around the broad range of practices related to worship and discipleship, the sodality represents an elite group particularly committed to a particular mission or vision. Monastic communities or movements of renewal within the Roman Catholic tradition represent some of the most striking examples of modalities and sodalities held in holistic tension. Winter conceived that the Believers' Church—the Anabaptist model of the sixteenth century—"stands in a certain sense, midway between a modality and a sodality, since it has the constituency of the modality (involving full families) and yet, in its earlier years, may have the vitality and selectivity of a sodality."[18]

---

16. Chilcote, *Recapturing the Wesleys' Vision*, 94.
17. See Winter, "Two Structures"; Winter and Beaver, *Warp and the Woof*.
18. Winter, "Two Structures," 129–30.

The Society: A Third Alternative to Church and Sect

Howard Snyder viewed Pietism, Moravianism, and Methodism in this same light.[19] There is no question that this dynamic connection between modalities and sodalities informed the Wesleys' conception of the church and the relation of their Methodist Societies to the established Church of England. From their perspective, maintenance/mission, modality/sodality, and church/sect dialectics interconnect in a dynamic way. Rupert Davies provides an incisive analysis of Wesleyan ecclesiology and identifies, perhaps, one of the most unique qualities of early Methodism. He plays off two of the three classic categories established by Weber and Troeltsch in their sociological treatises, namely, church and sect.[20] While the church "claims to confess objectively the width and depth of catholic tradition, to guarantee the grace of the sacraments, and to comprehend all genuine varieties of worship, spirituality, and faith within its generous embrace," the sect "cuts itself off from the life of the church" so defined "on the grounds of possessing the totality of Christian truth . . . and of embodying the only authentic form of Christian discipleship."[21]

Davies conceives early Methodism as a third alternative to these two classic types—a vision of Christian community that falls somewhere between the two and evinces some of the characteristics of both. He views the "Society" as a unique form of Christianity and provides his own classic definition as follows:

> A "society" acknowledges the truths proclaimed by the universal church and has no wish to separate from it, but claims to cultivate, by means of sacrament and fellowship, the type of inward holiness, which too great an objectivity can easily neglect and of which the church needs constantly to be reminded. A society does not unchurch the members of either church or sect . . . it calls its own members within the larger church to a special personal commitment which respects the commitment of others.[22]

To employ the classic language of Pietism, the Methodist Societies were *ecclesiolae in ecclesia* (little churches within the church).

---

19. Snyder, *Signs of the Spirit*, chs. 3–5, in particular.

20. The three concepts of church, sect, and mystic Christianity are given definitive expression by Troeltsch, *Social Teachings*.

21. J. Wesley, *Works*, 9:3. Davies does not discuss the third Troeltschian category of "mystic" Christianity as it is not directly germane to his analysis here.

22. J. Wesley, *Works*, 9:3.

At the Puritan and Westminster Conference in 1965 dedicated to the theme "Approaches to the Reformation of the Church," D.M. Lloyd-Jones provided a definitive discussion of "Ecclesiola in Ecclesia." According to his analysis,

> The idea of those who formed these little churches was not to form a new church. That is basic. They were not concerned at all about separation; indeed they were bitterly and violently opposed to it. They were not out to change the doctrine of the church . . . their position was that they were not so much dissatisfied with the nature as with the functioning of the church. They were not concerned about the church's doctrine, but were very concerned about its spiritual life and condition.[23]

Howard Snyder, among others, has traced the earliest conception of little churches within the church to Martin Luther, and to his preface to the German Mass of 1526, in particular, where he proposes an "evangelical order" within the life of the established church.[24] In his monumental study of *Ecclesiola in Ecclesia*, the German scholar Gerhard Hilbert argued that Luther envisaged a smaller voluntary covenantal community within the state church. Luther in his view, "never understood this 'ideal' as false, even though he had not embodied it practically."[25]

Under the influence of this Lutheran and later Pietist tradition, the Wesleys designed their United Societies to function like catalysts of renewal within the life of the larger church. Having rediscovered a mission-church paradigm within the life of their own *ecclesiolae in ecclesia,* their hope was that the leavening influence of these small groups of committed missioners would re-awaken the Church of England to its primary vocation in the world, namely, the *missio Dei*. The Methodist Societies were like little dynamos, spinning inside the church and building momentum in order to re-establish a centrifugal force in the church itself, spinning it out in turn in mission. The Societies under the leadership of the Wesleys, therefore, were neither church nor sect. Their members viewed themselves as part of a larger community of faith—the Church of England—but functioned as sodalities within that structure. They endorsed both the maintenance of the institutional church and God's mandate for mission in the world, and their intention was to do all in their power to effect a dynamic symbiosis between them. Early Methodists, and the women we will look at in particular, therefore, did not plant churches. They do not fall neatly into the categories of pioneer or saturation planters;

---

23. Lloyd-Jones, *Puritans*, 130.
24. Snyder, *Signs of the Spirit*, 35.
25. Quoted in Snyder, *Signs of the Spirit*, 37.

nor do they resemble replacement or even sectarian planters. Rather, they planted little churches within the church.

Planting *Ecclesiolae* in *Ecclesia*

Women were conspicuous as pioneers in the establishment and expansion of early Methodism. As I observed in *She Offered Them Christ*, "It was in large measure due to the activities of women that the network of societies under Wesley's direction quickly spread across the land. Women . . . founded prayer groups and societies on their own initiative."[26] Women employed two basic models in the efforts to plant *eccesiolae in ecclesia* during the eighteenth century. First, individual women planted Methodist Societies on the basis of their own entrepreneurial initiatives, most frequently by simply inviting John Wesley or one of his itinerant preachers to their communities and establishing a regular routine of preaching, fellowship, and service in their homes. Secondly, from time to time women drew themselves together into intentional communities in which the rhythms of mutual accountability and active social service modeled vital Christianity to the world around them. These women formed intentional, semi-monastic communities, not unlike the various forms of neo-monasticism in the life of the church today, but all within the larger matrix of the Church of England.

Individual *Ecclesiolae* Planters

The history of Methodism in many English towns and villages begins with the story of a woman who planted the first Society. A brief litany of examples must suffice here.[27] Smith House, the home of Mrs. Holmes of Halifax, became the chief center of religious revival after she invited John Wesley to preach there and organized a Society in the summer of 1742.[28] Mary Allison was the first to open her home to Methodist preachers in Teesdale;[29] the aunt of Mary Denny introduced Methodism to Maldon in the same way;[30] Mrs. Hosmer procured a room for preaching in Darlington.[31] In each of

---

26. Chilcote, *She Offered Them Christ*, 26.

27. For a full discussion of this pioneering work, see Chilcote, *John Wesley and Women*, 45–66.

28. Everett, *Methodism in Manchester*, 52.

29. Steele, *Methodism in Barnard Castle*, 41.

30. Church, *Early Methodist People*, 40.

31. Jackson, *Methodism in the Darlington*, 17.

these instances, illustrative of many other parallel activities, the connection between these women and itinerant evangelists was critical. But in other circumstances, women took the initiative in the actual formation of Societies without the support or authorization of Wesley or his itinerants. For example, several years before Wesley's first visit to Macclesfield, Mary Aldersley opened Shrigley-fold for religious services and led informal meetings for the purposes of prayer, Scripture reading, and religious conversation.[32] Martha Thompson, a wealthy widow who possessed a considerable estate at Rufforth, established her own Society and later pioneered Society planting in the nearby cathedral city of Yorkk, as well.[33]

The pioneering work of Dorothy Fisher illustrates in a more detailed manner the methodology employed by most of these women in their Society planting practices.

> Converted under Wesley's preaching in London, she joined the society there in 1779. About the year 1784 she moved to Great Gonerby in Lincolnshire, opened her house to preaching, and in 1786 purchased a small stone building to serve as a chapel. A small group of Methodists at Sturton heard of Dorothy's piety and observed her work . . . Sarah Parrot of Bracebridge, walked twenty-seven miles to Mrs. Fisher's home. She boldly proclaimed that Dorothy had been brought to their area by God in order to bring Methodism to Lincoln. Concluding that it must be a call from God, Dorothy consented, settled her affairs, moved to Lincoln, purchased a large home to accommodate preaching, and invited the traveling preachers to make it their base of operations . . . Dorothy formed a small society in an old lumber room near Gowt's Bridge. Not unexpectedly, it consisted of four women.[34]

The Society planting work of Fisher and these women reflects the "Pauline Cycle" developed by Hesselgrave in a number of ways.[35] Each of the women received something akin to a commission, more generally a direct impression or command from God, before they entered into their work. They contacted a specific group of people for the purpose of their making a deeper commitment (or a first-time commitment) to the gospel. They continued to meet together in a regular pattern of life, elevated leaders from their own ranks, sustained their relationships through active service and common

---

32. Smith, *Methodism in Macclesfield*, 17–19.
33. Lyth, *Methodism in York*, 53–54.
34. Chilcote, *She Offered Them Christ*, 28–29.
35. See Hesselgrave, *Planting Churches Cross-Culturally*, 47–51.

cause, and extended their mission into their community. Almost all of these women maintained a vital connection with the Anglican parish in which they worshipped regularly and received the sacraments.

Semi-Monastic *Ecclesiolae* Planters

The establishment of intentional communities of women in a cenobitic or semi-monastic style of life represents a second model of Society or *ecclesiolae* planting among early Methodist women. While only a few of these communities emerged over the course of the eighteenth century, their influence was pervasive. Mary Bosanquet was the center of one such community. We have already explored the rise and development of her Leytonstone community in chapter 8, above. Her work bore all the marks of a neo-monasticism in her own day. Her establishment of a "rule of life" provided the foundation for this thriving group of women. The decision-making processes reflected the egalitarian nature of life together, but the community clearly vested leadership in Mary and her successors. She functioned as an "abbess" of a religious community, and her influence extended to other Methodist communities, as well. Mary's community—established on a definitive pattern of life together on a semi-monastic model of austere communal life, disciplined religious contemplation, and service to the needy—maintained strong connections with the Foundery Society and the Anglican parish in which it was located.

Lessons Learned

The work of these women provides a unique example of church planting that breathed new life into the moribund ecclesial establishment of their own day. As part of the Wesleyan movement of renewal that sought to remain intimately connected to the Church of England, these endeavors modeled a symbiosis of modality and sodality, maintenance and mission. The planting of little churches within the church brought renewal to the church at a time when a rediscovery of a biblical, missional vision of life in Christ was sorely needed. This paradigm affords theological and practical lessons for the church today.

Theological Foundations

Stuart Murray provides a helpful theological framework for church planting that coincides nicely with the vision of the early Methodist women.[36] It consists of three primary concerns: *missio Dei*, Incarnation, and the reign of God.

The Mission of God

A robust theological foundation undergirded the missional vision that gave birth to the *ecclesiolae* planting of the early Methodist women. The Wesleys taught them that mission began with God and not with them. They conceived a "missionary God" because the God they had come to know in Jesus Christ was a God of love who was always reaching out from self to others—an expression of God's love and grace they described as God's prevenient action. The missional practices of the women mirrored this understanding of God's nature and character. Moreover, they firmly believed that God was active and at work in the world to save and restore all creation. These primary convictions led the early Methodist women to reclaim mission as the church's reason for being and evangelism as the heart of that mission in the world. They developed a holistic vision of mission and evangelism that refused to separate faith and works, personal salvation and social justice, physical and spiritual needs.

Incarnation

The way in which God entered human history in the person of Jesus Christ provided the primary metaphor shaping the church-planting practices of the women. The Incarnation, in other words, pointed to the "centrifugal nature" of God's activity, poignantly demonstrating this missional quality. The Wesleys and their followers, moreover, were drawn to the kenotic understanding of the Incarnation, owing in part, perhaps, to the influence of the Moravian Pietists. In his famous hymn entitled "Free Grace," Charles Wesley condensed the whole *kenotic* doctrine into a single line.

> He left his Father's throne above
> > (So free, so infinite his grace!),
> *Emptied himself of all but love,*

---

36. Murray, *Church Planting*, esp. 38–53.

And bled for Adam's helpless race.
'Tis mercy all, immense and free,
For, O my God, it found out me![37]

No image of self-emptying impresses itself with greater veracity than the pervasive and distinctive phrase, "Emptied himself of all but love," a poetic line found pervasively throughout the writings of the women. They sought to emulate this kenotic character in all they did. Servanthood became the keynote of their church-planting practice.

The Reign of God

The early Methodist women understood that Christian mission that flows from any source other than the good news of God's love in Jesus Christ is ultimately without substance and power. They were convinced that mission and evangelism must be held together without pitting personal salvation against social justice. Mary Bosanquet's Leytonstone community incarnated this vision. The biblical witness to God's reign functioned like the lens through which they viewed the world and their action in it. The church planting efforts of the women, therefore, were nothing other than an attempt to realize God's shalom in the world. Moreover, they found it impossible to speak of God's reign apart from Christ, or of Jesus without God's reign. The purpose of the communities they planted was to woo others into the loving embrace of God and then help them to see that their mission in life, in partnership with Christ, was to be the signpost of God's reign in this world. The little churches within the church that they established were something like kingdom demonstration and training plots in which the characteristics of Christian community that are absolutely necessary to the church's mission—acts of devotion and worship, acts of compassion and justice—were practiced and explored.

Practical Lessons

I believe that there are significant practical lessons to be learned from the ways in which the early Methodist women planted *ecclesiolae*, as well. I want to take my lead once again from Stuart Murray who discusses church planting models in terms of planting agency, motivation, and results.[38]

---

37. Wesley and Wesley, *Hymns and Sacred Poems* (1739), 118, st. 3.
38. See Murray, *Church Planting*, 229–30.

Using these categories in a slightly different way than Murray, I suggest that the women's dependence on the Holy Spirit, passion for a symbiotic ecclesiology, and vision of authentic discipleship provide relevant insights for the church today.

The Holy Spirit

In discussing one of the primary thrusts of Wesleyan theology, Albert Outler once observed that "the gospel is God's enacted promise in Christ that we can live intentionally, following the inner leadings of the Holy Spirit, obedient to what we are given to know of God's will."[39] In their efforts to plant new communities of faith in the church, the early Methodist women demonstrated their total dependence on the Holy Spirit. In their view, it was not so much owing to their own efforts that new communities of faith grew and flourished; rather, they pointed consistently to the all-sufficiency of the Spirit at work in the world. Dorothy Fisher, for example, began her work in Lincoln in response to a somewhat unconventional calling of the Spirit. Mary Bosanquet acknowledged that her work was based on an invitation from the Spirit, as well. This posture implies some practical lessons related to dependence upon prayer and openness to the movement of the Spirit. Isabella Wilson, one of the many *ecclesiolae* planters of her day, expressed this well in the form of a prayer offered in the midst of her work.

> My whole dependence is upon thee both for present and future blessings. I cannot distrust my blessed Jesus, who has dealt so lovingly with me. I can never sufficiently praise thy holy Name for the consolations of thy Spirit, and favours renewed day by day . . . let us live dependent on Thee our merciful God for the supply of every want.[40]

Symbiotic Ecclesiology

In many ways, the genius of the Wesleyan Revival was the absolute insistence on the part of the Wesleys that their Societies remain within the Church of England.[41] On multiple occasions, they resisted the natu-

---

39. Outler, *Theology*, 62–63.
40. Pipe, "Isabella Wilson," 468–69.
41. For a definitive discussion of the evolutionary process that transformed the Methodist Societies into a church independent of the Church of England, see Baker, *John Wesley*.

ral inclinations of many within their ranks to separate from the Church. As long as the symbiosis of Society and Church remained intact—as long as a dynamic tension was maintained between these two normative structures—spiritual renewal ensued. Not all, to be sure, but by far most of the early Methodist women were adamant about maintaining a close working relationship with the Anglican parishes in which they were immersed. This became increasingly clear toward the end of the eighteenth century, when the call for separation from the Church intensified. In the heat of this contentious situation, women like Mary Bosanquet (Fletcher by that time) styled themselves "Church Methodists" and did all in their power to stress the extraordinary nature of their mission inside the Church. Without question, intentionality more than anything else held them true to that course and required the practice of humility, forbearance, and love.[42]

Authentic Discipleship

The early Methodist women understood that authentic Christian discipleship requires community.[43] Their little churches within the church functioned as greenhouses in which Jesus' disciples were encouraged to grow and mature in their faith. As I have observed in *Making Disciples in a World Parish*, these Christian families became disciple-making communities "as they bore witness to the good news by making room and creating safe space for the other (hospitality), by offering reconciliation and peace to the broken-hearted and the oppressed (healing), and by living in and for God's shalom-vision for all humanity and creation (holiness)."[44] The primary lesson to be learned from their experience revolves around the profoundly personal nature of this work. The *ecclesiolae* provided an intimate context in which faith was born, and awakened sinners were encouraged to grow in grace, to be channels of love for others, and to enter a particular, revolutionary path of self-sacrificing love for the world. Early Methodist women planted *ecclesiolae* in order to experience the gift of God's reign, offer it to others, participate in it more fully, and help the larger church community rediscover the centrality of God's rule

---

42. In a discussion of Stephen Clark's *Unordained Elders and Renewal Communities*, Snyder observes, "Clark holds that subcommunities are and should be a normative pattern in the church, . . . 'movements [for him] in which the central thrust is towards a more fervent and effective living of the Christian life'" (Snyder, *Signs of the Spirit*, 54).

43. For a discussion of the formative nature of early Methodist small groups, see Matthaei, *Making Disciples*.

44. Chilcote, *Making Disciples*, 7.

in its life. A little-known hymn of Charles Wesley celebrates the resistless love that animated their practice.

> Love, which willest all should live,
> Love, which all to all would give,
> Love, that over all prevails,
> Love, that never, never fails.
> Love immense, and unconfined,
> Love to all of humankind.[45]

---

45. Kimbrough, *Songs for the Poor*, no. 1.

Chapter 18

Charles Wesley and the "Peaceable Reign" of Christ

Source note: An unpublished address delivered before the Charles Wesley Society Annual Meeting, held at Princeton University on September 29, 2017.

STUDENTS OF THE BIBLICAL witness have used a plethora of terms to capture the meaning of the kingdom of God—a theme that pervades Scripture and constitutes the central teaching of Jesus.[1] It is not my purpose here to provide an exhaustive exploration of this language; a couple well-known examples suffice and serve to locate Charles Wesley among other substantial theologians in this ongoing quest. In the wake of the recent tragedy in Charlottesville, Virginia, where racism and bigotry raised its ugly head, it is important to note that the vision of the "beloved community" was the central principle of the thought and activity of Martin Luther King Jr.[2] This was his language for the kingdom of God. In his seminal work, *Living Toward a Vision: Biblical Reflections on Shalom*, Walter Brueggemann identified God's rule with this singular Hebrew term—*shalom*—and thereby provided a vision of "a caring, sharing, rejoicing community with none to make them afraid."[3] For him, all aspects of God's kingdom may be subsumed under this overarching concept within the biblical narrative. For these disciples of Jesus, beloved community and shalom function as shorthand terms for their profound and dynamic conception of God's rule.

---

1. "The concept of the Kingdom of God involves, in a real sense," claimed John Bright, "the total message of the Bible" (Bright, *Kingdom of God*, 7).
2. Smith and Zepp, *Search for Beloved Community*, 119–40.
3. Brueggemann, *Living Toward a Vision*, 20.

Charles Wesley articulates a similarly compelling vision of God's kingdom in his lyrical theology.[4] One hymn, in particular, from his collection of *Hymns for the Nativity of Our Lord*, describes various dimensions of God's rule. He prays for God's kingdom to come; he celebrates its realization in the here and now; he admonishes everyone to live into this alternative reality with hope. In this hymn, he uses a noteworthy expression as he paints a lyrical portrait of God's dominion, somewhat unique for him but very contemporary in its sound. He describes God's kingdom in the language of a "quiet and peaceable reign."[5]

> All glory to God in the sky,
>   And peace upon earth be restor'd!
> O Jesus, exalted on high,
>   Appear our omnipotent Lord:
> Who meanly in Bethlehem born,
>   Didst stoop to redeem a lost race,
> Once more to thy creature return,
>   And reign in thy kingdom of grace.
>
> When thou in our flesh didst appear,
>   All nature acknowledg'd thy birth;
> Arose the acceptable year,
>   And heaven was open'd on earth:
> Receiving its Lord from above,
>   The world was united to bless
> The giver of concord and love,
>   The Prince and the author of peace.

---

4. See Chilcote, *Faith That Sings*, 106–21 (ch. 8: "Dominion: Situated in God's Shalom"). Many of the insights presented here depend greatly upon this earlier work.

5. Despite a pervasive reference to kingdom language and images, Wesley only uses this expression in one other hymn in his entire corpus, namely, in his lyrical exposition of Job 29:25, where he sings: "Thy sway among men to maintain, / Compassion and righteousness meet; / Thy reign is a peaceable reign, / Thy seat is a merciful seat" (*Scripture Hymns*, 1:242). A simple word search for the term "kingdom" in the Wesleyan corpus reveals some rather startling statistics: "In his two published volumes of *Scripture Hymns* the term appears more than 150 times. Likewise, in his manuscript hymns on Matthew's Gospel—a biblical document in which the kingdom of God figures quite prominently—Wesley appropriates the term in more than 100 instances. While the term itself is important, greater significance attaches to the major themes related to God's dominion in the biblical witness and the process by which God resituates the faithful in God's shalom" (Chilcote, *Faith That Sings*, 106).

O wouldst thou again be made known,
>   Again in thy Spirit descend,
And set up in each of thine own,
>   A kingdom that never shall end!
Thou only art able to bless,
>   And make the glad nations obey,
And bid the dire enmity cease,
>   And bow the whole world to thy sway.

Come then to thy servants again,
>   Who long thy appearing to know,
Thy quiet and peaceable reign
>   In mercy establish below:
All sorrow before thee shall fly,
>   And anger and hatred be o'er,
And envy and malice shall die,
>   And discord afflict us no more.

No horrid alarm of war
>   Shall break our eternal repose;
No sound of the trumpet is there,
>   Where Jesus's Spirit o'erflows:
Appeas'd by the charms of thy grace
>   We all shall in amity join,
And kindly each other embrace,
>   And love with a passion like thine.[6]

Wesley's use of the phrase "peaceable reign" undoubtedly resonates with the contemporary disciple of Jesus. Stanley Hauerwas popularized a term very similar to this—the "peaceable kingdom"—which he used as the title of his groundbreaking primer in Christian ethics, first published in 1991.[7] In an unpublished address, entitled "Artisans of a Peaceable Kingdom," his mentor, John Howard Yoder, demonstrated how this theme had been celebrated in the arts.[8] In 1820, for example, famous American Quaker artist, Edward Hicks,

---

6. C. Wesley, *Nativity Hymns*, 23–24.
7. Hauerwas, *Peaceable Kingdom*.
8. Yoder, "Artisans of a Peaceable Kingdom."

began a sixty-one-painting series on this theme. Hicks had taken Isaiah 11:6 as the biblical focus of his artistic reflections. Inspired by these paintings over a century later, composer Randall Thompson composed a choral work on "The Peaceable Kingdom." In 1954, Jon Silkin published a poetic collection on this same title. Given the vivid scriptural imagery attached to this vision, it has cried out for artistic expression over the years.

A constellation of biblical texts shapes this vision and this language. Leviticus 26:3–6 describes the peaceable reign among those who walk in obedient relationship to God. Creation imagery dominates. In this kingdom, rains water the land, the earth produces abundant crops, trees yield good fruit, people eat their fill, and no one lives in fear from wild beasts or human foes. According to the Psalmist, in God's peaceable reign, "steadfast love and faithfulness will meet; righteousness and peace will kiss each other" (85:10). In Hosea's vision, God abolishes the bow, the sword, and war from the land and enables everyone to lie down in safety (2:18–20). No biblical writer articulates this vision more pervasively and persuasively than the prophet Isaiah. In the peaceable kingdom, "they shall beat their swords into plowshares, and their spears into pruning hooks"; he proclaims, "nation shall not lift up sword against nation, neither shall they learn war anymore" (2:4). When God establishes the peaceable reign "the effect of righteousness will be peace and the result of righteousness, quietness and trust forever. My people will abide in a peaceful habitation, in secure dwellings, and in quiet resting places" (32:17–18).

Isaiah 11:6–9 provides the primary locus for the iconic vision.

> The wolf shall live with the lamb,
> > the leopard shall lie down with the kid,
> the calf and the lion and the fatling together,
> > and a little child shall lead them.
> The cow and the bear shall graze,
> > their young shall lie down together;
> > and the lion shall eat straw like the ox.
> The nursing child shall play over the hole of the asp,
> > and the weaned child shall put its hand on the adder's den.
> They will not hurt or destroy
> > on all my holy mountain;
> for the earth will be full of the knowledge of the LORD
> > as the waters cover the sea.

Jesus employs all these images and embodies the peaceable reign in his own life and ministry. These are the characteristics of his reign; the manifestation of this kingdom is his primary mission. The hymn of Charles Wesley, above, demonstrates the way in which all creation groans in anticipation of God's rule. His conception of the peaceable reign of Christ points to several key elements: the gift of reconciliation; Christ's dominion in the human heart; the fruits of peace, joy, and righteousness; the practices of justice and compassion; and the already-but-not-yet character of this rule.

"Your kingdom come!"

Matthew 6:10

Given the large space devoted to the kingdom in Charles's lyrical theology, it should be no surprise that the petition in the Lord's Prayer—"Your kingdom come. Your will be done, on earth as it is in heaven" (Matt 6:10)—figures prominently in his hymns. He refers to this verse explicitly sixteen times in the 1780 *Collection of Hymns for the Use of the People Called Methodists*. He identifies a dual focus related to God's dominion in this text, namely, the importance of both God's kingdom and God's will. St. Luke's version of the Lord's Prayer inspired Wesley to compose a composite hymn on the peaceable reign of Christ, combining two lyrical paraphrases of Luke 11:2.

> Father of me, and all mankind,
>   And all the hosts above,
> Let every understanding mind
>   Unite to praise thy love,
> To know thy nature and thy name,
>   One God in Persons Three,
> And glorify the great I AM
>   Through all eternity.
>
> Thy kingdom come, with power and grace,
>   To every heart of man,
> Thy peace and joy, and righteousness,
>   In all our bosoms reign!
> Thy righteousness our sin keep down,
>   Thy peace our passions bind,

And let us in thy joy unknown,
    The first dominion find.

The righteousness that never ends,
    But makes an end of sin,
The joy that human thought transcends,
    Into our souls bring in,
The kingdom of established peace,
    Which can no more remove,
The perfect power of godliness,
    The omnipotence of love.[9]

Charles yearns for all people to rediscover this "first dominion" which God's creatures rejected and ignored. As in his doctrine of redemption, the concepts of reconciliation and restoration play a central role in his concept of Christ's kingdom. People, in his view, do not build the kingdom; rather, God must restore the rule of Christ, and this entails reconciliation. Believers receive the kingdom into their hearts and then partner with God in this work in the world.

Reconciliation: The Foundation of the Peaceable Reign

2 Corinthians 5:19

St. Paul writes to the embattled church in Corinth: "God was in Christ, reconciling the world unto himself, not imputing their trespasses unto them; and hath committed unto us the word of reconciliation" (2 Cor. 5:19). This is the Authorized translation that would have been most familiar to Wesley, with this verse coming, of course, in the context of a larger discourse (namely, 2 Cor 5:11–21) in which the apostle discusses the ministry of reconciliation. Many of St. Paul's most familiar themes resound in this fifth chapter: new creation, imputation, the righteousness of God.

In summary statements like this one, St. Paul captures God's total mission to which, he believes, the entirety of the scriptural witness bears testimony. Friendship with God characterizes this vision of life. Those drawn into this realm love both God and neighbor. Christ makes this kind of existence possible by breaking down all the barriers that divide people

---

9. C. Wesley, *Scripture Hymns*, 2:220.

and disrupt God's intended harmony in the created order. Reconciliation itself is both the foundation and the sign of God's peaceable reign and the nearness of God's rule. While the reconciliation of the believer in Christ to God is an accomplished fact, the reconciliation of the cosmos is a continuing process into which the community of faith is invited as the representative of God's alternative vision in the world. God's people are called to stand in the juncture, as it were, between the old world which is passing away and the new world—the peaceable reign—that is being birthed in Christ, despite all appearances.

In a verse inspired by 2 Corinthians 5:17, Charles celebrates the momentous change in the believer's life effected by trust in Christ and the inbreaking rule of Christ.

> Thrice acceptable word,
>   I long to prove it true!
> Take me into thyself, O Lord,
>   By making me anew;
>   Me for thy mercy sake
>   Out of myself remove,
> Partaker of thy nature make,
>   Thy holiness and love.[10]

He describes this true foundation of the peaceable reign as the "reconciling word."

> See me, Saviour, from above,
>   Nor suffer me to die!
> Life, and happiness, and love,
>   Drop from thy gracious eye;
> Speak the reconciling word,
>   And let thy mercy melt me down;
> Turn, and look upon me, Lord,
>   And break my heart of stone.[11]

This reconciling word of God illuminates the soul with the gift of faith. God restores sight to the blind and rescues those who dwell in darkness. Those

---

10. C. Wesley, *Scripture Hymns*, 2:300.
11. C. Wesley, *Hymns and Sacred Poems* (1749), 1:122.

who entrust their lives to God through Christ by faith pray for all the fullness of God in their lives.

> The gift unspeakable impart:
>   Command the light of faith to shine,
> To shine in my dark, drooping heart,
>   And fill me with the life divine;
> Now bid the new creation be!
> O God, let there be faith in me!
>
> Thee without faith I cannot please,
>   Faith without thee I cannot have;
> But thou hast sent the Prince of peace
>   To seek my wandering soul, and save;
> O Father, glorify thy Son,
> And save me for his sake alone![12]

For those who are "reconciled by grace," God justifies through faith alone, opens mercy's door, offers assurance of forgiveness, relieves burdens, and prepares for heaven.[13] God's will is that all might be saved and the extent of God's love is so great that we "tremble at the word / Of reconciling grace."[14] This reconciling word composes the weary breast and sinks it into visions of eternity, but also raises believers to sing their Savior's praise, flows from their hearts, fills their tongues, permeates their life with purest love, and joins them to the communion of God's faithful throughout the ages.[15]

The Peaceable Reign in the Heart

Luke 17:21

For Charles Wesley, everything begins with the heart. He had been raised with the Authorized Version of Luke 17:21, "Neither shall they say, Lo here! or, lo there! for, behold, the kingdom of God is within you." Regardless of other translations which render *entos hymon* "among you" as opposed to

---

12. C. Wesley, *Redemption Hymns*, 18–19.
13. Wesley and Wesley, *Hymns and Sacred Poems* (1742), 130.
14. C. Wesley, *Hymns and Sacred Poems* (1749), 2:230.
15. C. Wesley, *Hymns and Sacred Poems* (1749), 1:92–93.

"within you," Charles never wavered from his conviction about the centrality of the human heart. His brother, John, had raised this very point in his reflections on this verse in his *Explanatory Notes upon the New Testament*: "*For behold the kingdom of God is within or among you*—look not for it in distant times or remote places: it is now in the midst of you: it is come: it is present in the soul of every believer: it is a spiritual kingdom, an internal principle. Wherever it exists, it exists in the heart."[16]

Charles's poetic rendering of Matthew 6:10 expresses his longing for God's dominion in the hearts of all people.

> When shall thy Spirit reign
> In every heart of man?
> Father, bring the kingdom near,
> Honor thy triumphant Son,
> God of heaven, on earth appear,
> Fix with us thy glorious throne.[17]

"Fix in every heart of man," he prays, "Thine everlasting throne."[18] He makes his appeal to the broken, to those whose hearts are still turned in on themselves. If any are to participate in God's rule, they must first turn their hearts to God. Before turning their attention outward, they must first attend to their deepest interior need. "Sinners, turn, believe, and find," he pleads, "The kingdom in your hearts."[19]

> God comes down on earth to reign,
> With dazzling majesty confessed:
> Every happy, pardoned man
> Contains him in his breast.

But Charles connects the interior life of the spirit intimately with the believer's engagement in "kingdom ministry." Urgency characterizes the singers' plea,

> I will, through grace I will;
> I do return to thee:

---

16. See C. Wesley, *Hymns and Sacred Poems* (1749); Wesley and Wesley, *Hymns and Sacred Poems* (1739), 174; and Wesley and Wesley, *Hymns and Sacred Poems* (1740), 65, 141.
17. C. Wesley, *Scripture Hymns*, 2:142.
18. C. Wesley, *Scripture Hymns*, 1:160.
19. C. Wesley, *MS Matthew*, 113.

> Take, empty it,
>> O Lord, and fill
>> My heart with purity:
>> For power I feebly pray;
>> Thy kingdom now restore,
> Today, while it is called today,
>> And I shall sin no more.[20]

Those who turn over their hearts to God for God's use receive God's power both to do so and to live as God's children (see 1 Cor 4:20). Whenever God imparts the Spirit, Wesley argues, "The kingdom restored is power in our hearts." But unlike the power of the world, this power is that of Christ's passion, "The strength of salvation, / the virtue of love."[21] Charles emphasizes the inextricable connection between this restored capacity and the cruciform nature of Christ's reign. In his reflections on 1 Corinthians 4:20, he identifies the origins and nature of the power of love in the peaceable reign.

> If Jesus doth reign, and save us from sin,
>> No words can explain his kingdom within,
> No boastful reflection on what we possess,
>> No talk of perfection, or flourish of grace.
>
> Wherever our Lord his Spirit imparts,
>> The kingdom restor'd is power in our hearts,
> The power of his passion, and rising we prove,
>> The strength of salvation, the virtue of love.
>
> With love we receive the power to obey,
>> Unspotted to live, unwearied to pray:
> His burthens we bear, while here we remain,
>> His agonies share, and suffer to reign.[22]

To describe the fruit of this transformation in the direction of God's rule, Wesley invariably alludes to Romans 14:17—the kingdom of God is

---

20. C. Wesley, *Scripture Hymns*, 1:11.
21. C. Wesley, *Scripture Hymns*, 2:29.
22. C. Wesley, *Hymns and Sacred Poems* (1749), 2:291.

righteousness and peace and joy. In his poetic corpus, he defines Christ's peaceable reign along the lines of this important trilogy.

Righteousness, Joy, and Peace

Romans 14:17

"For the kingdom of God," St. Paul claims, "is not food and drink but righteousness and peace and joy in the Holy Spirit" (Rom 14:17). Charles therefore prays,

> Bring in the kingdom of his peace,
> > Fill all our souls with joy unknown,
> And stablish us in righteousness,
> > And perfect all his saints in one.[23]

In a reflection on Hebrews 12:2, he simply implores,

> Speak gracious Lord, my sickness cure,
> Make my infected nature pure;
> Peace, righteousness and joy impart,
> And pour thyself into my heart.[24]

A lyrical paraphrase of Luke 17:20—Jesus' dialogue with the Pharisees about how and where the kingdom comes—elicits the grand trilogy:

> Love, the power of humble love
> > Constitutes thy kingdom here:
> Never, never to remove
> > Let it, Lord, in me appear,
> Let the pure, internal grace
> > Fill my new-created soul,
> Peace, and joy, and righteousness,
> > While eternal ages roll.[25]

---

23. Wesley, *Moral and Sacred Poems*, 3:241.
24. Wesley and Wesley, *Hymns and Sacred Poems* (1739), 92.
25. C. Wesley, *MS Luke*, 251–52.

Wesley's reflections on Matthew 5:3 celebrate the peaceable reign as "Glorious joy, / unutter'd peace, / All victorious righteousness."[26] In a hymn for "Christian Friends," he anticipates the in-breaking reign.

> Now wilt thou make an end of sin,
> > The kingdom of thy peace
> The joy unspeakable bring in,
> > Th'eternal righteousness![27]

In Christ's reign, peace displaces discord and anxiety, joy supplants sorrow and discouragement, and righteousness dislodges depravity and sin. The contrasts between the kingdoms of this world and the peaceable reign of Christ could not be more stark in Charles's poetry. For those who conform their lives to this world, "joy is all sadness," "mirth is all vain," "laughter is madness," and "pleasure is pain." But those who have the mind of Christ experience full and abundant life.

> All fulness of peace,
> > All fulness of joy,
> > > And spiritual bliss
> > > > That never shall cloy,
> > > > > To us it is given
> > > > > > In Jesus to know
> > > > > A kingdom of heaven,
> > > > > > An heaven below.[28]

While each of these constitutive elements of the peaceable reign relate directly to the individual at a deeply personal level, they also have a critical social dimension. Charles perceives a peculiar trajectory related to Christ's peaceable reign. God's dominion begins in the human heart most certainly, but extends into the church, and then expands yet further to the poor, the persecuted, and those pulverized by war and strife. "For Methodists this internal transformation was not enough," observes Andrew Winckles, "the true evidence of the kingdom of God in heart and life was in how it worked outward into community."[29]

> Still the great God resides below,

---

26. C. Wesley, *Hymns and Sacred Poems* (1749), 1:36.
27. C. Wesley, *Hymns and Sacred Poems* (1749), 2:326.
28. C. Wesley, *Redemption Hymns*, 32.
29. Winckles, "Kingdom of God."

> (And all his faithful people know
>   He will not from his church depart)
> The Father, Son, and Spirit dwells,
>   His kingdom in the poor reveals,
> And fills with heaven the humble heart.[30]

In his peaceable reign, Christ inextricably binds righteous, joy, and peace together with justice and compassion.

Justice and Compassion

Isaiah 11:6–9

Charles mandates that faithful disciples of Jesus translate the personal gifts of righteousness, joy, and peace, therefore, into concrete acts of justice and compassion in the world. In a hymn he composed for his wife on their wedding day, Charles affords a unique window into the aspects of Christian character shaped by the values of God's way and rule.

> Come, let us arise,
>   And press to the skies,
>   The summons obey,
> My friend, my beloved, and hasten away!
>   The master of all
>   For our service doth call,
>   And deigns to approve
> With smiles of acceptance our labor of love.[31]

The hymn encourages bride and groom to be accountable to one another in love and good works as a performance of God's rule in their lives. Their common witness to the peaceable reign meant attending to those who were distressed, afflicted, and oppressed. Their kingdom work entailed relieving prisoners, receiving strangers, and supplying all their wants. Kingdom ministry included acts of justice and compassion. The world depends on these works of mercy for there to be any hope of wolves and lambs to live together in peace and harmony.

---

30. C. Wesley, *Scripture Hymns*, 1:167.
31. C. Wesley, *Hymns and Sacred Poems* (1749), 2:280–281.

Various forms of injustice clamored for attention in Wesley's day. His hymns encouraged commitment to God's vision of the peaceable reign and active engagement in ministries of justice. In one of his *Hymns of Intercession for all Mankind*, in particular, Wesley paints a vivid portrait of a world gone wrong, but offers an alternative biblical vision for life as God intended it to be.

> Our earth we now lament to see
> With floods of wickedness overflowed,
> With violence, wrong, and cruelty,
> One wide-extended field of blood,
> Where men, like fiends, each other tear
> In all the hellish rage of war.

The singer intercedes on behalf of humanity with regard to the atrocities associated with a fallen world. Charles calls upon Jesus to intervene.

> O might the universal Friend
> This havoc of his creatures see!
> Bid our unnatural discord end,
> Declare us reconciled in thee!
> Write kindness on our inward parts
> And chase the murderer from our hearts.

He locates the hope for peace in the transformation of the human heart and calls on all faithful disciples of Jesus "To follow after peace, and prize / The blessings of thy righteous reign." This, and only this, will restore "The paradise of perfect love."[32]

Isaiah's iconic vision provides the imagery for many of his hymns in which he describes the reign of Christ. His brilliant lyrical paraphrase of Isaiah 11:6–7 provides a powerful illustration of the theme.

> Prince of universal peace,
> Destroy the enmity,
> Bid our jars and discords cease,
> Unite us all in thee.
> Cruel as wild beasts we are,
> 'Till vanquished by thy mercy's power,

---

32. C. Wesley, *Intercession Hymns*, 4.

> We, like wolves, each other tear,
>> And their own flesh devour.
>
> But if thou pronounce the word
>> That forms our souls again,
>
> Love and harmony restored
>> Throughout the earth shall reign;
>
> When thy wondrous love they feel,
> The human savages are tame,
>> Ravenous wolves, and leopards dwell
>>> And stable with the lamb.[33]

In Charles's poetry, war always represents the antithesis of this peaceable reign.

> Messias, Prince of Peace,
>> Where men each other tear,
>
> Where war is learnt, they must confess
>> Thy kingdom is not there:
>
> Fightings and wars shall cease,
>> And in thy Spirit given
>
> Pure joy, and everlasting peace
>> Shall turn our earth to heaven.[34]

There is also an amazing body of hymnody related to the poor in Wesley's collected works. Work alongside the poor requires both elements of the reign—justice and compassion. "Perhaps the uniqueness of his contribution lies," as Kimbrough has argued, "in the way he opened for the church to remember its responsibility to the dispossessed of the earth."[35] Wesley "creates a hymnic, poetically remembered theology," he claims, "that articulates the imperatives of ministry to the poor."[36] Charles's doctrine of the peaceable reign demonstrates God's love for the poor, their important role in the community of faith, and the responsibility of all faithful disciples to

---

33. C. Wesley, *Scripture Hymns*, 1:316.
34. C. Wesley, *Scripture Hymns*, 1:305.
35. Kimbrough, "Charles Wesley and the Poor," 148.
36. Kimbrough, "Charles Wesley and the Poor," 155.

engage in advocacy for all who are dispossessed. The following hymn well illustrates both Charles's attitude toward the poor and the actions that faithful Christians should take on their behalf, all modeled after Jesus.

> The poor as Jesus' bosom friends,
>> The poor he makes his latest care,
> To all his followers commends,
>> And wills us on our hands to bear;
> The poor our dearest care we make,
>> And love them for our Savior's sake.[37]

Charles depicts the compassionate character of those whose lives have been conformed to the image of Christ through their ministry alongside the marginalized. Mary Naylor was one such woman, an active leader of the Methodist Society in Bristol noted for God's rule in her life.

> The golden rule she has pursued,
> And did to others as she would
>> Others should do to her;
> Justice composed her upright soul,
> Justice did all her thoughts control,
>> And formed her character.
>
> Affliction, poverty, disease,
> Drew out her soul in soft distress,
>> The wretched to relieve;
> In all the works of love employed,
> Her sympathizing soul enjoyed
>> The blessedness to give.
>
> A nursing mother to the poor,
> For them she husbanded her store,
>> Her life, her all, bestowed;
> For them she labored day and night,
> In doing good her whole delight,
>> In copying after God.[38]

---

37. C. Wesley, *MS Acts*, 421.
38. C. Wesley, *Funeral Hymns*, 51.

An affective experience of God's rule and an outward performance of the kingdom defined Wesley's doctrine of the peaceable reign of Christ. As Winckles has observed, the genius of Methodism in this regard was "a subjectivity founded not upon individual autonomy and rights but on the freedom to do God's will, to enact the kingdom on earth."[39]

"Already but not yet"

Hebrews 2:8–9

Wesley encouraged the church, like the individual disciple, to strive for perfection. But he also acknowledged the elusive nature of perfect love. God's dominion has come in Jesus Christ, and yet the church still prays for it to come. With regard to the peaceable reign of Christ there is an "already but not yet" dynamic at work. George Eldon Ladd popularized this language in the 1950s, describing both a present and future dimension of the kingdom of God in Scripture.[40] Charles drew the same conclusions, basically conceiving a realm in which God rules in the present and a future fulfillment of God's reign that is not yet fully realized. He describes both realities in his hymns.

He bears witness to the present rule of Christ in a lyrical reflection on Daniel 7:18.[41] The present kingdom, he argues, is already given to all the saints below. "It is not of this world, we know, / But comes with Christ from heaven." He celebrates the fact that God's people live in this peaceable reign "Before we reach the sky" and in the present moment "With Christ triumphant live." The church celebrates this present reign, partners with God to cultivate its values, and proclaims God's vision of shalom. Times of trouble, in particular, elicit Charles's hopes for a fuller manifestation of the peaceable reign in the future.

> We know that his word
> > And promise are past;
> >
> > Thy kingdom, O Lord,
> >
> > Shall triumph at last:
> >
> > The kingdoms before thee
> >
> > And nations shall fall,

---

39. Winckles, "Kingdom of God."
40. See Ladd, *Gospel of the Kingdom*.
41. C. Wesley, *Scripture Hymns*, 2:63–64.

> And all men adore thee,
>
> > The monarch of all.[42]

Daniel's description of the God of heaven who destroys, breaks in pieces, and consumes all other kingdoms provides the graphic language that suits Charles's vision well. "Thy kingdom come," he prays, "All these worldly powers o'erthrow, / And scatter, and consume!" And he anticipates a divine monarchy that will be "Founded in perpetual grace."[43]

> Father, by right divine,
>
> Assert the kingdom thine;
>
> Jesus, power of God, subdue
>
> > Thine own universe to thee;
>
> Spirit of grace and glory too,
>
> > Reign through all eternity.[44]

Sometimes the present and future coalesce in Wesley's poetry. The imagery of the heavenly banquet in his Eucharistic hymns, in particular, evokes this eschatological fusion.

At the table, the community of faith dwells, as it were, in both kingdoms, present and future. Only a thin veil separates the one from the other.[45]

> The church triumphant in thy love
>
> > Their mighty joys we know,
>
> They sing the Lamb in hymns above,
>
> > And we in hymns below.
>
> Thee in thy glorious realm they praise,
>
> > And bow before thy throne,
>
> We in the kingdom of thy grace,
>
> > The kingdoms are but one.

Gathered around the table for "thy great kingdom feast," the faithful feel God's promise of "eternal rest." "Yet still an higher seat," Wesley proclaims, "We in thy kingdom claim."

---

42. Wesley and Wesley, *Hymns for Times of Trouble*, 9.
43. C. Wesley, *Scripture Hymns*, 2:58–59.
44. C. Wesley, *Scripture Hymns*, 2:143.
45. Wesley and Wesley, *Hymns on the Lord's Supper*, 84.

> That glorious heavenly prize
>> We surely shall attain,
> And in the palace of the skies
>> With thee for ever reign.

He articulates an inclusive vision of Christ's peaceable reign in a lyrical paraphrase of the parable of the great banquet in Luke 14:15-24. In this hymn, he sounds a note of eschatological urgency with regard to the ultimate victory of God's inclusive love. In the peaceable reign of Christ, God invites all to the table. God offers grace to every soul. God excludes none from the gracious offer of life in the reign of shalom to come. Wesley paints a compelling and dynamic portrait of the peaceable reign through the imagery related to this banquet.

> Come, sinners, to the gospel-feast,
> Let every soul be Jesu's guest,
> Ye need not one be left behind,
> For God hath bid all humankind.
>
> Sent by my Lord, on you I call,
> The invitation is to all.
> Come all the world: come, sinner, thou,
> All things in Christ are ready now.
>
> Come then ye souls, by sin oppressed,
> Ye restless wanderers after rest,
> Ye poor, and maimed, and halt, and blind,
> In Christ an hearty welcome find.
>
> This is the time, no more delay,
> This is the acceptable day,
> Come in, this moment, at his call,
> And live for him who died for all.[46]

Permanency characterizes the peaceable reign of Christ, and Wesley invests his life and places his hope in this ultimate promise of God.

---

46. C. Wesley, *Redemption Hymns*, 63–66 (selected verses).

> Earthly kingdoms soon decline,
>> Totter, fall, and pass away;
> Permanent, O Christ, is thine,
>> Cannot moulder, or decay;
> Every other power o'rethrown
>> Shall its destined period prove,
> Thy dominion stands alone,
>> Fixed as thine eternal love.[47]

In Charles's mind, this eternal reign is nothing less than "paradise restor'd,"[48] and he prays ultimately, with all creation, for the fullest possible realization of the peaceable reign of Christ in and for all.

> Come then to thy servants again,
>> Who long thy appearing to know,
> Thy quiet and peaceable reign
>> In mercy establish below:
>
> Appeas'd by the charms of thy grace
>> We all shall in amity join,
> And kindly each other embrace,
>> And love with a passion like thine.[49]

---

47. C. Wesley, *MS Luke*, 7.
48. C. Wesley, *Scripture Hymns*, 2:76.
49. C. Wesley, *Nativity Hymns*, 24.

Appendix A

A World Methodist Affirmation

Source note: First published in *The Wesleyan Tradition: A Paradigm for Renewal*, edited by Paul W. Chilcote, 19–21. Nashville: Abingdon, 2002.

FOLLOWING THE SIXTEENTH WORLD Methodist Conference in Singapore in 1991, the executive committee established a special work group for the task of developing a substantive theological paper on the question of diversity and pluralism, focusing in particular on the Wesleyan perspective. The consultative group met subsequently in the summer of 1995 under the leadership of Dr. Norman E. Dewire. One of the documents produced by this committee is entitled "Wesleyan Essentials of the Christian Faith." This statement, including affirmations about Wesleyan beliefs, service, common life, worship, and witness was adopted by the World Methodist Conference meeting in Rio de Janeiro in 1996.

Since I had been involved in laying a foundation for the work of this task force at the invitation of Dr. Dewire, and since I had an intimate knowledge of the process that led to the creation of this document, he invited me to prepare a "liturgical expression" of the approved Essentials statement. An initial draft of the litany was circulated and Schuyler Rhodes and Geoffrey Wainwright made helpful editorial comments that shaped the final product. It is appropriate to include this affirmation at the close of this volume on the Wesleyan Tradition.

> We confess the Christian faith, once delivered to the saints; shaped by the Holy Scriptures, guided by the apostolic teaching, and rooted in the grace of God which is ever transforming our lives and renewing our minds in the image of Christ.

SPIRIT OF FAITH COME DOWN,

REVEAL THE THINGS OF GOD.

We worship and give our allegiance to the Triune God; gracious to create and mighty to redeem, ever ready to comfort, lead, and guide, ever present to us in the means of grace, uniting us in Baptism and nourishing us in the Supper of the Lord, who calls us in our worship to become sacred instruments of justice and peace, to love and serve others with a faith that makes us dance and sing.

O FOR A THOUSAND TONGUES TO SING

MY GREAT REDEEMER'S PRAISE.

We bear witness to Jesus Christ in the world through word, deed, and sign, earnestly seeking to proclaim God's will for the salvation of all humankind, to embody God's love through acts of justice, peace, mercy, and healing, and to celebrate God's reign here and now, even as we anticipate the time when God's rule will have full sway throughout the world.

JESUS, THOU ART ALL COMPASSION,

PURE, UNBOUNDED LOVE THOU ART.

We will strive with God through the power of the Holy Spirit for a common heart and life, binding all believers together; and knowing that the love we share in Christ is stronger than our conflicts, broader than our opinions, and deeper than the wounds we inflict on one another, we commit ourselves to the solidarity of nurture, outreach, and witness, remembering our gospel commitment to love our neighbors whoever and wherever they may be.

HE BIDS US BUILD EACH OTHER UP,
AND GATHERED INTO ONE,

TO OUR HIGH CALLING'S GLORIOUS HOPE,
WE HAND IN HAND GO ON.

We will work together in God's name, believing that our commitment comes to life in our actions: Like Christ, we seek to serve, rather than to be served, and to be filled with the energy of love. With God's help we will express this love through our sensitivity to context and culture, our compassion for the last and the least, and our commitment to a holiness of heart and life that refuses to separate conversion and justice, piety and mercy, faith and love.

TO SERVE THE PRESENT AGE,
MY CALLING TO FULFILL,

O MAY IT ALL MY POWERS ENGAGE
TO DO MY MASTER'S WILL.

Appendix B

A Progressive Wesleyan Declaration

Source note: First published as the Epilogue for Paul W. Chilcote, *Active Faith: Resisting 4 Dangerous Ideologies with the Wesleyan Way*, 75–76. Nashville: Abingdon, 2019.

I PRAY THAT THE ideas upon which you have been reflecting and the practices in which you have engaged have formed truth, joy, peace, and love in your life. The core values of the progressive Wesleyan vision include the mandate to translate faith into action, to conform in attitude and action to the values of God's reign of shalom, and to grow in grace into the fullest possible love of God and others.

This vision and these critical commitments are compressed below in "A Progressive Wesleyan Declaration." My hope is that you will return to this statement often as a reminder of the Wesleyan way. If you study this book in a group, I highly recommend that you recite this statement together when you meet for conversation. The Declaration can also be used as well in corporate worship. Words have power. They shape us and give us our identity. So simply hearing these words and being reminded about these practices can further shape them in the core of your being. Hopefully, you will find this Declaration to be both convicting and inspirational. It provides yet another way to practice the Wesleyan way of humility, hospitality, healing, and holiness.

Appendix B: A Progressive Wesleyan Declaration

With confidence in the promises of God, faith in Jesus Christ, and in the power of the Holy Spirit, we declare:

We find Truth in Jesus.

> Being found in human form, he emptied himself of all but love.
>
> Like him, we seek to lift people up, assuming a posture of servanthood among all.
>
> We pray that our practice of humility helps to break down barriers of human hostility.

We find Joy in Jesus.

> He made room for others and invited all people into the sacred space of love.
>
> Like him, we seek to create safe spaces for others, turning enemies into friends.
>
> We pray that our practice of hospitality helps build bridges and tears down walls.

We find Peace in Jesus.

> He embraced a mission of love, caring for all and restoring God's world.
>
> Like him, we seek to partner with God in the recovery of God's vision of shalom.
>
> We pray that our practice of healing helps to restore peace with justice everywhere.

We find Love in Jesus.

> He demonstrated the fullest possible extent of the love of God and neighbor.
>
> Like him, we seek to live a life of faith working by love leading to holiness.
>
> We pray that our practice of holiness helps to inspire others to discover their true identity as the beloved children of God.

We embrace the holistic and all-inclusive vision of God's restoration of beloved community.

Bibliography

Albin, Tom. "An Empirical Study of Early Methodist Spirituality." In *Wesleyan Theology Today: A Bicentennial Theological Consultation*, edited by Theodore Runyon, 275-90. Nashville: Kingswood, 1985.
Ambrose. *On the Sacraments and on the Mysteries*. Edited by J.H. Strawley. London: SPCK, 1950.
Anderson, E. Byron. "The Power of Godliness to Know: Charles Wesley and the Means of Grace." *Wesleyan Theological Journal* 43.2 (Fall 2008) 7-27.
Appleby, R. Scott. *The Ambivalence of the Sacred: Religion, Violence, and Reconciliation*. Lanham: Rowman & Littlefield, 2000.
Athanasius. *On the Incarnation*. In *Christology of the Later Fathers*, edited by Edward R. Hardy and translated by Archibald Robertson, 55-110. Philadelphia: Westminster, 1954.
Avruch, Kevin, and Beatriz Vejarano. "Truth and Reconciliation Commissions: A Review Essay and Annotated Bibliography." *Online Journal of Peace and Conflict Resolution* 4.2 (Spring 2002).
Baillie, D.M. *God Was in Christ: An Essay on Incarnation and Atonement*. New York: Scribner & Sons, 1948.
Baker, Frank. *John Wesley and the Church of England*. New York: Abingdon, 1970.
———. "John Wesley's First Marriage." *London Quarterly and Holborn Review* 192 (October 1967) 33-41.
———. "The People Called Methodists, 3: Polity." In vol. 1, *A History of the Methodist Church in Great Britain*, edited by Rupert Davies, A. Raymond George, and Gordon Rupp, 211-55. 4 vols. London: Epworth, 1965-88.
Baker, Frank, and Fred Maser. "John Wesley's Only Marriage." *Methodist History* 16 (October 1977) 33-41.
Barry, Jonathan, and Kenneth Morgan, eds. *Reformation and Revival in Eighteenth-Century Bristol*. Stroud: Printed for the Bristol Record Society, 1994.
Bass, Dorothy C. *Practicing Our Faith: A Way of Life for a Searching People*. San Francisco: Jossey-Bass, 1997.
Battle, Michael. *Reconciliation: The Ubuntu Theology of Desmond Tutu*. Cleveland: Pilgrim, 1997.
Bebbington, David. *Evangelicalism in Modern Britain: A History from the 1730s to the 1980s*. Grand Rapids: Baker, 1989.
Beck, Brian E. "Rattenbury Revisited: The Theology of Charles Wesley's Hymns." *Epworth Review* 26.2 (April 1999) 71-81.

Begbie, Jeremy S. *Beholding the Glory: Incarnation Through the Arts*. Grand Rapids: Baker Academic, 2000.

———. *Resounding Truth: Christian Wisdom in the World of Music*. Grand Rapids: Baker Academic, 2007.

———. *Voicing Creation's Praise Towards a Theology of the Arts*. New York: T&T Clark, 2000.

Begbie, Jeremy S., and Steven R. Guthrie. *Resonant Witness: Conversations Between Music and Theology*. Grand Rapids: Eerdmans, 2011.

Benedict, Daniel, and Craig Miller. *Contemporary Worship for the Twenty-First Century: Worship or Evangelism?* Nashville: Discipleship Resources, 1995.

Bennet, William, ed. *Memoirs of Mrs. Grace Bennet*. Macclesfield: E. Bayley, 1803.

Berger, Teresa. *Theology in Hymns?: A Study of the Relationship of Doxology and Theology According to "A Collection of Hymns for the Use of the People Called Methodists"* (1780). Translated by Timothy E. Kimbrough. Nashville: Kingswood, 1995.

Bird, Warren. *Starting a New Church: How to Plant a High-Impact Church*. Kansas City: Beacon Hill, 2003.

Bishop, S.L., ed. *The Hymns of Isaac Watts*. Glasgow: Faith, 1962.

Bonhoeffer, Dietrich. *The Cost of Discipleship*. Translated by R.H. Fuller with some revision by Irmgard Booth. New York: Macmillan, 1963.

The Book of Common Prayer. Cambridge: John Baskerville, 1762.

The Book of Discipline of the United Methodist Church. Nashville: United Methodist Publishing House, 2016.

Borgen, Ole E. *John Wesley on the Sacraments: A Theological Study*. New York: Abingdon 1962.

Bosanquet, Mary. *An Account of the Rise and Progress of the Work of God in Latonstone, Essex*. Np: 1763

———. *An Aunt's Advice to Her Niece*. Leeds: J. Bowling, 1780.

———. *Jesus, Altogether Lovely: or A Letter to Some of the Single Women in the Methodist Society*. Bristol, 1764.

———. *A Letter to the Rev. Mr. John Wesley. By a Gentlewoman*. London: Foundery in Upper Moorfields, 1764.

Bottrall, Margaret. *George Herbert*. London: John Murry, 1954.

Bouteneff, Peter. "All Creation in United Thanksgiving: Gregory of Nyssa and the Wesleys on Salvation." In *Orthodox and Wesleyan Spirituality*, edited by ST Kimbrough Jr., 189–201. Crestwood: St. Vladimir's Seminary, 2002.

Bowie, Fiona, ed. *Beguine Spirituality*. New York: Crossroad, 1990.

Bowmer, John. *The Sacrament of the Lord's Supper in Early Methodism*. London: Dacre, 1951.

Boyd, Timothy L. *John Wesley's Christology: A Study in Its Practical Implications for Human Salvation, Transformation, and Its Influences for Preaching Christ*. Salem: Allegheny, 2004.

Bramwell, William. *A Short Account of the Life and Death of Ann Cutler*. York: John Hill, 1827.

Brevint, Daniel. *The Christian Sacrament and Sacrifice*. Oxford, 1673.

Bright, John. *The Kingdom of God: The Biblical Concept and Its Meaning for the Church*. New York: Abingdon-Cokesbury, 1953.

Brock, Charles. *Indigenous Church Planting: A Practical Journey*. Neosho: Church Growth International, 1994.

Brown, Earl Kent. "Standing in the Shadow: Women in Early Methodism." *Nexus* 17.2 (1974) 22–31.
———. *Women of Mr. Wesley's Methodism*. New York: Edwin Mellen, 1983.
———. "Women of the Word: Selected Leadership Roles of Women in Mr. Wesley's Methodism." In vol. 1, *Women in New Worlds: Historical Perspectives on the Wesleyan Tradition*, edited by Hilah F. Thomas and Rosemary Skinner Keller, 42–60. 2 vols. Nashville: Abingdon, 1981–82.
———. "Feminist Theology and the Women of Mr. Wesley's Methodism." In *Wesleyan Theology Today*, edited by Theodore Runyon, 145–50. Nashville: Kingswood, 1984.
Bruce, F.F. "Christ as Conqueror and Reconciler." *Bibliotheca Sacra* 141 (October/December 1984) 291–302.
Brueggemann, Walter. *Living Toward a Vision: Biblical Reflections on Shalom*. Cleveland: United Church, 1976.
Bulmer, Agnes, ed. *Memoirs of Mrs. Elizabeth Mortimer*. London: J. Mason, 1836.
Butler, David. *Methodists and Papists: John Wesley and the Catholic Church in the Eighteenth Century*. London: Darton, Longman, & Todd, 1995.
Campbell, Ted A. "Charles Wesley, 'Theologos.'" In *Charles Wesley Life, Legacy and Literature*, edited by Kenneth G.C. Newport and Ted A. Campbell, 264–78. Peterborough: Epworth, 2007.
Cannon, William R. *The Theology of John Wesley with Special Reference to the Doctrine of Justification*. Lanham: University Press of America, 1974.
Carroll, Thomas K., ed. *Jeremy Taylor*. New York: Paulist, 1990.
Carter, Kenneth H., Jr. *A Way of Life in the World: Spiritual Practices for United Methodists*. Nashville: Abingdon, 2004.
Cheyney, Tom, et al., eds. *Seven Steps for Planting Churches*. Alpharetta: North American Mission Board, 2003.
Chilcote, Paul W. "'All the Image of Thy Love': Charles Wesley's Vision of the One Thing Needful." *Proceedings of the Charles Wesley Society* 18 (2014) 21–40.
———. "Biblical Equality and the Spirituality of Early Methodist Women." *Priscilla Papers* 22.2 (Spring 2008) 11–16.
———. "Charles Wesley and Christian Practices." *Proceedings of the Charles Wesley Society* 12 (2008) 35–47.
———. "Charles Wesley and the Language of Faith." In *Charles Wesley Life, Legacy, and Literature*, edited by Kenneth G.C. Newport and Ted A. Campbell, 299–319. Peterborough: Epworth, 2007.
———. "Charles Wesley's Lyrical Credo." *Proceedings of the Charles Wesley Society* 15 (2011) 41–67.
———. "'Claim Me for Thy Service': Charles Wesley's Vision of Servant Vocation." *Proceedings of the Charles Wesley Society* 11 (2006–2007) 69–85.
———. "An Early Methodist Community of Women." *Methodist History* 38.4 (July 2000) 219–30.
———, ed. *Early Methodist Spirituality: Selected Women's Writings*. Nashville: Kingswood, 2007.
———. "The Empowerment of Women in Early Methodism." *Catalyst* 11.2 (January 1985) 1–3.
———. "Eucharist and Formation." In *A Wesleyan Theology of the Eucharist: The Presence of God for Christian Life and Ministry*, edited by Jason E. Vickers, 183–201. Nashville: General Board of Higher Education and Ministry, 2016.

———. "Evangelistic Practices of the Wesleyan Revival." In *Methodist Evangelism: Wesleyan Mission, Equipping Global Ministry, Wesleyan Studies Project, Session 8.* Curated by Laceye Warner. Washington: Wesley Theological Seminary, 2011.

———. *A Faith That Sings: Biblical Themes in the Lyrical Theology of Charles Wesley.* Eugene, OR: Cascade, 2016.

———. "A Faith That Sings: The Renewing Power of Lyrical Theology." In *The Wesleyan Tradition: A Paradigm for Renewal*, edited by Paul W. Chilcote, 148–62. Nashville: Abingdon, 2002.

———. *Her Own Story: Autobiographical Portraits of Early Methodist Women.* Nashville: Kingswood, 2001.

———. *The Imitation of Christ: Selections Annotated and Explained.* Woodstock: SkyLight Paths, 2012.

———. "The Integral Nature of Worship and Evangelism: Insights from the Wesleyan Tradition." *Asbury Theological Journal* 61.1 (Spring 2006) 7–23.

———., ed. *John and Charles Wesley: Selections from Their Writings and Hymns.* Woodstock: SkyLight Paths, 2011.

———. "John and Charles Wesley." In *Christian Theologies of the Sacraments: A Comparative Introduction*, edited by Justin S. Holcomb and David A. Johnson, 272–94. New York: New York University Press, 2017.

———. "John and Charles Wesley on 'God in Christ Reconciling.'" *Methodist History* 47.3 (April 2009) 132–45.

———. "John Wesley as Revealed by the Journal of Hester Ann Rogers." *Methodist History* 20.3 (April 1982) 111–23.

———. *John Wesley and the Women Preachers of Early Methodism.* Metuchen: Scarecrow, 1991.

———. "Lessons from the 'Society Planting' Paradigm of Early Methodist Women." *Witness: Journal of the Academy for Evangelism in Theological Education* 27 (2013) 5–30.

———, ed. *Making Disciples in a World Parish: Global Perspectives on Mission and Evangelism.* Eugene, OR: Pickwick., 2011.

———. "The Mission-Church Paradigm of the Wesleyan Revival." In *World Mission in the Wesleyan Spirit*, edited by Darrell L. Whiteman and Gerald H. Anderson, 151–64. Franklin: Providence House, 2009.

———. *Praying in the Wesleyan Spirit: 52 Prayers for Today.* Nashville: Upper Room, 2001.

———. "'Practical Christology' in John and Charles Wesley." In *Methodist Christology: From the Wesleys to the Twenty-First Century*, edited by Jason Vickers, 1–35. Nashville: Wesley's Foundery, 2020.

———. "Preliminary Explorations of Charles Wesley and Worship." *Proceedings of the Charles Wesley Society* 9 (2003–2004) 67–82.

———. *Recapturing the Wesleys' Vision: An Introduction to the Faith of John and Charles Wesley.* Downers Grove: InterVarsity, 2004.

———. "Rethinking the Wesleyan Quadrilateral." *Good News Magazine* 38.4 (January/February 2005) 22–23.

———. "Sanctification as Lived by Women in Early Methodism." *Methodist History* 34.2 (January 1996) 90–103.

———. "Servants of Shalom in the World." *Covenant Discipleship Quarterly* 18.3 (Summer 2003) 1–2.

———. *She Offered Them Christ*. Nashville: Abingdon, 1993. Reprint, Eugene, OR: Wipf & Stock, 2001.

———. *Wesley Speaks on Christian Vocation*. Nashville: Discipleship Resources, 1986.

———. "Wesleyan and Emergent Christians in Conversation: A Modest Proposal." *Epworth Review* 36.3 (July 2009) 6–25. Reprinted in *Journal of the Academy for Evangelism in Theological Education* 23 (2007–2009) 58–81.

———, ed. *The Wesleyan Tradition: A Paradigm for Renewal*. Nashville: Abingdon, 2002.

Chilcote, Paul W., with Katheru Gichara and Patrick Matsikenyiri. "A Singing and Dancing Church: Methodist Worship in Kenya and Zimbabwe." In *The Sunday Service of the Methodists: Twentieth-Century Worship in Worldwide Methodism*, edited by Karen B. Westerfield Tucker, 227–53. Nashville: Kingswood, 1996.

Church, Leslie. *The Early Methodist People*. London: Epworth, 1948.

———. *More about the Early Methodist People*. London: Epworth, 1949.

Clapper, Gregory S. *As if the Heart Mattered: A Wesleyan Spirituality*. Nashville: Upper Room, 1997.

Clarke, Adam, ed. *Memoirs of Mrs. Mary Cooper*. Halifax: William Nicholson and Sons, nd.

Cole, Joseph, ed. *Memorials of Hannah Ball*. 3rd ed. London: Wesleyan Conference Office, 1880.

Colledge, Eric. *Medieval Netherlands Religious Literature*. Leiden: E.J. Brill, 1965.

Collins, Kenneth J. *A Faithful Witness: John Wesley's Homiletical Theology*. Wilmore: Wesley Heritage, 1993.

———. *The Theology of John Wesley*. Nashville: Abingdon, 2007.

Crosby, Sarah. "An Account of Mrs. Crosby, of Leeds." *Methodist Magazine* 29 (1806) 418–23, 465–73, 517–21, 563–68, 610–17.

Curnock, Nehemiah, ed. *The Journal of the Rev. John Wesley, A.M.* 8 vols. London: Epworth, 1909–16.

Cushman, Robert E. "Baptism and the Family of God." In *The Doctrine of the Church*, edited by Dow Kirkpatrick, 74–89. Nashville: Abingdon, 1964.

———. *Faith Seeking Understanding*. Durham: Duke University Press, 1981.

———. "Worship as Acknowledgment." In *Faith Seeking Understanding: Essays Theological and Critical*, 181–97. Durham: Duke University Press, 1981.

Dale, James. "The Theological and Literary Qualities of the Poetry of Charles Wesley." PhD diss., Cambridge University, 1961.

Davies, A.P. *Isaac Watts: His Life and Works*. London: Tarrington, 1948.

Davies, Rupert, et al., eds. *A History of the Methodist Church in Great Britain*. 4 vols. London: Epworth, 1965–88.

DeGeorge, Rob. "Rehabilitating John Wesley's Christology in the Book of Hebrews: A Response to Hambrick and Lodahl." *Wesleyan Theological Journal* 53.2 (Fall 2018) 165–93.

Deschner, John. *Wesley's Christology: An Interpretation*. Dallas: Southern Methodist University Press, 1960.

Dixon, Neil. "The Wesleys' Conversion Hymn." *Proceedings of the Wesley Historical Society* 37 (February 1967) 43–47.

Doughty, W.L., ed. *The Prayers of Susanna Wesley*. London: Epworth, 1956.

Duffy, Eamon. "Wesley and the Counter Reformation." In *Revival and Religion Since 1700*, edited by Jane Garnett and Colin Matthew, 1–19. London: Bloomsbury Academic, 1993.

Dykstra, Craig. *Growing in the Life of Faith: Education and Christian Practices*. 2nd ed. Louisville: Westminster John Knox, 2005.

Dykstra, Craig, and Dorothy C. Bass. "A Theological Understanding of Christian Practices." In *Practicing Theology: Beliefs and Practices in Christian Life*, edited by Miroslav Volf and Dorothy Bass, 13–32. Grand Rapids: Eerdmans, 2001.

Dyrness, William A. *Poetic Theology: God and the Poetics of Everyday Life*. Grand Rapids: Eerdmans, 2010.

Entwisle, Mary. *Manuscript Journal*. Methodist Archives and Research Center, Rylands Library, Manchester.

Erb, Peter C., ed. *Pietists: Selected Writings*. New York: Paulist, 1983.

Everett, James. *Wesleyan Methodism in Manchester*. Manchester: S. Russell, 1827.

Felton, Gayle C. *This Gift of Water: The Practice and Theology of Baptism Among Methodists in America*. Nashville: Abingdon, 1992.

Fletcher, Mary. *Thoughts on Communion with Happy Spirits*. Birmingham: William Rickman King, nd.

Flew, R. Newton. *The Idea of Christian Perfection in Christian Theology: An Historical Study of the Christian Ideal for the Present Life*. New York: Humanities, 1968.

Frost, Francis. "The Christ-Mysticism of Charles Wesley: The Eucharist and the Heavenly Jerusalem." *Proceedings of the Charles Wesley Society* 9 (2003–04) 11–26.

———. "The Veiled Unveiling of the Glory of God in the Eucharistic Hymns of Charles Wesley: The Self-Emptying Glory of God." *Proceedings of the Charles Wesley Society* 2 (1995) 87–99.

Gallaway, Craig. "The Presence of Christ with the Worshiping Community." PhD diss., Emory University, 1988.

Galliers, Brian. "The Theology of Baptism in the Writings of John Wesley." MA thesis, Leeds University, 1957.

George, A. Raymond. "Review of John Deschner, 'Wesley's Christology.'" *Journal of Theological Studies, New Series* 12.2 (October 1961) 382.

Gilbert, Ann. "The Experience of Mrs. Ann Gilbert, of Gwinear, in Cornwall." *Arminian Magazine* 18 (1795) 42–46.

Gordon, James. *Evangelical Spirituality: From the Wesleys to John Stott*. London: SPCK, 1991.

Graham, David A. "The Chalcedonian Logic of John Wesley's Christology." *International Journal of Systematic Theology* 20.1 (January 2018) 84–103.

Greenman, Jeffrey P., and George R. Sumner. *Unwearied Praise: Exploring Christian Faith Through Classic Hymns*. Toronto: Clements, 2004.

Grislis, Egil. "The Wesleyan Doctrine of the Last Supper." *Duke Divinity School Review* 28 (1963) 99–110.

Guder, Darrell L., ed. *Missional Church: A Vision for the Sending of the Church in North America*. Grand Rapids: Eerdmans, 1998.

Gunter, W. Stephen, et al. *Wesley and the Quadrilateral: Renewing the Conversation*. Nashville: Abingdon, 1997.

Hall, Bathsheba. "An Extract from the Diary of Mrs. Bathsheba Hall." *Arminian Magazine* 4 (1781) 35–40, 94–97, 148–52, 195–98, 256–59, 309–11, 372–75.

Hambrick, Matthew, and Michael E. Lodahl. "Responsible Grace in Christology?: John Wesley's Rendering of Jesus in the Epistle to the Hebrews." *Wesleyan Theological Journal* 43.1 (Spring 2008) 86–103.
Harper, Steve. *Devotional Life in the Wesleyan Tradition*. Nashville: Upper Room, 1983.
———. "Works of Piety as Spiritual Formation." In *The Wesleyan Tradition*, edited by Paul W. Chilcote, 87–97. Nashville: Abingdon, 2002.
Hauerwas, Stanley. *The Peaceable Kingdom: A Primer in Christian Ethics*. South Bend: University of Notre Dame Press, 1991.
Hays, Richard B. *The Moral Vision of the New Testament: A Contemporary Introduction to New Testament Ethics*. San Francisco: HarperSanFrancisco, 1996.
Hellier, J.E. "The Mother Chapel of Leeds." *Methodist Recorder Winter Number* 36 (Christmas 1895) 61–72.
Henderson, D. Michael. *John Wesley's Class Meeting: A Model for Making Disciples*. Anderson: Francis Asbury, 1997.
Herbert, Chesley C. "Charles Wesley: The Poet-Theologian of Methodism." In *The Theologians of Methodism*, edited by W.F. Tillet, 36–45. Nashville: MECS, 1895.
Hesselgrave, David J. *Planting Churches Cross-Culturally: North America and Beyond*. Grand Rapids: Baker, 2000.
Hindmarsh, D. Bruce. *The Evangelical Conversion Narrative: Spiritual Autobiography in Early Modern England*. New York: Oxford University Press, 2005.
———. "'My chains fell off, my heart was free': Early Methodist Conversion Narratives in England." *Church History* 68 (1999) 910–29.
Holland, Bernard. *Baptism in Early Methodism*. London: Epworth, 1970.
———. "The Conversions of John and Charles Wesley." *Proceedings of the Wesley Historical Society* 38 (1971–72) 46–53, 51–65.
Hoon, Paul W. *The Integrity of Worship*. Nashville: Abingdon, 1971.
Hynson, Leon O. *To Reform the Nation*. Grand Rapids: Francis Asbury, 1984.
Hughes, H. Trevor. *The Piety of Jeremy Taylor*. London: Macmillan, 1960.
Hunt, Mary E. *Fierce Tenderness: A Feminist Theology of Friendship*. Minneapolis: Fortress, 2009.
Hynson, Leon O. *To Reform the Nation: Theological Foundations of Wesley's Ethics*. Grand Rapids: Francis Asbury, 1984.
Ives, A.G. *Kingswood School in Wesley's Day and Since*. London: Epworth, 1970.
Jackson, George. *Wesleyan Methodism in the Darlington Circuit*. Darlington: J. Manley, 1850.
Jackson, Thomas, ed. *The Journal of the Rev. Charles Wesley, M.A.* 2 vols. Grand Rapids: Baker, 1980.
Jeffrey, David Lyle, ed. *English Spirituality in the Age of Wesley*. Reprint, Grand Rapids: Eerdmans, 1994.
Jennings, Theodore W. *Good News to the Poor*. Nashville: Abingdon, 1990.
Jones, Ralph H. *Charles Albert Tindley, Prince of Preachers*. Nashville: Abingdon, 1982.
Kane, J. Herbert. *Christian Missions in Biblical Perspective*. Grand Rapids: Baker, 1976.
Keck, Leander. *The Church Confident*. Nashville: Abingdon, 1993.
Keller, Rosemary Skinner, ed. *Spirituality and Social Responsibility: The Vocational Vision of Women in the United Methodist Tradition*. Nashville: Abingdon, 1993.
Kempis, Thomas à. *The Imitation of Christ*. Edited by George Stanhope. London: W. Onley, 1699.

BIBLIOGRAPHY

Kent, John H.S. *Wesley and the Wesleyans: Religion in Eighteenth-Century Britain*. Cambridge: Cambridge University Press, 2002.
Khoo, Lorna. *Wesleyan Eucharistic Spirituality*. Hindmarsh, Australia: ATF, 2005.
Kiefert, Patrick *Welcoming the Stranger: A Public Theology of Worship and Evangelism*. Minneapolis: Fortress, 1992.
Kimbrough, ST, Jr., ed. *Charles Wesley: Poet and Theologian*. Nashville: Kingswood, 1992.
———."Charles Wesley and the Journey of Sanctification." *Evangelical Journal* 16 (Fall 1998) 49–75.
———. "Charles Wesley and the Poor." In *The Portion of the Poor: Good News to the Poor in the Wesleyan Tradition*, edited by M. Douglas Meeks, 147–67. Nashville: Kingswood, 1995.
———. "Charles Wesley and a Window to the East." In *Charles Wesley: Life, Literature and Legacy*, edited by Kenneth G.C. Newport and Ted A. Campbell, 165–83. Peterborough: Epworth, 2007.
———. "Charles Wesley's Dynamic, Lyrical Theology: The Power and Impact of Verbs." *Proceedings of the Charles Wesley Society* 11 (2006–2007) 15–34.
———. *Global Praise 1*. New York: GBGMusik, 1996.
———. *A Heart to Praise My God: Wesley Hymns for Today*. Nashville: Abingdon, 1996.
———. "Hymnody of Charles Wesley." In *T&T Clark Companion to Methodism*, edited by Charles Yrigoyen Jr., 36–60. New York: T&T Clark, 2010.
———. "Hymns Are Theology." *Theology Today* 42.1 (April 1985) 59–68.
———. "'Kenosis' in the Nativity Hymns of Ephrem the Syrian and Charles Wesley." In *Orthodox and Wesleyan Spirituality*, edited by ST Kimbrough Jr., 265–85. Crestwood: St. Vladimir's Seminary, 2002.
———. *Lost in Wonder*. Nashville: Upper Room, 1987.
———. "Lyrical Theology." *Journal of Theology* 98 (1994) 18–43.
———. "Lyrical Theology: Theology in Hymns." *Theology Today* 63.1 (April 2006) 22–37.
———. *The Lyrical Theology of Charles Wesley A Reader*. Eugene, OR: Cascade, 2011.
———. *Orthodox and Wesleyan Ecclesiology*. Crestwood: St. Vladimir's Seminary, 2007.
———. *Orthodox and Wesleyan Spirituality*. Crestwood: St. Vladimir's Seminary, 2002.
———. *Orthodox and Wesleyan Scriptural Understanding and Practice*. Crestwood: St. Vladimir's Seminary, 2006.
———. "Other Eastern Sources and Charles Wesley." In *Orthodox and Wesleyan Spirituality*, edited by ST Kimbrough Jr., 205–85. Crestwood: St. Vladimir's Seminary, 2002.
———. *Partakers of the Life Divine: Participation in the Divine Nature in the Writings of Charles Wesley*. Eugene, OR: Cascade, 2016.
———. *Songs for the Poor*. New York: GBGMusik, 1993.
———. "'Theosis' in the Writings of Charles Wesley." *St. Vladimir's Theological Seminary Quarterly* 52.2 (2008) 199–212.
Knight, Henry H. *Eight Life-Enriching Practices of United Methodists*. Nashville: Abingdon, 2001.
———. *The Presence of God in the Christian Life: John Wesley and the Means of Grace*. Lanham: Scarecrow, 1992.
Köberle, Adolf. *The Quest for Holiness: A Biblical, Historical, and Systematic Investigation*. St. Louis: Concordia, 1964.

Kolb, Robert, and Timothy J. Wengert, eds. *The Book of Concord: The Confessions of the Evangelical Lutheran Church*. Minneapolis: Fortress, 2000.

Ladd, George Eldon. *The Gospel of the Kingdom: Scriptural Studies in the Kingdom of God*. London: Paternoster, 1959.

Langford, Andy, and Sally Overby Langford. *Worship and Evangelism*. Nashville: Discipleship Resources, 1989.

Langford, Thomas A. "Charles Wesley as Theologian." In *Charles Wesley Poet and Theologian*, edited by ST Kimbrough Jr., 97–105. Nashville: Kingswood, 1992.

———. *Practical Divinity: Theology in the Wesleyan Tradition*. Nashville Abingdon, 1983.

Langford, Thomas A., ed. *Doctrine and Theology in the United Methodist Church*. Nashville: Kingswood, 2001.

Lawson, John. "Charles Wesley: A Man of the Prayer-Book." *Proceedings of the Charles Wesley Society* 1 (1994) 85–118.

———. *The Wesley Hymns as a Guide to Scriptural Teaching*. Grand Rapids: Francis Asbury, 1988.

Leaver, Robin A. "Charles Wesley and Anglicanism." In *Charles Wesley: Poet and Theologian*, edited by ST Kimbrough Jr., 157–75. Nashville: Kingswood, 1992.

Lederach, John Paul. *Building Peace: Sustainable Reconciliation in Divided Societies*. Herndon: United States Institute of Peace, 1997.

———. *The Journey Toward Reconciliation*. Scottsdale: Herald, 1999.

———. *The Moral Imagination: The Art and Soul of Building Peace*. New York: Oxford University Press, 2005.

Leger, Augustin. *John Wesley's Last Love*. London: J.M. Dent and Sons, 1910.

Lerch, David. *Heil und Heiligung bei John Wesley, Dargestellt unter Besonderer Berücksichtigung Seiner Ammerkungen zum Neuen Testament*. Zürich: Christlichen, 1941.

Lerner, Robert E. *The Heresy of the Free Spirit in the Later Middle Ages*. Los Angeles: University of California Press, 1972.

Lloyd-Jones, D.M. *The Puritans: Their Origins and Successors*. London: Banner of Truth Trust, 1987.

Long, D. Stephen. *John Wesley's Moral Theology: The Quest for God and Goodness*. Nashville: Abingdon, 2005.

Loyer, Kenneth M. "Memorial, Means, and Pledge Eucharist and Time in the Wesleys' 'Hymns on the Lord's Supper' 1745." *Proceedings of the Charles Wesley Society* 11 (2006–2007) 87–106.

Lyth, John. *Glimpses of Early Methodism in York*. York: Williams Sessions, 1885.

Maddox, Randy L. *Responsible Grace: John Wesley's Practical Theology*. Nashville: Kingswood, 1994.

———. "The Theology of John and Charles Wesley." In *T&T Clark Companion to Methodism*, edited by Charles Yrigoyen, 20–35. New York: T&T Clark, 2010.

Malphurs, Aubrey. *Planting Growing Churches for the 21st Century: A Comprehensive Guide for New Churches and Those Desiring Renewal*. 2nd ed. Grand Rapids: Baker, 1998.

Marquardt, Manfred. *John Wesley's Social Ethics: Praxis and Principles*. Translated by John E. Steely and W. Stephen Gunter. Nashville: Abingdon, 1992.

McAdoo, H.R. *The Spirit of Anglicanism*. London: Black, 1965.

McDonnel, Ernest W. *The Beguines and Beghards in Medieval Culture*. Brunswick: Rutgers University Press, 1954.
McVey, Kathleen E., ed. *Ephrem the Syrian: Hymns*. New York: Paulist, 1989.
Massa, Mark. "The Catholic Wesley: A Revisionist Prolegomenon." *Methodist History* 22.1 (October 1983) 38–53.
Matthaei, Sondra Higgins. *Making Disciples: Faith Formation in the Wesleyan Tradition*. Nashville: Abingdon, 2000.
Matthews, Rex D. "'With the Eyes of Faith': Spiritual Experience and the Knowledge of God in the Theology of John Wesley." In *Wesleyan Theology Today: A Bicentennial Theological Consultation*, edited by Theodore Runyon, 406–15. Nashville: Kingswood, 1985.
Meistad, Tore. "The Missiology of Charles Wesley: An Introduction." *Proceedings of the Charles Wesley Society* 5 (1998) 37–60.
———. "The Missiology of Charles Wesley and Its Links to the Eastern Church." In *Orthodox and Wesleyan Spirituality*, edited by ST Kimbrough Jr., 205–31. Crestwood: St. Vladimir's Seminary, 2002.
Miles, Rebekah. "Works of Mercy as Spiritual Formation: Why Wesley Feared for the Souls of the Rich." In *The Wesleyan Tradition: A Paradigm for Renewal*, edited by Paul W. Chilcote, 98–110. Nashville: Abingdon, 2002.
Monteiro, Simei. "Evangelization and Music in a Latin American Context from a Wesleyan Perspective." In *Evangelization, the Heart of Mission: A Wesleyan Perspective*, edited by ST Kimbrough Jr., 130–43. New York: GBGM, 1995.
Moore, Henry. *The Life of Mrs. Mary Fletcher*. 6th ed. London: J. Kershaw, 1824.
Morgenthaler, Sally. *Worship Evangelism*. Grand Rapids: Zondervan, 1995.
Mother Teresa. *In the Heart of the World: Thoughts, Stories and Prayers*. Norato: New World Library, 1997.
Murray, Stuart. *Church Planting: Laying Foundations*. Scottsdale: Herald, 2001.
Newport, Kenneth G.C. "Premillennialism in the Early Writings of Charles Wesley." *Wesleyan Theological Journal* 32.1 (Spring 1997) 85–106.
Newport, Kenneth G.C., ed. *The Sermons of Charles Wesley: A Critical Edition with Introduction and Notes*. Oxford: Oxford University Press, 2001.
Newport, Kenneth G.C., and Ted A. Campbell, eds. *Charles Wesley: Life, Literature and Legacy*. Peterborough: Epworth, 2007.
Newton, John A. *Faith Working by Love: The Methodist Tradition*. Maryknoll: Orbis, 2007.
Nicholson, Roy S. "The Holiness Emphasis in the Wesleys' Hymns." *Wesleyan Theological Journal* 5.1 (Spring 1970) 49–61.
Norris, John. *A Collection of Miscellanies: Consisting of Poems, Essays, Discourses, and Letters, Occasionally Written*. 2nd ed. London: Printed for J. Crosley and Samuel Manship, 1692.
Oden, Thomas C. *John Wesley's Scriptural Christianity: A Plain Exposition of His Teaching on Christian Doctrine*. Grand Rapids: Zondervan, 1994.
Orcibal, Jean. "The Theological Originality of John Wesley and Continental Spirituality." In *A History of the Methodist Church in Great Britain*, edited by Rupert Davies et al., 1:83–111. London: Epworth, 1965.
Ott, Craig, and Gene Wilson. *Global Church Planting: Biblical Principles and Best Practices for Multiplication*. Grand Rapids: Baker, 2011.
Outler, Albert C. *Evangelism in the Wesleyan Spirit*. Nashville: Tidings, 1971.

———. *Theology in the Wesleyan Spirit*. Nashville: Tidings, 1975.
Outler, Albert C., ed. *John Wesley*. New York: Oxford University Press, 1964.
Parris, John. *John Wesley's Doctrine of the Sacraments*. London: Epworth, 1963.
Payne, J.D. *Discovering Church Planting: An Introduction to the Whats, Whys, and Hows of Global Church Planting*. Colorado Springs: Paternoster, 2009.
Peters, George. *A Biblical Theology of Mission*. Chicago: Moody, 1972.
Peterson, Rodney L., and Raymond G. Helmick, eds. *Forgiveness and Reconciliation: Religion, Public Policy, and Conflict Transformation*. Philadelphia: Templeton Foundation, 2001.
Phillips, Dayton. *Beguines in Medieval Strasburg: A Study of the Social Aspect of Beguine Life*. Stanford: Stanford University Press, 1941.
Pipe, John. "Memoir of Miss Isabella Wilson." *Wesleyan Methodist Magazine* 31 (1808) 372–75, 410–15, 461–69, 516–18, 562–67, 595–97.
Pratt Green, Fred. *The Hymns and Ballads of Fred Pratt Green*. Carol Stream: Hope, 1982.
———. *Later Hymns and Ballads and Fifty Poems*. Carol Stream: Hope, 1989.
———. "Poet and Hymn Write." *Worship* 49.4 (April 1975) 192–93.
Quantrille, Wilma J. "The Triune God in the Hymns of Charles Wesley." PhD diss., Drew University, 1989.
Rack, Henry D. *Reasonable Enthusiast: John Wesley and the Rise of Methodism*. London: Epworth, 1993.
Rattenbury, J. Ernest. *The Conversion of the Wesleys*. London: Epworth, 1938.
———. *The Eucharistic Hymns of John and Charles Wesley*. London: Epworth, 1948. Facsimile edition, with an introdcution by Geoffrey Wainwright. Madison: Charles Wesley Society, 1995.
———. *The Evangelical Doctrines of Charles Wesley's Hymns*. London: Epworth, 1941.
Raymond, Janice G. *A Passion for Friends: Towards a Philosophy of Female Affection*. London: Women's Press, 1986.
Renshaw, John R. "The Atonement in the Theology and John and Charles Wesley." ThD thesis, Boston University, 1965.
Rice, Chris. *Reconciliation as the Mission of God: Christian Witness in a World of Destructive Conflicts*. Tacoma: World Vision International Peacebuilding and Reconciliation Department, [2005].
Ridderbos, Herman. *Paul: An Outline of His Theology*. Grand Rapids: Eerdmans, 1975.
Riss, Richard M. "John Wesley's Christology in Recent Literature." *Wesleyan Theological Journal* 45 (Spring 2010) 108–29.
Ritschl, Albrecht. *Geschichte des Pietismus*. 3 vols. Bonn, 1880–86.
Robert, Dana L. *Evangelism as the Heart of Mission*. Mission Evangelism Series 1. New York: General Board of Global Ministries, 1997.
———. *Friendships: Embracing Diversity in Christian Community; Embracing Diversity in Christian Community*. Grand Rapids: Eerdmans, 2019.
Rogers, Hester Ann. *An Account of the Experience of Hester Ann Rogers*. New York: Hunt & Eaton, 1893.
———. *Manuscript Journal*. Perkins Library, Duke University.
Rosado, Edgardo. *John Wesley's Christology: A Social Approach to the Presentation of the Gospel of Christ*. Independently published, 2019.
Ruffin, Bernard. *Fanny Crosby*. Philadelphia: United Church, 1976.

Runyon, Theodore, ed. *Wesleyan Theology Today: A Bicentennial Theological Consultation.* Nashville: Kingswood, 1985.
Ruth, Lester. "Word and Table." In *The Wesleyan Tradition: A Paradigm for Renewal,* edited by Paul W. Chilcote, 136–47. Nashville: Abingdon, 2002.
Ryan, Sarah. "Account of Sarah Ryan." *Arminian Magazine* 2 (1779) 296–310.
Saliers, Don. "Singing Our Lives." In *Practicing Our Faith: A Way of Life for a Searching People,* edited by Dorothy C. Bass, 179–93. San Francisco: Jossey-Bass, 1997.
Sanchez, Daniel R. "Review of 'Planting Growing Churches for the 21st Century: A Comprehensive Guide for New Churches and Those Desiring Renewal,' by Aubrey Malphurs." *Missiology* 21.3 (July 1993) 359.
Sanders, Paul. "John Wesley and Baptismal Regeneration." *Religion in Life* 23 (1953–54) 591–603.
———. "Wesley's Eucharistic Faith and Practice." *Anglican Theological Review* 48.2 (April 1966) 157–74.
Sattler, Gary R. *God's Glory, Neighbor's Good: A Brief Introduction to the Life and Writings of August Hermann Francke.* Chicago: Covenant, 1982.
Schaller, Lyle F. *Forty-four Questions for Church Planters.* Nashville: Abingdon, 1991.
Schmidt, Martin. *John Wesley: A Theological Biography.* Translated by Norman Goldhawk and Denis Inman. 3 vols. New York: Abingdon, 1966.
———. *Pietismus.* Stuttgart: W. Kohlhammer, 1972.
Scougal, Henry. *The Life of God in the Soul of Man.* Edited by W.S. Hudson. Philadelphia: Westminster, 1958.
Scroggs, Robin. "John Wesley as Biblical Scholar." *Journal of Bible and Religion* 28.4 (October 1960) 415–22.
Sheldrake, Philip. *Spirituality and History.* 2nd ed. London: SPCK, 1995.
Smith, Benjamin. *The History of Methodism in Macclesfield.* London: Wesleyan Conference, 1875.
Smith, Edward, ed. *The Extraordinary Life and Christian Experience of Margaret Davidson, as Dictated by Herself.* Dublin: Dugdale, 1782.
Smith, Kenneth L., and Ira G. Zepp, Jr. *Search for the Beloved Community: The Thinking of Martin Luther King, Jr.* Valley Forge: Judson, 1974.
Snyder, Howard. *The Radical Wesley.* Downers Grove: InterVarsity, 1980.
———. *Signs of the Spirit: How God Reshapes the Church.* Grand Rapids: Academic, 1989.
Sound the Bamboo: CCA Hymnal 1990. Quezon City: Christian Conference of Asia and The Asian Institute for Liturgy and Music, 1990.
Southern, R.W. *Western Society and the Church in the Middle Ages.* Harmondsworth: Penguin, 1970.
Stanwood, Paul G. *William Law.* New York: Paulist, 1978.
Staples, Rob. *Outward Sign and Inward Grace: The Place of Sacraments in Wesleyan Spirituality.* Kansas City: Beacon Hill, 1991.
Steele, Anthony. *History of Methodism in Barnard Castle and the Dales Circuit.* London: George Vickers, 1857.
Stevenson, John, ed. *A New Eusebius.* London: SPCK, 1957.
Stevick, Daniel B. *The Altar's Fire: Charles Wesley's Hymns on the Lord's Supper, 1745 Introduction and Exposition.* Peterborough: Epworth, 2004.
Stoeffler, Ernest. *German Pietism During the Eighteenth Century.* Leiden: E.J. Brill, 1973.
———. *The Rise of Evangelical Pietism.* Leiden: E.J. Brill, 1963.

Stone, Ronald. *John Wesley's Life and Ethics*. Nashville: Abingdon, 2001.
Stranks, C.J. *Anglican Devotion*. London: SPCK, 1961.
Summer, Joseph. *George Herbert: His Religion and Art*. Cambridge: Harvard University Press, 1954.
Taft, Zechariah. *Biographical Sketches of the Lives and Public Ministry of Various Holy Women*. 2 vols. London: Kershaw, 1825; Leeds: Stephens, 1828.
Telford, John, ed. *The Journal of the Rev. Charles Wesley*. 2 vols. London: Robert Culley, 1910.
———, ed. *The Letters of the Rev. John Wesley, A.M.* 8 vols. London: Epworth, 1931.
Thornton, Martin. "The Caroline Divines and the Cambridge Platonists." In *The Study of Spirituality*, edited by Cheslyn Jones et al., 431–37. New York: Oxford University Press, 1986.
———. *English Spirituality*. London: SPCK, 1963.
Tooth, Mary. *A Letter to the Loving and Beloved People of the Parish of Madeley*. Shiffnal: A. Edmonds, n.d.
Towlson, Clifford W. *Moravian and Methodist*. London: Epworth, 1957.
Troeltsch. Ernst. *The Social Teachings of the Christian Churches*. Translated by Olive Wyon. 2 vols. Louisville: Westminster John Knox, 1992.
Tuttle, Robert. *Mysticism in the Wesleyan Tradition*. Grand Rapids: Frances Asbury, 1989.
Tyson, John R. *Charles Wesley on Sanctification*. Grand Rapids: Zondervan, 1986.
———. "Charles Wesley's Theology of the Cross." PhD diss., Drew University, 1983.
———. "The Lord of Life Is Risen: Theological Reflections on 'Hymns for our Lord's Resurrection' (1746)." *Proceedings of the Charles Wesley Society* 7 (2001) 81–99.
———. "'The One Things Needful': Charles Wesley on Sanctification." *Wesleyan Theological Journal* 45.2 (Fall 2010) 177–95.
———. "The Theology of Charles Wesley's Hymns." *Wesleyan Theological Journal* 44.2 (Fall 2007) 58–75.
———. *The Way of the Wesleys: A Short Introduction*. Grand Rapids: Eerdmans, 2014.
Tyson, John R., ed. *Charles Wesley: A Reader*. New York: Oxford University Press, 1989.
Underwood, Joel, ed. *Banquet of Praise*. New York: Bread for the World, 1990.
Van Kuiken, Jerome. "Deschner's Wesley and the Monophysite Meme." *Wesleyan Theological Journal* 54.2 (Fall 2019) 37–55.
Vickers, Jason E. "Charles Wesley and the Revival of the Doctrine of the Trinity: A Methodist Contribution to Modern Theology." In *Charles Wesley: Life, Literature and Legacy*, edited by Kenneth G.C. Newport and Ted A. Campbell, 278–98. Peterborough: Epworth, 2007.
———. "The Making of a Trinitarian Theology: The Holy Spirit in Charles Wesley's Hymns." *Pneuma* 31.2 (2009) 213–24.
Volf, Miroslav. *Exclusion and Embrace: A Theological Exploration of Identity, Otherness, and Reconciliation*. Nashville: Abingdon, 1996.
Wainwright, Geoffrey. "Review of John Deschner, *Wesley's Christology*." *Perkins Journal* 39.2 (April 1986) 55.
———. "The Sacraments in Wesleyan Perspective." *Doxology* 5 (1988) 5–20.
———. "Types of Spirituality." In *The Study of Spirituality*, edited by Cheslyn Jones et al., 592–605. New York: Oxford University Press, 1986.
Wakefield, Gordon. *Fire of Love: The Spirituality of John Wesley*. London: Epworth, 1976.

BIBLIOGRAPHY

———. *Methodist Devotion: The Spiritual Life in the Methodist Tradition*. London: Epworth, 1966.
———. *Methodist Spirituality*. Peterborough: Epworth, 1999.
———. "The Puritans." In *The Study of Spirituality*, edited by Cheslyn Jones et al., 437–45. New York: Oxford University Press, 1986.
Wakefield, Gordon, ed. *The Westminster Dictionary of Christian Spirituality*. Philadelphia: Westminster, 1983.
Wall, John N., Jr., ed. *George Herbert*. New York: Paulist, 1981.
Walther, Johann. *Geystliche gesangk Buchleyn*. Wittenberg, 1524.
Warren, Robert. *Building Missionary Congregations*. London: Church House, 1995.
Watson, David Lowes. *Accountable Discipleship*. Nashville: Discipleship Resources, 1985.
———. "Methodist Spirituality." In *Protestant Spiritual Traditions*, edited by Frank Senn, 217–73. New York: Paulist, 1986.
Watson, J. Richard. "'Experimental and Practical Divinity': Charles Wesley and John Norris." *Proceedings of the Charles Wesley Society* 6 (1999–2000) 59–72.
———. "The Presentation of Holiness and the Concept of Christian Perfection in the Sermons and Hymns of the Wesleys, 1730–1780." In *Transforming Holiness*, edited by Irene Visser and Helen Wilcox, 81–94. Dudley: Peeters, 2006.
Watts, Isaac. *Hymns and Spiritual Songs*. London: W. Strahan, 1763.
Webber, Robert. *Worship Is a Verb*. Waco: Word, 1985.
Wesley, Charles. *Elegy on the Death of Robert Jones, Esq. of Fonmon Castle in Glamorganshire, South Wales*. Bristol: Farley, 1742.
———. *Hymns on God's Everlasting Love*. 2nd series. London: Strahan, 1742.
———. *Hymns on the Great Festivals*. London: M. Cooper, 1746.
———. *Funeral Hymns*. London: Strahan, 1759.
———. *Hymns and Sacred Poems*. 2 vols. Bristol: Farley, 1749.
———. *Hymns for Children*. Bristol: Farley, 1763.
———. *Hymns of Intercession for all Mankind* [*Intercession Hymns*]. Bristol: Farley, 1758.
———. *Hymns for the Nativity of Our Lord* [*Nativity Hymns*]. London: Strahan, 1745.
———. *Hymns for Those That Seek and Those That Have Redemption in the Blood of Jesus Christ* [*Redemption Hymns*]. London: Strahan, 1747.
———. *Hymns on the Trinity* [*Trinity Hymns*]. Bristol: Pine, 1767.
———. *Hymns for the Use of Families* [*Family Hymns*]. Bristol: Pine, 1767.
———. *The Manuscript Journal of the Reverend Charles Wesley, M.A.* Edited by ST Kimbrough Jr. and Kenneth G.C. Newport. 2 vols. Nashville: Kingswood, 2008.
———. *MS Acts*. Methodist Archive and Research Centre, MA 1977/555 (Charles Wesley Notebooks Box 1).
———. *MS Cheshunt*. The Cheshunt Foundation, Westminster College, Cambridge.
———. *MS Funeral Hymns* [1756–82]. Methodist Archive and Research Centre, MA 1977/578 (Charles Wesley Notebooks Box 3).
———. *MS Henderson*. Methodist Archive and Research Centre, MA 1977/594/1 (Charles Wesley Notebooks Box 6).
———. *MS Luke*. Methodist Archive and Research Centre, MA 1977/575 (Charles Wesley Notebooks Box 3).
———. *MS Matthew*. Methodist Archive and Research Centre, MA 1977/577 (Charles Wesley Notebooks Box 3).

———. *MS Richmond*. Methodist Archive and Research Centre, MA 1977/551 (Charles Wesley Notebooks Box 1).
———. *MS Scripture Hymns*. Methodist Archive and Research Centre, MA 1977/576 (Charles Wesley Notebooks Box 3).
———. *Preparation for Death, in Several Hymns*. London, 1772.
———. "The Promise of Sanctification." In *Christian Perfection, a Sermon*, by John Wesley, 44–48. London: Strahan, 1741.
———. *Short Hymns on Select Passages of the Holy Scriptures* [*Scripture Hymns*]. 2 vols. Bristol: Farley, 1762.
Wesley, John. *A Christian Library*. 50 vols. Bristol: Farley, 1749–55.
———. "Some Account of Sarah Peters." *Arminian Magazine* 5 (1782) 128–36.
———. *Christian Perfection, a Sermon*. London: Strahan, 1741.
———. *Explanatory Notes upon the New Testament*. London: Boyer, 1755.
———. *Instructions for Children*. London: Printed by G. Paramore, 1791.
———. *Select Hymns with Tunes Annext*. London: n.p., 1761.
———. *The Sunday Service of the Methodists in North America*. Edited by James F. White. Nashville: United Methodist Publishing House, 1984.
———. *Thoughts upon Methodism*. In *The Works of the Rev. John Wesley, AM*, edited by Thomas Jackson. London: Methodist Publishing House, 1831.
———. *The Works of John Wesley*. Vol. 1, *Sermons I (1–33)*. Edited by Albert C. Outler. Nashville: Abindgon, 1984.
———. *The Works of John Wesley*. Vol. 2, *Sermons I (34–70)*. Edited by Albert C. Outler. Nashville: Abindgon, 1985.
———. *The Works of John Wesley*. Vol. 3, *Sermons III (71–114)*. Edited by Albert C. Outler. Nashville: Abingdon, 1986.
———. *The Works of John Wesley*. Vol. 4, *Sermons IV (115–51)*. Edited by Albert C. Outler. Nashville: Abingdon, 1987.
———. *The Works of John Wesley*. Vol. 7, *A Collection of Hymns for the Use of the People Called Methodists*. Edited by Franz Hildebrandt and Oliver A. Beckerlegge. Oxford: Clarendon, 1983.
———. *The Works of John Wesley*. Vol. 9, *The Methodist Societies: History, Nature, and Design*. Edited by Rupert E. Davies. Nashville: Abingdon, 1989.
———. *The Works of John Wesley*. Vol. 12, *Doctrinal and Controversial Treatises I*. Edited by Randy L. Maddox. Nashville: Abingdon, 2012.
———. *The Works of John Wesley*. Vol. 13, *Doctrinal and Controversial Treatises II*. Edited by Paul Wesley Chilcote and Kenneth J. Collins. Nashville: Abingdon, 2013.
———. *The Works of John Wesley*. Vol. 18, *Journal and Diaries I (1735–1738)*. Edited by W. Reginald Ward and Richard P. Heitzenrater. Nashville: Abingdon, 1988.
———. *The Works of John Wesley*. Vol. 19, *Journal and Diaries I (1738–1743)*. Edited by W. Reginald Ward and Richard P. Heitzenrater. Nashville: Abingdon, 1990.
———. *The Works of John Wesley*. Vol. 25, *Letters I (1721–1739)*. Edited by Frank Baker. Oxford: Clarendon, 1980.
———. *The Works of John Wesley*. Vol. 26, *Letters I (1740–1755)*. Edited by Frank Baker. Oxford: Clarendon, 1982.
Wesley, John, and Charles Wesley. *Collection of Psalms and Hymns*. London: Strahan, 1743.
———. *Hymns and Sacred Poems*. London: Strahan, 1739.
———. *Hymns and Sacred* Poems. London: Strahan, 1740.

———. *Hymns and Sacred Poems*. Bristol: Farley, 1742.
———. *Hymns and Spiritual Songs*. London: Strahan, 1753.
———. *Hymns on the Lord's Supper*. Bristol: Farley, 1745.
———. *Hymns of Petition and Thanksgiving for the Promise of Father*. Bristol: Farley, 1746.
———. *Hymns for Times of Trouble*. London: Strahan, 1744.
Whaling, Frank, ed. *John and Charles Wesley: Selected Prayers, Hymns, Journal Notes, Sermons, Letters and Treatises*. New York: Paulist, 1981.
Willard, Dallas. *Renovation of the Heart: Putting on the Character of Christ*. Colorado Springs: NavPress, 2002.
Wilson, Charles R. "Christology." In *A Contemporary Wesleyan Theology*, edited by Charles W. Carter, 331–69. Grand Rapids: Francis Asbury, 1983.
Wink, Walter. *When the Powers Fall: Reconciliation in the Healing of Nations*. Minneapolis: Fortress, 1998.
Winckles, Andrew. "Kingdom of God—Kingdom of Man: Freedom, Identity, and Justice in Charles Wesley and William Blake." Unpublished paper presented at the North American Society for the Study of Romanticism Conference, Park City, Utah, August 12, 2011.
Winter, Ralph D. "The Two Structures of God's Redemptive Mission." *Missiology* 2.1 (January 1974) 121–39.
Winter, Ralph D., and R. Pierce Beaver. *The Warp and the Woof: Organizing for Mission*. South Pasadena: William Carey Library, 1970.
Yoder, John Howard. "Artisans of a Peaceable Kingdom." Paper presented at the Whitworth University Forum, 1984.
Yrigoyen, Charles, Jr. *Praising the God of Grace: The Theology of Charles Wesley's Hymns*. Nashville: Abingdon, 2005.
Zinzendorf, Nikolaus Ludwig von. *Gesang-Buch der Herrnhuter und anderer Brüder-Gemeinen*. Herrnhut, 1741.